MADE IN MEXICO

HOLLYWOOD SOUTH OF THE BORDER

Published in 2018 by Applause Theatre & Cinema Books
An Imprint of Hal Leonard LLC
7777 West Bluemound Road
Milwaukee, WI 53213

Trade Book Division Editorial Offices
33 Plymouth St., Montclair, NJ 07042

All images are from the author's collection unless otherwise noted.

Printed in the United States of America

Book design by Damien Castaneda

Library of Congress Cataloging-in-Publication DataNames: Reyes, Luis, 1953- author.Title: Made in Mexico : Hollywood south of the border / Luis I. Reyes ; foreword by Jorge Rivero ; edited by Frank Thompson and Jan Pippins.Description: Milwaukee : Applause Theatre & Cinema Books, 2019. | Includes bibliographical references and index.Identifiers: LCCN 2018020736 | ISBN 9781495097898 (pbk.)Subjects: LCSH: Motion picture locations--Mexico--History--20th century. | Motion pictures--United States--History--20th century. | Western films--History and criticism. Classification: LCC PN1995.67.M6 R49 2019 | DDC 791.430250972--dc23LC record available at https://lccn.loc.gov/2018020736

ISBN 978-1-4950-9789-8

www.applausebooks.com

Made in Mexico / Hecho en Mexico: Hollywood South of the Border is dedicated to **Pedro Armendáriz Jr.** (1940–2011) and the Mexican film industry. For me, it was always special to work in Mexico and have the good fortune to be on a picture in which "Pedrito," as I affectionately called him, would be working. His infectious smile, his charisma, his lack of pretense, made you feel welcome. "Un Fuerte Abrazo" (hug), as we say in Spanish. Though good-natured, he was a very serious professional who took his acting seriously and worked continuously in Mexican and American movies, television shows, telenovelas, and on the stage for more than four decades. He was a fearless actor and took on every acting assignment and relished the particular challenges that the roles presented to him. The last time we worked together, in March of 2010, we spent a couple of hours talking on a commuter train from Philadelphia to Washington, D.C., en route to location, where he captivated me with stories of his acting and life experiences. His father, Pedro Armendáriz, was an icon of the Golden Age of Mexican cinema. His son Pedro walked in his father's footsteps and, just like his father, touched everyone with his work on the screen. He left us all too soon.

Also dedicated to: the late Tony Scott (1944–2012), an extraordinary director. I had the opportunity to accompany him on a filmmaker's journey through Mexico, meeting the people and places he loved, while working on two films, *Revenge* and *Man on Fire*.

CONTENTS

Acknowledgments

Michael Donnelly   Satir Gonzalez

Nick Redman   Jerry Velasco

Martin Blythe   Mike Gomez

Frank Thompson   Bel Hernandez

Anna Roth   Jimmy Smits

Jan Pippins   Chon Noriega

Jorge Rivero   David Maciel

Jesus "Chucho" Duran   Fernando Ulloa

Jeff Mantor   Conrad Hool

Larry Edmunds Bookstore   Lance Hool

Michael Singer   Miluka Rivera

Sergio Gutierrez, Durango Film Commission   Nancy de Los Santos

C. P. Jorge Herrera Caldera Gobernador Del Estado   Scott Solakian

De Durango   Alfonso Rosas Priego

Lic. José Angel Reinosa Gonzalez- Secretario De   Patrick Wayne

Turismo De Durango   Lon Davis Applause books

Lic. Martin Gamboa / Vice-presidente Zona Norte   Marybeth Keating Applause books

Zita Quintero Montgomery   Emilia Arau

George R. Padilla   The staff of the County of Los Angeles Norwood

Academy of Motion Pictures Arts and Sciences: Library in El Monte, CA

Margaret Herrick Library   Marc Wanamaker

Pepe Serna   Bison Archives

And finally, a very special thank you to my wife,
Maria Martha Reyes, and my agent, Leticia Gomez

NOTE

Because of corporate mergers, buyouts, and transfer of rights over a period of a hundred years, film copyrights are reserved and are listed in this book by their original U.S. studio release dates and original releasing or distribution companies.

Whenever possible, the author has referred to primary sources, such as original books and archived film publicity material, press books, press kits, newspapers, magazines, and trade clippings from the files of the Academy of Motion Pictures Arts and Sciences Margaret Herrick Library in Los Angeles, the Chicano Studies Research Center at University at California Los Angeles, University of Southern California Cinema Library, and The American Film Institute Library and Catalogue of Feature Films. Due to the nature of modern research, the author utilized the Internet with its innumerable film, Western, and Mexican film history–related websites, from which information was drawn and cross-referenced. Interviews were conducted with individuals who are knowledgeable on the subject.

FOREWORD

As a young actor starting a film career in Mexico, all I wanted to do was work and carve out a name for myself in my chosen profession. At the time, I gave little thought to the fact that I was starring with Maria Felix and Emilio "El Indio" Fernández and working with the famed cameraman Gabriel Figueroa, some of the legendary icons of the Mexican film industry in the last days of the so called "Golden Age." Of course, I knew who they were and I had grown up watching their work on the screen, but when you are on the set together and cameras are rolling, you are equals engaged as film artists, playing roles to the demands of the script, the director, and the cameraman.

My first two films were with the popular masked wrestler El Santo, whose films are truly the only genre that is uniquely Mexican. Never in my wildest dreams did I realize the power of world cinema and the characters and images we create until I went to Spain and Italy for the first time, and, everywhere I went, I was recognized from the El Santo movies.

As a leading man, I got to kiss a lot of beautiful ladies on the screen and fight off a lot of bad guys. I even starred in and produced *Indio*, a western filmed in Durango, Mexico, which was a tremendous box-office success. My agent told me about a western to be filmed in Mexico called *Soldier Blue*, directed by Ralph Nelson and starring Candice Bergen. Would I be interested in a part in the movie? I said, "Yes!" I was cast by the director Ralph Nelson in the role of the Cheyenne Indian warrior Spotted Wolf, who valiantly tries to save his tribe from annihilation by the United States Cavalry.

This was my first experience with a big-budget Hollywood production, even though most of the crewmembers were Mexican, and with whom I had worked before on many films. Mexican film crews are the best in the world and really give their all to make a production work with efficiency, talent, and artistry. The only difference between Hollywood and Mexico is the tremendous financial and technological resources that Hollywood brings to a film.

Hollywood director Howard Hawks saw me at a rodeo in Houston and asked me if I was an actor and would I like to be in his upcoming movie. Again, I said, "Yes!" Next thing I know, I am on a plane to Los Angeles, where a studio has been set up in a banquet room at the Sportsman's Lodge; this was where I was to do a screen test. I did not know much English, but I learned my lines in the script phonetically.

Into the studio, standing there bigger than life, walks John Wayne, the biggest and most famous star of his era. He comes up to me extends his hand and introduces himself: "Hi, I'm John Wayne." All I could say was: "Like I don't know who you are! Of course you are John Wayne!" He just laughed and turned to Mr.

Jorge Rivero goes over the script with John Wayne at the Cuernavaca location of *Rio Lobo* **(1970).** *Courtesy of Jorge Rivero*

Hawks and said, "I like the kid, already."

I was to play a Southern rebel soldier of mixed Mexican and French parentage, Pierre Cardona, in the western *Rio Lobo*. The Late Mexican screen idol Pedro Armendáriz had blazed a trail for me some twenty years before when he played the half-Mexican, half-Southern Union Cavalry Sgt. Beufort in *Fort Apache*, also with Wayne.

One of my leading ladies in the movie, Sherry Lansing, years later became the first woman to run both 20th Century-Fox and, later, Paramount Studios. Another young actress in the film, Susana Dosamantes, continues to work in film and is very popular to this day. In 1984, after six years as a number one box-office star, I could see that the gravy days in Mexican cinema were coming to an end, and I sought to expand my opportunities in both the United States and Europe.

The world, the movies, and I have changed considerably since I first entered the industry more than five decades ago, but the need to tell our stories, to entertain, to understand one another through the great art form of movies, remains unchanged. Technological advancements have transformed the cinema and the manner in which we watch these visual narratives have taken on new forms and formats. My movies are being seen by new generations who have discovered my work.

Looking back now, I realize how fortunate I was to have had the experience of working with these legendary talents from both Mexico and Hollywood at a time of great transition in the cinema. In some small measure, like the others who came before me, my being here has made it possible to open welcoming doors to a new generation of Mexican and U.S. visual and performing artists who contribute to the art and language of motion pictures, where creativity and imagination have no borders.

JORGE RIVERO

Jorge Rivero *Satir Gonzalez*

Jorge Rivero is the last of the leading men of Mexican cinema's golden age. Since making his film debut in 1964, Rivero has starred in more than 150 films in Mexico, Latin America, and Europe. Born and raised in Mexico City, the actor became the number-one box-office star in Mexican films for six years consecutively, and a leading male sex symbol. Jorge appeared in American movies such as Rio Lobo *with John Wayne,* Soldier Blue *with Candice Bergen, and* The Last Hard Men *with Charlton Heston and James Coburn. He has acted opposite such actresses as Isela Vega, Sasha Montenegro, and the legendary Ava Gardner. Rivero was a guest star on the epic twenty-six-hour NBC Universal Television miniseries adaptation of James H. Michener's* Centennial. *Jorge makes his residence in Hollywood with his wife, the former Betty Moran, a screenwriter, but maintains homes in his native Mexico. He remains active as a producer and actor on several ongoing media projects in both Mexico and the United States.*

INTRODUCTION

Hollywood movies made in Mexico have left an indelible imprint on the cinematic imaginings of movie-goers and filmmakers worldwide for generations. Motion pictures, the modern nation of Mexico, and Hollywood filmmaking all came of age during the first two decades of the twentieth century. For over a hundred years, cinema as an art form has been recognized as a vital part of a nation's culture. Beyond being a source of entertainment, films serve as cultural artifacts that help us understand the society that created the films and reflect the presiding ideas and values of the times.

The cowboy persona of U.S. President Theodore Roosevelt (whose term in office lasted from 1901–1908), and the prominence of Mexican bandit-turned-revolutionary hero Pancho Villa (during the years 1910–1916) captured the public's imagination. They could be considered the first of the so-called modern "media stars." Roosevelt and Villa had "charisma and cojones," politely translated as "charm and daring." They were two of the most photographed and written about figures of their time. Roosevelt, who made headlines during and after his presidency, was a larger-than-life American figure. A new American man for a new American century, he embodied manifest destiny, expansionism, and American hemispheric intervention as dictated by the Monroe Doctrine. Even though Roosevelt's presidency was over by the time Villa rose to prominence, his influence loomed large in the American psyche. In many ways his counterpart, Pancho Villa's larger-than-life figure was born out of the Mexican Revolution. Though an uneducated outlaw, Villa instinctively understood the power of photographic images and motion pictures to convey ideas as well as create a distinctive persona. He became, not only a national hero, but a worldwide celebrity. The Mexican Revolution (1910–1920) was the first large-scale and nationalistic revolution of the twentieth century. It is estimated that more than a million people perished in the multi-phase, devastating factional warfare that prompted massive immigration from Mexico into the U.S. through El Paso, Texas. Because the Mexican Revolution took place along the southern United States border, it inspired immense newspaper and photographic media coverage, not only in the United States, but from all over the world. The Mexican Revolution was also the first modern conflict to have access to the developing medium of moving pictures, even though crude motion picture cameras had covered (in a very limited fashion) the Spanish-American War and the Balkan Wars. In 1914, Villa signed a $25,000 contract with the Mutual Film Company of New York for exclusive rights to film him and his battles. (The contract resides in a museum in Mexico City at the Archivo Federico Gonzalez Garza, folio 3057, and according to Friedrich Katz, a leading Villa historian, what "the contract did specify was that Mutual Film Company was granted exclusive rights to film Villa's troops in battle and that Villa would receive 20 percent of all revenues that the films produced.") Mutual's D. W. Griffith, an American film pioneer, sent his young protégé Raoul Walsh (who later became a director in his own right) with five thousand dollars, a general's costume, and a small camera crew to Mexico.

This would be the first of many varied cinematic projects shot in that country over the next century. Since then, more than one hundred major Hollywood film productions have gathered up their star actors and crews and traveled south of the border to make movies. A significant number of these films have become classics and, though they differ, they all embrace Mexico, its culture, its people, and its exquisite locations. The country's respective backdrops have proven alluring to American film producers and moviegoers everywhere. However, the majority of these films are about Americans or foreigners in Mexico, not about Mexicans themselves. More often than not, they are from the gringo's point of view and generally do not go beyond national or individual stereotypes. Mexico has had a long and turbulent history with the United States, making for an uneasy relationship between the two countries to the present time. At the turn of the twentieth century, Mexico was identified by its proximity to the U.S., a country torn by violence and revolution and peopled by noble peasants, beautiful señoritas, and bandidos. Mexico, both real and romanticized, is a cinematic extension and manifestation of the mythic Old West. In European films, especially the spaghetti westerns of the sixties, Mexico and the American West are part of a reimagined mythic Old West that has nothing to do with actual history or authenticity and more to do with post-war European Politics.

Philip French in his book, *Westerns: Aspects of a Movie Genre*, states: "[G]enre films like Westerns express the political moods of their times more accessibly than any other genre because of their conventions."

Glenn Erickson, on his DVD Savant webpage, writes about foreign intervention in the American Western and espouses his own thoughts on a subgenre of Westerns about gun-toting Americans adventuring in Mexico. Such films "can be seen as an ever changing record of U. S. attitudes toward military intervention overseas, our real 'foreign policy,' as it were. Nothing defines Americans better than how they comport themselves overseas." Some of the films cited by Erickson for inclusion in this subgenre are *Vera Cruz* (1954), *The Magnificent Seven* (1960), *Major Dundee* (1965), and *The Wild Bunch* (1969), all of which were filmed in Mexico.

The global image of Mexico in the first two decades of the twenty-first century, as perceived through American popular culture and fueled by the media, is a country characterized by drug wars, immigration, and spring break vacation paradises. Ironically, in 1913, the most famous Mexican was Pancho Villa, a hundred years later the most famous Mexican is the powerful drug cartel leader Joaquin "El Chapo" (Shorty) Guzman. Hollywood courted both of them in order to bring their exploits to the screen.

On October 2, 2015, popular Mexican actress Kate del Castillo and two-time Oscar-wining American actor Sean Penn caused an international furor when they arranged for a secret meeting in Mexico with El Chapo, in order to secure his cooperation for a proposed film biography. El Chapo had recently escaped from a maximum-security prison and was eluding authorities on both sides of the border. He posed for a picture with the two stars that went viral on the Internet, and the colorful shirt El Chapo sported became a most sought-after fashion item. From bandidos to narco trafficantes and drug cartel leaders, this is a distorted image of Mexico and its people through the prism of Hollywood's lens, clouded by history, language, cultural differences, ignorance, and prejudice. But, on both sides of the Rio Grande, filmmakers' romance with the real and "reel" Mexico continues to nurture the visual narrative of both countries through technological advances in multimedia platforms into the twenty-first century.

Made in Mexico documents and examines more than one hundred major Hollywood theatrical feature films that have been made in Mexico between 1914 and the present, and how Hollywood filmmakers influenced Mexican films, and how Mexican filmmakers influenced Hollywood. From its formative years there has always been a vital exchange of talents between Hollywood and Mexico, including actors, artists, and technicians. *Dolores Tierney in Emilio Fernández: Pictures in the Margin* (Manchester University Press, 2007) states: "In the case of Mexico, examining U.S.

work alongside Mexican films deepens our understanding of the country's cinematic history where border crossings have shaped the national cinema" of both countries. The majority of Hollywood films made on actual Mexican locations commenced in earnest right after World War II, with the advent of better transportation, lighter film cameras, lower labor costs, and the availability of a skilled Mexican film industry work force. Technological advancements in widescreen processes, such as CinemaScope, needed unique, unspoiled, never-before-seen vistas for the cameras to serve as backdrops for the stories. Prior to that time, an imaginary Mexico, filmed primarily as a backdrop for westerns, was cobbled together from makeshift Mexican village sets of adobe and red-tiled roofs on studio ranches and Hollywood backlots. *Made in Mexico* lists each motion picture chronologically, with cast, credits, synopsis, and critical reviews along with a production history. This book will also examine how Hollywood films depicted Mexico and how Mexico represented itself on film in relation to the films shot on location. Mexico also was used by Hollywood as a backdrop for non-Mexican locales. *Made in Mexico* will also provide a historical perspective in order to understand the socioeconomics and politics of the film industries of both countries in order to better comprehend the external forces at play in selecting Mexican production venues. For purposes of this book, Hollywood films are classified as primarily English-language theatrical feature motion pictures that were partially or totally filmed in Mexico, produced by a major Hollywood studio or independent American releasing company.

Some of the greatest names in American cinema have worked in Mexico. Every major Hollywood star, from Clark Gable to Paul Newman, from Brad Pitt to Angelina Jolie, has worked in Mexico. Classic Hollywood directors, such as John Ford, Howard Hawks, Orson Welles, and John Huston, as well as more contemporary helmers John Schlesinger, Tony Scott, and Oscar-winning directors James Cameron, Oliver Stone, and Mel Gibson have all made films in Mexico. *The Treasure of the Sierra Madre*; *The Fugitive*; *The Lady From Shanghai*; *Captain from Castile*; *The Sun Also Rises*; *The Magnificent Seven*; *The Wild Bunch*; *Dune*; *Honey, I Shrunk the Kids*, and *Apocalypto* are just some of the diverse movies made in Mexico that have left an indelible mark on film history. The 1997 Academy Award–winning Best Picture *Titanic*, based on the twentieth century's most famous maritime disaster, was filmed entirely in Mexico, as was a segment of the Oscar-nominated *Babel* and the Jack Black comedy *Nacho Libre*.

Estudios Churubusco, the largest production studio in Mexico and in Latin America to this day, was built with the assistance of RKO Pictures during the 1940s as part of then-President Franklin D. Roosevelt's "Good Neighbor Policy." Mexico's long history with film and television production, along with its proximity to Hollywood and lower labor costs, has made it a viable option for American film productions.

With the increasing international nature of filmmaking and the growing importance of the U.S. Hispanic population, which is primarily of Mexican origin, it is time to examine the aesthetic, political, and economic influences of the creative talents who have crossed international borders with the universal language of film. In 2007 alone, three Mexican-born directors and their films received fourteen Academy Award nominations.

Most recently, Mexican born directors Alfonso Cuaron, Alejandro Gonzalez Inarritu and Guillermo Del Toro have dominated the Academy Awards four years consecutively by receiving Oscars for Best Director for the films *Gravity* (2014), *Birdman* (2015), *The Revenant* (2016) and *The Shape of Water* (2017). Mexican cinematographer Emmanuel Lubezki won Oscars a record three years in a row for his work on *Gravity, Birdman, and The Revenant*. The Oscar-winning cinematographer Guillermo Navarro (*Pan's Labyrinth*, 2007), as well as the Oscar-nominated Mexican actors Salma Hayek, Adriana Barraza, and Demian Bichir, have all impacted Hollywood and the international filmmaking community in a globalized media environment and transnational filmmaking.

CHAPTER 1

A Brief History of the Relationship Between the Hollywood and Mexican Film Industry

Magic, he on whose heart the dust of Mexico has lain, will find no peace in any other land. . . . There is nothing more real than magic.

—FERMIN, THE EX-BRITISH CONSUL IN JOHN
HUSTON'S FILM OF *UNDER THE VOLCANO*

***

The country of Mexico is a Federal Republic made up of thirty-one states and one federal district (Mexico City). Mexico City is the oldest and most populated city in North America with an estimated population in 2015 of 20 million people. Mexico shares a two thousand–mile border with the United States along Texas, New Mexico, Arizona, and California to the north; Belize and Guatemala in Central America to the south. Mexico has varied geography with different climate zones. Towering mountains alternate with high plateaus and scenic highlands, vast stretches of northern deserts and jungles. Mexico is bounded on two sides by expanses of water, to the west, the Pacific Ocean and, to the east, the Gulf of Mexico.

In 1889, William Kennedy Laurie Dickson developed the first motion picture cameras while working for Thomas Alva Edison in America. In 1891, Edison made patent applications for a camera called the Kinetograph and started making films in his New Jersey studio. He also patented W. K. L. Dickson's invention the Kinetoscope, an individual viewing machine. Essentially a large box

Churubusco Studios

in which a role of film—the 35mm celluloid film stock was the contribution of George Eastman—moved on spools. The viewer could drop a coin in the box and watch a very brief movie through a peephole at the top.

Edison failed to file a patent in Europe, which led the Lumiére brothers in Paris, France, to develop the first portable hand-cranked cameras and a projection device. This quickly expanded the audience for moving pictures from the individual nickelodeon viewer and laid the foundation for modern cinema and movie houses. In 1896, the first motion pictures were exhibited at the Chicago Exposition in America. Representatives of the Lumiéres exhibited films in Mexico City just a few months later, in August of 1896, to Mexican President Porfirio Diaz at Chapultepec Castle. Motion pictures became a successful entertainment industry in less than a decade. At first, moving pictures were only concerned with capturing movement, such as a man sneezing, a girl dancing, or a train arriving in a station; soon after, the art of film storytelling began to develop. With the mass-media culture that has permeated twenty-first century life, it is nearly impossible to imagine the impact those early flickering moving images projected onto a screen had on audiences of the day. In 1902, French filmmaker Georges Méliés made the film *A Trip to The Moon*, incorporating narrative and primitive special effects. The following year saw the release of a seminal American western with 1903's *The Great Train Robbery* (a one-reel film directed by Edwin S. Porter for the Edison Company, shot on the East Coast, in Dover, New Jersey). In the early 1900s, Edison's Motion Picture

Patents Company in New Jersey tried to control the use of his invention of film cameras and projectors in the emerging film industry in America. Eastern filmmakers relocated to California to get away from the strict rules imposed by Edison. Los Angeles and the tiny nearby community of Hollywood proved attractive locations due to the warm and sunny climate, diverse terrain, and available cheap labor. In the early days of filmmaking with slow film stock, sunlight was a necessary asset, with "interiors" filmed on open-air sets. Colonel William Selig, a pioneering producer in Chicago, sent a company to shoot moving pictures in Los Angeles in the fall of 1907; the Biograph Company, headed by the visionary director D. W. Griffith, arrived in 1910, followed by the Nestor Film Studio in 1911, Cecil B. DeMille in 1913, and many others. From time to time when Edison's goons came to California to strong-arm patent enforcement, the filmmakers would slip across the border into Mexico.

During the silent era, there was no Mexican film industry as such: individuals and small companies there produced movies sporadically. Salvador Toscano Barragán is considered the first Mexican filmmaker of note; he was preceded by Enrique Rosas, who began exhibiting films in Mexico at the beginning of the twentieth century. However, before the Mexican Revolution (1910–1920) caused a major upheaval in the country, thirty years of stability under the tyrannical rule of President Porfirio Diáz (1876–1910) allowed for economic and social Euro-centric artistic growth. The Mexican Revolution provided a canvas for photographers of both still and moving pictures. Photographs would be reprinted in newspapers, and moving pictures would be exhibited in nickelodeons, small theaters, auditoriums, or in tents with white bed sheets as makeshift screens. These cameramen worked for showmen and businessmen who were interested in selling tickets to audiences on both sides of the border.

Movies' popularity grew rapidly as the proliferation of nickelodeons soared after 1908; an estimated 49 million tickets had been sold each week in the United States by 1914. At the same time, artists were developing longer narratives told with increasing emotional and technical sophistication. The enormous success of D. W. Griffith's *The Birth of a Nation* in 1915 led to a rash of longer features being produced; the number reached one thousand features in 1917 alone. Such overproduction resulted in lower rental fees. Production companies and movie theater owners joined forces, creating an oligopoly of a small number of large studios. This allowed for higher rental fees on fewer, more profitable, films.

After World War I ended in late 1918, the film industry was adversely impacted by the Spanish Flu pandemic, which killed an estimated 50 to 100 million people over a two-year period. Thousands of theaters shut their doors; in the East, all filming came to a standstill; in Hollywood, production was cut at least by half. A major recession hit America in 1921, forcing many film companies into bankruptcy. Product output fell again, reaching an all-time low (just six hundred features) in 1923. This gradually improved with the advent of Hollywood's Poverty Row studios cranking out films with lower budgets.

By the mid-twenties, opulent theaters, at least in the major cities, became the norm. These movie palaces served as escapist fantasy settings for large audiences. By the later part of the decade, moviegoers were becoming acclimated to sound films, thanks to the sound-on-disc Vitaphone system, developed by Warner Bros. and its sister studio First National. Feature films and nearly a thousand short subjects were produced in this commercially successful and widely used format between 1926 and 1931.

The brothers Rodríguez—José "Joselito" and Roberto Rodríguez Ruelas—developed the first motion picture optical synchronized sound-recording system used in Mexico. In 1923, they left Mexico for Los Angeles and managed to land employment at the Metro studios. The jobs were short-lived, and the rest of the devoutly Catholic family moved to Los Angeles to escape the Mexican Cristeros Wars. They opened a bakery near the city's Mexican center on Olvera Street and were met with unprecedented success. While working at the bakery, José refined his optical-sound invention and made a short film about the sights and, most importantly, the sounds of the Spanish/Mexican Olvera Street. The film generated an enthusiastic response. When independent Mexican producers decided to come to Hollywood to license a sound system, the Rodríguez brothers demonstrated their invention and convinced the producers of the long-term viability of the equipment—and themselves as technicians and operators. With the advent of sound, Mexico was one of only three countries to develop a fully operational sound system.

José and Roberto returned to Mexico City in 1931 and worked on the first Mexican sound film, *Santa*, starring Lupita Tovar and directed by Spanish-born silent film Hollywood matinee idol Antonio Moreno. (Santa, sensitively portrayed by Tovar, is a naïve young village girl who has an affair with a young soldier. She is kicked out of her village and, in desperation, becomes a prostitute. Santa finds herself torn between her love for an arrogant bullfighter and a blind pianist.) Another brother, Ismael Rodríguez, as a writer, director, and producer, became one of the most important figures of the Mexican cinema's golden age. Enrique Rodríguez maintained recording studios in Mexico and Los Angeles, and a sister, Consuelo, was the first female sound engineer in Mexico. A younger sister, Emma, became an actress in Mexican cinema.

After a succession of post-revolutionary presidents, Mexican stability was brought about by the nationalistic government of President Lazaro Cardenas (1934–1940), the first president to serve a full six-year term. Literature, music, poetry, photography, and painting flourished during the decades of the 1930s and '40s. This allowed the motion picture industry in Mexico to also coalesce and develop with many of those in the industry who received their training or apprenticeship in Hollywood. With the release of *Santa* in 1931, Mexican films became popular abroad in the neighboring Spanish-speaking countries. It also jump-started the Mexican film industry.

For a few years, Hollywood tried to make Spanish-language versions of some of its English-language films as well as some original productions (most famously, the Spanish-language version of Universal's *Dracula* in 1931, with *Santa*'s leading actress, Lupita Tovar, and the Spanish actor Carlos Villarias in the title role).

An art form was emerging from a modern state that was about to discover the meaning of what it meant to be Mexican. A Mexican national identity was born out of the revolution, celebrating the indigenous and mestizo culture. A post-revolutionary visual culture was led, to a large degree, by the Mexican muralists Diego Rivera, David Alfardo Siqueiros, and José Clemente Orozco.

Mexico and Argentina were the only two Latin-American countries with a movie making infrastructure and the only ones with significant film production during the golden age, commonly identified as the years 1931–1960. As film historian Michael Donnelly states, "The Golden Age is a categorization supposedly given after the fact. Those making movies at the time were not aware of a Golden Age; they were going about doing what they were doing."

The Mexican film industry adopted many of the established Hollywood film genres, with slight variations, and made them their own, such as westerns, women's pictures, melodramas, films noirs, comedies, and musicals. The singing cowboy, personified in America by Gene Autry and Roy Rogers, was only made possible with the invention of sound, and became a popular genre that easily coincided with the Mexican *La Comedia Ranchera*/rural comedies. These incorporated music, comedy, drama, and nationalistic themes set in a mythical ranch populated by kind cattle barons, beautiful señoritas, and handsome cowboys who were equally adept with a guitar, a horse, and a gun. *Alla en el Rancho Grande* (*Out on the Big Ranch*), released in 1936 and starring Mexican singer Tito Guizar as a *charro* (a Mexican cowboy, usually in elaborate, traditional dress), paved the way for such Mexican singing idols as Pedro Infante and Jorge Negrete. The *charro* film character soon developed as a more traditional *vaquero* (a cattle driver) western hero, with such stars as Pedro Armendáriz and, later, Tony Aguilar and Vicente Fernández personifying the role.

In the 1950s a series of B-westerns were produced by Alfonso and Enrique Rosas Priego, stripped of their Mexican traits and filmed as *vaquero* westerns, featuring Mexican leading men. The Rosas Priego family has been involved in film production since 1906 and is still active in domestic film production to the present day.

Mexican screen comedians included Mario "Cantinflas" Moreno (1911–1993) and German "Tin Tan" Valdes. Cantinflas, who hailed from a type of Mexican vaudeville called *carpas* (tent shows), found tremendous success in Mexico and Latin America. Cantinflas added a verbal aspect to the downtrodden everyman character first cultivated

Cantinflas

in the silent cinema successfully by Charlie Chaplin, except that Chaplin's Little Tramp belonged to the entire world and Cantinflas's roles as a *pelado* (a term for "urban bum") identified strongly in Mexico and transcended into the Spanish-speaking world. RKO Pictures courted him in the mid-1940's, but he did not enter Hollywood films until 1956, when he was cast as Passepartout, the resourceful assistant to British gentleman Phileas Fogg (David Niven) in Michael Todd's Oscar-winning adaptation of Jules Verne's novel *Around the World in 80 Days*.

Sweeping historical films commenced with director Fernando Des Fuentes's realistic Mexican Revolution epic *Vamonos con Pancho Villa* (*Let's Go with Pancho Villa*) in 1936, and expanded with Emilio "El Indio" Fernández's romantic *Flor Silvestre* (*Wild Flower*, 1943) and *Maria Candelaria* (1944).

Former Mexican Hollywood star Dolores del Rio achieved even greater fame through serious and diverse film roles in her native Mexico; she was rivaled by the beautiful and tempestuous Mexican star Maria Felix. Post–World War II American urban film noir was reflected in films, directed by Julio Bracho and Roberto Gavaldon, which dealt with the rural migration to Mexico City and the corruption inherent to that locale.

The *cabaretera* (cabaret) films, such as *Sálon México* (1949), are an example of Mexican urban film noir that incorporate aspects of the melodrama and the popular tropical music emanating largely from Cuba.

The masked wrestler adventure film genre, *lucha libre* (freestyle wrestling), stands alone as truly unique to Mexican cinema, born as it was out of Mexican culture. It fuses together iconic elements of Mayan and Aztec culture with mythic Catholic-Hispanic ritual pitting good against evil. The closest American incarnation is the recent rash of superhero films that have their origins in comic books and graphic novels, such as the Marvel Super Heroes series. *Lucha libre* can be described as intensely cultural with social value that goes beyond the actual sport itself. Mexican rural and urban poor working classes in the mid-1940s gave prominence to the development of the Greco-Roman freestyle *lucha libre* as a form of mass entertainment in large and small arenas throughout the nation, events which are popular to this day.

In Carlos Avila's 2013 American documentary, *Tales of Masked Men*, there is a segment on El Santo, once a journeyman wrestler who struggled to find a place in the *lucha libre* world. El Santo (a phantom-like masked hero called "The Sainted One") rose to prominence in the ring, becoming an international film and television star in a series of films that frequently gave him supernatural powers. There also developed a star system, similar to that of Hollywood, which included such now-legendary names as Pedro Infante, Jorge Negrete, Pedro Armendàriz, María Félix, Dolores del Rio, Cantinflas, Emilio "El Indio" Fernández, Arturo de Córdova, and many others.

Estudios Churubusco, constructed in a suburb of Mexico City with the financial assistance of RKO Pictures in the mid-1940s, housed hundreds of productions. A postwar Hollywood alignment with the rising Mexican film industry seemed likely to advance American economic and political influence in Latin America. RKO provided a great deal of technical support and money, and production quality shifted to a different type of industry. Film production became more organized, artistic, polished, and reflected a national pride. It was based on the Hollywood business model in which films were shot in the studio or on nearby locations. Without having to go far out of Mexico City, productions could find fields, desert landscapes, old haciendas, forests, and lakes.

The advantages of the studio system meant a large permanent staff of competent craftsmen, research and legal departments, makeup, standing sets, props, camera, and costume departments. Motion pictures are by nature a collaborative enterprise. During World War II, Mexican cinema blossomed into an industry almost to rival Hollywood. In 1943, Gilbert Johnson, of Atlas Theatres, opened two movie houses in New York City's Times Square to show Mexican movies. These movies were reviewed by the *New York Times* and the show business trade paper *Variety* on a regular basis. Mexican films gained serious attention both in the United States and abroad for their unique style and visual expression reflecting Mexican culture and post-revolutionary ideals.

Because of economic advantages, technical capabilities (RKO's Estudios Churubusco in Mexico City, for example), and scenic locations, many Hollywood productions were filmed in Mexico beginning in the late 1940s, right after World War II. Better transportation and lighter cameras and equipment, facilitated by the war effort, also made location filming more feasible.

However, just prior to and after World War II, actors, directors, craftspeople, and technicians began to unionize. In 1948, in a landmark anti-trust decision, the United States Supreme Court ruled that studios could not own the theaters where they exhibited their films made with personnel under contract to the studios.

With the rise of the industry in Mexico, there also was union organizing by the many artists and technicians involved in the industry under ANDA (the actors union) and STPC (technicians union). Artists and social activists, such as Gabriel Figueroa and Cantinflas, championed better wages and working conditions for those in the industry; they also rooted out corruption in the upper ranks.

In the new, independent Hollywood era after World War II, the financing, making and marketing of individual films became larger and more difficult. Also, as in the United States, television was introduced in Mexico in the late '40s and early '50s, leading to a dramatic drop in movie theater attendance. To rectify this situation, U.S. producers began to offer epic films in Technicolor and various widescreen formats (e.g., CinemaScope, VistaVision, Cinerama) as well as stories with dramatic location backdrops. With its experienced crews, lower labor costs, and close proximity to the United States, Mexico was perfectly poised to take part economically and artistically in the new U.S. productions. Spain and Italy were able to benefit for the same reason.

The decline of the Mexican film industry started with the death of its leading stars—Pedro Infante, Jorge Negrete, and Pedro Armendàriz—in the latter part of the fifties and early sixties. For more than thirty years (roughly 1940–1970), Spanish-speaking audiences could count on seeing at least one of their favorite stars in films at their local cinema.

Mexican producers put profit before art, and thus started to engage in the production of films recycling themes and genres with less and less creativity. Mexico in the 1950s was emerging with a new, educated middle class, and a growing intelligentsia. Films were not keeping up with their audiences.

A number of American film actors went south of the border to work in Mexican film productions in the 1960s, including Boris Karloff, John Carradine, Jack Palance, Glenn Ford, Cameron Mitchell, Nick Adams, Robert Conrad, Jeffrey Hunter, Martha Hyer, and Shirley Jones. Just as Latin performers found themselves typecast in Hollywood, Anglos working in Mexico were limited to certain roles in Mexican movies. Jean Franco, in her book *Plotting Women: Women, Gender and Representation in Mexico* (Columbia University Press, 1989), writes: "The coda used to represent gringos continues the conventions used in the classic period. These conventions were stereotypes that fall into two categories: unscrupulous and greedy villains (*La Perla/The Pearl*) and inoffensive and unmanly objects of ridicule." A number of films produced in Mexico by American directors with Mexican crews have aesthetic Mexican sensibilities, making them virtually indistinguisible from a Mexican production.

MARILYN MONROE MYSTIQUE IN MEXICO

The legend of the enduring 1950s American blonde bombshell and screen icon Marilyn Monroe (1926–1962) extends itself to Mexico. Monroe visited Mexico on a shopping trip from February 20 to March 3, 1962, to furnish the new home she had purchased in the Brentwood area of Los Angeles, California, six months before her untimely death. Richard Meryman described Marilyn's trip to Mexico in a *Life* magazine article published twelve days after the actress's passing, on August 17, 1962: "She [Marilyn] carefully searched in roadside stands and shops and even factories to find the right things to put in her three-bedroom Mexican style home." On February 22, 1962, she stayed at the Continental Hilton Hotel in Mexico City and held a press conference for the Mexican press. Monroe wore a tight cocktail dress and sat in a chair after standing for a press photo opportunity. The crush of Mexican press photographers, TV crews, and reporters surrounded her and took countless photos. One photographer, Antonio Caballero, found himself nearly at her feet and did not realize until he developed the pictures that Marilyn was not wearing any underwear; when she uncrossed her legs, her pubic hair revealed that she was not a natural blonde. The photos appeared in a censored version in the

Marilyn Monroe in Mexico.

Mexican newspapers two days later, and worldwide the following week. She visited Estudios Churubusco and met with famed Mexican cinematographer Gabriel Figueroa, who was working with Spanish director Luis Buñuel on the set of *The Exterminating Angel*. The star also visited with famed Mexican director Emilio Fernàndez, who held a dinner party at his home in her honor. She spent two days in Taxco and stayed at the Hotel La Borda, where her constant escort, José Bolaños, a Mexican screenwriter (*La Cucaracha*, 1961) and producer hired mariachis to serenade her. She stopped in Acapulco for a brief stay, after which she returned to Los Angeles. The Hollywood Foreign Press awarded her a Golden Globe as Female Star of the Year at the awards ceremony in Beverly Hills on March 5, which she attended with Bolaños. The actress immortalized a brown-and-white Mexican sweater she posed in on a cold, windswept Santa Monica beach, in her last photo session for famed photographer George Barris in July of 1962. Monroe was found dead at her home of a drug overdose, at age thirty-six, on August 5, 1962. She was buried in the short, lime-green Emilio Pucci dress she wore at the press conference in Mexico. Legend has it that she bought the sweater for 130 pesos in the little town of Chiconcuac, near Cuernavaca, Mexico. In fact, that Mexican sweater belonged to a woman named Katie, who had purchased it from Mexican sweater artisan and designer Rosario Martinez. Katie was an acquaintance of Monroe's and gifted the sweater to the actress. Monroe wore the sweater in her last photo session in July, just days before her passing. Marilyn had been to Mexico previously in, Juarez, for her divorce from her third husband, Pulitzer Prize–winning playwright Arthur Miller, on January 20, 1961. After the divorce decree, she rode around Juarez and stopped at the famous (Prohibition era) Kentucky Club bar, where she bought all the customers a round of drinks to celebrate her divorce. Monroe was 20th Century-Fox Studios most important female star of the era and she starred in such box-office hits as *Gentelemen Prefer Blondes* (1953), *Niagara* (1953), *Bus Stop* (1956), *How To Marry a Milionaire* (1955), and *Some Like It Hot* (1959). (Interesting to note that seven years prior to Monroe's passing, another curvaceous and troubled star, sultry blonde Czech-born Mexican actress Miroslava Stern (1925–1955), who appeared in some thirty Mexican, and two American, films, died of a drug overdose at her Mexico City home; she was twenty-nine.)

In 1960, *Macario*, directed by Roberto Gavaldon, an allegorical Day of the Dead tale set in Colonial Mexico was based on "The Third Guest," a short story by B. Traven. The story centered on a poor woodcarver named Macario, who meets God, the Devil, and Death. Photographed by Gabriel Figueroa, the film became the first Mexican production nominated for an Academy Award in the Best Foreign Language category.

Mexican President Luis Echeverria (who served in that capacity from 1970–1976) took over the film industry, which was in serious decline, and appointed his brother, actor Rodolfo Echeverria, to run it. This meant big-budget productions but, by this time, the companies had lost worldwide distribution to the growing dominance of Hollywood films and lack of production. "A slow pace of production made it difficult to establish a loyal audience—something that was key to success in Latin cinema years ago," remarks Mexican film historian Michael Donnelly. "You need a consistency in production, otherwise you just have the opportunistic film that does well when it comes out." Mexican-born producers Lance and Conrad Hool, along with Pancho Kohner, produced a number of films with star actors for the international market, including *St. Ives*, *Cabo Blanco*, and *Crocodile Dundee in Los Angeles*. *Gaby: A True Story* (1987), directed by Luis Mandoki, is a U.S.–Mexico collaboration that captured an Academy Award nomination for Best Supporting Actress Norma Aleandro, as well as Golden Globe nominations. Mexican films were being exported to Latino communities in the United States and, since they were grossing dollars, not pesos, the U.S. became a prime market for exploitation films containing sex and violence. Raunchy comedies and border/ drug-trafficking dramas reigned at the box office during the eighties.

In the 1990s, a new generation of Mexican filmmakers, like Maria Novarro and Alfonso Arau, with the critically acclaimed magic realism of the worldwide hit *Like Water for Chocolate* (1991) and Nicholas Echevarria's *Cabeza De Vaca* (1991), spurred film activity through international co-productions. Alfonso Arau followed with the Hollywood production of *A Walk in the Clouds* starring Keaneu Reeves and Anthony Quinn, a remake of a 1942 Italian film. For *A Walk in the Clouds*, Arau gave cinematographer Emmauel Lubeski his first Hollywood feature film assignment.

Influenced by Hollywood and golden age Mexican cinema, "Chicano" (second generation Mexican-Americans with social and artistic concerns borne out of the civil rights movement) produced a number of independent and Hollywood-based feature films that reflected their U. S. bicultural experience. Beginning with Jesus Treviño's *Raices de Sange / Roots of Blood* (1978), in which filmmakers from Mexico and the U. S. jointly produced a dramatic film about labor organizing along the Mexico/U. S. Border. The film, which launched Treviño on a career in television directing, featured Pepe Serna (*Scarface*, 1983) and Richard Yniguez (*Boulevard Nights*, 1979) in leading roles. These films addressed the social history of Mexican-Americans in the U. S., with themes that reflected a new American identity rooted in the American experience, including those of Luis Valdez (*Zoot Suit*, 1983; *La Bamba*, 1987), Gregory Nava (*El Norte*, 1983; *My Family/Mi Familia* (1995); *Selena* (1997), Edward James Olmos (*American Me*, 1992), Ramon Menendez (*Stand and Deliver*, 1988), Moctesuma Esparza (*The Milagro Beanfield War*, 1988, directed by Robert Redford), Cheech Marin (*Born in East L. A.*, 1987), Robert M. Young (*The Ballad of Gregorio Cortez*, 1982), Carlos Avila (*Price of Glory*, 2000), and Patricia Cardoso's/Josefina Lopez (*Real Women Have Curves*, 2002). Cuban-American Leon Ichasso directed the independently produced *El Super* (1979), *Crossover Dreams* (1985), *Piñero* (2001), and *El Cantante* (2006). New York–born Puerto Rican filmmaker Franc Reyes directed *Empire* (2002) and *Illegal Tender* (2007). Texas-born Robert Rodriguez, who was influenced by Sergio Leone westerns and John Carpenter's *Escape from New York* (1981), made his debut in 1992 with the 16mm $7,000 feature *El Mariachi*; this brought him to the attention of Hollywood, where he made his reputation with stylish, money-making action films, such as *Desperado* (1995), *From Dusk Till Dawn* (1996), *Once Upon a Time in Mexico* (2003), and a rare yet successful foray into family fare (Spy Kids franchise, 2001–2011).

Amores Perros (2000), *Y Tu Mama Tambien* (2001), and *Cronos* (2003) sparked a renaissance in Mexican cinema in the early 2000s and set in motion the careers of a new generation of Mexican filmmakers, directors, actors, and screenwriters who have crossed over to Hollywood. Alfonso Cuaron, Guillermo del Toro, and Alejandro Gutierrez Iñárritu are part of a talented wave of directors who came to prominence with their Spanish-language films. Alfonso Cuaron (*Harry Potter and the Prisoner of Azkaban*, 2004; *Gravity*, 2013) is noted for his mainstream filmmaking; Alejandro Gonzalez Iñárritu (*Babel*, 2006; *Birdman*, 2014) makes highly personal, quirky mainstream films; Del Toro is known for his fantasy and horror films (*Cronos*, 1993; *Pan's Hellboy*, 2004; *Pan's Labyrinth*, 2006). These auteurs have influenced Hollywood aesthetics through Iñárritu's multiple interlocking stories converging in one incident (*Crash*, 2004; *Syriana*, 2005), extensive hand-held or Steadicam camera work (*The Bourne Ultimatum*, 2007), and digital desaturation of the color palettes. These techniques are not exclusive to Mexico and indeed have their foundations in the independent cinema of the sixties. Actors such as Gael Garcia Bernal, Diego Luna, and Oscar nominees Salma Hayek and Demian Bichir have chosen to work in Mexico and in Hollywood on international productions.

20th Century Fox leased forty acres of seaside land in Rosarito Baja California, just south of Tijuana, and constructed two huge outdoor water tanks with the actual ocean horizon behind it, along with sound stages and offices for James Cameron's *Titanic* (1997). For this mammoth production, Cameron utilized the services of hundreds of Mexican technicians, laborers, workers, and extras. Sebastian Silva was the lead Mexican assistant director on the film. With only one of three outdoor water tanks in the world—the other two being in Malta and Australia—Fox Baja Studio has hosted such productions as *Pearl Harbor* (2001) and *Master and Commander: The Far Side of the World* (2003). When Fox sold its interest in the studio the facility passed on to private Mexican investors and as Baja Studios continues to serve such productions as Robert Redford's seafaring vehicle *All Is Lost* (2013) and the 2015 remake of *Point Break* (1991).

Pantelion Films, a division of Mexico's media giant Televisa, launched a filmmaking arm with U.S.-based Lionsgate Films to produce Latin-themed films for Mexico and U.S. audience consumption. The company's first breakout hit, *Instructions Not Included* (2013), starring popular Mexican comedian Eugenio Derbez—who also wrote the screenplay, as well as produced and directed—became the highest grossing independent Spanish-language film in U.S. history, with a domestic box-office gross of $44.5 million dollars. This was followed in 2014 with the Mexican-Spanish co-production *Cantinflas*, based on the life of the famous Mexican comedic screen idol, grossing $6.5 million in the United States alone.

There is an ever-growing influx of cinematic Mexican talent such as Gael Garcia Bernal, Diego Luna, and producer Pablo Cruz along with Oscar nominees Salma Hayek and Demian Bichir, with the ability to traverse on a transnational level both their native film industry and Hollywood. As actor/director Alfonso Arau remarked to an audience at the Guadalajara Film Festival in Los Angeles, "If you are a filmmaker, you need to be at the center of the film world, which is Hollywood." Mexican screenwriter Guillermo Arriaga (*21 Grams*, 2003) wrote the screenplay for the modern-day western *The Three Burials of Melquiades Estrada* (2005) that was made into a film directed by and starring Tommy Lee Jones. The film has parallels to Peckinpah's *Bring Me the Head of Alfredo Garcia* (1974) and clearly shows that film's influences. Gerardo Naranjo directed the gritty tale of a beauty contestant who gets involved with the Mexican crime underworld in *Miss Bala* (2011), a tremendous box-office hit in Mexico that gained notoriety in the United States. Naranjo's reputation caught the attention of young American actress Dakota Fanning, who starred in his most recent film, *Viena and the Fantomes* (2016). Gabriel Ripstein, the nephew of famed Mexican director Arturo Ripstein, directed his first feature, *600 Miles* (2016), starring Tim Roth. Mexican-born director Patricia Riggen made her film debut with the Fox Searchlight release *Bajo la Misma/Luna Under the Same Moon* (2007), which was a box-office hit in both Mexico and the United States, and led to her directing the big-budget feature *The 33* (2015), starring Antonio Banderas. The story of the trapped Chilean miners, *The 33* was filmed in Colombia and Chile, with Riggen's husband, Checco Varese, as the cinematographer.

Today, Mexico City is the center of domestic Mexican film production. It is where more than 85 percent of the country's film industry is based, including more than twenty sound stages, ninety-five rental companies, eight laboratories and forty-eight casting agencies. Twenty-eight films were made in Mexico in 2000; in 2014, that number rose to 130. Since 2014, Mexican-born filmmakers working in Hollywood have dominated the Academy Awards. Collectively "the Three Amigos" (Inarritu, Cuaron, and del Toro) as they have been dubbed by the press, have won eight competitive Oscars and one for Special Achievement and have a total of seventeen Oscar nominations plus three nominations for Mexico in the Best Foreign Language film category.

Alejandro Gonzalez Inarritu made history as the first Mexican to win the Oscar for Best Director two years in a row for *Birdman* in 2015 and *The Revenant* in 2016. It is somehow fitting that actor Leonardo Di Caprio, who was catapulted to stardom with the Mexico-filmed *Titanic*, won his Academy Award as Best Actor for his performance in *The Revenant* under the direction of Inarritu. Alfonso Cuaron won Oscars in 2014 as Best Director and for Best picture (*Gravity*). This winning streak continued at the 90th Academy Awards ceremony with Guillermo del Toro's win for Best Director and Best Picture (*The Shape of Water*).

Mexico City born cinematographer Emmanuel Lubeski is a three-time Academy Award winner: *Gravity* (2014), *Birdman* (2015), and *The Revenant* (2017). Cinematographer Rodrigo Prieto was nominated for an Oscar for Martin Scorsese's *Silence* (2016).

Carne y Arena/Flesh and Sand (2017), Inarritu's extraordinary and immersive virtual reality short film which details the experience of an immigrant illegally entering the United States, earned him a Special Achievement Oscar for his collaboration with cinematographer Emmanuel Lubeski. A press release issued by the Academy on October 27, 2017 states: " More than even a creative breakthrough in the still emerging form of virtual reality, it viscerally connects us to the hot button political and social realities of the U.S.-Mexico border."

According to John Hecht, Mexican correspondent for *The Hollywood Reporter*, "The common thread is that they (Cuaron, Inarritu, and del Toro) all took risks . . . They push the limits of technology, the limits of photography, and the limits of storytelling."

Pixar's *Coco* (2017), directed by Lee Unkrich and Adrian Molina, which highlights the Mexican cultural tradition of the Day of The Dead, won the Oscar for Best Animated Feature Film. The film also won an Oscar for Best Song—"Remember Me", written by Robert Lopez and his wife Kristen Anderson-Lopez. *Coco* became the highest grossing Mexican film of all time and was a global hit, featuring an impressive voice cast of Latino actors from both Mexico and the United States.

In his Oscar acceptance speech, Guillermo del Toro said, " I think the greatest thing our industry does is erase the lines in the sand. We should keep doing that as the world tries to make them deeper."

CHAPTER 2

CULTURAL TRADITIONS AND NATIONAL SELF IDENTITY

JOHN FORD (1894–1973) AND EMILIO FERNÁNDEZ (1904–1986)

Film directors John Ford, in the United States, and Emilio "El Indio" Fernández, in Mexico, forged evocative and enduring images of their respective countries, histories, landscapes, and peoples. Ford and Fernández shared an instinctive sense of cinema and societies, though the Old West and Mexico never really existed as they are presented on film. Fernández once remarked, "Only one Mexico exists, the one I invented." Such an invention would not have been possible without the faces of actors like Dolores del Rio, Pedro Armendáriz, the scripts of Mauricio Magdaleno, the editing of Gloria Schoemann, and the cinematography of Gabriel Figueroa. Figueroa's skies, clouds, haciendas, and chiaroscuro became, for better or worse, the national image of Mexico on the world's screens.

Ford created iconic cinematic images of America's frontier and its people, which helped forge a national identity for America during the first half of the twentieth century through films like *The Iron Horse* (1924), *Young Mr. Lincoln, Stagecoach* (1939), *The Grapes of Wrath* (1940), *My Darling Clementine* (1946), *Fort Apache* (1948), and *The Searchers* (1956). Ford and other pioneering film directors helped establish Americans' sense of their own popular history (particularly the Mythic Old West), which influenced generations. "No American director has ranged across the landscape of the American past, the worlds of Lincoln, Lee, Twain, O'Neill, the three great wars, the Western and Trans-Atlantic migration, the horseless Indians of the Mohawk Valley and the Sioux and Comanche, cavalries of the West, the Irish and Spanish incursions and the delicately balanced politics of polyglot cities and border states," wrote Andrew Sarris in *Film Culture* (No. 25, Summer 1962).

Emilio Fernandez and John Ford on the set of *The Fugitive* (1947).

This blending of cultures, myth vs. reality, profoundly influenced American and Mexican film. The American dream and its mythology was played out on the big screens and acted as a unifying factor, especially with the distinctive image of the American cowboy. Ford's use of Monument Valley in Utah, his stirring cavalry charges, his evocation of Frederic Remington's western paintings coincide with Mexico's Emilio Fernández. Fernández celebrated Mexico's indigenous and mestizo cultures, and gained inspiration from such Mexican muralists as Diego Rivera, Alfardo Siqueiros, and José Clemente Orozco. Ford used actors John Wayne, Henry Fonda, Victor McLaglen, and Maureen O'Hara in the same way that Fernández used Dolores del Rio, Pedro Armendáriz, Maria Felix, and others as personifications of national figures. "Mexican cinema has practiced celluloid Imperialism just as Hollywood is so often accused of doing," observes Carl J. Mora in *Mexican Cinema: Reflections of a Society 1896–1998* (Berkeley, CA: Berkeley University Press, 1992). The images, the music, and the stars created by the Mexican cinema during its golden age dominated film screens throughout Latin America and reinforced a national identity throughout the world. So much so that, despite the "Good Neighbor Policy," Mexico and the rest of Latina America, with the exception of Peron's Argentina and perhaps Cuba, were in the American popular culture as one, large south of the border extension of Mexico.

Emilio Fernández was born in Coahuila, Mexico, in 1904, of a Spanish father and an Indian mother, thus the affectionate sobriquet "El Indio." As a youth, Fernández joined the rebels against Adolfo De La Huerta during the Mexican Revolution and was captured and sentenced to twenty years in prison. He escaped and made his way to the U.S. and headed to Chicago in 1923.

He ultimately settled in Los Angeles in 1924, where he began his career in film as an actor's double (stand-in) and extra in Hollywood. According to Fernández, while "working extra" on the Douglas Fairbanks starrer *The Thief of Bagdad* (1924), he gave director Raoul Walsh the idea for the opening sequence during a lunch break when he noticed that Walsh was experiencing difficulty with it.

During his stay in Hollywood, Fernández became friends with Dolores del Rio, who had become a film star in Hollywood and later married the celebrated MGM art director Cedric Gibbons (they were married from 1930–1941). When the Academy of Motion Pictures Arts and Sciences was founded in 1927, Gibbons was given the assignment of designing an award statuette. He sketched a knight with a sword standing on top of reels of film. Gibbons needed a life model to pose nude for the statuette and Del Rio suggested Fernández, who, in need of money, agreed. The Oscar statuette's square chest and broad shoulders closely resemble Fernández's young physique as documented in pictures of Fernández of that era. The first Academy Awards of Merit Oscars were handed out in 1929 and is, today, one of the most recognized trophies in the world.

Fernández and Del Rio nurtured a friendship, and, years later, when she returned to Mexico to make movies, she did so with Emilio Fernández as her director. The fact that Del Rio was already an established international film star gave prominence to Mexican cinema worldwide. "I got tired of being a star, I wanted to be an actress and I found it difficult to reveal myself as a serious actress," she remarked during an onstage tribute at the San Francisco Film Festival on October 11, 1981, referring to the Hollywood typecasting that led her to participate in the films of her native country.

She enjoyed immediate success in her first two films under Fernández's direction in Mexico, *Flor Silvestre* and *Maria Candelaria*. Curiously, the plot of the latter film involves a simple peasant woman who poses for an artist and enrages the town with her supposed nudity. During his time in Hollywood, Fernández was influenced by Russian director and film theorist Sergei Eisenstein (*Battleship Potemkin*, 1925), who was courted by Paramount Studios and accepted a short-term contract from that studio that ran from May through October of 1930. Invited by Dolores del Rio and Eisenstein's Mexican assistant director Luciano "Chano" Urueta to a screening at Paramount, Fernández was impressed with the rushes he saw from Eisenstein's *Que Viva Mexico!* that was shot in Mexico in 1930 and 1931. The proposed film was to be an episodic portrayal of Mexican culture and politics from pre-conquest civilization to the present. The contract stated that the film could not show or imply anything that could be construed as insulting to, or critical of, post-revolution Mexico (a condition imposed by the Mexican government before it would allow Eisenstein and his two associates entry into Mexico. Eisenstein shot somewhere between thirty to fifty hours of footage. It was the only film Eisenstein was able to make outside the constraints of the Soviet Union. Leftist progressive American millionaire author Upton Sinclair financed the film but stopped the funding at the crucial editing stage. Joseph Stalin ordered Eisenstein back to the Soviet Union, and *Que Viva Mexico!* remained unfinished.

When the Mexican government gave a general amnesty to all revolutionaries, Fernández went home to Mexico. Even though he loved the United States, it was not his country. He therefore took what he learned

Pedro Armendariz and Dolores Del Rio in Emilio Fernandez's
Flor Silvestre/Wildflower **(1943).**

in Hollywood and related it to Mexico. Like John Ford, he gave his films "a perceived and emotional reality that audiences in both Mexico and the United States related to," according to film historian Michael Donnelly.

Upon his return in 1934, Fernández began his career in the local movie industry as an actor in *Corazon Bandolero* and *Janitizio*, the latter his first starring role. He was also a writer and assistant director on a number of films. *La Isla De La Passion* (1941) marked Fernández's debut as a director, actor, and writer. The artistic partnership of Fernández, cinematographer Gabriel Figueroa, and screenwriter Mauricio Magdaleno began in 1943 with the film *Flor Silvestre*, followed by *Las Abadonadas, Bugambilia,* and *Maria Candelaria,* all released in 1944. Fernández's relationship with his cinematographer Gabriel Figueroa compares with that of Ford and Gregg Toland, Bert Glennon, or Winton C. Hoch, in which their respective visions complemented each other.

Maria Candelaria won the Grand Prix, now known as the Palme D'or prize, as Best Film at France's Cannes Film Festival in 1946. It was picked up for U.S. distribution by MGM, dubbed into English, and released under the title *Portrait of Maria*. In 1945, Fernández adapted John Steinbeck's *The Pearl* for the screen with the help of the novel's author. Figueroa's cinematography on location in Acapulco earned him a Golden Globe award.

After the revolution, Mexico was a country searching for itself. The Mexican muralists and other prominent artists were in the vanguard to establish *Mexicanidad* (Mexican Identity). The artists' nationalism was reflected in cultural touchstones, traditions of the indigenous people, popular traditions, and distinctly Mexican landscapes. Ford's use of Monument Valley's landscapes defined the image of the American West that is still in use today. Some of Ford's films reflected social issues, such as themes of race and Native Americans. The social, historical, and political context of the Mexican Revolution and the films emerging with stories from that recent conflict (1910–1921) were familiar to Mexican audiences of the thirties and forties as the Civil War and the American West were to Americans. The western hero and the Mexican *charro vaquero* are subjects, whose roots are in history, whose images have been transformed into myth, and whose chief function for contemporary audiences was to provide popular entertainment.

Fernández's best work grew out of a partnership with his leading actors, cinematographer, and writers in much the same way that John Ford did with his so-called "stock company," including Harry Carey, George O'Brien, Victor McLaglen, Henry Fonda, Maureen O'Hara, and John Wayne. The charismatic but volatile

Fernández, like John Ford, inspired amazing loyalties from many talented film artists. Fernández had little formal education, and everything he undertook was self-taught. He understood the film business, the workings of the camera, how to delegate, and most of all, he understood his limitations.

✳✳✳

In 1946, John Ford went to Mexico to film *The Fugitive*, Dudley Nichols's adaptation of Graham Greene's anti-clerical novel, *The Labyrinthine Ways* (a.k.a. *The Power and the Glory*), the story of a priest on the run in an anti-clerical Central American country, who determines to honor his religious duties while eluding the military and his own fall from grace. The movie, like the Greene novel, illustrated a part of Mexican history beginning in 1926, when President Plutarco Elias Calles began strict enforcement of the anti-clerical provisions of the Constitution of 1917 and the expansion of further restrictive laws. Since colonial times, the Catholic Church was a major landowner and asserted power and influence in Mexico. Calles's strict enforcement of anti-clerical laws sparked opposition from the Catholic Church, which resulted in regional internal uprisings in Mexico against the government by Catholics. The long, bloody fight resulted in diplomatic U.S. intervention in order to end the crisis that was destabilizing the country and affecting U.S. interests. In retrospect, it is somewhat amazing that *The Fugitive* was made in Mexico at all considering that this little-known chapter was a relatively recent and sensitive situation. Mexican President Miguel Aleman Valdez (who served between 1946–1952) approved *The Fugitive* after a meeting with Figueroa, Del Rio, and RKO executives.

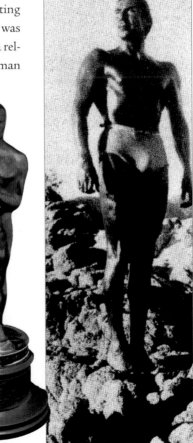

Although *The Fugitive* was made in Mexico and events obviously took place there, the location is never identified as such in the film. The anti-clerical stance in the movie is never explained and comes off like postwar communist totalitarianism. There was criticism within Mexico about the version of the anti-clerical campaign portrayed in the film. *The Fugitive* was filmed entirely on Mexican locations and at Estudios Churubusco in Mexico City from November 4, 1946 through January 27, 1947. Ford wisely surrounded himself with some of the country's finest filmmaking talent, including leading star Armendáriz and Del Rio. Emilio Fernández, who had directed the pair in the 1944 hit *Maria Candelaria*, was Ford's associate producer and assistant director. In spite of its flaws,

When he was still working as an extra in Hollywood, Emilio Fernandez served as the nude model for the Oscar statue, designed by Cedric Gibbons. *A.M.P.A.S. Fernandez from Janitzio (1934).*

The Fugitive allowed people of great talent, knowledge, and experience to work together in a transnational cinematic enterprise.

"It came out the way I wanted it to, that's why it is one of my favorite pictures," John Ford explained in a 1966 interview. "To me it was perfect. It wasn't popular, the critics got at it, and evidently, it had no appeal to the public, but I was very proud of my work."

Upon completing *The Fugitive*, Ford put Pedro Armendáriz under contract to his newly formed Argosy Pictures and co-starred him with John Wayne as a Mexican outlaw in *3 Godfathers* (1948). That same year, Ford's Cavalry picture *Fort Apache* starred Wayne as Captain Kirby York, Henry Fonda as Colonel Owen Thursday, Miguel Inclán as Cochise, and Armendáriz as Sergeant Beaufort. Casting Mexico's leading actor opposite John Wayne simply made good business sense to Ford, who was able to profitably sell his films to all of Latin America, as well as the world. Armendáriz, who was raised in Mexico but schooled in the United States, spoke perfect English. Ford, Wayne, and Armendáriz became fast friends.

The first two decades of the twentieth century in America saw the closing of the West, industrialization, waves of immigrants from Europe, the Mexican Revolution, and World War I. Films were originally seen as an entertainment for the masses and, in America's case, it was largely an uneducated though literate (20 percent of the U.S. population was illiterate, as compared with Mexico, which had an 85 percent illiteracy rate in 1910), rural population that was being infused with European immigrants concentrated in Eastern industrial cities but soon migrated across the country. This changed the character of America and its sense of identity. Filmmakers quickly saw motion pictures as a way to unify American audiences, as did filmmakers in Mexico. These early films provided Mexican audiences, for the first time, with glimpses not only of the outside world but of their own country. The Mexican Revolution caused mass movements of people, not only across Mexico but also into the southwestern United States as refugees and political exiles escaping the bloody conflict.

John Ford was born John "Jack" Martin O'Feeney on February 1, 1894, in St. Elizabeth, Maine, the son of Irish immigrants. After high school and a short time in college, he followed his older brother, Francis Ford, to Hollywood, where Francis had found success as an actor/director beginning in 1909. John began as an actor, stuntman, and assistant director in the film industry and was given the opportunity to direct a series of westerns with actor Harry Carey; these proved to be quite popular. Ford's reputation was cemented with his direction of the 1924 silent western epic *The Iron Horse*. During a career that spanned over fifty years and 146 films, from 1917–1966, Ford won seven Oscars, four for directing, one for Best Picture, and two for Best Documentary.

Emilio Fernández directed 43 films, twenty-four with his closest collaborator, Gabriel Figueroa. In later years he began repeating himself as a director. None of his films after 1960 are highly regarded, although he continued directing until 1979. Ford's last highly regarded movie was *The Man Who Shot Liberty Valence* in 1962, though he completed three more afterward: *Donovan's Reef* (1963), *Cheyenne Autumn* (1964), and *7 Women* (1966). Fernández returned to acting in 1958 at the request of director Ismael Rodríguez for his epic story of the revolution, *La Cucaracha*, which also starred Pedro Armendáriz and paired, for the only time, rival screen divas Dolores del Rio and Maria Felix.

Hollywood directors who filmed there understood that Mexican union rules required that any foreign production hire Mexican assistant directors, and Emilio Fernández, who knew the film business, found regular employment in Hollywood productions as an assistant director. American directors discovered Fernán-

Key elements from *The Bravados* (1958) including a lone rider silhouetted against Mexican adobes inspired Sergio Leone's *For a Few Dollars More* (1965).

dez as an actor in the early sixties and he began appearing in more and more Hollywood films, shot both in and out of Mexico. His volatile temper (he once shot a film critic) and alcoholism soon made this respected director an object of derision. This man, who had helped to create the most beautiful images of Mexico, created, in later life, a most memorable stereotypical portrayal as the violent and drunken General Mapache in Peckinpah's *The Wild Bunch* (1969). On the other hand, he vowed to bring authenticity to spaghetti westerns and films made in Spain with a Mexican setting when he and Rudy Acosta were hired as actors for *Return of the Seven* (1966). Fernández also made a cameo appearance as a shepherd in Peckinpah's *Pat Garrett and Billy the Kid* (1973) and played a significant role in *Bring Me the Head of Alfredo Garcia* (1974). He was last seen on American screens in Huston's *Under the Volcano* (1984).

Over their lifetimes, Ford and Fernández became functioning real-life caricatures or cultural stereotypes. Ford transformed into the functional "drunken Irish poet," while Fernández became the outgoing yet disturbing macho image of the Mexican *charro*. Ford died in 1973, at the age of seventy-nine in Palm Desert, California, his body ravaged by cancer and years of alcohol abuse. Fernández passed away into legend in 1986 after a remarkable life of artistic achievements combined with hard living and hard drinking.

In John Ford's masterpiece *The Searchers* (1956), the director paid homage to his respected colleagues in Mexico by having the one Mexican character in the film (played by actor Antonio Moreno) who helps Ethan Edwards (John Wayne) find Chief Scar introduce himself as Emilio Gabriel Figueroa Y Fernández. Ford and Fernández's film images continue to be fostered in all forms of media to this day because they are so elemental to American and Mexican popular culture and each nation's perception of itself. American film director Martin Scorsese introduced a restored print of Fernandez's *Enamorada* (1947) at a screening at the 2018 Canees Film Festival where he acknowledged "an appreciation and fascination with Mexican cinema," and considers the late director "one of the best in world cinema."

CHAPTER 3

THE GOOD NEIGHBOR POLICY

GABRIEL FIGUEROA (1907–1997) AND GREGG TOLAND (1904–1948)

Born in Mexico City in 1907, Gabriel Figueroa trained as a painter and violinist. The young artist made his living as a photographer. He entered the motion picture industry as a stills photographer shortly after the advent of sound, under the tutelage of cinematographer Alex Phillips Sr. In 1933, director Howard Hawks and his MGM troupe arrived in Mexico to film *Viva Villa!*, a highly fictionalized account of the bandit revolutionary hero Francisco "Pancho" Villa, with gringo Wallace Beery in the title role. Hawks and his famed Chinese-American cameraman James Wong Howe required twenty cameras and cameramen for a particular sequence. Figueroa obtained a motion picture camera and got his first Hollywood experience as a cameraman. During the location shoot, one of the actors, while inebriated, urinated from his hotel balcony on a passing parade of soldiers; the company was forced to return to Hollywood, where director Jack Conway completed the film.

In 1935, Gabriel Figueroa received financial support from the Cinematografica Latino Americano (CSLA) to study cinematography with Gregg Toland (1904–1948) in Hollywood. Toland was noted for his innovative lighting techniques, including deep focus and chiaroscuro (stark contrasts between illuminated spaces and dark shadows) in such films *as Wuthering Heights* (1939), *The Grapes of Wrath* (1940), *Citizen Kane* (1941), and *The Best Years of Our Lives* (1946).

Figueroa went to see Toland with a letter of introduction from his friend, cinematographer Alex Phillips. Figueroa claims he learned everything about lighting from Toland. In an *American Cinematographer* interview with Tom Dey (March 1995), Figueroa recalled, "Toland was making *Splendor* (1935) with star Miriam Hopkins and I was lucky enough to have him take me on as a student. I stood on the set and I watched him work through the entire picture." He returned to Mexico the following year after observing other filmmakers at work in Hollywood, including a stay at Hal Roach Studios. In 1936, after working as an operator on three films for cameraman Jack Draper (another American living and working in Mexico), he received the opportunity as cameraman on a film which became a huge international hit, *Alla En El Rancho Grande*, starring Tito Guizar.

Gabriel Figueroa's cinematography reflected a visual culture in a post-revolutionary Mexico that was influenced to a large degree by the Mexican muralists Diego Rivera, David

Alfardo Siqueiros, and José Clemente Orozco. In an interview with the author, Figueroa described his first meeting with Diego Rivera at an Academy Tribute in Los Angeles in 1994: "Rivera said to me, 'I am in awe of you and your work.' I humbly replied, "But Maestro, *you* in awe of *me*? You are the great painter of such brilliant murals.' 'Yes, that's true,' Rivera replied, 'but I am in awe of you because you paint murals that move.'"

Toland continued to give Figueroa advice through the years and once, en route to Acapulco, he stopped at the studios in Mexico City and visited with him. "Toland saw something in me I had never seen," remarked the cinematographer in the same interview.

In 1941, the United States was on the verge of entering World War II. Concern over Axis influence in Latin America was intense as countries with powerful right wing parties considered "neutrality." The Roosevelt administration tried to win the sympathies of the Latin American nations, many of which were dictatorships and had more in common with the Axis powers than the democratic United States. Securing the "southern front" was a major goal of wartime psychology, embodied in Roosevelt's "Good Neighbor Policy." This policy, enacted in 1933, was a pact between the United States and Latin American countries to end the "gunboat diplomacy," long practiced by the United States to protect its interests in Latin America. Now, with the Good Neighbor Policy, cultural-exchange programs were set up and business ventures were encouraged. This pushed Mexico and the U.S. out of a detrimental cycle characterized by wars, conflict, and intervention. For the first time, the two countries began to work together for their own best interests against the Axis powers.

The possibilities of a transnational motion picture culture between Mexico and the U.S. had been nurtured during World War II, when Hollywood, Washington, and Mexico City collaborated to expand Mexican moviemaking to serve the anti-Axis cause in the Americas. Mexico and the U.S. had strained cultural relations cinematically due to the preponderance of negative Mexican stereotypes (bandidos, greasers, gigolos, etc.) in Hollywood films. During the 1920s, Mexico banned the showing of Hollywood films because of such negative cultural images. At a time when revenues from Europe were in decline or non-existent due to the war in Europe, Mexico, Central and South America offered a lucrative marketplace for Hollywood films. The slapstick comedy team of Stan Laurel and Oliver Hardy, known as *El Flaco y el Goldo* ("Skinny and Fat") in Mexico and Latin America, appeared at the Mexico City Motion Picture Industry Film Festival from April 12–15, 1941, as guests of President Avila Camacho. Their silent films and, later, Spanish-language sound shorts helped maintain their popularity in Latin America. Mexico City audiences could not understand why Laurel and Hardy could not speak Spanish in person since they spoke it in the movies. The comedians spoke only minimal Spanish and learned their lines phonetically for the Spanish-language versions of their mostly physical comedy shorts; they were also surrounded by Spanish-speaking supporting players. While in Mexico, they were approached by Azteca studios of Mexico City to do a series of Spanish-language films for Latin America, but the deal never materialized. They also made a promotional personal appearance in Ensenada, Baja Mexico, the following March.

In 1941, Walt Disney and his staff made a goodwill trip to Latin America, and a year and hundreds of sketches later, photographs and film recordings were reworked into a part-animated, part-live action travelogue called *Saludos Amigos* (1943), which was followed by *The Three Caballeros* (1945). The latter featured music by Mexican composer Agustin Lara, dancer Carmen Molina who performed the "Jesusita," and singer Dora Luz. Ace cameraman Ray Rennahan photographed the live-action sequences. Panchito, a Mexican *charro* rooster is a cartoon character who joins the animated Brazilian toucan José Carioca and Donald Duck through a visual tapestry of Mexican history, traditions, and folklore. These two films were initially released in Latin America, where they were among the few Hollywood productions to enjoy wide acceptance and success.

In 1942, Figueroa attended a seminar at Disney Studios in Burbank as part of Nelson Rockefeller's program of visual education in Latin America. Rockefeller was the coordinator of Inter-American affairs, appointed by President Roosevelt in 1940. Under the auspices of the Good Neighbor Policy, *Citizen Kane* director Orson Welles was asked to go to Brazil to make a documentary film. Figueroa was invited to dinner at the home of the resident young genius, as were Dolores del Rio, editor Robert Wise, and writer/producer/actor William Alland. A member of Welles's Mercury Theater Company, Alland had played the reporter in *Citizen Kane* (1941). In an after-dinner conversation, Figueroa related a story about a half-man half-fish that, once a year, came out of the Amazon River to claim a maiden from a nearby village. The cinematographer swore it was a true story. Alland later developed the tale into a story he called "The Sea Monster." Twelve years later, his story became the basis for Maurice Zimm's screenplay of Universal's 3D horror hit, *The Creature From the Black Lagoon*

Spanish release poster for *The Creature From The Black Lagoon* (1954).

(1953), which Jack Arnold directed and Alland produced. However, it was not filmed in either the Amazon or Mexico, but at Universal Studios' backlot in Universal City, California, and with underwater sequences filmed off the coast of Florida. When future director Guillermo del Torro was seven years old, he saw *The Creature From the Black Lagoon*, an important event for his burgeoning creativity. "The creature was the most beautiful design I've ever seen," he recalls. "And I saw him swimming under [actress] Julie Adams, and I loved that the creature was in love with her, and I felt an almost existential desire for them to end up together. Of course, it didn't happen." In 2017, with the release of his highly acclaimed fantasy film, *The Shape of Water*, del Torro made his wish come true. The film, a front-runner nominee for Best Picture, and Best Director involves a captured sea creature who falls in love with a female research scientist, a love that is reciprocated.

Many Latino performers were brought to U.S. screens during the "Good Neighbor Policy" years in hopes of engaging American and South American audiences, with such stellar names as Tito Guizar, Carmen Miranda, Maria Montez, Arturo de Córdoba, Desi Arnaz, Xavier Cugat, Esther Fernández, and a handsome new discovery who was put under contract to MGM in 1947, Ricardo Montalban. Though born and raised in Mexico, Ricardo attended high school in Los Angeles and pursued a career on the New York stage before returning to his native country and finding work in the film industry. In 1940, in his senior year at Fairfax High School, he was screen tested by MGM in Culver City for the leading role opposite Irish-American Spencer Tracy that eventually went to the Jewish-American John Garfield in the screen adaptation of John Steinbeck's tale of Monterey Bay's Mexican-American community, *Tortilla Flat* (1942). The casting director told Montalban, to his disbelief, that he was "not Mexican enough for the role." In Hollywood, when there were rare Latino leading roles, they almost always went to white actors wearing brown makeup and sporting phony accents (e.g., Wallace Beery, *Viva Villa!*), Hedy Lamarr (*Tortilla Flat*), Warner Baxter (*The Cisco Kid*), Jennifer Jones (*Duel in the Sun*), even though established Hispanic stars—Dolores del Rio, Lupe Velez, Gilbert Roland, Cesar Romero, and Rita Hayworth—were available.

"Hollywood provided a space for my professional development and an opportunity to get to know the work of and become friends with other photographers," remarked Figueroa to Dey in the aforementioned *American Cinematographer* interview. During the shooting of *Enamorada/Beloved*, in 1945, Figueroa was visited in Mexico by Merian C. Cooper, producer of the original *King Kong* (1933), who had just set up an independent production company, Argosy Pictures, with John Ford. Cooper explained that he wanted to sign Figueroa to photograph a John Ford film called *The Fugitive* in Mexico. Having already been asked by Toland to join his crew on *The Fugitive*, Figueroa was surprised to learn that he would be replacing him.

Toland had to drop out of the film due to a contractual commitment with the Samuel Goldwyn Company that would not allow him to take on outside assignments. When John Ford asked Toland if there was someone else who could photograph the picture with the strength of Mexican painting and engraving, Toland replied, "In Mexico there is only one cameraman stronger than I am: Gabriel Figueroa." *New York Times* film critic Bosley Crowther, in his review of *The Fugitive*, called "it a symphony of light and shade, of deafening din and silence, of sweeping movement and repose."

Toland died unexpectedly of a heart attack, at the age of forty-four, at his Hollywood home in 1948. A true innovator, he was always in the forefront of his profession, applying new technological advances to creative film narratives, and introducing lens and lighting modifications that strongly influenced and inspired his colleagues. This edited quote taken from an article by Gregg Toland in *Theater Arts Magazine* (September 1941) could be applied to Gabriel Figueroa's work as well.

> The Cameraman should always work in close collaboration with the scriptwriter and director before production. Each film should have its own particular style. A comedy and a tragedy should not be photographed in the same way: *The Grapes of Wrath*, a harsh film, *The Long Voyage home*, a character film, *Citizen Kane*, a psychological story in which the external realities were very important. Camera movements should not be apparent because they distract attention from the actors and from what is happening.

Figueroa's expressionistic lighting techniques and infrared filtering enanbled him to develop a unigue style of black-and-white cinematography which helped define the Mexican cinema. His career spanned six decades and included cinematography on more than two hundred films in all genres, showcasing many of the most brilliant Mexican stars. Figueroa's cinematography went on to serve the distinctive styles of several world-renowned filmmakers, including John Ford (*The Fugitive*) Luis Buñuel (*Los Olvidados, Nazarin*) John Huston (*The Night of the Iguana, Under the Volcano*), Roberto Gavaldon (*Macario*), and Don Siegel (*Two Mules for Sister Sara*).

Gilbert Roland walks down a Mexican street.

CHAPTER 4

DALTON TRUMBO, THE HOLLYWOOD BLACKLIST, STEINBECK, AND MEXICO

The Hollywood blacklist (1946–1960) was a shameful chapter in the history of America and American film, affecting hundreds of creative personnel and their families. One director, one producer, and eight screenwriters, known collectively as the "Hollywood Ten," refused to testify in the HUAC (House Un-American Activities Committee) hearing of 1947 in Washington D.C. This committee, overseen by Senator Joseph McCarthy (R-Wisconsin), investigated alleged Communist influence in Hollywood. They were charged with contempt for using their constitutional right granted in the Fifth Amendment and were sentenced to a year in prison. A second set of HUAC hearings were initiated in 1951.

The Hollywood blacklist unofficially denied employment in the U.S. film industry to those suspected of Communist leanings or associations. It was a reaction to the rise of post–World War II labor organizing in Hollywood. Prominent screenwriter Dalton Trumbo (1905–1976), who began his career in 1934, was noted for his work in such successful films as *A Man to Remember* (1938), *Kitty Foyle* (1940), *A Guy Named Joe* (1943), *Thirty Seconds Over Tokyo* (1944), and *Our Vines Have Tender Grapes* (1945). Trumbo refused to answer questions about his political associations; he was later convicted of contempt of Congress and served ten months in a federal prison. Virtually unemployable, blacklisted from the Hollywood studios and in increasingly dire financial circumstances after his release, he continued to write scripts under a pseudonym and soon moved to Mexico City with his wife, Cleo, and their three children. They remained there for two years while he continued writing along with fellow blacklisted writers Hugo Butler and Albert Maltz. Many such writers left for Mexico and Europe to continue their careers under assumed names or had their scripts fronted by others. Blacklisted American director/writer Jules Dassin's low-budget French-produced heist drama *Rififi* (1955) was so influential that, when it played in Mexico, thieves used the film as a guidepost to commit an actual robbery, prompting the Mexican government to ban the film. Cinematographer Gabriel Figueroa opened his home in Mexico to blacklisted Americans while other sympathetic industry colleagues, like Dalton Trumbo's friend and fellow screenwriter Ian McLellan Hunter, volunteered to front for blacklisted screenwriters submitting screenplays to the studios, using assumed names on their behalf. Trumbo's screenplay for the hit film *Roman Holiday* (1953) starring Gregory Peck and a young Audrey Hepburn, won an Academy Award. Hunter was on

Trumbo press book art from *The Brave One* (1951).

hand to accept the award, and it was not until 1993 that the Academy credited the win to Trumbo. When he exhausted his savings, Trumbo returned to the United States in 1954 and settled in the Highland Park area of Los Angeles. His hope of working with Luis Buñuel in Mexico never came to fruition, but while he was there he wrote what eventually became *The Brave One* (1956). "I enclose herewith 'The Boy and the Bull,' Mexico City, April 1953," reads one entry in *Additional Dialogue: The Letters of Dalton Trumbo, 1942–1962* (Los Angeles, CA: L. A. Theatre Works, p. 270).

Inspired by Trumbo's experiences in Mexico, the screenplay resembled Robert J. Flaherty's "My Friend Benito," which was based on a true incident in a Mexican bullring. Slated as part of Orson Welles's *It's All True* Good Neighbor Policy documentary for RKO, the segment was directed by Norman Foster in Mexico under Welles's personal supervision, from September to December 1941. Although it was later abandoned by RKO, the studio retained the story rights. When King Brothers Productions decided to pursue the project, they sought a production and distribution deal with RKO. *The Brave One* went on to win an Oscar for Best Original Story in 1957; Dalton Trumbo had written it under the pseudonym Robert Rich. When the press could not find anyone by that name in the Writers Guild, Trumbo seized on the opportunity to reveal the hypocrisy of the blacklist. In January 1960, director/producer Otto Preminger announced that Trumbo would receive screen credit for his screenplay for *Exodus* and, in August of that year, actor/producer Kirk Douglas announced that Trumbo would receive screenplay credit for *Spartacus*, officially bringing the blacklist to an end.

Albert Maltz, another blacklisted American screenwriter and member of the Hollywood Ten, lived in Mexico from 1952 to 1962. In 1970, he was commissioned by Universal Studios to write a screenplay for Budd Boetticher's story idea for *Two Mules for Sister Sara*. Shot in Mexico, the film was directed by Don Siegel, photographed in color by Gabriel Figueroa, and paired rising star Clint Eastwood with veteran actress Shirley Maclaine in a spaghetti-style western with comedic overtones.

Despite Dolores del Rio's long career in Hollywood and the success of her Mexican films, she was not welcome in the United States in early 1954 because of entanglements in the infamous Cold War–McCarthy hearings. Claims that she aided anti-Franco refugees from the Spanish Civil War and associated with well-known socialist artists Frida Kahlo and Diego Rivera, along with her support of an anti-nuclear proliferation Stockholm peace appeal in 1950, were used by the U.S. State Department to deny her a visa.

In 1954, Del Rio was again denied a work visa, this time to star opposite Spencer Tracy in 20th Century-Fox's *Broken Lance* (1954). The role went to Mexican actress Katy Jurado (fresh from her memorable performance as saloon owner Helen Ramirez in *High Noon*), who earned an Oscar nomination. Del Rio was able to reenter the United States in 1956 for a theatrical engagement of the play *Anastasia*. While in America, she visited an old friend, director John Ford, on the sound stages of RKO, where he was filming interiors for *The Searchers* and where she had her greatest commercial success, *Flying Down to Rio* (1933). The actress returned to Hollywood movie making in 1960 when she portrayed Elvis Presley's Native American mother in Don Siegel's *Flaming Star*; in 1963, she played another Native American, alongside Gilbert Roland and Ricardo Montalban in John Ford's last epic western, *Cheyenne Autumn*.

In January 1953, young Mexican actress Rosaura Revueltas, with only a few films to her credit, entered the United States with a proper work visa. She had been cast as the female lead, Esperanza Quintero, the wife of a Mexican-American Zinc miner who becomes involved in the struggle for workers' rights in *The Salt of the Earth* (1954). The film, based on a true story about striking Zinc miners, was being independently produced by a group of blacklisted Hollywood talent in New Mexico.

The movie was beset with problems because the anti-Communist political climate prevented access to Hollywood talent and resources. Local state and federal government agencies, as well as vigilantes, tried to deter filming, which utilized many of the actual miners who had bargained for better wages and working conditions. A few weeks before completion of the film, U.S. immigration officials came for Revueltas with concerns over her visa. Threatened with deportation, she was charged with entering the United States illegally. When Revueltas chose not to contest the charges against her and left voluntarily, the case was dropped. Her forced return caused an international incident in which the Mexican government retaliated by reexamining documents for all American actors working in Mexico, including Gary Cooper.

The producers of *The Salt of the Earth* had to use a stand-in for Revueltas when shooting certain sequences; she later completed her scenes in Mexico, after which the footage was smuggled back across the border to prevent confiscation by U.S. customs officials. Today, *The Salt of the Earth* is considered an American classic of independent cinema.

STEINBECK, *THE PEARL* AND *ZAPATA*

Celebrated American author John Steinbeck (1902–1968) had been traveling to Mexico since 1935 and, in March of 1940, he and his associate Ed Ricketts spent time on a scientific expedition to Baja California's Sea of Cortez. As a result of the trip, Steinbeck wanted to make a film without Hollywood interference. Teaming with documentarian Herbert Kline and working with a budget of $35,000, Steinbeck produced a semi-documentary called *The Forgotten Village*, which was filmed in La Paz, Baja, California, Mexico. The film was released in January 1941, but ran afoul of censors who objected to a raw natural-childbirth scene. Clearing the censors, the film went into limited release in the fall of 1941 with little fanfare from either critics or the public.

In January 1944, Steinbeck traveled to Mexico, where he fashioned the idea for *The Pearl*, based on his Baja trips and the Mexican folktales he had read. Set in part in the then-impoverished fishing village of La Paz in Baja California Sur, *The Pearl* is the story of an Mexican-Indian diver named Kino whose discovery of a magnificent pearl from the Gulf of Mexico means the promise of a better life for his needy family. His dreams blind him to the greed and suspicion the pearl arouses in him and his neighbors, and even his loving wife, Juana, cannot temper his obsession or stem the events leading to tragedy. With the help of director Lewis Milestone (*All Quiet on the Western Front*, 1930) and his Hollywood and Mexican connections, Steinbeck made a deal for *La Perla/The Pearl*. During the summer of 1945, he worked on the script in Mexico with director Emilio Fernández. Together they developed both English- and Spanish-language scripts, which they proceeded to film simultaneously. Production commenced in October of 1945, with bilingual Mexican actors Pedro Armendàriz and Marìa Elena Marqués on location in Acapulco, Guerrero, and Estudios Churubusco in Mexico City. Cameraman Gabriel Figueroa captured the extraordinary narrative visuals.

On location in Acapulco, Pedro Armendáriz and Maria Elena Margués are the leads in Emilio Fernandez's *The Pearl* (1947). John Steinbeck wrote the screenplay based on his story idea, with Emilio Fernandez and Jack Wagner, and later turned it into a published novel.

Steinbeck's script outline was serialized in *Woman's Home Companion* in December 1945 as "Pearl of the World." RKO put up half of the $400,000 budget financing. According to *The Hollywood Reporter*, it was the first Mexican-made English-language picture to be distributed in the U.S. The film was well received in the States, where it was a moderate success. *La Perla/The Pearl* won the Ariel Award, Mexico's equivalent to the Academy Award, for Best Picture, Best Actor, and Best Cinematography. It also won awards at the Venice International Film Festival. Initially, Steinbeck's outline was serialized in *Woman's Home Companion* (December 1945) as "Pearl of the World"; in 1947, he published *The Pearl* as a novella.

Steinbeck was drawn to Mexico and Mexican themes, including those based on actual events. Pan-American films had approached him in 1944 about writing a screenplay based on the life of Zapotec Indian revolutionary Emiliano Zapata (1879–1919). The prospective project grabbed Steinbeck's interest and held it. Zapata was a mestizo leader who united with Pancho Villa to rout the thirty-year ruling tyrant Porfirio Diaz from the presidency in 1911. Eight years later, still fighting for land reform against Diaz's successors, he was killed in an ambush, succumbing to the same fate as Pancho Villa in 1923. Having conducted research through his many travels in Mexico, Steinbeck realized he would have a number of hurdles to overcome if a movie of Zapata's life was to be filmed on location in Mexico. He met Elia Kazan, a Broadway actor/director who had come to Hollywood and had success with two socially themed films: *Pinky* (1949) deals with racial prejudice, and *Gentlemen's Agreement* (1947) with anti-Semitism. Kazan had received rave ws for his stage direction of Tennessee Williams's play *A Streetcar Named Desire* (1947), starring a young actor who electrified audiences, Marlon Brando. Steinbeck and Kazan's relationship with Fox head of production Darryl F. Zanuck provided them with the assistance of a scenarist to develop a screenplay from a 337-page treatment, written by Steinbeck.

In *Kazan: The Master Director Discusses His Films* (New York: New Market Press, 1979, p. 92), Kazan recounts to Young:

> John and I wanted to [film in Mexico]. We went down there and met with a guy named [Gabriel] Figueroa. He was a very well-known cameraman, the darling of Mexican films, but very old-fashioned, always photographing fifty women holding candles and stuff like that. He also happened to be the head of the Mexican Union of stagehands, a Communist and very political. After he read the script, he was cordial and sweet, but he said, "No, this must be this way." Whenever I heard the word "must," that was about the end of it. John was even more opposed to what he said than I was.

In his autobiography *Kazan: A Life* (New York, NY: Alfred A. Knopf, 1988, p. 400), the director further stated:

> The Mexican communists were using Zapata as a symbol of the struggle for land and bread, then he said, "We would be proud to have you make a film in Mexico, Señor Kazan. We know your work but on this"—he indicated the manuscript, which he had read, just as I expected. "No."

Gabriel Figueroa came under McCarthy era scrutiny because of his union organizing activities in Mexico and for the assistance he had provided to Hollywood blacklisted writers who had moved there. The main objection to the script by the Mexican government representatives was that Zapata gives up the presidency when in actual historical fact he never held that position. Zapata is also shown to be illiterate when in fact he was not. *Viva Zapata* was finally filmed in 1951 near the Mexican border in and around Roma, and Del Rio, Texas, and at the 20th Century-Fox Ranch with interiors on the studio sound stages. Marlon Brando was chosen to play Zapata and the actor spent time in Anencuilco, Mexico, the town where Zapata was born near Ayala Morelos to prepare himself for the role. Anthony Quinn, who was born in Mexico in a railroad boxcar during the Mexican Revolution and whose parents actually fought for Pancho Villa, played Emiliano Zapata's brother Eufemio.

The cameraman on *Zapata*, Joe McDonald, called Figueroa and asked him for advice which Figueroa gave to his colleague. You can see Figueroa's influence in the framing of the peasant faces and the end shot with Zapata's horse in the mountains. Kazan and McDonald pored over hundreds of photographs of the Mexican Revolution trying to capture cinematically the look of the period photos and did so successfully.

CHAPTER 5

Sam Peckinpah and John Huston

Mexico has always meant something special to me.... My Mexican experience is never over... Everything important in my life has been linked to Mexico, in one way or another. The country has a special effect on me.

—*SAM PECKINPAH, PLAYBOY MAGAZINE, AUGUST 1972*

✱✱✱

THE OLD IGUANA AND THE LION

Filmmakers Sam Peckinpah (1925–1985) and John Huston (1906–1987) shaped the public perception of Mexico and Mexicans in the second half of the twentieth century. These two directors transformed celluloid images which had originated, not with these men, but in the mutual histories, politics, and culture represented in American frontier novels and, later, in films and on television. In Paul Schrader's article for *Cinema*, "Sam Peckinpah Going to Mexico," he states, "Huston's characterization of Mexicans was not so much incisive (*The Treasure of the Sierra Madre*) as it was stereotypical, a fault which Peckinpah unfortunately shares." He added, "Peckinpah's Mexico is much more powerfully drawn than Huston's and more accurately resembles the Mexico of Luis Buñuel's films."

Mexico serves not only as a setting for the filmic stories, but takes a central role as a mythic space and character. Peckinpah's Mexico is a place where gringos can play out their fantasies, a never-never land of sex, violence, and ultra-machismo. It is a place to escape from American law, and a place of spiritual renewal. With the closing of the American West at the turn of the nineteenth century, Mexico became an extension of the lawless frontier and an oasis for those whose way of life was ending. Women were to serve the needs of the men, usually sexual. Most Mexican women in Peckinpah's films are portrayed as whores, or as easily available sexual creatures of one type or another. His films are about gringos in Mexico, not about Mexicans in Mexico. Peckinpah captured images of the turmoil and violence of a Mexico in the midst of a revolution, in *The Wild Bunch*, that sting with accuracy and truth. Peckinpah directed fourteen films in his career, six of which are westerns.

Gabrielle Murray, in the May 2002 issue of *Great Directors*, writes,

> The personal mythology surrounding Peckinpah is inscribed in much of the writing generated by these films. A drunk, a coke addict, a sentimental romantic, possibly schizophrenic, a little man with a big chip on his shoulder—Peckinpah is said to be many things. Yet it is obvious that the large body of critical literature, which includes reviews, articles and numerous books, both critical and biographical, that Peckinpah is not a neglected filmmaker, rather, there is an unwillingness to deal with the paradoxical nature of his films.

David Samuel Peckinpah was born in Fresno, California, on February 21, 1925, to a family whose history was part of the pioneer fabric of that area. He enlisted in the U. S. Marine Corps in 1943 and served in China at the end of World War II. His battalion was in charge of disarming Japanese soldiers and civilians and returning them to Japan. After receiving his discharge at the end of 1946 he wanted to return to China, but the Communist takeover made that impossible. Peckinpah and many members of his generation were influenced by the writings of American writer Jack Kerouac, who stated, "The only people for me are the mad ones. The ones who are mad to live, mad to talk, desirous of everything at the same time." This passage from *On the Road*, Kerouac's quintessentially American novel of the post–World War II Beat Generation, aptly describes the life and career of Sam Peckinpah. In *On the Road*, when Sal Paradiso and Dean Moriarity reach the U.S.–Mexico border, they find what they already knew: "Just across the street Mexico began. We looked with wonder. To our amazement, it looked exactly like Mexico." That statement echoes what the Gorches say to Angel (the only Mexican member of *The Wild Bunch*) in Peckinpah's movie as they cross the Rio Grande into Mexico: "Looks just like more Texas."

"You have no eyes," responds Angel.

Peckinpah's first trip to Mexico resulted in a three-month stay. He fell in love with the country and its people. He returned from the war and entered college, where he discovered theater arts. Upon graduation, he went to Los Angeles and secured work at a television station as an assistant to director/editor Don Siegel. Siegel recommended Peckinpah for a writing job. That led to his work as a writer on such popular 1950s western TV series as *Gunsmoke, Broken Arrow* (for which he penned three episodes), and *The Rifleman* (Peckinpah wrote the pilot script and directed and wrote several episodes during the first season and one during the second). He drew on his own experiences growing up on a ranch in rural Fresno, and his background easily gravitated into the western genre. He knew cowboys firsthand: his   **Sam Peckinpah.**

grandfather was a hanging judge, and the town of North Fork used on *The Rifleman* is actually located in the Sierra foothills, near Fresno—not in the series' New Mexico setting. On the strength of his television work, Peckinpah moved on to feature films, with *The Deadly Companions* (1961) and *Ride the High Country* (1962). *Ride the High Country* was treated as a B-western by MGM, but it found a warm reception from a few U.S. critics. It did respectable business at the nation's box office and became very popular in Europe, winning an award at the Cannes Film Festival. The film starred two aging western film stars, Joel McCrea and Randolph Scott, paired for the first and only time. It was a buddy movie, played straight.

✶✶✶

Peckinpah was hired by producer Jerry Bresler to co-write and direct the western *Major Dundee* for Columbia Pictures. Working closely with Oscar Saul, he completely rewrote an early draft of the script by Harry Julian Fink in 1ate 1963; this new version would ultimately be used for the film. Charlton Heston stars as the glory-hungry Union major, and Richard Harris is the antagonistic Confederate Colonel Tyreen. The story follows the opponents as they ride into French-occupied Mexico, pursuing Apache Indians responsible for a massacre. *Major Dundee* went into production in Mexico without a finished script. The sprawling epic created many production hurdles for the inexperienced Peckinpah, who was accustomed to more contained television productions. The studio wanted a more traditional cavalry western, star Heston wanted a Civil War epic, and Peckinpah was intent on bringing a more violent, mature, and modern perspective to the western genre; differences between filmmakers, studio heads, and producers quickly became apparent. Heston had numerous run-ins with Peckinpah, which he detailed in his autobiography, *In the Arena* (New York, NY: Berkley Trade, 1997). He noted that Peckinpah's erratic behavior and all-night drunken binges did not help him, his actors, or the production. The director finished the film, which ran over budget, and the final cut was taken away from him and recut by Jerry Bresler after several disastrous previews. A condensed version was released, in March 1965, and met with lukewarm audience response. *Major Dundee* has moments of greatness and one can see themes Peckinpah would further explore in *The Wild Bunch* (1969). In hindsight, Heston wrote, "One of the most crucial, though none of us realized it at the time . . . Sam, though he never said anything like this, really wanted to make *The Wild Bunch*. That's the movie that was steaming in his psyche." Following the personal debacle of *Major Dundee*, Peckinpah was fired by MGM a few days into directing *The Cincinnati Kid* (1969) starring Steve McQueen.

"I put in a lot of time in Mexico and I knew Mexican history," Peckinpah said, referring to his script for 1968's *Villa Rides*. He had submitted the screenplay to Paramount with the understanding that he would direct, but the film's star, Yul Brynner, did not like Peckinpah's dark and complex portrait of Villa. The director and the script were jettisoned for a more traditional, favorable heroic tale. However, in comparing the scripts with the final product, some elements of Peckinpah's original script remain. Robert Towne and William Douglas Lansford, who also wrote *Pancho Villa*, the book upon which the screenplay was based, rewrote it. *Villa Rides* was filmed in Spain, not Mexico, at the end of the Italian spaghetti western era, with Buzz Kulik, a director, like Peckinpah, versed in television.

His return to feature filmmaking after the debacle of *Major Dundee* was prompted by his sensitive direction of the television adaptation of Katherine Anne Porter's novella *Noon Wine*, in 1966, for ABC's *Stage*

67. Film historian Nick Redman states, "There were two Sam Peckinpahs that were conflicted in his film-making, as in his own life. The poetic side and the notorious self-destructive nature fueled by alcohol and drugs." He followed the career-defining *The Wild Bunch* with the touching comedy-western *The Ballad of Cable Hogue*—which was virtually ignored at the time of its release—then struck violent box-office gold again, this time with *Straw Dogs*, which cemented his image as "Bloody Sam." Nick Redman states, "Unfortunately, he began to play the image of 'Bloody Sam' offscreen as well." The character of Pike Bishop in *The Wild Bunch* resembles Peckinpah's true character the most in that he lived by a code but ultimately let everyone down." Heavily controversial and criticized upon its release, *The Wild Bunch* is now considered Peckinpah's revisionist western masterpiece because of its originality, vision, and its subsequent influence, not only on other films of that era, but on today's films.

Stephen Price wrote in 1999, "*The Wild Bunch* is an epic work, and it has had an impact on American cinema." He further noted Martin Scorsese's description of the film as "savage poetry." Paul Seydor has described *The Wild Bunch* "as one of the great masterpieces of World Cinema. It's a western about the betrayal of friendship . . . and it's very violent." The director himself, in a 1969 interview for *Films and Filming* (October 1969, no. 1) acknowledged the picture's brutality: "During the first preview, thirty-two people walked out during the first ten minutes. *Wild Bunch* is not a pretty picture. It's the story of violent people in violent times. I think a lot of people are going to be shocked, [at] least I hope so. I hate an audience that just sits there." Violence in westerns up to that time tended to be unrealistic and devoid of consequences, but Peckinpah's violent realism and slow-motion "bullet ballet of death" aroused controversy and criticism, not unlike that which surrounded Arthur Penn's *Bonnie and Clyde* (1967). These two films opened up a portal in the depiction of explicit onscreen violence in American and world cinema.

Peckinpah was nominated for an Academy Award for Best Adapted Screenplay for *The Wild Bunch*. In his violent action-packed heist film *The Getaway* (1972), bank robber Doc McCoy (Steve McQueen) and his wife, Carol (Ali MacGraw), make their way through Texas landscapes, eluding U.S. lawmen and pursuing gunmen while making their way to Mexico and freedom. The final sequence was filmed east of El Paso, Texas, in the village of Caseta, Mexico, at the southern end of Texas. Peckinpah, in an October 10, 1972, *Rolling Stone* interview with Grover Lewis, said, "I was married to a Mexican woman and asked her one time to tell me all about Mexico. 'Don't be silly,' she said. Nobody knows all about Mexico.' She was right, of course."

Peckinpah wanted to shoot *Pat Garrett and Billy the Kid* in New Mexico for the sake of authenticity, but Metro-Goldwyn-Mayer wanted it filmed in Mexico, to cut costs. Sam went over budget by $1. 5 million and ran afoul of MGM president Jim Aubrey. Director Andrew V. McLaglen remarked to an audience at a British Film Institute tribute, "I went down To Durango, Mexico, to film *Chisum* [in which the Billy the Kid legend plays a part in the story]. Apparently, Sam Peckinpah was already down there and had been there for a while, working on *Pat Garett and Billy the Kid*. By the time *Chisum* was wrapped, Peckinpah was still there." Peckinpah lost a week's worth of footage due to a technical problem with the camera, and had to reshoot. He had wanted a technician on set to take care of the cameras, protecting them from the extreme dust and weather conditions in Durango, but Aubrey wouldn't allow it. At MGM, the film edit he presented was taken from him and was reedited. *Pat Garrett and Billy the Kid* was released in July of 1973 in a truncated version as a direct result of his altercations with Jim Aubrey; it did only average business. In October 1973, MGM ceased film production, causing Aubrey to resign.

Peckinpah's *Bring Me the Head of Alfredo Garcia* (1974) involves greed, revenge, and murder in Mexico. El Jefe (Emilio Fernández), a rich landowner, puts a bounty on the head of a man named Alfredo Garcia, who seduced and impregnated his young daughter. However, El Jefe does not know that the perpetrator is already dead. Bennie (Warren Oates), an American in Mexico, and his Mexican girlfriend, Elita (Isela Vega), are offered money to help two henchmen find Garcia. Elita, a prostitute, secretly knows that Garcia was killed and was buried in an unmarked grave. Benny and his girlfriend are losers with this one last chance to succeed. They go off in search of the body, but soon find themselves in a nightmarish situation that ultimately leads to drastic consequences—and death. Peckinpah was able to make the film on a low-budget in Mexico, with a largely Mexican crew, without studio interference. This grim and graphically violent film was poorly received by critics and rejected by audiences at the time of its release, but now is considered a cult classic and a prominent entry in the Peckinpah canon. Peckinpah described *Alfredo Garcia* this way, "I did the film straight and it's mine. It is not the Mexico that people want to see, but it's the Mexico I know."

Alfredo Garcia could be considered the third film in the Peckinpah Mexico Trilogy, beginning with *Major Dundee*, and followed by *The Wild Bunch*. During the filming of *Major Dundee* in 1964, Peckinpah began a friendship with Emilio Fernández, a friendship that would grow through the years. Peckinpah said that Emilio Fernández gave him the idea for the children's game involving ants and scorpions that is seen at the beginning of *The Wild Bunch*. Fernández also suggested various Mexican actors for parts in the film, including Jorge Russek and Alfonso Arau, who play Leiutenants Zamorra and Herrera, respectively. Arau remarked to the author, "I was sent to wardrobe and makeup and they darkened my teeth and I thought, What's up with that? Peckinpah came over to me and said that he wanted a character actor like Alfonso Bedoya in *The Treasure of the Sierra Madre*. Peckinpah knew that I directed my first film in Mexico the previous year, so he kind of adopted me." Arau worked as an actor in several American films, including *The Three Amigos* and *Romancing the Stone*; after expanding his directing skills, he was responsible for the international hit *Like Water for Chocolate* (1991). Another distinguished Mexican director, Luciano "Chano" Urueta (1904–1979), then in his sixties, was cast as the elder in Angel's village in *The Wild Bunch*.

Returning from a trip to Mexico, Peckinpah fell ill and died of heart failure, on December 28, 1984, in Inglewood, California. Mexican cinema costume designer Lupita Peckinpah (Sam's daughter with actress Begoñia Palacios, whom he met on the set of *Major Dundee*; they married the same year) remarked in an interview with Paul Rowlands, of the Money Into Light website, "My father found love and freedom in certain aspects in his life here in Mexico."

At the Directors Guild of America memorial service for Sam Peckinpah, actor James Coburn said of the late director, "He pushed me over the abyss and then jumped in after me. He took me on some great adventures." Author/film historian Paul Seydor remarked in a 2015 Q&A with Neil Fulwood on The Agitation of Mind website, "Sam was a deeply complex, complicated, and troubled man. That he was able to translate so much of what troubled him into his films is part of which gives those films their edge, intensity, their beauty, and their truthfulness."

With his violent nature, bouts with alcohol and drugs, fights with the establishment studio executives, Peckinpah was often referred to in Mexico as "The Old Iguana" in that he   **John Huston.**

had assumed many characteristics of that lizard: keen vision, skin that would change colors depending on his mood, aggressiveness, grumpiness, and a constitution that made him equally adept in the tropics and in the deserts. In his alcoholic, self-destructive nature, Peckinpah resembled the characters of John Huston's Mexico.

Huston, unlike Peckinpah's lizard, was "The Old Lion." This moniker reflected his larger-than-life, leonine, strong, domineering personality. By all accounts he was fiercely protective of his filmmaking team. He was clearly in charge, taking bold risks in his choice of material and subject matter. His films encompass a wide range of geographical settings: *The Asphalt Jungle* (America's Midwest), *The Red Badge of Courage* (America's Deep South), *The African Queen* (Uganda and the Congo), *Moulin Rouge* (Paris, France), *The Misfits* (western Nevada), and *Prizzi's Honor* (Brooklyn, New York). But of all the locales in which he filmed, none meant more to him than Mexico. As he stated in a featurette on the making of *The Night of Iguana*: "My name is John Huston; I am a director of motion pictures. I've been in Mexico for a long time now, not consecutively, but I always return to Mexico. It's one of the countries I like best in the world."

Huston was a vital and creative force in the film industry for more than fifty years; he was still making movies at the time of his death, in 1987. Mexico influenced Huston's life and work. His classic *The Treasure of the Sierra Madre* was one of the first Hollywood films made largely on location in Mexico. Huston adapted Tennessee Williams's 1961 play *The Night of the Iguana* to film in 1964, partly because he could shoot it in Mexico. The resulting Puerto Vallarta location became his final home. The Oscar-winning director/writer spent his last years at his Las Caletas retreat where the jungle meets the sea, south of Puerto Vallarta, and only accessible by boat.

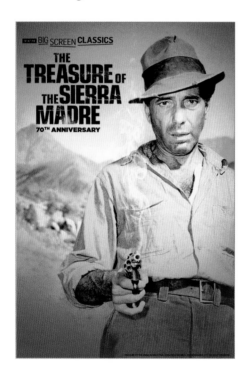

Hunphrey Bogart is featured in the 70th anniversary TCM poster celebrating the classic film directed by John Huston.

In a 1984 interview with the author during a promotional tour for *Under the Volcano*, Huston revealed his feelings about Mexico: "I never wanted to make a travelogue of clichés about Mexico, the tourism. Mexico is a country with so many faces, and only through living there and going around can you get to know something about its heart—or hearts, I should say." He continued, "There's a savage face to Mexico, and another, benign and gentle, a deep humanity. There's the history, too."

In 1926, after an ear infection and an operation to repair his jawbone, twenty-one-year-old John Huston recuperated by going to Mexico. He traveled from New York to Veracruz, and then traveled by train from Veracruz to Mexico City. He saw a country still reeling from the aftermath of the revolution, with abject poverty all around, going about rebuilding itself. He stayed in Mexico City for a year and, indulging in his passion for horses, took riding lessons. When he ran out of money, his riding teacher suggested he accept an honorary commission in the Mexican Army as a member of the equestrian team.

Huston wrote in his memoirs, *An Open Book* (Boston, MA: DaCapo Press, 1994): "There would be no pay of course, but I could have meals at the barracks, a place to sleep if I wanted and the best horses in Mexico to ride. I jumped at the offer and [was?] given the temporary rank of lieutenant."

Jeffrey Meyers, in his book *John Huston, Courage and Art* (New York, NY: Crown Archetype, 2011), writes: "It's odd considering his love of Mexico and a year in the Mexican Cavalry that Huston never bothered to learn the language. Despite his lack of Spanish, Mexico had a powerful impact on his life. He learned that he could get away with anything there, no matter how outrageous. Later he would make four movies in that highly charged country: he collected pre-Columbian art, both real and fake, and often smuggled it into America. He built his last home near Puerto Vallarta, where at the end of his life, he was cared for by a devoted Mexican servant."

John Marcellus Huston was born in Nevada, Missouri, on August 5, 1906, into a theatrical family. His Canadian-born father, Walter, was a noted stage and, later, film actor (*Dodsworth*, 1936); he and John's mother, Rhea, separated when John was twelve. John spent time with his father on tour, but lived mostly with his mother, who later settled in Los Angeles. In high school, John became quite an accomplished amateur boxer. Choosing not to attend college, he instead tried his hand at writing and acting. He drifted through a number of occupations until a car accident in Los Angeles turned his life around. Huston went to New York and settled into a writing position at a newspaper, but shortly thereafter returned to California, where his father helped him secure a job at Warner Bros. Studios. John quickly found success writing or co-writing scripts for such films as *The Amazing Dr. Clitterhouse* (1938), *Sergeant York* (1940), and *High Sierra* (1941).

In his autobiography, Huston recalled his work on the script for the film *Juarez* at Warner Bros. in 1939: "Henry Blanke asked if I would be interested in writing a screenplay about Benito Juárez, the father of the Mexican Republic. I couldn't have asked for a more attractive assignment. It seemed almost providential, tying in with my knowledge of Mexico and my love for the country. The story was of the conflict between the deposed Mexican president Benito Juárez and the French puppet, Emperor Maximillian."

Though a screenwriter, he scored the opportunity to direct his own screenplay of the twice-before-filmed *The Maltese Falcon*, which became a commercial and critical hit in 1941, with Humphrey Bogart in the lead as Dashiell Hammett's tough-talking detective Sam Spade. The film established Huston as a major talent and fused a professional and personal bond with star Humphrey Bogart. John's career was interrupted by service in World War II, in which he filmed three documentaries for the War Department under combat conditions in the Italian campaign and at home.

Upon his return from war service, he adapted and scripted B. Traven's 1927 novel *The Treasure of the Sierra Madre* and convinced studio chief Jack Warner to let him direct the film largely on location in Mexico. *The Treasure of the Sierra Madre*, released in 1948, was a personal triumph for Huston, both father and son: John won an Academy Award as Best Director; Walter walked away with an Academy Award as Best Supporting Actor for his role as Howard, the old prospector. Film critics regard *The Treasure of the Sierra Madre* as one of the best and most influential American movies ever made. In all, John Huston made four movies in Mexico: *The Treasure of the Sierra Madre*, *The Unforgiven*, *The Night of the Iguana*, and *Under the Volcano*. Except for *The Unforgiven*, filmed in Durango but set in Texas, three of the four films could be considered Huston's Mexican Trilogy.

**Sam Peckinpah and
Charlton Heston.**

In her essay *"Under The Volcano*: Before The Stillness"* (translated from the French by Ellen Scwihek in 2007), Christian Vivani perceptively states that the three Mexican-made films "all concern characters in exile searching for a new beginning. Here at the border with the United States, Mexico offers the fantasy of an imaginary geography where Hustonian 'Misfits' wander between adventure (*The Treasure of the Sierra Madre*) and sex (*The Night of the Iguana*) before accepting death (*Under the Volcano*)." The backdrop for *Under the Volcano* is the Day of the Dead Festival in Mexico, on the eve of World War II in 1939, and was adapted for the screen from Malcolm Lowery's novel of the same name.

In Huston's films, Mexicans are in control of their own universe. Americans in Mexico are not superior as in many other films, but instead fragile, vulnerable, often flawed humans, in a harsh but hospitable environment. Huston's Mexico is not a place for gringos to go for spiritual renewal. These Anglos carry their demons with them, and whoever they are, or whatever they did in their place of origin or across the border, eventually catches up with them in Mexico.

Treasure's Fred C. Dobbs (Humphrey Bogart) allows greed and suspicion to sacrifice friendship and camaraderie as he spirals into murder and self-destruction. Both Reverend Shannon (Richard Burton), in *Iguana*, and the ex-British consul Geoffrey Firmin (Albert Finney), in *Volcano*, are self-destructive alcoholics who have disgraced themselves in their former professions.

Huston brought to *Volcano* a number of legendary talents of the Mexican film industry's golden age, including cameraman Gabriel Figueroa, director/actor Emilio "El Indio" Fernández, production designer Gunther Gerzo, and Oscar-nominated veteran actress Katy Jurado.

CHAPTER 6

DURANGO, PANCHO VILLA, THE MOVIES, AND JOHN WAYNE

Western movie heroes, from John Wayne to Kevin Costner, and heroines, from Jane Russell to Salma Hayek, have ridden across Durango's Western landscapes into endless sunsets, where gunplay and magnificent natural scenery highlight simple morality plays in which the good guys almost always win.

The state of Durango lies in the northwest central area of Mexico. It encompasses an area of 121,776 square kilometers and is the fourth-largest of the thirty-one Mexican states comprising the Republic of Mexico. Spectacular outdoor locations, including the majestic Sierra Madre Mountains, rock formations, and extensive deserts are all within an hour's drive from the colonial capital city, also named Durango, which was founded in 1540 as a mining town.

Los Organos State Park, used as a backdrop for dozens of westerns, is located halfway between Durango and Zacatecas, and contains spectacular rock formations resembling church organ pipes which surround a high desert valley. Towering desert sand dunes "Las Dunas De Bilbao," located north of Durango near the city of Torreon, are recognizable to moviegoers from key sequences in Peckinpah's *The Wild Bunch* and John Wayne's *The Train Robbers* (1973).

Durango's rich and prolific filming heritage goes back to the year 1898, when Edison Company cameras filmed a travel short subject, *A Train Arriving in Durango*, along with some of its people and customs. In 1913, at the height of the Mexican Revolution, General Francisco "Pancho" Villa, was perhaps the most photographed newsmaker of his time. Though he was born in a small village in the state of Durango, and his early forays as a bandit occurred there, his legendary exploits as a hero of the Mexican Revolution took place largely in the adjacent state of Chihuahua. Nevertheless, Durango claims him as its native son. Villa was paid $25,000 in gold by D. W. Griffith's Mutual

Film Company of New York to allow cameras to film him and the battles at Ojinanga, Torreon, and Zacatecas for a film called *The Life of General Villa* (1914). One of Griffith's assistants, the future director Raoul Walsh, was a member of the film crew that traveled to Durango, Mexico, for the assignment. It was nearly suicidal to shoot battles with early film cameras under combat conditions. Villa played for the cameras and, on several occasions, had his troops don enemy uniforms so Walsh could get better shots. Walsh brought Villa a uniform to wear on camera that matched what the public *thought* a general should look like. Back in Los Angeles, Walsh played the young Villa in dramatized scenes filmed in and around the San Fernando Mission. Those scenes, directed by W. Christy Cabanne, were incorporated into the location footage of Villa and his battles for *The Life of General Villa*. The film was released at the height of Villa's popularity in the United States and had its premiere in New York City on May 9, 1914. It was a tremendous box-office hit for the time and, unfortunately, is believed to be a lost film, although unedited fragments and scene stills do exist. Raoul Walsh became one of the leading pioneering directors in Hollywood during the first half of the twentieth century. Among his more than 150 film credits, spanning from the silent era to sound, are *The Thief of Bagdad* (1924), *What Price Glory?* (1926), *The Big Trail* (1930), *The Roaring Twenties* (1939), *High Sierra* (1941), *They Died With Their Boots On* (1941), *White Heat* (1949), *and The Naked and The Dead* (1958).

Dolores del Rio and her cousin Ramon Novarro were forced to flee their Durango birthplace when Villa's forces overtook the city. They sought refuge with relatives in Mexico City, since their aristocratic family was not in favor with Villa, and resided there until destiny led them to the United States and Hollywood stardom. Durango was largely unknown as a filming location until 1954, when various factors led to discovery by Hollywood.

Hollywood movies prior to 1945 were mostly made at studios with enormous backlots and ranches. That changed dramatically in the years following World War II. The surge in suburban housing developments encroached on previously unspoiled locations just as improved modes of travel and technological advancements made long-distance transportation of people and equipment easier. Armed with newer, lighter-weight cameras, lenses, and better film stock that required less lighting, major Hollywood movies were being shot on location in Mexico, including *Tarzan and The Mermaids*, *Captain from Castille*, *The Fugitive*, *The Treasure of the Sierra Madre*, and *Fiesta*, all of which were in production from 1947 to 1948. 20th Century-Fox developed a widescreen format known as "CinemaScope," which was introduced with enormous success in the biblical film blockbuster *The Robe* (1953). Studios clamored for new, never-before-seen eye-popping locales for CinemaScope and other widescreen formats that followed.

Mexico's vast interior offered rich, natural locations, and colonial architecture perfect for that Hollywood staple, the western. Close proximity to the United States, a favorable monetary exchange rate, trained crews, and lower labor costs enhanced the appeal. The Mexican film industry boomed during and immediately after the Second World War. Based on the U.S. studio business model, most Mexican films were shot in and around Mexico City's newly constructed Estudios Churubusco.

Miguel Alemán Velasco partnered in a film production company along with Melchior Perrusquia, the enterprising son of the former president of Mexico (1946–1952), Miguel Alemán. In 1954, Hollywood producer Robert L. Jacks, who was affiliated with 20th Century-Fox, approached them about co-producing a proposed western film, *White Feather*. The film had nothing to do with Mexico but the locations scouted in

Durango could easily pass for the American Southwest. The partners agreed and *White Feather* went into production with an American cast headed by young Fox contract stars Robert Wagner, Debra Paget, and Jeffrey Hunter; the crew was made up mostly of Mexicans. Robert Wagner remarked in a 2006 interview with *Wildest Westerns Magazine*: "I did a western called *White Feather* that they built an entire set in Durango, Mexico. We were the first company that was ever down there . . . I had single combat with Jeff Hunter and Hugh O'Brian in that picture, and we did most of the stunts. We did some pretty quick stuff on that, a lot with horses, a lot on bareback."

Ranching and cattle, supported by expansive ranch lands, were—and are to this day—a major economic force in the state of Durango. Hundreds of locals were employed as extras portraying Indians, cowboys, and soldiers. Local craftsmen were utilized to make leather goods, saddles, and costumes. Merchants supplied food and goods for the production company. The few nearby hotels were filled with actors and technicians. Livestock from nearby ranches were rented, and skilled horsemen were employed as wranglers. Film production quickly became a major component of economic development in the region.

White Feather (1955) turned out to be a rather dull, routine western, but Durango locations filmed in CinemaScope and Technicolor by cinematographer Lucien Ballard raised awareness of the filming sites. Five- to seven-thousand-foot mountain ranges, high deserts, verdant river valleys, vivid blue skies and cloud formations offered the filmmakers unparalled opportunities. Motion pictures could be completed in a shorter period of time because extended periods of daylight in the southern hemisphere allowed for more exterior filming. The scenery was stunning, the economic advantages obvious, the people welcoming, and Durango is steeped in history. Previously famous mostly for the scorpions that inhabit its deserts, Durango was smitten with the Hollywood bug. This was no unrequited love: Hollywood reciprocated by bringing stars, dollars, and recognition to Durango.

The following year, in April of 1955, 20th Century-Fox sent the biggest Hollywood star of his day, Clark Gable, along with fellow leading lights Jane Russell and Robert Ryan, to Durango and filmed the western adventure *The Tall Men* (1955) under the direction of Raoul Walsh (making his first return since working on the 1914 film *The Life of General Villa*). Next came *Comanche* (1957) starring Dana Andrews and Linda Cristal, followed by *Geronimo* (1960), with Chuck Connors, and *The Unforgiven* (1960), directed by John Huston and starring a powerhouse cast of stars: Burt Lancaster, Audrey Hepburn, Audie Murphy, Joseph Wiseman, and Lillian Gish.

✳ ✳ ✳

Superstar John Wayne (1907–1979) had roles in more than 172 films during a career that spanned five decades. For several generations he symbolized rugged American masculinity in the form of a western hero or military soldier. At six four, with his distinctive walk, laconic speech, charismatic personality, and athletic abilities, the "Duke" galvanized audiences with his screen persona. His career is inextricably linked with his mentor, director John Ford, who crafted his screen image and best screen performances in a series of now classic films, including *Stagecoach* (1939), *They Were Expendable*, *The Quiet Man* (1952), *The Searchers* (1956), and *The Man Who Shot Liberty Valance* (1962).

In 1965, Wayne brought national and international attention to the state of Durango when he made his first film there, *The Sons of Katie Elder*. News media from around the world focused on the fact that the fifty-seven-year-old actor was recovering from a highly publicized operation to remove his left lung due to cancer. The strenuous role of gunfighter John Elder required Wayne to do some hard riding, fall off his horse, and dive into a frigid river. Could he do it? he was asked. "Well, I didn't get famous for doing drawing room comedies," he answered with a smile.

Life magazine featured a cover story on Wayne and the film from the Durango locations. The small adobe village of Chupaderos, a onetime Pancho Villa stronghold, was given a makeover for the cameras. With the aid of false fronts and imaginative art direction, it was changed into a typical period-movie western town.

Once Wayne successfully completed production of *The Sons of Katie Elder*, directed by veteran Henry Hathaway and produced by Hal Wallis, it seemed like every producer in Hollywood wanted to shoot a Western in Durango.

Wayne had been traveling to Mexico since 1926 and had sailed along the coast on his friend John Ford's yacht, *The Araner*, stopping at Mazatlán and Acapulco. When Wayne took over the producing reins on some of his films beginning in the late 1940s, one of his first projects was Budd Boetticher's *The Bullfighter and the Lady* (1951), made in Mexico City for Republic Pictures. Through his Wayne-Fellows Productions, the Duke produced and starred in the Western *Hondo* (1953), filmed in Camargo, Mexico, and produced *Plunder of the Sun* (1953) starring Glenn Ford, also in Mexico. Wayne became part-owner of the Boca Chica and Flamingo Hotel in Acapulco and was also part-owner of the Belmar Hotel in Mazatlán.

Wayne's dream project of *The Alamo* (1960) was originally to be filmed in Mexico to control the epic film's cost, but the actor fell victim to international politics on both sides of the border: Texans said they would boycott the movie if it was made in Mexico; the Mexican government objected to some of the script's historical inaccuracies and gringo point of view. In the end, Wayne shot it on a sprawling ranch in Brackettville, Texas, and made a concerted effort to portray General Santa Ana and the Mexican army with restraint and great dignity. Ranch owner Happy Shahan and Wayne built the western town of San Antonio and the Alamo mission compound on his property as fully functional interior and exterior sets. They had hoped to draw more films to the site, but *The Alamo*'s limited success and the far-off Brackettville location near the Texas-Mexico border proved too much of a costly obstacle for many Hollywood productions. Five years later, Wayne's dream of a western filmmaking mecca became a reality in Durango.

The success of *The Sons of Katie Elder* enabled Wayne to finance, through his own Batjac Productions, a series of undemanding yet entertaining westerns shot in Durango, including *The War Wagon* (1967) and *The Undefeated* (1969). *Rio Lobo* (1970), directed by Howard Hawks, was originally set to be shot in Durango, but a scheduling conflict made the Western town set unavailable, and Hawks filmed most of it in Old Tucson, Arizona. A Civil War prologue sequence with a vintage train was the only part of *Rio Lobo* to be shot near Cuernavaca, Mexico. Wayne was in the middle of filming *Rio Lobo* when he won his Oscar as Best Actor in 1969 for his portrayal of the fat old sheriff Rooster Cogburn in *True Grit*. The Duke enjoyed the process of moviemaking and the camaraderie with cast and crew. The company would commence filming by 6:30 a.m. and would finish shooting on most days around 4:00 p.m. This gave *Katie Elder* co-star Dean Martin time for a round of golf at the exclusive private golf and country club, Campo Campestre, in Durango.

Through a new production and distribution agreement with Warner Bros., Wayne purchased a ranch in Durango called "La Joya," to use as a location for the Batjac production of *Chisum* (1970). At the foot of a magnificent canyon he constructed a Western town with a connecting vintage railroad line that he used for an additional three films—*Big Jake* (1971), *The Train Robbers* (1973), and *Cahill U.S. Marshall* (1973)—and rented out to other productions. In a June 2015 interview with the author, Patrick Wayne, who co-starred with his father in *Big Jake*, stated, "It made a lot of sense to shoot in Mexico, fundamentally a better choice for producers, for it was cheaper, the number of productions filming there created an experienced crew base in which all that was needed from Hollywood were the principal cast members and a few department heads." About his famous father, he said, "My dad was strong-willed, a strong persona, and not shy about expressing his feelings, but understood everyone's collaboration in making a motion picture. He was a huge presence, and on *Big Jake*, director George Sherman on the set was in control." He added, "*Big Jake* was really an excellent film to work on and it was a true family affair. Besides working with my dad and all his friends, my brother Michael Wayne was the producer and my little brother Ethan was the grandson who gets kidnapped [in the story]. I was able to bring my immediate family to the Durango location."

The Duke's youngest son, Ethan Wayne, in a December 13, 2011, interview with the *Orange County Register*, recalled, "I loved being with my dad in Mexico. In the wilderness, you are in John Wayne country. For me, as a youngster, it was like growing up on a ranch or summer camp. John Wayne loved Mexico. There he got the same recognition, if not more so, than back home." In a 1969 *Time* magazine interview, Wayne was quoted as saying, "I would like to be remembered, well, the Mexicans have a phrase, 'Feo, Fuerte y Formal,' which means: he was ugly, strong, and had dignity," though in actuality the Mexican epitaph is "Fuerte, Audaz y Valiente." Mexico is the country Wayne loved, second only to his own. That love was reciprocated by the Mexican crewmembers and his co-stars. Ed Faulkner, who appeared in three films with Wayne in Durango, recalled that John Wayne "was the first on the set and usually the last to leave, and when he walked on that set he brought along a certain ambiance—the actors respected the man for what he'd done and how he'd done it."

In 1965, Durango retained the feeling of the imaginary old Wild West for Hollywood actors and producers. Men walked around with guns strapped to their sides, horses were commonplace, and tequila flowed in the local bars. Actors could stroll through the town and not be bothered by fans. Dusty streets, adobe structures, haciendas, and colonial buildings adorned the capital city and its surrounding environments. Wayne could be observed walking through town shopping or visiting local restaurants and watering holes. One resident recalls running into a slightly inebriated, bigger-than-life Wayne on the street dressed in his cowboy outfit. Another resident fondly remembers Wayne standing outside the local movie house in Durango, personally handing out free tickets to the local kids and their families to a Sunday matinee special showing of his family-oriented adventure film *Hatari!* (1962).

At that time, housing could only be found in the one nineteenth century hotel built in the center of town, and the Mexico Courts Motel on the outskirts where Wayne and most film crews stayed. One castmember described Durango and the location filming as an eight-week-long summer camp experience for old screen veterans—without their wives. The male cast and crew would get drunk, play cards and fool around, all under the guise of making a movie. In 1980, a five-star hotel, El Gobernador, was built on the grounds of a former prison.

So popular had Durango become that, in 1967, three western films had to adjust their schedules to accommodate one another while shooting there at the same time: *Hour of the Gun*, *Guns for San Sebastian*, and *The Scalphunters*.

Mexican productions began to discover Durango as early as 1959 with *La Cucaracha*, which reunited such stars of the Mexican Golden Age of Cinema as Dolores del Rio, Pedro Armendáriz, Emilio "El Indio" Fernández, and Maria Felix. Many Spanish-language films were to follow, including *Los Dorados De Pancho Villa* (1961) with Fernández, *El Tunco Maclovio* (1969) and *Indio* (1972) with Jorge Rivero. *Rage* (1966), a Mexican-American co-production with Columbia Pictures, featured American actor Glenn Ford working with a Mexican director and a largely Mexican cast. Mexican actors as well as assistant directors and technicians found regular employment in Hollywood productions that brought them to Durango from Mexico City. A pool of behind-the-camera talent could provide skilled crews, massive sets, convenient services, and breathtaking locations. In the seventies alone, Durango hosted a record forty-nine American film productions.

Durango was the destination not only for the stars of Hollywood's golden age—John Wayne, Burt Lancaster, Glenn Ford, et. al—but for the quirky actors of Hollywood's new generation: Jack Nicholson (*Goin' South*, 1978), Dennis Hopper (*Kid Blue*, 1973), and even singer-songwriter Bob Dylan (*Pat Garrett and Billy the Kid*, 1973).

Influenced by the spaghetti westerns and the success of Peckinpah's *The Wild Bunch*, filmmakers more and more began producing counter-culture stories involving graphic violence. *Soldier Blue* (1970), the story of an Indian massacre perpetrated by the U.S. Cavalry, echoed the Mai Lai Massacre of civilians by U.S. troops in Vietnam and a student massacre by police in Mexico City. *A Man Called Horse* (1970) tells the harrowing story of an Englishman (Richard Harris) who is captured and tortured by Sioux Indians. Sidney Poitier's *Buck and the Preacher* (1972) mirrored the civil rights movement in America with its story of African-American pioneers. Alexandro Jodorowskys'

John Wayne on horseback, overlooking the Durango landscape.

Penelope Cruz and Salma Hayek in poster art from the film *Bandidas* (2006).

avant garde cult classic *El Topo* (1970) also utilized Durango locations.

In the 1980s, twenty-eight motion pictures were filmed in Durango. *Caveman* (1980) starring Beatle-turned-actor Ringo Starr, utilized the desolate rock formations of Mexiquillo, which served as a prehistoric setting. Before his breakout roles in *Saturday Night Fever* (1977) and *Grease* (1978), John Travolta made his film acting debut in Durango with the horror film *Devil's Rain*, which was not released until 1979.

Tony Scott shot *Revenge* (1988) starring a then-up-and-coming Kevin Costner and veteran actor Anthony Quinn on Durango locations. New Mexico's Los Alamos Research Laboratory was duplicated in a wooded Durango valley for the World War II–era atom bomb story *Fatman and Little Boy* (1988) with Paul Newman. *Old Gringo* (1988), an epic production starring Jane Fonda, Gregory Peck, and Jimmy Smits, was shot at an old mine and hanging bridge called Puente de Ojuela in Mapimi. Durango's deserts served as the setting for the international television mini-series *Samson and Delilah* (1983), and the El Saltito waterfalls were used for a short sequence in the medieval-era feature film *First Knight* (1995) with Richard Gere and Sean Connery. Several films made for Turner Network Television (TNT) featured Dorango settings, among them: *The Cisco Kid* (1993) starring Jimmy Smits; *The Warden* (1999) starring James Caan; *The King of Texas* (2002) starring Patrick Stewart in an updating of Shakespeare's King Lear; and a French made-for-TV western, *Blueberry* (2002).

Nonetheless, the near demise of the western film and the death in 1979 of its leading practitioner, John Wayne, caused Durango's popularity to spiral downward beginning in the 1990s.

The Mexican film industry, after a long period of artistic and economic decline, began a new era of cinema in 1999 with the Oscar-nominated (for Best Foreign Language feature) *Cabeza de Vaca*. The film, which is based on the early Spanish explorers' travels through the American wilderness, was shot in Durango, as was the Mexican drama *Pueblo De Madera* (1990).

Durango's fifty-year anniversary as a locale for film productions was celebrated with the arrival of Mexican actress Salma Hayek and Spanish actress Penelope Cruz to film the bawdy gal-pal western *Bandidas* (2006) from French director Luc Besson. Then-governor of Durango, Ismael Hernandez Deras, honored the filmmakers with a special welcoming ceremony at the Official Governor's residence.

Futuristic landscapes were found in Durango for the science fiction film saga *Dragonball* (2008), based on the wildly popular Japanese anime. It was because of factors influencing the making of the movie that for the first time, an empty, abandoned industrial complex was transformed into a complete production facility with space for sets, mills, and sound stages. Prior to *Dragonball*, interior scenes shot in Durango were made in makeshift stages in a local warehouse as cover sets, which were used in case of inclement weather or other delays. In most cases, the production companies would schedule interior filming on corresponding sets at Estudios Churubusco in Mexico City.

Due to drug-related violence and kidnappings in the region, fueled by a declaration of war on the drug cartels by the administration of President Calderon in 2009, Hollywood productions have been increasingly reluctant to film in Mexico due to safety concerns and insurance regulations. Among the few films made in Durango in recent years is *For Greater Glory: The True Story of Cristiada* (2012), a historical epic starring Andy Garcia and Eva Longoria, about Mexico's bloody 1920s anti-clerical conflict. Though directed by an American, Dean Wright, *For Greater Glory* was a Mexican production, so We Insurance regulations regarding films produced outside the United States did not restrict it.

Although not as popular as they once were, westerns continue to be made in Durango, including *Texas Rising* (2015), an epic ten-hour mini-series directed by Oscar-nominated Roland Joffé (*The Killing Fields*, *The Mission*) for the Arts and Entertainment (A&E) cable channel.

Durango is in the process of reinventing itself as the state can double for the Middle East, Afghanistan, the Pacific Northwest of North America, England, or virtually any imaginary cinematic world. In the global business of location filmmaking, Durango faces stiff competition from film commissions, not only within Mexico, but those from outside who have come to realize the local economic benefits of motion picture production.

The present-day Durango Film Commission, a state government–run agency, offers tax and monetary filming incentives, as well as low-cost cooperation from local, state, and federal agencies and municipalities. The film industry provides employment for hundreds of local people and those in support services. Moviemaking also provides Durango with unparalled exposure and marketing opportunities for tourism. A modern airport connects Durango with Mexico City and major cities of the southwestern United States.

Rita Haworth in *Acapulco*.

CHAPTER 7

FILMS MADE IN MEXICO

THE LIFE OF GENERAL VILLA (1914)

Director: W. Christy Cabanne, Raoul Walsh (uncredited)

Producer: D. W. Griffith, Mutual Film Corporation

Cast: Pancho Villa (as himself), Raoul Walsh (young Villa), Teddy Sampson (Villa's sister), Irene Hunt (Villa's sister), Walter Long (federal officer)

Story: The highly fictionalized story of the early life of bandit-turned-revolutionary hero Pancho Villa and his victories in Nortrhern Mexico.

Production: On January 5, 1914, Villa signed a contract with the Mutual Film Corporation, represented by partner Harry E. Aitken. Mutual's D. W. Griffith sent his protégé Raoul Walsh to Mexico where he filmed actual battle scenes and reenacted some for the cameras and even shot footage of Villa. Back in Los Angeles, Walsh was recruited to play a young Villa for the film's early scenes; these were shot in and around the San Fernando Mission, located just north of Los Angeles. A success when it was first released in 1914, *The Life of General Villa* is one of the first films we would identify, in modern contemporary terms, as a "docu-drama," combining documentary footage with dramatic renencaments. This film, along with an estimated 73 percent of American films, shot on visually stunning but unstable silver nitrate stock in the silent era, are now considered lost. Many perished in studio fires, some were scrapped for their silver content, and others simply disintegrated with time.

KINKAID, GAMBLER (UNIVERSAL FILM MANUFACTURING CO., 1916)

Director: Raymond Wells

Screenplay: Fred Myers

Producer: Carl Laemmle

Cast: Ruth Stonehouse (Nellie Gleason), R. A. Cavin (Jim Kinkaid), Raymond Whittaker (George Arnold), Noble Johnson (Romero Valdez)

Story: Female detective Nellie Gleason follows gambler Jim Kinkaid to Mexico after he robs the estate of millionaire George Arnold. She then discovers that Arnold is a crook who swindles immigrants and that

Kinkaid robbed him to pay back the people Arnold had cheated. Nellie decides to let Kinkaid escape.

Production: Photographic still evidence indicates that some scenes for the *Kinkaid, Gambler* were shot partly on location in Mexico. No prints of the film are known to exist.

LA VENGANZA DE PANCHO VILLA (THE REVENGE OF PANCHO VILLA) (1930)

Director: Felix Padilla and Edmundo Padilla

Story: A condensed film story of Pancho Villa and his triumphs that offers an alternative point of view to that of the U.S.

Production: In 2003, after an exhaustive two-year multi-national search for a possible surviving copy of *The Life of General Villa*, documentary filmmaker Gregorio Rocha stumbled on a hidden treasure at the University of Texas in El Paso. He had found, not the original film he was looking for but another film, *La Venganza De Pancho Villa (The Revenge of Pancho Villa)*, most of it intact, that included a few scenes from *The Life of General Villa*. Footage also used from the five-reel New York Motion Picture Corp./Triangle production *Lieutenant Danny, U.S.A.* (1916), and a twenty-part Universal western serial, *Liberty: A Daughter of the U.S.A.* (1916).

La Venganza de Pancho Villa is a compilation silent film, with both English and Spanish intertitles, which consists of footage from American features, serials, newsreel footage from both the U.S. and Mexico. Also included are still photographs and original scenes made by Felix Padilla and his son Edmundo, who were film exhibitors along the Tex-Mex border. In a published article by Laura Isabel Serna, PhD, citing a press release issued by the National Film Registry on February 17, 2009, declared that the film provides evidence of a "vital Mexican-American film presence during the 1910–1930s."

THE SEA BAT (METRO-GOLDWYN-MAYER, 1930)

Director: Wesley Ruggles

Screenplay: Bess Meredyth, John Howard Lawson, Dorothy Yost

Producer: Wesley Ruggles

Cast: Charles Bickford (Sims), Raquel Torres (Nina), Nils Asther (Carl), John Miljan (Juan), George F. Marion (Antone) Boris Karloff (Corsican), Gibson Gowland (Limey), Edmund Breese (Maddocks), Mathilde Comont (Mimba), Mack Swain (Dutchy)

Story: A beautiful West Indian girl, Nina, loses her husband, a sponge diver, to a giant manta ray. Vowing vengeance, she offers herself to the first man who kills the evil "sea bat." She finds herself attracted to a visiting minister who, unbeknownst to her, is an escaped convict from Devil's Island. Together, they unravel the mystery surrounding her husband's death and the deadly manta ray exacts its moral justice on the perpetrator.

Production: *The Sea Bat* was shot on location off the coast and near Mazatlán, Mexico, substituting for a fictional island called Portuga in the West Indies and pseudo island culture. The movie was originally intended as a vehicle for star Lon Chaney (*The Hunchback of Notre Dame*, 1923; *The Phantom of the Opera*, 1925), known as the "Man of a Thousand Faces," for his ability to morph into grotesque and deformed—yet still very human—characters. Chaney died of lung cancer shortly before the film went into production. This was an early talking film that offered excellent location camera work and water special effects. The eponymous

Wesley Ruggles gives directions to Mexican extras on location in Mazatlán, Mexico, for MGM's *The Sea Bat* (1930).

sea bat prefigures Steven Spielberg's Bruce, the great white shark in *Jaws* (1975), forty-five years later. The giant Atlantic manta (*Manta birostris*) is a type of devil fish and is characterized by its large flapping fins and two horns protruding near the mouth, giving it a diabolic appearance. It lives in the warmer waters, where it eats small fish and plankton. The Atlantic manta can grow to twenty-three feet, from fin tip to fin tip, and can weigh up to 2,200 pounds. Despite its sinister appearance, it is, in fact, a gentle creature and does not attack humans in the water. Director Wesley Ruggles found himself instructing more than five hundred Mexican natives of Mazatlán for the big camera shots. The following year, Ruggles directed the Academy Award–winning Best Picture, the epic western *Cimarron* (1931), based on the Edna Ferber novel. Raquel Torres (1908–1987) was a Mexican American actress who had starred as an island maiden in Robert Flaherty's semi-documentary silent film *White Shadows in the South Seas* (1929), which was filmed on location in Tahiti and the Marquesas. Floyd Crosby won an Oscar for Best Cinematography. Her screen career was short lived; after a half-dozen films, she retired. *The Sea Bat*'s script has the literary influences of Herman Melville and W.

Somerset Maugham in its melodramatic plot. Charles Bickford was promoted as a leading man by MGM in the early 1930s, but he met with poor audience approval; he did, however, succeed as a character actor later, in such films as *Duel in the Sun* (1946) and *The Big Country* (1958). Boris Karloff, who would soon find fame as the Monster in James Whale's *Frankenstein* (1931), has a small role as the Corsican, one of Nina's suitors.

VIVA VILLA! (1934)

Director: Howard Hawks, Jack Conway, William A. Wellman
Screenplay: Ben Hecht
Producer: David O. Selznick
Cast: Wallace Beery (Pancho Villa), Leo Carrillo (Sierra), Stuart Erwin (Johnny Sykes) Fay Wray (Teresa), Katherine DeMille (Rosita Morales)
Story: *Viva Villa!* is a fictional interpretation of the historical Mexican figure Francisco "Pancho" Villa (1878–1923), born Doroteo Arango, who is considered simultaneously a hero of the Mexican Revolution, a bandit, a womanizer, a terrorist, a military strategist, and a murderer. The film concentrates on Villa's achievements in freeing the poor, dethroning the tyrants, and restoring peace to Mexico; it ends with his assassination.
Production: *Viva Villa!* was produced by David O. Selznick (*Gone With the Wind*); newly installed MGM production executive Irving Thalberg spearheaded the project. The film went into production in 1933, just ten years after Pancho Villa's assassination, which had been orchestrated by members of the prevailing government in 1923. The film follows key factual events in Villa's life in a highly fictionalized and historically inaccurate manner. MGM was trying to capitalize on the popularity of the western at the beginning of the sound era, which started with the heroic Cisco Kid in Fox's *In Old Arizona* (1929). MGM decided to film on location in Mexico not only for authenticity but also because the studio had "frozen funds" there. These were profits generated in Mexico that could only be spent there.

The historical Villa was one of the most celebrated and photographed men of his time. He had a natural instinct for celebrity and

On location in Mexico, a film crew readies a shot of Wallace Beery in Jack Conway's *Viva Villa!* (1934).

understood the power of moving pictures. While the accepted image of the bandit leader showed him with sombrero and bandoliers, Villa sometimes undermined the stereotype by appearing in photos wearing a general's uniform (provided by the Mutual Film Company), campaign hat, or a pith helmet. The images of Villa still resonate to the present day in both Mexico and the United States. Americans considered the Mexican Revolution to be a romantic adventure and Villa a charismatic hero as the military leader of the armies of Northern Mexico. American journalist John Reed wrote of Villa and the Revolution as a romantic undertaking. Celebrated American writer/author/journalist Ambrose Bierce traveled to Mexico as an observer in Villa's army and disappeared on the battlefield, presumed dead and never to be heard from again. Villa brought his Division del Norte from the north, and Emiliano Zapata from the south, to the capital, Mexico City. Villa's forces temporarily disbanded and were later assaulted by various factions. When Villa started attacking American business interests, the Hearst newspapers, owned by William Randolph Hearst who also held property in Mexico, decried Villa. On March 9, 1916, Villa crossed the border in a daring raid on the small community of Columbus, New Mexico, in retaliation supposedly for an arms deal gone bad and for President Wilson's support of the Carranza government that Villa had fought against. Villa's men burned and looted the New Mexico border town, leaving ten U.S. civilians and eight U.S. Cavalrymen and a hundred of their own dead. Villa's violent invasion of United States soil turned U.S. public opinion against him with the permission of the Carranza Government. President Wilson sent General Pershing and six thousand American troops into Mexico to find and capture the elusive Villa, a mission that did not meet with success. Thus, Pancho Villa eluded the Americanos and rode into legend.

Viva Villa! was filmed in 1933, largely on location in Mexico, including San Marcos, a town just north of Mexico City. The Hollywood troupe was thrown out of Mexico when, in a state of intoxication, actor Lee Tracy who originally played the American newspaperman, urinated from his hotel balcony on a passing parade of soldiers. MGM studio head Louis B. Mayer sent a telegram to Mexican president Abelardo Rodríguez, apologizing for the deplorable conduct of Tracy, which he said "shocked his company as deeply as it did Mexico." As a result, MGM dismissed Lee Tracy and canceled his contract. Stuart Erwin replaced Tracy in the film. (A consistent theme in all Hollywood film productions about Villa is that he is seen through the eyes of an American, such as a journalist, a newspaperman, a mercenary, an outlaw, or an ex-soldier.)

Cinematographer James Wong Howe hired some twenty Mexican cameramen, including Gabriel Figueroa, to handle multiple camera shots; this exposed Mexican cameramen for the first time to the opulent and chaotic style of Hollywood filmmaking. James Wong Howe (1899–1976), a famed Chinese-American cinematographer (*Yankee Doodle Dandy*, 1942; *Body and Soul*, 1947; *Funny Girl*, 1968), whose career spanned the twenties to the seventies. He was nominated nine times for an Academy Award for Best Cinematography, winning for *The Rose Tattoo* (1955) and *Hud* (1963). Wong Howe would later return to Mexico to work on Robert Rossen's *The Brave Bulls* (1951) and Arnold Laven's *The Glory Guys* (1965).

Director Howard Hawks told interviewer Joseph McBride (*Hawks on Hawks*, University of California Press, 1982) that he and Mayer physically fought it out when Mayer disapproved of his shooting pace. Depending on the source, Hawks was either fired or he quit. *Viva Villa!* was completed by director Jack Conway at the MGM studios and at a ranch location in California's San Fernando Valley. Hundreds of Mexican and Mexican American extras worked on the production. Ironically, Conway had been the studio's first choice as

Charles Rosher, one of several Mutual cameramen sent to Mexico to cover Pancho Villa and the Mexican Revolution. Rosher went on to win the first Academy Award for Best Cinematography in 1929, an honor he shared with Karl Struss. *Courtesy Marc Wanamaker/Bison Archives*

director; announcements were made to that effect in the trade papers before production began. In December 1933, Conway came down with the flu and prolific director William A. Wellman took over as director for one week.

Rugged, rough-hewn and bear-like, MGM star Wallace Beery (*The Big House, 1930; Dinner at Eight*, 1933; Oscar-winning Best Actor for *The Champ*, 1931) plays Pancho Villa as a likeable, overgrown, buffoon child who has great difficulty in understanding why people try to dissuade him from slaughtering his defeated adversaries. (Beery is also credited as having played Villa in the partially lost fifteen-chapter Pathé serial *Patria* (1917), a story about a woman involved in a plot by Japan and Germany to ally with Mexico in order to invade the United States.) Leo Carrillo (1881–1961) plays Sierra, who was based on the historical figure actually named Fierro. Carrillo is best remembered for his portrayal of Pancho, the Cisco Kid's loveable sidekick in the fifties television series. The actor was the only Hispanic or Latin hero figure in the early days of television in America. Born in an adobe building on Olvera Street in Los Angeles, Carrillo was a direct descendent of one of the original Spanish/Mexican Californio families. He had a long and successful career on

in his essay for the Criterion DVD release of *Redes*, "Its collectivist pro-union story about the consciousness raising of exploited fishermen resonated with the left-leaning politics in international artistic circles in the 1930s." The film met with a poor reception from Mexican audiences upon its release in 1936, perhaps due to its new stylistic narrative, its serious subject matter, and its downbeat ending. In 1937, it was released in America, where it enjoyed limited success. The musical score, composed by Silvestre Revueltas, influenced American composer Aaron Copland.

Redes is considered a forerunner of the Italian postwar neorealism reflected in Luchino Visconti's similar film *La Tierra Trema* (*The Earth Trembles*, 1948) about Sicilian fishermen.

IN OLD MEXICO (PARAMOUNT PICTURES, 1938)

Director: Edward D. Venturini

Screenplay: Harrison Jacobs, based on characters created by Clarence E. Mulford

Producer: Harry Sherman

Cast: William Boyd (Hopalong Cassidy), George "Gabby" Hayes (Windy Halliday), Russell Hayden (Lucky Jenkins), Paul Sutton (The Fox), Allan Ernest Garcia (Don Carlos), Trevor Bardette (Colonel Lopez)

Story: "The Fox" escapes from a Mexican prison and vows vengeance on Hopalong Cassidy and the rurale Colonel Lopez, who imprisoned him. He lures them into a trap by sending a false message of mutual aid for a rendezvous at Lopez's family ranch in Mexico.

Production: *In Old Mexico* was the twentieth film in the popular Hopalong Cassidy B-Western series, comprising sixty-six black-and-white features (1935–1946). It was a sequel to the previous installment, *Borderlands* (1937). Outdoor exteriors of *In Old Mexico* were shot on location at Joshua Tree National Desert, in Eastern California. The Hacienda scenes were filmed at Boca Del Toro Ranch, owned by Jose Villarreal, near Mexicali, Baja California Norte. Novelist Clarence L. Mulford created the fictional Western character of Hopalong Cassidy in 1905. William Boyd (1895–1972) was a silent screen star for pioneering director Cecil B. DeMille. Boyd's career faltered during the transition from silent to sound movies when an actor with a similar name was involved in a public scandal. Beginning in 1935 with the first feature *Hop-along Cassidy*, Boyd and producer Harry Sherman transformed the hard-cussing cowboy created by Mulford into "Hoppy," the likable, urbane, silver-haired, black hat–wearing wrangler with his white horse, Topper. In 1948, Boyd purchased the rights to his Cassidy films and licensed them to television. A new generation discovered the character with which Boyd had become closely identified. Allan Ernest Garcia (1887–1938), who plays Don Carlos, was a casting director and actor for comic genius Charlie Chaplin on a number of his films, including *The Circus* (1928), *City Lights* (1931), and *Modern Times* (1936). Director Venturini was born in Argentina.

BLOOD AND SAND (20TH CENTURY-FOX, 1941)

Director: Rouben Mamoulian

Screenplay: Jo Swerling, based on the novel *Sangre y Arena* by Vicente Blasco Ibáñez

Producer: Darryl F. Zanuck

Cast: Tyrone Power (Juan Gallardo), Linda Darnell (Carmen Espinosa), Rita Hayworth (Doña Sol), Nazimova (Señora Gallardo), John Carradine (Nacional) Anthony Quinn (Manolo de Palma), Laird Cregar (Natalio

Curio), J. Carol Naish (Garabato), Lynn Bari (Encarnacion)

Story: The story of farm boy Juan Gallardo's rise as one of Spain's greatest bullfighters. When he falls under the spell of Doña Sol, it leads to his downfall.

Production: This lavish sound Technicolor production was a remake of the 1922 Rudolph Valentino silent feature of the same name. Set in Spain, the 1941 film was shot at 20th Century-Fox studios in West Los Angeles, and the bullfight sequences were filmed on location at the Plaza de Toros in Mexico City, D. F., as was as other background material. With Spain in the middle of a civil war on the eve of World War II, location filming in Spain would have been impossible, let alone impractical. While scouting locations in Mexico, the film's director, Rouben Mamoulian, hired a young American bullfighter by the name of Oscar "Budd" Boetticher as the credited "Bullfighting Advisor." One of his duties was to teach Tyrone Power (1914–1958) the intricacies and movements of bullfighting. Boetticher also recommended the renowned bullfighter Armilita to serve as Power's onscreen double in the bullfighting sequence in Plaza de Toros. (Power was the only principal cast member to work in Mexico.) Back at the studio, Boetticher assisted choreographer Gene Sawyer in creating the Torero's Paso Doble, a sensual dance sequence performed by Anthony Quinn and Rita Hayworth, two young actors on the verge of stardom. (Hayworth was a trained dancer; Quinn had prior experience as both a ballroom dancer and a boxer.) Boetticher also advised screenwriter Jo Swerling on bullfighting details, and editor Barbara Mclean on their correct sequencing. This fascination with bullfighting inadvertently led him to a career in motion pictures. Years later, he would write and direct a semi-autobiographical film, *The Bullfighter and the Lady*, which earned him an Academy Award nomination for Best Story of 1951. Boetticher is best known for his direction of a series of six spare, hard-edged Westerns, starring Randolph Scott, in the late 1950s. *Blood and Sand* won the Academy Award in 1942 for Best Color Cinematography (Ernest Palmer and Ray Rennahan). Mamoulian, who directed the first three-strip Technicolor film, *Becky Sharp* (1935), was a consummate visual stylist who patterned *Blood and Sand*'s look on many of the famed paintings by Goya. Power returned to Mexico for an extended stay in 1947 to star in *Captain from Castille*. He met Mexican-born actress Linda Christian while shooting scenes for the film in Acapulco and married her in 1949. He returned to Mexico one last time, in 1956, for his role in *The Sun Also Rises*.

FIVE WERE CHOSEN/CINCO FUERON ESCOGIDOS (RKO PICTURES, 1944)

Director: Herbert Kline, Augustin P. Delgado

Screenplay: Budd Schulberg, Rafael M. Munoz, Xavier Villanueva

Producer: Herbert Kline

Cast: Victor Killian, Howard Da Silva, Ricardo Montalban (Stefan), Rosa Harvan (Stojak)

Story: A group of Yugoslavian villagers attempt to free five of their citizens held by the Nazis during World War II.

Production: *Five Were Chosen* was filmed in Mexico in two versions, one in English and one in Spanish *(Cinco Fueron Escogidos)*. It was filmed in November 1942 and released in Mexico in 1943, with a subsequent U.S. release in 1944. Jack Draper was responsible for the black-and-white cinematography on both versions. The bilingual Mexican actor Ricardo Montalban is the film's star. In 1947, he was signed as a contract player at

MGM. Originally, the rising American film star Frances Farmer (1913–1970) was to be the female lead in *Five Were Chosen*, but her outrageous behavior torpedoed that. The cast was staying at the posh Maria Isabel Hotel in downtown Mexico City. One night at the beginning of production, Farmer became drunk, ran through the hotel in a state of intoxication, spraying other guests with a seltzer bottle, then stripped naked and sprinted outside to the main thoroughfare. There, she mooned the revered San Angel Monument in plain sight of the police, shocking onlookers. Montalban dashed outside, quickly covered her naked body with an overcoat, and escorted her back into the hotel, but it was too late. She was arrested and swiftly deported to the United States. Farmer's alcoholism and mental instability killed her once-promising career.

Herbert Kline, Budd Schulberg, and several members of the English-language cast had been members of the leftist and progressive American Group Theatre. Writer Budd Schulberg wrote a novel, *What Makes Sammy Run*, which was a scathing indictment of Hollywood in 1941. Schulberg went on to win Academy Awards for *On the Waterfront* (1954), *The Harder They Fall* (1956), and *A Face in the Crowd* (1957). Kline collaborated with John Steinbeck on the Mexican documentary *The Forgotten Village* (1941), but was later blacklisted in Hollywood when he refused to testify before the House Un-American Activities Committee. In 1970, Kline resumed filmmaking when he directed *Walls of Fire*, a documentary about Mexican artists Diego Rivera and David Alfaro Siqueiros, for which he earned an Academy Award nomination.

THE MACOMBER AFFAIR (UNITED ARTISTS, 1947)

Director: Zoltan Korda

Screenplay: Casey Robinson, from the 1936 Ernest Hemingway story "The Short Happy Life of Francis Macomber"

Producer: Benedict Borgeaus

Cast: Gregory Peck (Robert Wilson), Joan Bennett (Margaret "Margo" Macomber), Robert Preston (Francis Macomber)

Story: Francis Macomber and his wife, Margaret, hire experienced hunter Robert Wilson as their guide on an African safari. The seemingly happy couple's problems come to the forefront on the safari as Margaret becomes openly attracted to the hunter. This causes tension among the three, especially when Robert refuses Margaret's advances.

Production: *The Macomber Affair* was filmed in black and white over a six-week period in and around Tecate, Baja California Norte (Southeast of Tijuana, halfway to Ensenada), and on soundstages in Hollywood. Three camera crews were reportedly sent to Africa for to photograph wildlife in order to match shots of the actors firing weapons into the distance. Gregory Peck had made his film debut with *Days of Glory* (1944), which was written and produced by Casey Robinson. Peck achieved stardom with his next role, that of a devoted priest, in *The Keys of the Kingdom* (1944), which earned him an Academy Award nomination. He followed this triumph with *The Yearling* (1945), *Gentlemen's Agreement (*1947), and Hitchcock's *Spellbound* (1948). Casey Robinson (*Captain Blood*, 1935; *Saratoga Trunk*, 1945) had optioned Ernest Hemingway's story and adapted it into a screenplay. Peck, a friend of Robinson's, agreed to be in the film. Five years later, he starred as a Hunter in Casey Robinsons' screen adaptation of Hemingway's *The Snows of Kilimanjaro* (1952) opposite Susan Hayward and Ava Gardner. Benedict Bogeaus (1904–1968) was a Chicago real estate magnate and entrepreneur who became an independent Hollywood producer. He produced above-average B-movies featuring name actors. Of the many films he produced, four were shot in Mexico: *The Macomber Affair*, *My Outlaw Brother*, *The River's Edge*, and *Enchanted Island*.

THE FUGITIVE (RKO PICTURES, 1947)

Director: John Ford

Screenplay: Dudley Nichols, based on the novel *The Labyrinthine Ways* by Graham Greene

Producer: Merian C. Cooper, John Ford

Cast: Henry Fonda (a fugitive), Dolores del Rio (Maria Dolores), Pedro Armendáriz (Lieutenant of Police), J. Carrol Naish (a police informant), Leo Carrillo (Chief of Police), Ward Bond (El Gringo), Miguel Inclán (a hostage)

Story: In a fictional Latin American country, seized by anti-clerical fever, a fanatical young lieutenant, who

Henry Fonda and J. Carol Naish on location in Taxco de Alarcon, México, for John Ford's *The Fugitive* (1947).

has also fathered the Magdalene's illegitimate baby, pursues the last priest with revolutionary zeal. The Magdalene, "Maria Dolores," hides the priest with the unsolicited help from Barabbas, who ambushes the military and aids the priest in his ultimately futile escape across a mountain. The priest finds redemption only after he is betrayed by a perversely comical Judas, and shot by a revolutionary firing squad.

Production: Filmed on locations in Taxco-Cholula Cuernavaca, El Perote, and Veracruz, Mexico. English writer Graham Greene departed for Mexico to write about religious persecution in 1928, when President Plutarco Calles ruled Mexico. "I had seen the devotion of peasants praying in the priestless churches," recalled Greene in his travel memoirs *Ways of Escape*, "and I had attended Masses in upper rooms where the Sanctus bell could not sound for fear of police." Greene's hatred of Mexico started with his disgust at a ceremonial cockfight in San Luis Potosi and was reinforced by the policies of the Calles government. In Villahermosa, decrees were passed that priests should marry. Priests in Tabasco were hunted down and eventually shot, all except one, who wandered the forests and swamps for ten years, becoming known as the elusive "Whiskey Priest."

In 1947, John Ford went to Mexico to film Dudley Nichols's adaptation of Graham Greene's anti-clerical novel *The Labyrinthine Ways* (also known as *The Power and the Glory*). *The Fugitive* was the first postwar undertaking of the director's independent production company, Argosy Pictures. *The Fugitive* was an international production combining Hollywood and Mexican talent in front of and behind the camera. The famed Mexican filmmaking team of director Emilio "El Indio" Fernández and cinematographer Gabriel Figueroa co-produced and photographed Ford's film. Mexican actors Pedro Armendáriz and Dolores del Rio (who had begun her movie career in Hollywood) joined Henry Fonda as the film's leads. Ford shot and produced *The Fugitive* out of Mexico City's Estudios Churubusco, co-owned by RKO, which also distributed the film.

FIESTA (METRO-GOLDWYN-MAYER, 1947)

Director: Richard Thorpe
Screenplay: George Bruce, Lester Cole
Producer: Jack Cummings
Cast: Ricardo Montalban (Mario Morales), Esther Williams (Maria Morales), Akim Tamiroff (Chato Vasquez), Fortunio Bonanova (Antonio Morales), Mary Astor (Señora Morales), Cyd Charisse (Conchita)
Story: Mario Morales (Montalban) is a bullfighter who wants to be a composer. His twin sister, Maria, wants to be a bullfighter in a male-dominated tradition.
Production: Filmed in Puebla, Mexico. The symphonic composition used in the film, *El Salon Mexico*, was written by Aaron Copland (1900–1990), a distinctly American classical composer, in 1936. It was based on Mexican folk music, which Copland began researching in 1932. It created a new sound, one that was based on Mexican folk music, which led to more popular symphonic works. The Mexican Symphony Orchestra inaugurated the work in 1937, and debuted it in the United States in 1938.

ADVENTURES OF CASANOVA (EAGLE-LION FILMS, 1948)

Director: Roberto Gavaldon
Screenplay: Crane Wilbur, Walter Bullock, Karen DeWolfe
Producer: Leonard S. Picker

Cast: Arturo de Cordóva (Casanova), Lucille Bremer (Zanetta), Turhan Bey (Lorenzo), John Sutton (De Brisac), George Tobias (Jacopo), Nestor Paiva (De Gaetano), Jorje Treviño (Angelino), Jacqueline Dalya (Lady Andrea), Miroslava (Signore Vallento), Fernando Wagner (Commander)

Story: Set in 1793, this fictional account of the great lover Casanova focuses on his patriotic fight to free Sicily from Austrian rule.

Production: Bryan Foy, head of production for Eagle-Lion Films, produced this lavish production (in both English and Spanish versions), filmed in and around Mexico City's Churubusco Studios. Second-unit photography was assigned to Jack Draper; set design was by Alfred Ybarra and Jorje Fernandez. The film followed the success of the similar *Adventures of Don Juan* (1948), starring Warner Bros. leading romantic star, Errol Flynn. Mexican actor Arturo de Córdova (1908–1973) appeared in more than a hundred films, beginning in 1935. Roberto Gavaldon was one of Mexico's most noted directors and is best known for the award-winning *Macario* (1961). Edwin Schallert, in his *Los Angeles Times* review of February 18, 1948, wrote that "special distinction was undoubtedly given the picture by the scenic backgrounds and the direction of Roberto Gavaldon."

MYSTERY IN MEXICO (RKO PICTURES, 1948)

Director: Robert Wise

Screenplay: Lawrence Kimble, from a story by Muriel Roy Bolton

Producer: Sid Rogell, Joseph Noriega (Associate Producer)

Cast: William Lundigan (Steve Hastings), Jacqueline White (Victoria Ames), Ricardo Cortez (Joe Norcross), Tony Barrett (Carlos), Jaqueline Dalya (Dolores), Walter Reed (Glenn Ames), José Torvay (Swigart), Jaime Jimenez (Pancho Gomez), Antonio Frusto (Pancho's father), Dolores Camerillo (Pancho's mother), Eduardo Casado (Commandante Rodríguez), Thalia Draper (Florecita), Carlos Muzquiz (Luis Otero), Freddie Romero (José), Alfonso Jimenez (Lopez), Conchita Gentil (Benny's mother). Lilia Blanchard (Benny's sister), Suzi Crandall and Marilyn Mercer (flight hostesses), William Forrest (Powers)

Story: American insurance investigator Glenn Ames disappears in Mexico City with a necklace worth $200,000. An insurance agency sends Steve Hastings to locate Ames and recover the jewels by posing as a tourist and following Ames's sister to Mexico.

Production: In *Robert Wise on His Films* by Sergio Leemann (Los Angeles, CA: Sillman-James Press, 1995), Wise recalled, "At the time RKO owned forty-nine percent of Estudios Churubusco in Mexico City. Was asked to go down there and make a film using all their people. I didn't take anybody from the States at all. It was an enjoyable experience for me, my first living out of the country and my only one working with an almost exclusively foreign crew. Originally we planned to do all the post production down there, but we got a little behind and it was decided to bring the film back to Hollywood and do all the finishing up—editing, music, score, sound effects—at RKO. Because we went somewhat over budget, I think, in the final analysis, it seemed to cost as much to make the film down there as it would have cost here. The studio wanted to know if it could make more reasonably priced movies in Mexico and it turned out not to be so."

Jaime Contreras served as assistant director on the film and the art direction was by celebrated Mexican artist Gunther Gerzso.

THE LADY FROM SHANGHAI (COLUMBIA PICTURES, 1948)

Director: Orson Welles

Screenplay: Orson Welles

Producer: Orson Welles

Cast: Orson Welles (Michael O'Hara), Rita Hayworth (Elsa Bannister), Everett Sloane (Arthur Bannister)

Story: Thriller about a seaman, a crippled lawyer, and his homicidal wife pursuing one another through a world of infidelity, deception, and murder.

Production: Baffling murders, fascinating plot twists, and remarkable camerawork all contribute to this dazzling film noir. In 1946, when Orson Welles (*Citizen Kane*, 1941) needed cash in a hurry to save his stage production of *Around the World in 80 Days*, he phoned the boss of Columbia Pictures, Harry Cohn. Welles claimed that when he went to Cohn's office to pitch the idea he grabbed a random volume of the shelf and said, "There's this great book, *If I Die Before I Wake*, by Sherwood King. I'll make the movie for you." Cohn agreed and, indeed, the book served as the basis of the script. Cohn had groomed star Rita Hayworth (*You Were Never Lovelier*, 1942; *Cover Girl*, 1944; *Gilda*, 1946) throughout her career at Columbia. Hayworth, whose real name was Margarita Cansino, had risen from bit player and was transformed into the all-American actress, dancer, and sex symbol of the 1940s. Born in Brooklyn, the daughter of a Spanish-dancer father and Irish mother, she became Columbia Pictures' top box-office female star. Cohn approved a budget of $2 million for the film, which would star Hayworth with her then-estranged husband Welles. The cast and crew went to Mexico in October 1946 and shot on Errol Flynn's yacht in and around Acapulco. Errol Flynn appears in the film as an extra in a scene outside a cantina in Acapulco. Just a few years earlier, Acapulco had been a fishing village with fewer than five thousand inhabitants.

In *This is Orson Welles* (Cambridge, MA: DaCapo Press, 1998), Welles told Peter Bogdanovich, "In those days, there was a clear distrust of all locations. They did let us go in the first place, but then just three days too early, they yanked us all back to Gower Gulch [Gower Street is where Columbia was located]. Three days more and we would have wrapped up the whole thing in Mexico." Having to finish in bits and pieces at the studio gave the Acapulco section of the film a dreamlike quality with which Welles actually found favor. A rumor that filming necessitated the moving of an entire village in Mexico was untrue, according to Welles. In an interview with Bogadanovich, he protested, "I used Acapulco just as we found it." Location work inspired Welles and he used it to great effect in this film, which contained scenes that are reminiscent of footage he shot for his aborted Latin-American documentary, "It's All True." Individual character interactions take place amid everyday life among the people in Mexico; landscapes of ocean cliffs and bluff, shot from unusual angles, are also used. Most effective are shots of Rita Hayworth on the beach, as well as tracking shots of her running through the Acapulco streets at night, highlighted by the archways.

Additional filming took place in San Francisco, Sausalito, and the Columbia Ranch in Burbank, California; principal photography wrapped in March of 1947. The film is lauded for its atmospheric photography and its climactic hall of mirrors scene that takes place in a San Francisco amusement park. Cohn was horrified when he saw a blonde Rita Hayworth with her long auburn hair clipped short. After seeing the film he remarked, "I'll give a thousand dollars to anyone who can explain the story to me." The film was cut from 156 minutes to 82 minutes. The film's release was delayed by more than a year, and critics and audiences

A lobby card featuring Orson Welles and Rita Hayworth in a scene filmed in Acapulco from Welles's *The Lady from Shanghai* **(1947).**

alike disliked it. Orson Welles—the boy genius with the success of *Citizen Kane* at age twenty-five, the failure of his follow-up film *The Magnificent Andersons* (1942) and now the disaster of *The Lady from Shanghai*—alienated studio chief Harry Cohn and his fellow moguls. It effectively ended Welles's Hollywood studio directing career, although he did direct a version of *Macbeth* (1948) for Republic Studios, following which he was divorced from Hayworth. He continued to act in films and his career was resurrected by his performance as Harry Lime in Carol Reed's 1949 British production of *The Third Man*. Universal Pictures and Charlton Heston (*The Ten Commandments* 1956; *Ben Hur*, 1959) gave him the opportunity to direct once again in Hollywood, as well as co-star, in *Touch of Evil* (1958), a low-budget Universal-International drama set in a Mexican border town. Though changed in the final editing by the studio, *Touch of Evil* met with lukewarm box-office returns. Years later, it became highly regarded by film critics, as did *The Lady From Shanghai*. Welles died in 1985, at the age of seventy.

TARZAN AND THE MERMAIDS
(RKO PICTURES, 1948)

Director: Robert Florey

Screenplay: Carroll Young

Producer: Sol Lesser

Cast: Johnny Weissmuller (Tarzan), Fernando Wagner (Vargas), Brenda Joyce (Jane) George Zucco (Palanth), Andrea Palma (Luana), Linda Christian (Mara) Gustavo Rojo (Tiko)

Story: A tribe of coastal people named the Aquatanians is forced to dive for pearls under the rule of a white trader who poses as a god. When he forces a young girl to be his bride, she flees the tribe and encounters Tarzan, who helps her and the tribe. In the ensuing struggles to free the girl and his wife from harm, Tarzan fights a giant underwater octopus and native warriors as well as the potentate himself.

Production: Most of the reviewers noted that many of the characters in the film set in Africa looked Mexican not African, which is no surprise since the film was shot in Acapulco, Mexico. The Acapulco scenery was breathtaking throughout the movie and the high-dive photography from overhead angles and from the beaches below are magnificently captured by cinematographer Jack Draper, with uncredited assistance from Gabriel Figueroa. Most of the story takes place in a coastal village of the Aquatanians, Calita Beach in Acapulco, and the caverned lagoon located at nearby Pie De La Cuesta lagoon. The river by Tarzan's home was shot at Puerto Marques, and the high dives were filmed at the cliffs of La Quebrada.

Interiors and underwater scenes were filmed at Mexico City's Estudios Churubusco. The exteriors of Balu's temple were filmed at the Aztec ruins of San Juan de Teotihuacan. Mexican actress Andrea Palma, who starred in the early Mexican hit movie *A Woman of*

The Aquatanian island village set in Acapulco for *Tarzan and the Mermaids* (1948).

72

the Port (1934), has a supporting role as Luana. Mexican-born starlet Linda Christian plays the beautiful Aguatanian girl Mara.

Tarzan is one of the best-known fictional literary characters. Created by Edgar Rice Burroughs in a series of adventure novels that first appeared in *All-Story Magazine* in October 1912, Tarzan has been interpreted by many actors over decades of large- and small-screen adaptations. The Tarzan story begins with Lord and Lady Greystoke, of England, becoming marooned in the western coastal jungles of equatorial Africa in 1888. It is there that their son, John Clayton, is born. When the baby is little more than a year old, his mother dies, and his father is killed. The infant is then adopted by Kala, a she-ape, who teaches him the ways of the jungle.

The most famous movie Tarzan, Johnny Weissmiuller, starred in twelve films beginning in 1932 with MGM's *Tarzan, the Ape-Man*, and ending with *Tarzan and the Mermaids* in 1948. Weissmuller, a three-time Olympic swimming champion, fell in love with Mexico while making this film; later in life, he returned to become a permanent resident of Acapulco, dying there at the age of seventy-nine, in 1984. From 1933–1939, Weissmuller was married to Mexican actress Lupe Vélez. A contemporary *Tarzan* TV series (1966–1968) was produced for the NBC Television Network in Mexico, with locales there doubling for Africa. It starred Ron Ely as Tarzan, and Manuel Padilla Jr. as his adopted son, Jai.

THE TREASURE OF THE SIERRA MADRE (WARNER BROS., 1948)

Director: John Huston

Screenplay: John Huston, based on the novel by B. Traven

Producer: Henry Blanke

Cast: Humphrey Bogart (Fred C. Dobbs), Walter Huston (Howard), Tim Holt (Curtin) Bruce Bennett (Cody), Alfonso Bedoya (Gold Hat), Manuel Donde (El Jefe), José Torvay (Pablo), Margarito Luna (Pancho), A. Soto Rangel (Presidente), Jaqueline Dalya (flashy girl), Robert "Bobby" Blake (Mexican boy with lottery tickets)

Story: In 1925, three down-on-their-luck Americans in Mexico decide to pool their meager resources and prospect for gold in the savage wilderness of the Sierra Madre Mountains. The trio finds the elusive gold but must evade bandits and confront their own greed and human frailties in the process.

Production: The film takes place in Durango, Mexico, but director John Huston found the Durango locations unsuitable for his vision of the story. Instead, he shot in and around San Jose de Perua (140 miles south of Mexico City), the municipality of Jungapeo in the state of Michoacán, the town of Lazaro Cardenas, and the village of San Francisco de Morales. John Ford had just finished shooting *The Fugitive* a few months before Huston arrived to shoot *Treasure*. Huston and producer Henry Blanke convinced Warner Bros. studio chief Jack Warner to allow them to film in Mexico.

"The Good Neighbor Policy," started by the Franklin D. Roosevelt administration in the late thirties, encouraged American studios to consider filming in Mexico. Even so, the studio had to obtain script clearance and permission from the Mexican government. The production had to take great care to make sure that the script did not depict Mexico in an unflattering light.

In San Jose de Perua, Huston found deserts, mountain ranges, and jungles, all within a close range. The location was remote for its time; although the town did have natural mineral springs, a resort spa, and a

hotel used to house cast and crew.

Versatile Warner Bros. cameraman Ted McCord, who made his reputation with outdoor Western photography but was equally adept at working on sound stages, blended real locations, studio sets, and process photography for *Treasure*. McCord began his career in 1921 and, in addition to *The Treasure of the Sierra Madre*, is known for his work on *Johnny Belinda* (1948), *Flamingo Road* (1948), *East of Eden* (1955), and *The Sound of Music* (1965). In *Treasure*, McCord shows the influence of the Mexican muralist and cinematographer Gabriel Figueroa in his lighting and composition. This is most obvious in scenes in the native Indian village when Howard (Walter Huston) is trying to resuscitate a stricken boy. The scene has an almost churchlike ceremonial quality, highlighted by the indigenous faces.

Huston started filming background location scenes in Tampico, with stand-ins, in February 1947. Principal photography began on April 10, 1947, in San Jose de Perua, in the state of Michoacán. Waterfalls, rock formations, canyons, native villages, colonial towns, and the meandering Tuxpan River in the Michoacán region provided a striking backdrop.

The bandit scenes, with Mexican actor Alfonso Bedoya as Gold Hat, were filmed both on locations in Mexico and at the Warner Bros. Burbank studio. Upon their arrival in California, actors Bedoya and José Torvay were made to join the Screen Actors Guild. Gold Hat and his gang attack a train and then, later, stumble upon Dobbs, Curtin, and Howard's mining camp, leading to a gunfight. Bedoya's brief but memorable appearance made him highly sought after, and he was cast in a number of Hollywood westerns. He will, however, always be remembered for the following exchange in *The Treasure of the Sierra Madre*:

> *Dobbs:* If you're federales, where are your badges?
> *Gold Hat: Badges*? We ain't got no badges . . . We don't need no badges . . . I don't
> have to show you no stinkin' badges!

In an unusual move for the time, the Mexican characters speak to each other in un-subtitled Spanish. When necessary, Huston's character translates to English. A. Soto Rangel, a respected actor with over two hundred Mexican film credits, plays Presidente, the old man in the town.

Forty-two crewmembers were brought in from Mexico City to supplement the American crew on location. Production ended in Mexico on May 30, and resumed at Warner Bros. studio until July 20.

The Treasure of the Sierra Madre won three Academy Awards, two for John Huston (Best Director, Best Screenplay) and one for his father, Walter Huston, as Best Supporting Actor. The film was a critical but not a commercial success because it broke with many conventions of audience expectations. There was no attractive or sympathetic leading man; it was a grim, depressing story with an unhappy ending, and there was no female love interest or leading lady. Its cynical edge and great performances from its cast, especially Humphrey Bogart (whose gradual descent into madness and paranoia as Dobbs brought him new recognition as a serious actor), were not enough to offset audience disappointment. The public preferred Bogart as the traditional urban tough guy.

John Huston (center) and the camera crew on location in Mexico for *The Treasure of The Sierra Madre* (1948)

The film was a major influence on such directors as Stanley Kubrick, Paul Thomas Anderson, (*There Will Be Blood*, 2007), and Sam Peckinpah (*The Wild Bunch*, 1969). It has withstood the test of time and is now considered one of the best American films of the twentieth century.

CAPTAIN FROM CASTILLE (20TH CENTURY-FOX, 1948)

Director: Henry King

Screenplay: Lamar Trotti

Producer: Lamar Trotti

Cast: Tyrone Power (Pedro de Vargas), Jean Peters (Catana Perez), Lee J. Cobb (Juan Garcia), Cesar Romero (Hernán Cortés), Thomas Gomez (Father Bartolome de Olmedo), John Sutton (Diego de Silva), Jay Silverheels (Coatl), Antonio Moreno (Don Francisco de Vargas)

Story: Set in the sixteenth century, the story begins with Castilian hidalgo Pedro de Vargas leaving Jaen, Spain, after the Inquisition falsely accuses him and his family of heresy. The fleeing de Vargas joins the Cortés expedition to Mexico in 1519.

Production: At a budget of $4.5 million, *Captain from Castille* is the first and only motion picture made by Hollywood about the Spanish conquest of Mexico (1519–1521). Darryl F. Zanuck, head of production at 20th Century-Fox, purchased the bestselling novel by Samuel Shellabarger in 1945 for $100,000 and immediately proceeded to develop the literary property for the screen, with plans to film in Mexico. In order to do so, 20th Century-Fox needed approval from the Mexican government. Because of the "Good Neighbor Policy," this approval was easily granted. For Fox, shooting in Mexico meant not only giving the film authenticity but also a way to minimize costs. Advances in transportation, due to the war, made it possible to shoot the film in remote areas of Mexico. The rise of the Mexican film industry, offering a pool of experienced technicians and craftsman, provided additional incentive. The Mexican government representative Arturo Ortiz Mugica, a member of the Departamento de Informacion del Extranjero (Exterior Relations and Information Ministry), reviewed a version of the script and recommended some factual changes. The studio complied.

In late November 1946, 20th Century-Fox sent eight railroad cars to Mexico, carrying supplies, costumes, and film equipment. The shipment included a special dry cleaning department for the

(*Left to right*)**: Cesar Romero as Hernando Cortes, Ramon Sanchez as an Aztec, Jay Silverheels as Coatl, Stella Inda as Doña Marina, and Gilbert Gonzales as Ambassador Cacamatzin in a scene from Henry King's *Captain from Castile* (1947).**

78

costumes, and refrigeration to store the Technicolor film stock.

The film opens with a title card: "Grateful acknowledgment is made to the Mexican Government and to the National Museum of Mexico for their advice and cooperation in the reenactment of the historical sequences. All scenes associated with the Cortez Expedition were photographed in Mexico, and whenever possible on the actual locations." This claim is false. While location shooting *was* done in Mexico, none of the sites were "actual locations." Locations used in the movie were Acapulco, Guerrero, Uruapan, and Morelia. Morelia, 350 miles south of Mexico City, was used for sequences which took place in Spain. Some of the exteriors for these scenes were filmed in Patzcuaro, Michoacán.

The volcano Paricutin, which erupted in 1943 and was still active at the time of filming, doubled for the Popocatepetl volcano, which was active at the time of the Conquest. The smoke, fire, and ash are clearly seen coming from the cinder cones in several scenes, adding to the Technicolor photography. As many as three thousand extras were used in the crowd scenes at the finale to depict the expedition and its Indian porters marching on Paricutin's lava beds toward Tenochtitlan, Montezuma's Aztec kingdom. Acapulco, on the Pacific coast, served as the filmic base of the Cortés's expedition into the New World; in actuality, the Conquistadors came ashore on the Eastern Gulf coast's Yucatan Peninsula. This story of the Conquest was told mostly from the European-Spanish point of view. The actual conflict with Montezuma, and the taking of Tenochtitlan, was never seen in the film. It rather abruptly ends in midstream, since only half of the actual novel was filmed.

Mexican actress Stella Inda plays the historical character of Dona Marina, Cortés's native interpreter and lover, otherwise known as "La Malinche." Inda had to learn to speak Nahuatl (Aztec language) for her dialogue. Director Henry King and the Mexican censors insisted on that authenticity of language instead of the Native American gibberish made up by actors and writers in many a Hollywood western. Handsome Tyrone Power was Fox's star player and had played a Spaniard in the hit *Blood and Sand* (1941), and a Spanish/Californio in *The Mark of Zorro* (1940). He was a natural to play the role of Pedro de Vargas, and Zanuck had purchased the novel with Power in mind to star. Prior to filming *Captain from Castille*, Tyrone and his close friend, fellow Fox contract player Cesar Romero, went on a Good Will tour of Mexico, Central and South America. Power, who had served as a pilot in the U.S. Marine Corps during World War II, flew their aircraft across Latin America. They were received by heads of state of each country (including Argentina's Evita and Juan Peron) and mobbed by fans. Zanuck cast Romero as Spanish explorer Hernán Cortés, at the suggestion of Power. Romero received critical acclaim for his portrayal and, in a retrospective interview with the author, considered it the best role of his long career. Jean Peters, a talent- and beauty-contest winner who was put under contract, acquitted herself well in her first major screen role, as the beautiful Spanish wench Catana Perez. She would go on to play another Latina, a Mexican in Elia Kazan's *Viva Zapata!* (1952), opposite Marlon Brando.

THE PEARL/ LA PERLA (RKO, F.A.M.A. AGUILA 1948)
Director: Emilio Fernandez
Screenplay: John Steinbeck, Emilio Fernandez, and Jack Wagner
Producer: Oscar Dancigers
For complete information see Steinbeck, The Pearl *and Zapata in chapter 4.*

THE BIG STEAL (RKO PICTURES, 1949)

Director: Don Siegel

Screenplay: Geoffrey Homes, Gerald Drayson Adams

Producer: Jack J. Gross, Sid Rogell

Cast: Robert Mitchum (Lieutenant Duke Halliday), Jane Greer (Joan "Chiquita" Graham), William Bendix (Captain Blake), Patric Knowles (Jim Fiske), Ramon Novarro (Colonel Ortega), Don Alvarado (Lieutenant Ruiz), Pascual Garcia Pena (Manuel), John Qualen (Julius Seton)

Story: Lt. Duke Halliday transports cash for an army payroll. After he is robbed of $300,000, he begins a wild chase through Mexico to recover the money from the thief. His accomplice is Jean "Chiquita' Graham, who is tart-tongued, daring, and fearless. Detective Capt. Blake, in turn, pursues them.

Production: Don Siegel (*Invasion of the Body Snatchers*, 1956; *Dirty Harry*, 1971) directed this black-and-white film on location in Veracruz, Tehuacan, and Mexico City. This is one of Siegel's first directing efforts, following his tenure at Warner Bros. as a montage editor and second-unit director. Veracruz is an important port city on the Gulf Coast. Tehuacan is known for its natural mineral springs and is located 120 miles from Puebla City in the state of Puebla. *The Big Steal* is a crime-thriller that takes place in the late 1940s and offers a contemporary view of Mexican life largely free of stereotypes.

Siegel went to Mexico in December 1948 to shoot background footage. Principal photography was to start in January 1949, but was delayed when star Robert Mitchum was arrested for marijuana possession in Los Angeles and served a sixty-day jail sentence. Mitchum's arrest, in the company of three women, cemented his bad boy image; the resulting newspaper headlines made him an even bigger box-office attraction. *The Big Steal* reunited Mitchum with his leading lady Jane Greer from *Out of the Past* (1947). Former MGM silent screen romantic star, Mexican-born Ramon Novarro (*Ben-Hur: A Tale of the Christ*, 1925) returned to the screen after a long absence. Director Don Siegel returned to Mexico twenty years later to direct *Two Mules for Sister Sara* (1970) starring Clint Eastwood and Shirley MacLaine.

Bosley Crowther (*New York Times*, July 11, 1949) described *The Big Steal* as "a breathtaking scenic excursion across the landscape of Mexico following pursued and pursuer through villages, on lovely open roads and over towering mountains on switchback highways at a fast and sizzling pace."

THE TORCH (EAGLE-LION FILMS, 1950)

Director: Emilio Fernández

Screenplay: Igo de Martinez Noriega Emilio Fernández; adaptation by Bert Granet

Producer: Bert Granet

Cast: Pedro Armendáriz (Juan José Reyes), Paulette Goddard (Maria Dolores) Gilbert Roland (Father Sierra), Carlos Musquiz (Fidel), Robert Reed (Dr. Stanley), Don Carlos (Julio Villareal)

Story: A dashing young Mexican revolutionary takes over a small town, only to fall in love with the daughter of a wealthy landowner.

Production: *The Torch* is an English-language remake of the 1946 Mexican hit *Enamorada* starring Pedro Armendáriz and Maria Felix. *Enamorada* opened in Mexico City on December 25, 1946, and was released in New York in an English-subtitled version in December of 1947. When American actress Paulette Goddard

(*Modern Times*, 1936; *Reap the Wild Wind*, 1942) saw the film, she remarked that she would love to have played the lead female role. It took producer Bert Granet three years to set up a production deal in Mexico for an English-language version with all the key creative people involved and starring Goddard. She also became an associate producer. Armendáriz reprised his role in English, and Mexican-born former silent screen star Gilbert Roland played the priest replacing José Mojica from the original film. *The Torch* was filmed in Cholula, Mexico, in black and white by Gabriel Figueroa, and directed by Emilio (who also directed *Enamorada*) on the very locations used by Fernández. Even though the film had the same creative team, the English-language version did not work; U.S. audiences stayed away.

PANCHO VILLA RETURNS (RENOWN PICTURES–HISPANIC CONTINENTAL, 1950)

Director: Miguel Angel Contreras

Screenplay: Miguel Angel Contreras

Producer: Miguel Angel Contreras

Cast: Leo Carrillo (Pancho Villa), Esther Fernández (Teresa), Rodolfo Acosta (Martin), Jeanette Comber (Rosario), Rafael Alcayde (Reyna), Jorge Trevino (Colonel Lopez)

Story: A soldier in the army of Pancho Villa is ordered to lead a band of men into a town which is primed to fall into the hands of Pancho Villa. At that moment, the soldier learns that his sweetheart is about to sacrifice herself by marrying a man who threatens to do harm to her mother and the local priest if she refuses to wed him. The soldier finds himself in a dilemma—does he obey Villa's orders or return to his own town to rescue the girl he loves?

Production: Produced by a London-based film financing, distribution, and production company, Renown Pictures Corporation, in Mexico in association with Miguel Angel Torres. Alex Phillips was the cinematographer of this black-and-white feature, made at authentic locations with a totally Mexican crew. It was shot bilingually for the world market since the principal actors spoke fluent Spanish and English. Leo Carrillo, a well-known veteran American character actor who could trace his lineage to the original Spanish/Mexican settlers of California, plays the title role. Even though Carrillo was almost seventy years old when he assumed the role, he effectively played the younger, historical Villa. In 1934's *Viva Villa!*, also filmed in Mexico, Carrillo played Sierra, Villa's murderous second in command. Carrillo portrayed Villa just before he memorably played the Cisco Kid's bumbling sidekick, Pancho, opposite Duncan Renaldo's Cisco, in a long-running television series, *The Cisco Kid* (1950–1957).

MY OUTLAW BROTHER (EAGLE-LION FILMS, 1951)

Director: Elliott Nugent

Screenplay: Gene Fowler, based on a Max Brand short story

Producer: Benedict Bogeaus

Cast: Mickey Rooney (Dennis O'Moore), Wanda Hendrix (Señorita Alvarado), Robert Preston (Joe Waldner), Robert Stack (Patrick O'Moore), José Torvay (Enrique Ortiz), Carlos Musquiz (Col. Sanchez), Fernando Wagner (Burger), Hilda Moreno (Señora Alvarado)

Story: A young man travels to Mexico in search of his brother who disappeared many years earlier. He is joined by a lawman who has crossed the border to search for a desperado who, in the end, turns out to be the same outlaw brother.

Production: This English-language, low-budget production was made at Estudios Tepeyac in Mexico City, with a largely Mexican crew. The black-and-white cinematography is by José Ortiz Ramos. It is the only western made by musical-comedy actor and former MGM star Mickey Rooney.

THE BULLFIGHTER AND THE LADY (REPUBLIC PICTURES, 1951)
Director: Budd Boetticher

Producer John Wayne (*center*) and actor Gilbert Roland (*right*) with bullfight crew members on the set of *Bullfighter and the Lady* (1951).

Screenplay: James Edward Grant, Budd Boetticher, Ray Nazarro
Producer: John Wayne
Cast: Robert Stack (Johnny Regan), Joy Page (Anita De La Vega), Gilbert Roland (Manolo Estrada), Katy Jurado (Chelo), Rodolfo Acosta (Juan)
Story: A spoiled, young American in Mexico discovers his manhood, with its inherent flaws and strengths, when he takes an unprecedented life turn and trains to be a matador under the tutelage of Mexico's premier bullfighter.

Production: Oscar "Budd" Boetticher Jr. (1916– 2001) is best known today as the director of this autobiographical bullfighting film and a series of seven stylish low-budget westerns in the late fifties starring Randolph Scott. J. Hoberman wrote in the *Village Voice* (September 19, 2000): "Boetticher made the [Randolph] Scott westerns as ritualized as a bullfight and anticipated the western milieus associated with Sam Peckinpah, Sergio Leone, and Monte Hellman." Boetticher was an athlete in college where he suffered a football injury in the mid-thirties, prompting him to go to Mexico to recuperate. He became fascinated with the art of bullfighting, which grew into the defining passion of his life and work. He learned the skills of bullfighting and became a professional matador for a time. The young Boetticher wound up with a job in Mexico as a technical advisor on the 1941 version of *Blood and Sand*, directed by Rouben Mamoulian. This was his entry into the movie industry, after which he worked as an assistant director and served apprenticeships under directors Charles Vidor and George Stevens. He directed his first feature film in 1944, *One Mysterious Night*, but was relegated to B-pictures for the rest of the decade.

In 1950, he was given the chance to write and direct Republic Pictures' *The Bullfighter and the Lady*, based on his own experiences as an American who became enamored with Mexico and the art of bullfighting. The film starred young actor Robert Stack in his first leading role. Stack is best remembered today for his role as government agent Eliott Ness, who had battled Al Capone and the Chicago mob during Prohibition, on the popular TV series *The Untouchables* (1959–1963). John Wayne, who was Republic Pictures' biggest star at the time, had just started producing his own films. Originally, the studio wanted Wayne to star in his production of *The Bullfighter and the Lady*, but he remarked that he "was too big to fit into the Matador's pants." Wayne wanted Boetticher to use Mexican cinematographer Gabriel Figueroa, but Boetticher did not like his style. He used another cameraman, Jack Draper, whom he felt suited the romantic but semi-documentary style of picture he wanted to make. Republic studio chief Herbert Yates agreed to a budget of $350,000. The film was shot entirely in Mexico, from May until July, with a largely Mexican crew. Locations included Queretaro and the village of Xayai, as well as Mexico City locations and Estudios Churubusco. Actual bullfighting venues were used in the film, including Plaza Mexico in Mexico City, and real-life matadors Luis and Miguel Briones participated in the filming. The movie was released in the United States in an 87-minute version edited by John Ford after the studio deemed Boetticher's 124-minute version too long. The full-length cut had been released in South American territories prior to Ford's edit under the title *Tarde de Toros* (*Afternoon of the Bulls*). Budd's restored cut premiered in the U.S. decades later, to great acclaim. Mexican-born Katy Jurado made her American film debut with this film just a year before she would co-star in the Academy Award–winning *High Noon* starring Gary Cooper. Boetticher took great pains to show his love for Mexico and the Mexican people, who are truly shown as fully realized characters in a contemporary setting. Veteran actor Gilbert Roland, whose father had been a matador, drew upon his own background and gave one of the best performances of his career, as the older matador Manolo. An incident occurred during filming for which Roland never forgave Boetticher; years later, he refused to attend a screening of the restored film at which Boetticher was honored. Roland had asked Boetticher for an additional close-up of his death scene and the director said it wasn't necessary, but Roland insisted. Finally, Boetticher reluctantly agreed. Roland believed he had filmed the scene, only to learn at the following day's dailies that no such footage existed. He had been tricked. Not wanting to shoot more film, Boetticher had Roland go through the scene as if it was being filmed, all the while knowing the camera was empty.

In a *Los Angeles Times* article by Philip K. Scheuer (April 15, 1951), Robert Stack is quoted as saying, "I had never been further south than Tijuana, and the first real bullfight I saw was in Plaza Mexico with the bullfighters Luis and Felix Briones. It was the Academy Award performance of the year, and I mean literally. They have them, you know. It was brilliant and it was theater. Theatrical in the cynical approach to death, the courage without the bravado, the understanding of fear but the overcoming of fear. These fighters are more important than movie stars or politicos. Such matadors as Manolete, who was killed the year before, are revered in a way we can hardly understand. The bull has to be killed; the only doubt is whether the man will be killed. It is not a sport but a ritual, one that goes back almost to amphitheater days. To those who disapprove or condemn from a distance I can only say, see it first and then judge. I lived and trained with them for weeks and learned how they think and feel."

The Bullfighter and the Lady received an Academy Award nomination for Best Story for Budd Boetticher and Ray Nazarro. The film was favorably compared with Robert Rossen's *The Brave Bulls*, which had a high-profile director, a bigger budget, and was released at the same time.

STRONGHOLD/FURIA ROJA (LIPPERT PICTURES, 1951)

Director: Steve Sleekly, Victor Umuchua
Screenplay: Wells Root
Producer: Ollalo Rubio Gandora
Cast: Veronica Lake (Maria Stevens), Zachary Scott (Don Miguel), Arturo de Córdova (Don Pedro Alvarez), Alfonso Bedoya (Nacho)
Story: In 1865, Mexican-American Maria Stevens, widow of a Southern aristocrat who lost his life and plantation during the Civil War, returns to Mexico hoping to find stability under Emperor Maximillian. Mary, her mother, and her manservant are captured by bandits. They are held for ransom in exchange for silver from the family mine that will be used by the rebels to support Benito Juarez.
Production: Filmed in Mexico City and in Taxco by veteran American cinematographer Stanley Cortez (*The Magnificent Ambersons*, 1942; *Since You Went Away*, 1945). Cortez toiled on many films during the fifties, his best-known work of the period being Charles Laughton's *Night of the Hunter* (1955). Cortez easily adapted to the Mexican style of photography established by Gabriel Figueroa. Jorje Stahl Jr. did some second-unit photography. *Stronghold* was filmed in English and Spanish simultaneously, with two separate casts, although some principal bilingual players, such as de Cordova and Bedoya, were retained for both versions. Maria Stevens was played by Veronica Lake (1922–1973) in the English-language version. Lake was a golden-haired

actress who was under contract to Paramount Pictures during the forties and was successful for most of the decade in urban crime dramas and light comedies (*This Gun For Hire*, 1942; *Sullivan's Travels,* 1941). *Stronghold* represented a downward slide in her career. In the Spanish-language version, *Furia Roja*, actress/singer Sara Montiel (1928–2013) played Maria Stevens. Montiel entered the film industry in Spain, but acted quite frequently in Mexican films.

THE BRAVE BULLS (COLUMBIA PICTURES, 1951)

Director: Robert Rossen

Screenplay: John Bright, from the novel by Tom Lea

Producer: Robert Rossen

Cast: Mel Ferrer (Luis Bello), Miroslava (Linda), Eugene Iglesias (Pepe Bello), Anthony Quinn (Raul Fuentes), José Torvay (Eladio Gomez), Charlita (Raquelita)

Story: The story of Luis Bello, who rose from rags to riches as Mexico's best bullfighter, and the accompanying fears he develops at the height of his career after facing years of life-and-death situations in the bullring. His confidence shaken, he confides in his manager, Fuentes, who arranges for him to take an interest in the beautiful Linda (who is, unbeknown to Bello, his manager's girlfriend). Bello falls in love with her. When she and Fuentes are killed in a car crash, Bello finds out about their true relationship and feels betrayed. The once-adoring crowds turn on the matador, and the press labels Luis a coward. Through all this, he is buoyed by his younger brother Pepe, who is his protégé, and takes his turn as lead matador until once again Luis can prove himself in the ring.

Production: Filmed entirely in and around Mexico City, including the famous bullring Plaza Mexico, and also in San Miguel De Allende. *The Brave Bulls* was the anticipated next film from young director/producer/ writer Robert Rossen who, in 1949, won critical acclaim for his Academy Award–winning *All the King's Men*. Rossen had previously directed the celebrated boxing drama *Body and Soul* (1947) with John Garfield. *The Brave Bulls* would turn out to be Rossen's last studio film for ten years. He not only argued with Harry Cohn over the film, he was also subjected to investigation by the House Un-American Activities Committee. The Hollywood studios blacklisted him during the fifties after HUAC witnesses identified him as a Communist. Rossen refused to answer questions when summoned before the committee. Though filmed in the spring of 1950, the film's release was delayed until 1951 due to the political climate. Released with little support from Columbia Pictures, the film failed miserably at the box office, despite uniformly excellent reviews.

In Mexico, during filming, actor Mel Ferrer was instructed to enter the ring at San Miguel de Allende, where he had to appear in actual shots with the bull. Legendary cameramen James Wong Howe and Floyd Crosby— Academy Award winner for *Tabu* (1931) and *High Noon* (1952), respectively—placed a camera in a barricaded wooden cage with an aperture for the lens. Ferrer went through the necessary motions in front of the bull for the cameras; luckily, the bull did not charge. Eugene Iglesias, who co-starred as the younger brother Pepe, recalled in an interview with Miluka Rivera for her book *Legado Puertorrigueno en Hollywood: Famosos y Olvidados*: "Robert Rossen was a wonderful director and an innovator. He would find unconventional ways to do the filming with the bull scenes, under difficult and often dangerous conditions."

Anthony Quinn, Miroslava, and Mel Ferrer at the Plaza de Toros in Mexico City in Robert Rossen's *The Brave Bulls* (1951).

THE ADVENTURES OF ROBINSON CRUSOE (UNITED ARTISTS, 1952)

Director: Luis Buñuel

Screenplay: Philip Ansel Roll (Hugo Butler), Luis Buñuel, from the Daniel Defoe novel

Producer: Oscar Dancigers

Cast: Dan O'Herlihy (Robinson Crusoe), Jaime Fernández (Friday), Felipe De Alba

Story: On his way to pick up a shipment of slaves, Robinson Crusoe is shipwrecked. He lands on a desert island where he spends years alone until he saves Friday, a native from a nearby island, from a tribe of cannibals. Through his relationship with Friday and his time on the island, Crusoe learns about himself and humanity.

Production: Filmed in 1952 on location in Manzanillo, Mexico, a small Pacific seaport town north of Acapulco, it was not released in the U.S. until 1954. The lush color cinematography is by Alex Phillips.

Spanish-born surrealist Luis Buñuel, after his auspicious debut with *Un Chien Andalou* (1929), developed as a filmmaker during his long exile in Mexico during the fifties and early sixties, where he tackled a number of different subjects. Buñuel's work in Mexico include the English-language movies *The Adventures of Robinson Crusoe* (1952) and *The Young One* (1960). Because producer Oscar Dancigers hoped to capture the international market after the success of the director's *Los Olvidados* (1950), Buñuel simultaneously shot both English and Spanish versions. Relatively unknown Irish actor Daniel O'Herlihy (1919–2005) received an Academy Award nomination as Best Actor in 1954 for his role as Crusoe, but lost to Marlon Brando for *On the Waterfront*. (He was in good company: the other nominees were Humphrey Bogart, Bing Crosby, and James Mason.) Buñuel cast him while watching Orson Welles's *Macbeth* (1948), when it was suggested that Welles play Crusoe. Buñuel didn't think Welles was right for the role, but the moment he saw the tall, blond O'Herlihy onscreen as Macduff, he knew he had found the right actor. For more than half of the film O'Herlihy is alone onscreen, dealing with the various emotional and physical situations he must face while marooned on the island. O'Herlihy went on to a fifty-year career in Hollywood, usually as a supporting actor. The film was co-written by Hugo Butler, a blacklisted Hollywood writer living in Mexico who did not return to the United States until the sixties (he also wrote Buñuel's *The Young One*). Butler wrote under the pseudonym of Philip Ansel Roll.

SECOND CHANCE (RKO PICTURES, 1953)

Director: Rudolph Maté

Screenplay: Oscar Millard, Sydney Boehm

Producer: Sam Wiesenthal

Cast: Robert Mitchum (Russ Lambert), Linda Darnell (Clare Shepard), Jack Palance (Cappy Gordon), Rudolfo Hoyos Jr. (Vasco), Fortunio Bonanova (hotel manager), Milburn Stone (Edward Dawson), Salvador Baguez (Officer Hernandez), Sandro Giglio (cable car conductor), Roy Roberts (Charley Malloy)

Story: An American prizefighter goes on a barnstorming tour of Latin America in order to forget an unfortunate ring accident. He meets up with a mobster's ex-girlfriend who is on the run from a hit man dispatched to kill her.

Linda Darnell is pursued by a hit man through the streets of Taxco in *Second Chance* (1953).

Production: The Technicolor film was shot in Taxco and Cuernavaca, Mexico. It was the first 3-Dimension feature made by RKO; it was also a box-office hit. The Mexican government gave permission for the film to be shot on location but asked that two lines of dialogue be deleted from the script: references to Latin women as "Tamales," and Mitchum's line, "Latin American men beat their women once a week regularly, and if they did not, the women would miss the beatings." Though the film was shot in Mexico, the location is never specifically identified. It is possibly supposed to be Peru, since the Andes are prominently featured. The hair-raising climax takes place on a cable car, high above the mountains.

SOMBRERO (METRO-GOLDWYN-MAYER, 1953)

Director: Norman Foster

Screenplay: Norman Foster, Josefina Niggli, based on her novel

Producer: Jack Cummings

Cast: Ricardo Montalban (Pepe Gonzalez), Pier Angeli (Eufemia Calderon), Vittorio Gassman (Alejandro), Yvonne De Carlo (Maria), Rick Jason (Ruben), Thomas Gomez (Don Calderon), Cyd Charisse (Lola de Torrano)

Story: Three intertwined love stories take place in a Mexican village. Maria and Alejandro wish to marry, but their respective families disapprove of the union.

Production: Filmed in 1952 in Tepotzlan, Cuernavaca, Tetecala, and Mexico City, *Sombrero* features the music of famed Mexican composer Augustin Lara. Josefina Niggli co-wrote the screenplay with Norman Foster, based on her own novel *Mexican Village*. Norman Foster directed in the Mexican film industry from 1943–1946 and had worked previously with Montalban, who was, in fact, his brother-in-law: Foster was married to Sally Blane, the half-sister of Montalban's wife, Georgiana Young. (Actress Loretta Young was Sally Blane's sister, as well.) Foster, who started his career as an actor, became a journeyman studio director (the Mr. Moto and Charlie Chan series, Universal's feature *Kiss the Blood off My Hands* with Burt Lancaster in 1948; he then found new success in the young medium of television, working for Walt Disney as an in-house director on such series as *Davy Crockett* and *Zorro*. He also directed the unfinished "Benito and the Bull" Mexican segment of the ill-fated Orson Welles documentary "It's All True," and directed Welles in *Journey into Fear* (1942).

Pier Angeli and Ricardo Montalban in the musical/romance *Sombrero* (1953), filmed at Churubusco Studios, Cuernavaca, Tetecala, and Tepotzlan. This was an adaptation of Josefine Niggli's book *Mexican Village*.

BLOWING WILD (WARNER BROS., 1953)

Director: Hugo Fregonese
Screenplay: Philip Yordan
Producer: Milton Sperling
Cast: Gary Cooper (Jeff Dawson), Anthony Quinn (Ward "Paco" Conway), Barbara Stanwyck (Marina Conway), Ruth Roman (Sal Donnelly), Ward Bond (Dutch Peterson), Juan Garcia (El Gavilan)
Story: In 1930s Mexico, American oil wildcatters Jeff Dawson and Dutch Peterson find their oil-drilling operation destroyed by bandits. Desperate and broke, they accept an assignment to drive a truck full of explosive nitroglycerin through the mountains—all the while eluding bandits. When they are cheated out of their money, they turn to old friend and employer Ward "Paco" Conway for help. Conway at first refuses because his wife, Marina, was once Dawson's former lover and she still carries a torch for him. In a turn of events, bandits threaten Conway's operation, causing him to ask Dawson for help. All the while, the scheming Maria plots to kill Paco and rekindle the relationship with Dawson.
Production: *Blowing Wild* was filmed on location in Cuernavaca and at Estudios Churubusco in Mexico City, with black-and-white cinematography by Sydney Hickox. It was directed by Argentine-born Hugo Fregonese, who worked successfully in Hollywood after being placed under contract at MGM and Universal in 1949 after his hit Argentinean film *Apenas Un Delincuente* (*Hardly a Criminal*) caught the attention of studio executives.

Though the opening title card states that the story takes place in South America, the setting is clearly Mexico. It borrows elements from films as disparate as *The Treasure of the Sierra Madre*, Billy Wilder's *Double Indemnity* (1944), and Henri Clouzot's French film *Wages of Fear* (1953).

In 1953, Gary Cooper and Anthony Quinn were working together in Mexico making *Blowing Wild* in Cuernavaca, where they were informed by telephone that they had both won Academy Awards, Cooper as Best Actor for *High Noon*, and Quinn as Best Supporting Actor for *Viva Zapata!*

Blowing Wild was the first of three Mexican-filmed westerns in a row for Cooper, who would soon return for Henry Hathaway's *Garden of Evil* and Robert Aldrich's edgy buddy film *Vera Cruz*. In a career that spanned from 1929 until his passing in 1960, Cooper was one of Hollywood's most beloved stars, whose onscreen persona represented the best aspects of the American character. Cooper had won the Best Actor Academy Award previously for *Sergeant York (1941)*. Anthony Quinn was born in a railroad boxcar in Chihuahua, Mexico, in 1915. His mother and father had fought in the Mexican Revolution with Pancho Villa. Quinn spent his formative years in the United States and, in 1936, began a film career which lasted over fifty years and included two Academy Awards (*Viva Zapata!*, *Lust for Life*) and international (*La Strada*, *Zorba the Greek*, *Guns of Navarone*) renown. He worked in Mexico on such films as *The Brave Bulls*, *Blowing Wild*, *Seven Cities of Gold*, *The Magnificent Matador*, *Guns for San Sebastian*, *Revenge*, and *High Risk*.

HONDO (WARNER BROS., 1953)

Director: John Farrow
Screenplay: James Edward Grant, from the novel by Louis L'Amour

Richard Karlen as Henderson, Anthony Quinn as Paco, and Gary Cooper as Dawson argue over oil rig procedures on the Cuernavaca location of Warner Bros. *Blowing Wild* (1953).

Producer: John Wayne, Robert Fellows

Cast: John Wayne (Hondo Lane), Geraldine Page (Angie Lowe), Ward Bond (Buffalo Baker), Michael Pate (Vittorio), James Arness (Lenny), Rodolfo Acosta (Silva), Leo Gordon (Ed Lowe)

Story: A half-Indian army dispatch rider comes to the aid of a widow and her young son who are under threat by local Indian tribes in the Arizona desert territory.

Production: Although he is generally regarded as a movie star, Wayne was also a pioneer of independent filmmaking who directed and produced. Based on a short story ("The Gift of Cochise") by famed western novelist Louis L'Amour, *Hondo* was the first film that John Wayne made in Mexico; he had traveled there for years and had produced, but not acted, in *The Bullfighter and the Lady*. Prior to *Hondo*, Wayne produced *Plunder of the Sun*, directed by John Farrow and starring Glenn Ford. He had friends and associates in the Mexican motion picture industry, which was then at its height. Mexico's artists and technicians were as skilled as any in Hollywood and more than able to meet the needs of big productions. *Hondo* was filmed in Camargo, Mexico, in the state of Chihuahua, four hundred miles south of El Paso, Texas. Camargo is situated in rough sagebrush country with vast panoramic blue skies and desert landscapes, the perfect backdrop for this story of the Western frontier. Filmed in the heat of summer, from June through August of 1953, this was the first of eight films that Wayne's production company, first Wayne-Fellows, and then later Batjac, would produce in Mexico. It marked the blossoming of Wayne's professional love affair with Mexico, its film industry, and its people. Wayne decided to shoot *Hondo* in Warner Color and in the then-new 3-D process, on Mexican locations that heretofore had never been filmed. Filming on a hot, dusty, remote desert with the bulky 3-D cameras was a major learning experience for the production company. Robert Burke and Archie Stout shared cinematography credits and found that the cameras were hard to operate, especially on moving shots. Equipment would frequently break down, as it was susceptible to the intense heat, dust, wind, and rain, causing delays in shooting. All of the weighty equipment had to be physically carried by the Mexican crew to remote outdoor locations. On one particularly intense day of shooting, a sudden rainstorm caused a flashflood, stranding crewmembers who had been wrapping up at the site. After word of the group's dilemma reached Wayne, he led a team to their rescue and then provided a hot meal and tequila afterward. The celebrated screen canine star Lassie, a Collie, was disguised with makeup to play Hondo's dog Sam. Early in the production, Lassie was kidnapped and held for ransom by some local thugs, but the ransom was paid and the dog was returned unharmed. John Ford performed uncredited work as a second-unit director on the film's final action sequence.

PLUNDER OF THE SUN (WARNER BROS., 1953)

Director: John Farrow

Screenplay: David Dodge, Jonathan Latimer

Producer: John Wayne, Robert Fellows

Cast: Glenn Ford (Al Colby), Diana Lynn (Julie Barnes), Patricia Medina (Anna Luz), Francis L. Sullivan (Thomas Berrien), Sean McClure (Jefferson), Eduardo Noriega (Raul Cornejo)

Story: Al Colby is a stranded American insurance adjustor in Havana. At the instigation of an exotic beauty and her elderly husband, Colby sails to Mexico on a quest for Aztec riches hidden near the town of Oaxaca.

Along the way, Colby meets an assortment of colorful characters, including a lusty alcoholic blonde and ruthless villains.

Production: Locations included the port city of Veracruz, Oaxaca, the Zapotec ruins of Monte Alban, and the Churubusco Studios in Mexico City. The film was shot from November 3, 1952 through January 5, 1953. *Plunder of the Sun* was based on a 1949 novel by David Dodge, which was set among the Incan ruins of Peru. Producers John Wayne and Robert Fellows, under their Wayne-Fellows partnership at Warner Bros., developed the screenplay. Glenn Ford (1916–2006), a dependable, underrated actor with a long, successful career as a leading man (*Gilda*, 1946; *The Big Heat*, 1953; *Blackboard Jungle*, 1955; *The Rounders*, 1965), starred in the film but reportedly butted heads with director John Farrow. Farrow built a solid reputation during his career with such credits as *The Big Clock* (1948), *His Kind of Woman* (1951), *Where Danger Lives* (1959), and the John Wayne western *Hondo* (1953), which was filmed shortly after *Plunder of the Sun*. The black-and-white cinematography was by Jack Draper.

THE WHITE ORCHID (UNITED ARTISTS, 1954)

Director: Reginald Le Borg

Screenplay: David Duncan, Reginald Le Borg

Producer: Reginald Le Borg, James O. Radford

Cast: William Lundigan (Robert Burton), Peggie Castle (Kathryn Williams), Armando Silvestre (Juan), Rosenda Monteros (Lupita), Jorje Trevino (Arturo)

Story: An American archaeologist hopes to contact an isolated primitive tribe in Mexico. A stateside magazine sends an attractive woman photographer to document the journey. The archeologist runs into a roadblock when the local guide refuses to take him. The persuasive charms of the photographer, however, change his mind, and the guide agrees to lead them into the unknown tribal land. The archaeologist has fallen for the photographer, and jealousy ensues.

Production: *The White Orchid* was filmed in Papantla, Tecolutla, and Poza Rica, in the state of Veracruz. (The actual archaeological site of El Tajin was, despite the narration at the beginning, neither built by the Tolteca, Azteca, nor Maya, but by Huastecan Indians of Eastern Veracruz. It was declared a World Heritage site in 1992.) Interiors were shot at Estudios Churubusco in Mexico City. Although a B-movie, it was filmed in color; the costumes, though, look cheap and unconvincing. It is sexist (by modern standards) due to the fact that the male archaeologist won't accept a woman magazine photographer to accompany him into such a primitive jungle. (For a better-realized, contemporary version of this story see the dramedy *Medicine Man* (1992) with Sean Connery and Loraine Bracco.) *The White Orchids* stars the wooden William Lundigan, who had previously starred in RKO's *Mystery in Mexico* (1948). Peggie Castle was an up-and-coming actress who appeared in many films but is best known for her role on the American television series *Lawman* of the early sixties. Though the credits read "Introducing Armando Silvestre," the San Diego–born actor had already established himself in supporting roles in both Mexican and Hollywood films. Screenwriter David Duncan would go on to write such classic science fiction films as *The Black Scorpion* (1957), George Pal's production of *The Time Machine* (1960), and *Fantastic Voyage* (1966). Music composer Antonio Diaz Conde scored 280 films in his career, including *Santa Claus* (1959).

SITTING BULL (UNITED ARTISTS, 1954)

Director: Sidney Salkow

Screenplay: Jack De Witt, Sidney Salkow

Producer: W. R. Frank

Cast: J. Carrol Naish (Sitting Bull), Dale Robertson (Major Parrish), Douglas Kennedy (George Armstrong (Custer), Mary Murphy (Kathy Howell), John Litel (General Wilford Howell), Iron Eyes Cody (Crazy Horse), Joel Fluellen (Sam)

Story: President Grant orders Cavalry Major Parrish to guard an Indian agency, where he clashes with George Armstrong Custer over Indian policy. A full-scale uprising erupts, led by Chief Sitting Bull, after his son is killed in an escape attempt at the agency. General Custer leads his men against Sitting Bull, but the entire regiment is slain by the massive tribal alliance at Little Big Horn. With the United States Cavalry in pursuit, Parrish, in order to protect the Indians, leads Sitting Bull and his tribes to Canada before they can be ambushed. Considered a traitor, Parrish is court-martialed and sentenced to be shot. Sitting Bull returns to the United States to convince President Grant to spare Parrish's life.

Production: Filmed in Mexico, with many of the Native Americans played by Mexicans. The Cavalry fort outpost used in the movie is the same fort exterior located outside of Mexico City, near Mt. Popocapetl, utilized for the subsequent films *7th Calvary* and *The Last Frontier* (both 1956). Though the film is somewhat sympathetic toward Native Americans, the script does not delve into the story of the title character. Instead, this is a standard Cavalry-versus-Indians movie, with the title character circling the interactions of the other characters. An interesting side note is that the major is aided by an African-American scout, Sam (played by Joel Fluellen), a former slave who lived with the Indians. It was the first independently produced color film shot in widescreen CinemaScope. The cinematographers were Victor Herrera and Charles Van Enger.

VERA CRUZ (UNITED ARTISTS, 1954)

Director: Robert Aldrich

Screenplay: Roland Kibbee, James R. Webb, from a story by Borden Chase

Producer: James Hill

Cast: Gary Cooper (Ben Trane), Burt Lancaster (Joe Erin), Denise Darcel (Countess), Sarita Montiel (Nina), Cesar Romero (Marquis de Labordere), Henry Brandon (Danette), Morris Ankrum (General Aguilar), Ernest Borgnine (Donnegan), Jack Elam (Tex), Charles Bronson, billed as Charles Buchinsky (Pittsburg)

Story: In Mexico during the revolution of 1866, Civil War veteran Benjamin Trane meets Joe Erin, a fellow soldier of fortune who invites Trane to join his gang of renegades and fight on the side that offers the most money. They meet up with Nina, who falls for Trane and tries to talk him into fighting for the rebels. They also meet the Marquis de Labordere, aide to the Emperor Maximillian, who persuades them to fight for the emperor. At the emperor's ball, they encounter the countess, who asks them to accompany her on a perilous journey to Vera Cruz. En route, she reveals that she is carrying gold to the emperor's forces, and agrees to steal it and split it three ways. The marquis overhears the plans and informs the emperor. Later, when Trane and Erin, along with the rebels, storm the fort, Erin runs off with the gold. Convinced by Nina that the gold rightfully belongs to the people, Trane is forced to kill Erin when he refuses to turn it over. Saddened by

Gary Cooper and Burt Lancaster film a scene in Mexico for Robert Aldrich's *Vera Cruz* (1954).

having to kill his friend, Trane gives the money back to the people.

Production: Athletic, former circus acrobat and army veteran, Burt Lancaster was one of the first of the emerging post–World War II film stars who took control of his career by producing and starring in a number of film projects of his own choosing. His company, Hecht-Hill-Lancaster, allowed him to reap artistic and financial rewards. Discovered by producer Hal Wallis, Lancaster made a stunning film debut in *The Killers* (1946, an adaptation of Ernest Hemingway's short story); his stardom was assured in a succession of films: *Brute Force* (1947); *I Walk Alone* (1947); *Sorry, Wrong Number* (1948); *The Crimson Pirate* (1952), and *From Here To Eternity* (1953), the latter of which earned him an Oscar nomination for Best Actor. For *Vera Cruz*, he wisely teamed with screen icon Gary Cooper and created one of the first modern buddy movies. Its violent and cynical storyline predated the work of Sam Peckinpah and Sergio Leone by ten years. *Vera Cruz* was directed by Robert Aldrich, a former assistant director who rose through the ranks and had directed Lancaster the year previously in the hit western film *Apache*. Lavishly filmed in SuperScope and Technicolor by cinematographer Ernest Laszlo, *Vera Cruz* was one of the first Hollywood films to be shot completely in Mexico. It was a tremendous box-office winner. About one hundred people, including cast and crew, were brought from Hollywood, and another two hundred (not counting extras) were hired in Mexico. The tropical lowlands of the road to the real Veracruz, with its rainy weather, were too hazardous for the production schedule, so the dusty Cuernavaca area south of Mexico City was chosen instead. The production team filmed near the Pyramids of Teotihuacan and outside Chapultepec Castle; the company was also granted the right to film key sequences at the former palace of Emperor Maximillian. Climactic battle scenes were filmed at the historic El Molino de las Flores hacienda, just outside Mexico City, in the area off the highway to Toluca. At Estudios Churubusco, an elaborate set was constructed to represent the interior of Maximillian's palace. The sequence took only two days to shoot, but employed five hundred elaborately dressed extras. Spanish actress Sarita Montiel made her Hollywood film debut as the Mexican girl Nina Papayas. Former 20th Century-Fox contract star Cesar Romero plays a villainous French count. A number of western character actors also worked in the picture, including Ernest Borgnine, a year before his Oscar-winning Best Actor performance in the Hecht-Lancaster production of *Marty*; a young Charles Bronson (billed as Charles Buchinsky); Jack Elam; and African-American former champion boxer Archie Moore. Morris Ankrum plays the Juarista General Ramírez; there are no Mexicans in principal roles.

GARDEN OF EVIL (20TH CENTURY-FOX, 1954)

Director: Henry Hathaway

Screenplay: Frank Fenton, from a story by Fred Freiberger and William Tunberg

Producer: Charles Brackett

Cast: Gary Cooper (Hooker), Susan Hayward (Leah Fuller), Richard Widmark (Fiske), Cameron Mitchell (Luke Daly), Rita Moreno (Cantina singer), Victor Manuel Mendoza (Vicente Madariaga)

Story: Stranded in the coastal town of Puerto Miguel, three American gold hunters and a Mexican *vaquero* are hired by a desperate, beautiful American woman, Lela Fuller, to rescue her husband trapped in a goldmine. In order to reach it, they will have to take a three-day ride, deep in dangerous Apache country.

Production: For *Garden of Evil*, 20th Century-Fox sent a compa-

(*Left to right*) Director Henry Hathaway, actors Victor Manuel Mendoza, Susan Hayward, and Gary Cooper discuss an upcoming scene during a break in filming on the Mexican location of *Garden of Evil* (1954).

ny of key crew department members, three of its most important star players (Cooper, Hayward, and Widmark), and veteran director Henry Hathaway to Mexico for three months of location filming.

Mexican cinematographer Jorge Stahl shot the film, along with Milton Krasner. It was filmed in Technicolor and CinemaScope, near Tepotzlan, Uruapan, and Guanajuato. Locations seen on the screen are the teeming banana jungles along the Los Concheros River Valley near Acapulco, and the devilish black sands around Paracutin Volcanic Mountain. The Paracutin volcano erupted in 1944 and the lava flow swallowed up the surrounding community. The ancient village and church of San Juan de Las Colchas, built in the fifteenth century, is still surrounded by a forty-foot wall of lava rock. Built of adobe walls five feet thick, the church withstood the tremendous force of lava flow. Its strength to survive the catastrophe made the church a revered shrine. The volcano is now dormant and the site can be reached through the town of Angahuan, in Uruapan.

The petite yet tough-minded redhead Susan Hayward (1917–1975) rose from starlet status in the forties to become one of the most important dramatic actresses of the 1950s, earning an Academy Award in 1959 for her searing performance in *I Want To Live* (1958). Richard Widmark (1914–2008) was a postwar Fox contract player who gained stardom with menacing portrayals in urban films noirs, such as *Kiss of Death* (1947), who graduated to tough-guy leading man status for most of his five-decade-long career. A young Rita Moreno plays the cantina singer in Puerto Miguel at the beginning of the film. The boat captain at the beginning is Fernando Wagner (1905–1973) who would later play the German advisor Mohrr in Sam Peckinpah's *The Wild Bunch*. Mexican actor Víctor Manuel Mendoza (1913–1993) had notable roles in Buñuel's *Los Olvidados* (*The Forgotten Ones*, 1950) and *Susana* (1951), and *The Wonderful Country* (1959).

WHITE FEATHER (20TH CENTURY-FOX, 1955)
Director: Robert D. Webb
Screenplay: Leo Townsend, Delmer Daves
Producer: Robert L. Jacks, Miguel Aleman Velasco, Melchor Perrusquia
Cast: Robert Wagner (Josh Tanner), Debra Paget (Appearing Day), John Lund (Colonel Lindsay), Jeffrey Hunter (Little Dog), Hugh O'Brian (American Horse), Eduard Franz (Chief Broken Hand), Iron Eyes Cody (Chief)
Story: In 1870 Wyoming, a peace treaty with the Cheyenne Indians is threatened when a young surveyor accompanied by the United States Cavalry arrives in Indian Territory. He is tasked with mapping out a town which is planned for the territory when it is opened up for gold mining. Complications arise when the surveyor falls in love with the chief's daughter and the Indians are asked to relocate to a reservation.
Production: Filmed in 1954, *White Feather* was the first American film to be made in Durango, Mexico. Mexican cameraman Jorje Stahl served as assistant to cinematographer Lucien Ballard. Delmer Daves co-wrote the screenplay. The story is similar to that of his film *Broken Arrow*, which Daves directed in 1950. Robert Wagner, a young contract player at 20th Century-Fox, was actively being promoted with leading and supporting roles in *Beneath the 12 Mile Reef* (1953), *Titanic* (1953), and *Between Heaven and Hell* (1955). A star of screen and television, with a career that spans more than sixty years, Wagner went on to appear in *The Longest Day* (1962), *The War Lover* (1962), *The Pink Panther* (1964), *Harper* (1966), *The Towering Inferno* (1974) and all three of Mike Myers's *Austin Powers* films, beginning in 1997. Wagner also starred in three television

Robert Wagner, star of *White Feather* (1955), the first Hollywood Western feature made in Durango.

series and continues to make guest appearances on episodic television, Debra Paget, another of Fox's young contract players, portrays an Indian maiden in the film. *White Feather* could be described as a youth-oriented version of *Broken Arrow*. The locally hired Mexican assistant directors were Rene Cardona and Jaime Contreras.

ROBBERS ROOST (UNITED ARTISTS, 1955)

Director: Sidney Salkow

Screenplay: John O'Dea, Maurice Geraghty, Sidney Salkow, from a novel by Zane Grey

Producer: Robert Goldstein

Cast: George Montgomery (Jim "Tex" Wall), Richard Boone (Hank Hayes), Bruce Bennett (Bull Herrick), Peter Graves (Heesman), Warren Stevens (Smokey), Leo Gordon (Jeff)

Story: After an outlaw finds a job on a ranch, two warring outlaws kidnap the daughter of a crippled rancher and he is forced to rescue the girl.

Production: A low-budget western shot in less than a month in Durango, Mexico, with a small team of thirty crewmembers on Rancho Weiker. Photographed by Jack Draper in Eastmancolor, for Leonard Goldstein productions.

THE TALL MEN (20TH CENTURY-FOX, 1955)

Director: Raoul Walsh

Screenplay: Frank Nugent

Producer: William A. Bacher, William B. Hawks

Cast: Clark Gable (Ben Allison), Robert Ryan (Nathan Stark), Jane Russell (Nella Turner), Cameron Mitchell (Clint Allison), Juan Garcia (Luis Estrada)

Story: After the Civil War, brothers Ben and Clint Allison rob wealthy gambler Nathan Stark. Stark strikes a business deal with the brothers whereby they will bring cattle herds from their home state of Texas to beef-starved Montana. Their journey is complicated by the rivalry of Ben and Nathan for the love of the adventurous, opportunistic, beautiful Nella Turner. With the help of old friends and Mexican *vaqueros*, they embark on the fifteen hundred–mile cattle drive, crossing treacherous terrain and encountering outlaws and Indians on the warpath.

Production: The opening snowy sequences, set in Montana, were filmed in Sun Valley, Idaho. The rest of the film (set in Texas) was filmed in Durango, Mexico. Fifty-eight actors and crewmembers from the United States were augmented with one hundred Mexican film technicians. Four hundred extras were required. Thirty-five hundred head of longhorn cattle and 250 horses were brought in by rail from Zacatecas. An airstrip was built in Los Organos Valley, just north of Durango, to transport the actors to and from Durango. Cinematographer Leo Tover shot the film in CinemaScope and Technicolor, making excellent use of the Durango locations. Prolific director Raoul Walsh had been in Mexico as a young man and in 1914 was sent to Durango as an assistant for D. W. Griffith's Mutual Film Company to obtain footage of Pancho Villa for *The Life of General Villa* (now considered a lost film). Clark Gable (1900–1960), an Academy Award winner for Best Actor in *It Happened One Night* (1934), and a Best Actor nominee for *Mutiny on the Bounty* (1935), and *Gone With The Wind* (1939), was known simply as "The King."

On location in Durango: Robert Ryan, Clark Gable, Jane Russell and her husband, Bob Westerfield, take a break while filming *The Tall Men* (1955).

At the time of *The Tall Men*, Gable was the highest paid actor in Hollywood; he had just ended his twenty-two-year contract with Metro-Goldwyn-Mayer and signed with 20th Century-Fox for two films. Jane Russell was a leading sex symbol of the late forties and early fifties. Robert Ryan was considered an important leading and supporting actor in Hollywood; he returned to Durango and Torreon several times in his career, most notably for *The Wild Bunch*. Juan Garcia (1905–1980), who plays the *vaquero* Luis, had extensive credits in Mexican and American films, including *The Pearl* (1948), *Vera Cruz* (1954), *The Bravados* (1958), and *something big* (1971). *The Tall Men* grossed $6 million at the U.S. box office upon its opening in October 1955.

A LIFE IN THE BALANCE (20TH CENTURY-FOX, 1955)
Director: Harry Horner, Rafael Portillo
Screenplay: Robert Presnell Jr., Leo Townsend
Producer: Leonard Goldstein
Cast: Ricardo Montalban (Antonio Gomez), Anne Bancroft (Maria Ibinia), José Perez (Paco Gomez), Lee Marvin (The Killer), Rodolfo Acosta (Lieutenant Fernando), Carlos Múzquiz (Captain Saldana), Tamara Gerina (Dona Lucrecia)
Story: An unemployed musician, who is also a single father, is suspected of murdering his ex-girlfriend. His

(*Left to right*) **Rodolfo Acosta, Ann Bancroft, Ricardo Montalban, and Jose Perez in a scene from** *A Life in the Balance*
(1955), filmed at the newly opened UNAM (Universidad Nacional Autonoma de Mexico) in Mexico City, D. F.

eleven-year-old son witnessed the actual crime and goes in pursuit of the real killer. Before long, the killer is in pursuit of the boy.

Production: *A Life in the Balance* was filmed entirely in Mexico City and featured sequences shot at the recently constructed Universidad Nacional Autonoma de Mexico. Famous Mexican artist Gunther Gerzo was the art director on the film. The movie is unusual in that it offers a modern and non-stereotypical view of life in circa 1955 Mexico City. It gave Ricardo Montalban a challenging leading role, which was a welcome change from the Latin lovers he was usually saddled with. Mexican actor Rudy Acosta (1920–1974), usually cast as a heavy, portrays a police detective. Supporting actor Lee Marvin (1924–1987), after an impressive number of film portrayals, including a star-making turn opposite Spencer Tracy in 1955's *Bad Day at Black Rock*, went on to win a Best Actor Academy Award for the comedy-western *Cat Ballou* (1965), and starring in such hit films as *The Professionals* (1966), *The Dirty Dozen* (1967), and *Point Blank* (1967).

THE MAGNIFICENT MATADOR (20TH CENTURY-FOX, 1955)

Director: Budd Boetticher
Screenplay: Charles Lang, from a story by Budd Boetticher
Producer: Edward L. Alperson

Cast: Maureen O'Hara (Karen Harrison), Anthony Quinn (Luis Santos), Richard Denning (Mark Russell), Thomas Gomez (Don David), Manuel Rojas (Rafael Reyes), Anthony Caruso (Emiliano), Eduardo Noriega (Miguel)

Story: A spoiled, rich American woman, Karen Harrison, is infatuated with famed matador Luis Briones, who inexplicably leaves the ring during a bullfight. Harrison follows the tormented Briones to a Mexican estate where, during her visit, he saves her from an attacking bull. It is later revealed that the reason for his brooding lies in the fact that an up-and-coming matador is his illegitimate son.

Production: Filmed in Mexico City and Cuernavaca and based on a Budd Boetticher story idea, it was the director/writer's second bullring-themed drama set in Mexico. *The Magnificent Matador* plays like a melodrama but is elevated by its beautiful location footage, shot in Eastmancolor by cinematographer Lucien Ballard. Ballard, over his long career, would return to Mexico to work on a number of films. In 1955 alone, along with *The Magnicent Matador*, he also filmed *White Feather* and *Seven Cities of Gold*. More than any movie, *The Magnificent Matador* suffered from the U.S. film production code that did not allow for the killing of the bull to be shown onscreen.

THE LAST FRONTIER (COLUMBIA PICTURES, 1955)

Director: Anthony Mann

Screenplay: Phillip Yordan, Russell S. Hughes

Producer: William Fadiman

Cast: Victor Mature (Jed Cooper), Guy Madison (Captain Riordan), Robert Preston (Colonel Marston), Ann Bancroft (Corrina), James Whitmore (Gus), Pat Hogan (Mungo), Manuel Donde (Chief Red Cloud)

Story: Two rugged trappers, Jed Cooper and Gus Hideout, and their Indian guide, Mungo, become scouts at a remote frontier fort, tenuously defended by a young officer and an Indian-hating colonel at a time when tensions with local tribes are running high. The brutish, uncivilized but charismatic Jed falls in love with the colonel's wife. Complications ensue when the colonel decides to attack an Indian tribe. It is up to the trappers to try to avert disaster.

Production: Director Anthony Mann's reputation now rests on his urban film noir of the late forties and his westerns of the fifties, the best of which star James Stewart in intense, psychological, and often violent roles. *The Last Frontier* is not highly regarded and is now nearly forgotten. Set in the Oregon wilderness just after the American Civil War, it was filmed in Mexico near snowcapped Mt. Popocatepetl, which looms in the background even though much of the action takes place at night. Columbia Pictures utilized the same sets and Mexican locations for Joseph H. Lewis's *7th Cavalry* starring Randolph Scott; the two films were shot back to back. The fort set and location was also used earlier, for *Sitting Bull*.

THE LITTLEST OUTLAW (BUENA VISTA, 1955)

Director: Roberto Gavaldón

Screenplay: Bill Walsh, from a story by Larry Lansburgh

Producer: Larry Lansburgh

Cast: Pedro Armendáriz (General Torres), Joseph Calleia (Padre), Rodolfo Acosta (Chato) Andres Velasquez

(Pablito), Gilberto Gonzales (Tigre), José Torvay (Vulture)

Story: Pablito is a young stable boy who takes care of General Torres's prized jumping horse, Conquistador. After an unfortunate set of circumstances involving an accident with the general's daughter, the general orders the horse destroyed. Pablito, devoted to Conquistador, runs away with the horse and is caught by local bandits who plan to kill the boy and sell the horse. Meanwhile, Chato, an unscrupulous horse trainer, searches for the boy and the horse. The boy is rescued through the intervention of a local priest. A further series of incidents leads the boy and the horse back to the general's ranch and reconciliation through a new understanding of the meaning of courage, love, and devotion.

Production: Filmed at the Estudios Churubusco in Mexico City. Outdoor location scenes were filmed in and around San Miguel de Allende in the Mexican state of Guanajuato. Though a Disney film, it is essentially a Mexican production, filmed in English under the direction of Roberto Gavaldón (*La Escondida* [*The Hidden One*], 1956; *Macario*, 1960) with an all-Mexican cast and crew, except for Joseph Calleia (a veteran American character actor, born in Malta). Alex Phillips photographed it in Technicolor, with second-unit photography by Carlos Caracal. Production manager was Luis Sanchez Tello; the assistant director was Jesus Marin; sound was by Manuel Topete; and set decoration was by Rafael Suarez. The production acknowledged the cooperation of General and Señora R. Rodriquez Familiar of the Rancho Meson del Prado, the Mexican Army Equestrian Team, Colonel Hernandez Zarazua, and General Humberto Mariles, as well as the people of San Miguel de Allende. Ten-year-old Andres Velasquez, who had no prior acting experience, was discovered in a Mexico City hotel by producer Larry Lansburgh and was given a screen test. The filmed test was sent to Hollywood, where Walt Disney approved the casting of Andres. *The Littlest Outlaw* is similar in plot to the King Brothers' *The Brave One* (1956), which was filmed two years later, with a bull replacing a horse in the boy's affection.

SEVEN CITIES OF GOLD (20TH CENTURY-FOX, 1955)

Director: Robert D. Webb

Screenplay: Richard L. Breen, John C. Higgins, from a novel by Isabel Gibson Zeigler

Producer: Barbara Mclean

Cast: Anthony Quinn (Captain Gaspar de Portolá), Richard Egan (José Mendoza), Michael Rennie (Padre Junipero Serra), Jeffrey Hunter (Matuwir), Rita Moreno (Ula) Eduardo Noriega (Sergeant), Victor Juncos, Julio Villareal, Guillermo Calles, Miguel Inclán

Story: In 1769, Spanish explorer Gaspar de Portoá sets off on an expedition to Alta-California, seeking the fabled Seven Cities of Gold. Father Junipero Serra, a peace-loving missionary who wishes to convert the local Indians to Christianity and establish missions, accompanies de Portolá. At the San Diego Bay settlement, Captain Mendoza saves the life of a native chief but then seduces his sister, who is accidentally killed in a lovers' quarrel with Mendoza. The whole expedition and settlement is threatened when the chief threatens war unless Mendoza is released to him for punishment. Against de Portolá's orders, Mendoza willingly gives himself up to the chieftain in order to save the lives of the explorers. Miraculously, the Spanish supply ship arrives in time.

Production: Filmed in CinemaScope and Deluxe color in the deserts near Guadalajara, Jalisco, Mexico. The

Rita Moreno and Richard Egan before the cameras at a beach in Manzanillo for *Seven Cities of Gold* 1955).

West Coast beaches near Manzanillo doubled for Baja California Norte and the Spanish settlement of San Diego, California. Jorge Stahl was camera operator for cinematographer Lucien Ballard and possibly shot some second-unit footage. Rene Cardona was credited as co-director, although his contributions might have been dictated by Mexican Union rules on foreign productions. *Seven Cities of Gold* is set during the period of Spanish exploration of Mexico and the settling of its borderland territories. Gaspar de Portolá's 1769 expedition surveyed the western coast of California. The expedition accompanied by Franciscan priest Junipero Serra resulted in the founding of the first California presidio and mission in San Diego. The fabled Seven Cities of Cibola were believed to be paved with gold and located in Alta, California. In the end, there were no cities of gold, only agrarian Native American communities.

Anthony Quinn is a commanding presence as the Spanish explorer de Portolá, and Michael Rennie brings dignity and strength to his Father Serra. Rita Moreno (1931-   ), a contract player at 20th Century-Fox, played Ula, the tragic Native American girl. Although Moreno appeared in sixteen films over a six-year-period beginning in 1949, she would not achieve critical recognition until her role as Tuptim in Walter Lang's film version of the stage hit *The King and I* (1956). She would later win a Best Supporting Actress Oscar as the fiery Anita in *West Side Story* (1961). With a career spanning seven decades, the Puerto Rican–born Moreno is one of the few performers (and the *only* Latina) to win four of the most prestigious awards in the entertainment industry: the Oscar, the Emmy, a Tony, and a Grammy.

Mexican actors and extras played Spanish explorers, soldiers, and Native Americans.

THE TREASURE OF PANCHO VILLA (RKO, 1955)

Director: George Sherman

Screenplay: Niven Busch, from a story by J. Robert Bren and Gladys Atwater

Producer: Edmund Grainger

Cast: Rory Calhoun (Tom Bryan), Gilbert Roland, (Colonel Castro), Shelley Winters (Ruth), Joseph Calleia (Captain Pablo), Fanny Schiller (Laria), Pasqual Pena (Ricardo), Tony Carvajal (Farolito)

Story: In Mexico in 1915, a former outlaw and American soldier of for-

tune decides there is more money in gold than in fighting for the Mexican Revolution, despite the example set by dedicated Mexican Villa supporter Colonel Castro.

Production: The Mexican Revolution served as historical background for this western, filmed in Technicolor against rugged locations in and around Cuernavaca in the state of Morelos, Mexico. The film's ends credits read: "Appreciation is gratefully acknowledged to the Direccion General de Turismo of Mexico and General Lopez de Nova, Governor of the state of Morelos, Mexico, for their assistance and cooperation in the production of this picture." Despite the title, Pancho Villa is never seen in the film. There is instead a Villa-like character, Colonel Castro, played by Gilbert Roland (1905–1994). Roland was born in Juarez, Mexico, as Luis Alonso. His family moved to El Paso, Texas, during the Mexican Revolution when Pancho Villa threatened the lives of all Mexicans of Spanish ancestry (both his parents were Spanish born). As a young boy, Roland made his way to Los Angeles where he worked as a film extra. He was discovered and found stardom in silent films as a matinee idol. After transitioning to sound movies he played mostly supporting roles. His credits include *Camille* (1927), *Juarez* (1939), *The Sea Hawk* (1939), *We Were Strangers* (1949), *The Furies* (1950), *The Bad and the Beautiful* (1952), *Bullfighter and the Lady* (1951), *The Miracle of Our Lady of Fatima* (1952), *The Big Circus* (1959) and *Barbarosa* (1982). Calhoun's Tom Bryan prefigures the screen prototype of many lone, gun toting, American mercenaries in Mexico featured in latter sixties Westerns. *The Treasure of Pancho Villa* was produced by RKO during its last years of ownership by eccentric self-made millionaire Howard Hughes.

FURY IN PARADISE (1955)

Director: George Bruce
Screenplay: George Bruce
Producer: George Bruce, Alfonso Sanchez Tello, Henri A. Lube
Cast: Peter Thompson (Jim Gregg), Rebecca Iturbide (Consuelo Alvarez), Eduardo Noriega (Captain Vasquez), Felipe Nolan (Don Alvarez), Fani Schiller (Dona Mercedes), Carlos Rivas (General Lopez), Claude Brooks (guard), Roberto Contreras (servant)

Story: During the Mexican Revolution an American in Mexico finds himself in the middle of a conflict between Zapatista rebels fighting for land reform and a rich landowner. The situation is further complicated when he falls in love with the landowner's daughter.

Production: The production was filmed in its entirety at the Hacienda Vista Hermosa at Tequesquiteengo, Morelos, in 1953, but was not released in the U.S. until 1955. The executive producer of the film was Howard Coldren, a retired North American lumberman who regarded the film as a way of improving friendly realtions between the U.S. and Latin America. Jaime Contreras was the assistant director and the Mexican producer was Alfonso Sànchez Tello, with Eastmancolor cinematography by Jack Draper, and film editing by Charles Kimball. Gonzalo Curiel composed the film's score, which was recorded by the Mexico City Philharmonic Orchestra. Mexican actor Roberto Contreras, who hails from a famous film family (his brother Jaime is the assistant director on this film), has a small role as a servant; he went on to appear in numerous American films, mostly westerns made in Mexico. Relocating to Hollywood, he appeared in such films as *The Magnificent Seven* (1960). He is best known, however, for his regular role on the popular television western *The High Chapparral*.

Randolph Scott leads a troop in *7th Cavalry* (1956), filmed in Amecameca, near the Popocatepetl Volcano, which is passing for the Northern Montana plains.

7TH CAVALRY (COLUMBIA PICTURES, 1956)

Director: Joseph H. Lewis

Screenplay: Peter Packer, based on a story by Glendon F. Swarthout

Producer: Harry Joe Brown, Randolph Scott

Cast: Randolph Scott (Captain Benson), Barbara Hale (Martha Kellogg), J. C. Flippen (Sergeant Bates), Denver Pyle (Dixon), Leo Gordon (Vogel), Pat Hogan (Young Hawk), Harry Carey Jr. (Corporal Morrison)

Story: In 1876, Captain Benson, with permission from General Custer, leaves Fort Lincoln to fetch his fiancée from a nearby post. Upon his return to the outpost with his bride-to-be, he discovers that General Custer had left to fight the Sioux and Cheyenne and was slain along with his regiment at the Little Big Horn. Questioned as to the unusual timing of his departure, he is suspected of cowardice by the remaining officers. To prove his courageousness, Benson volunteers for a suicidal mission with a band of misfit soldiers. They intend to ride into hostile territory to retrieve the remains of Custer and his men from the battlefield that the Native American warriors now believe to be sacred ground.

Production: Filmed on location near Mexico City, not far from the Popocapetl Volcano, the second-highest Volcano in Mexico, at 17,930 feet, which borders the states of Mexico, Morelos, and Puebla. *Popocapétl* is the Aztec Nahuatl word for Smoking Mountain. The snow-capped cinder-cone mountain looms large in nearly every exterior shot captured in gorgeous three-strip Technicolor by famed American Oscar-winning cameraman Ray Rennahan (*Gone With the Wind*, 1939; *Blood and Sand*, 1941). Interiors were filmed at Estudios

Churubusco. The production utilized the same log-stockade set previously used in *Sitting Bull* and *The Last Frontier*. Except for the presence of Popocapétl, the location was very believable as the Dakotas and Wyoming Territory setting. Randolph Scott, a perfunctory leading man who began his film career in the mid-thirties, settled comfortably into a cowboy persona from the mid-forties until his retirement after 1962's *Ride the High Country*. He produced this film with his partner, Harry Joe Brown, through Columbia Pictures in Mexico, to take advantage of the scenery as well as the lower labor and production costs. Mexican extras portrayed cavalrymen and Native Americans.

BANDIDO (UNITED ARTISTS, 1956)

Director: Richard Fleisher

Screenplay: Earl Felton

Producer: Robert L. Jacks

Cast: Robert Mitchum (Wilson), Gilbert Roland (Colonel Escobar), Ursula Thiess (Lisa Kennedy), Zachary Scott (Kennedy), Rodolfo Acosta (Sebastian), José Torvay (Gonzalez), Victor Junco (General Lorenzo), Miguel Inclán (priest)

Story: Wilson, an American arms dealer, gets involved in the Mexican Revolution of 1916 by selling badly needed arms to a rebel leader. Wilson falls in love with the wife of a rival arms dealer. Complications ensue when he tries to sell a cache of hidden munitions to the rebel leader and the military forces at the same time, playing one side against the other.

Production: Exteriors were shot on coastal locations in Acapulco, Cuernavaca, and at the Dominican Cathedral in nearby Tepotzlan, Yautepec, and Cocoyoc Hacienda; interiors were filmed at Estudios Churubusco. *Bandido* was a logistically complicated production, involving explosions, dangerous stunt work, and hundreds of extra players and horses. Filmed in Deluxe color and CinemaScope by Ernest Laszlo, who had photographed *Vera Cruz* in Mexico three years earlier, with many of the same production requirements.

During filming, Fidel Castro, future leader of the Cuban Revolution, was in exile for eighteen months in Mexico. While plotting and seeking funds for his return to Cuba, Castro worked as an extra in *Bandido*. He organized the extra stunt players and demanded better wages because of the potentially numerous hazards.

RUN FOR THE SUN (UNITED ARTISTS, 1956)

Director: Roy Boulting

Screenplay: Roy Boulting, Dudley Nichols, based on a short story by Richard Connell

Producer: Harry Tatelman

Cast: Richard Widmark (Michael Latimer), Trevor Howard (Browne), Jane Greer (Katherine Connors), Peter Van Eyck (Dr. Van Anders), Juan Garcia (Fernández), José Antonio Carbajal (Paco), B. Carlos Henning

Story: A British traitor hides out in a South American jungle with Nazi war criminals. When an American writer crashes his plane near their hideout, he and his passenger at first are rescued by the criminals. Then, while attempting to escape, they become human prey in a savage hunt through teeming jungles.

Production: Filmed in Mexico, in Technicolor, *Run for the Sun* is loosely based on the Richard Connell short story "The Most Dangerous Game," filmed previously at RKO in 1933. Widmark's character, writer Mike

Latimer, seems to be based on a combination of two real-life authors, the mysterious B. Traven (*The Treasure of the Sierra Madre*) and the macho American Ernest Hemingway. Jane Greer's previous onscreen Mexican adventures were on the backlot of RKO studios in Hollywood with *Out of the Past*, and on location with The *Big Steal*. On location in a jungle river while making *Run for the Sun*, she caught a deadly virus, which required an early form of open-heart surgery in order to save her life.

Run for the Sun was filmed on location over five weeks, fifty miles from Acapulco, on the southwestern coast of Mexico and in an old hacienda that was later converted into a hotel in Atlacomulco, near Cuernavaca. The interiors of the hacienda and patio, as well as a seaside cantina, were constructed at Estudios Churubusco, where the company worked for an additional three weeks. The Mexican locations, at first, appear beautiful and romantic in the seaside town of San Marcos and then turn wild and deadly as the characters are hunted.

Mexican actors in featured roles include taxi driver Hernandez, played by actor Juan Garcia (who also appeared in *Vera Cruz*) and fisherman José Chavez Towe (later featured in *The Wild Bunch*); Spanish actor Francisco Reiguera portrayed the hotelier. An exiled actor from Franco's Spain, Reiguera later worked on Luis Buñuel's *Simon of the Desert* in Mexico, and appeared in Peckinpah's *Major Dundee*, both in 1965.

SERENADE (WARNER BROS., 1956)

Director: Anthony Mann
Screenplay: Ivan Goff, Ben Roberts, John Twist, based on the novel by James M. Cain
Producer: Henry Blanke
Cast: Mario Lanza (Damon Vicente), Joan Fontaine (Kendall Hale), Vincent Price (Charles Winthrop), Sarita Montiel (Juana Montes)
Story: A young California vineyard worker with a beautiful tenor voice becomes a rising star in the opera world due to the help of a beautiful society woman and her impresario. The tenor falls in love with the beautiful socialite, who uses and then discards him. Depressed, he abruptly leaves for Mexico to find another life—and, perhaps, true love.
Production: Filmed in Mexico for five weeks in late summer of 1955, on location in San Miguel De Allende. Locations included the church interior at the Templo de San Felipe Neri, built in 1712; La Parroquia church, a two hundred-year-old hacienda owned by bullfighter Pepe Ortiz; and the Palace of Fine Arts in Mexico City. Scenes taking place in San Francisco and New York were filmed at the Warner Bros. studios in Burbank, California.

Popular Italian-American tenor Mario Lanza (1921–1959) made his film debut at MGM in 1949; parts in five movies made him a star. He then took a three-year hiatus before returning for the lead in *Serenade*, based on a 1937 novel by James M. Cain. Racy for its time, the novel is about a bisexual opera singer who falls in love with his male impresario and then flees to Mexico, where he then falls in love with a Mexican prostitute. Because of the Production Code, the novel could not be filmed. It was nearly twenty years before a cleaned-up script was approved for filming.

Lanza was teamed with Oscar-winning actress Joan Fontaine and the equally beautiful Spanish actress Sarita Montiel, who had made her career as a leading lady in Spanish and Mexican films. Montiel's American

Sarita Montiel and Mario Lanza in San Miguel de Allende, Guanajuato, for Anthony Mann's melodrama *Serenade* (1956), based on James M. Caine's novel.

film debut was with Gary Cooper and Burt Lancaster in *Vera Cruz*. Lanza made two more films before he died of a heart attack in 1959, at the age of thirty-eight. Producer Henry Blanke also made *The Treasure of the Sierra Madre* in Mexico.

THE BRAVE ONE (RKO, 1956)

Director: Irving Rapper
Screenplay: Harry Franklin, Merril G. White, based on a story by Robert Rich (Dalton Trumbo)
Producer: Frank and Maurice King
Cast: Michel Ray (Leonardo), Rodolfo Hoyos (Rafael Rosillo), Elsa Cardenas (Maria), Carlos Navarro (Don Alejandro), Joi Lansing (Marion), George Trevino (Salvador), Carlos Fernández (Manuel), Fermin Rivera (Fermin)
Story: Leonardo and his family live on a ranch owned by wealthy Don Alejandro; it is on this ranch that the bull Gitano was calved. Don Alejandro, while retaining ownership of the bull, has allowed Leonardo to raise Gitano. This is a satisfactory arrangement until Don Alejandro, a racing enthusiast, is killed in an automobile accident. Gitano has attracted attention for his size and strength and it seems inevitable that Leonardo's pet bull will be sent to Mexico City for a fatal showdown with a matador.
Production: Based on a true incident that occurred in Barcelona, Spain, in 1936, the story has certain similarities to "Benito the Bull" by Robert Flaherty (which was an episode of Orson Welles's unfinished documentary "It's All True"). Legendary Oscar-winning British cinematographer Jack Cardiff (*Black Narcissus*, 1947; *The Red Shoes*, 1948) filmed *The Brave One* on location in and around Plaza Mexico Bullring, in Mexico City. Fermin Rivera, a respected matador of the time, plays himself. The film remains the King Brothers' (*Gun Crazy*,1950;*The Ring*, 1952) most prestigious and highly regarded achievement as producers. It won an Oscar for Best Motion Picture Story and nominations for Film Editing and Sound Recording. Blacklisted writer Dalton Trumbo wrote the screenplay for *The Brave One* and won the Oscar for Best Motion Picture Story, under the name of Robert Rich. Trumbo admitted that he was Robert Rich two years later when the Academy repealed its ruling that blacklisted writers were not eligible for Academy Awards; they then publicly acknowledged him and gave him proper credit as ascreenwriter for *Exodus* and *Spartacus*. In May of 1975, Academy president Walter Mirisch gave a belated Oscar for *The Brave One*, inscribed with the screenwriter's real name. Director Irving Rapper (*Now Voyager*, 1942; *The Corn is Green*, 1945) said in an interview with Charles Higham, "One picture of mine wasn't compromised: *The Brave One*. They all said, 'What do you see in it?' And I said, 'It's so simple, it reads like a fairy tale.' And it cost $430,000 to make and grossed $8½ million." The King Brothers cast a young French boy, twelve-year-old Michel Ray, whom they had seen in an English film called *The Divided Heart*, to play the young Mexican boy Leonardo.

DANIEL BOONE, TRAILBLAZER (REPUBLIC PICTURES, 1956)

Director: Albert C. Gannaway, Ismael Rodríguez
Screenplay: Tom Hubbard, John Patrick
Producer: Albert C. Gannaway
Cast: Bruce Bennett (Daniel Boone), Lon Chaney Jr. (Chief Blackfish) Claudio Brook (James Boone), Eduar-

do Noriega (Squire Boone)

Story: After leading settlers into Kentucky, Daniel Boone must fight the Shawnee Indians and the British, who are inciting the Indians to kill settlers.

Production: This low-budget, competently produced feature film was made to capitalize on the "Davey Crockett craze" that swept America in February 1955 after the television broadcast of Disney's live-action shows on the American frontiersman. As Daniel Boone, Bruce Bennett played a similar frontier hero from Kentucky. Bennett had made two prior films in Mexico, *The Treasure of the Sierra Madre* and *Robbers Roost*. Cameraman Jack Draper shot in the economical Trucolor process. Jaime Contreras served as assistant to veteran director Ismael Rodríguez, who actually directed the film. *Daniel Boone, Trailblazer* was filmed in the mountainous, wooded forest area outside of Mexico City, doubling for the Kentucky frontier. Mexican actors played Native Americans and white settlers.

COMANCHE (UNITED ARTISTS, 1956)

Director: George Sherman
Screenplay: Carl Krueger

Kent Smith, Linda Cristal, and Dana Andrews in Durango for the Western/romance *Comanche* (1956).

Producer: Carl Krueger

Cast: Dana Andrews (Jim Read), Linda Cristal (Margarita), Nestor Paiva (Puffer), Kent Smith (Chief Quanah Parker), Henry Brandon (Black Cloud), John Litel (General Nelson A. Miles)

Story: An army cavalry scout, Jim Read, is asked to broker a treaty between Mexico and the United States to stop Comanche raids on both sides of the border, led by half-white, half-Comanche Chief Quanah Parker.

Production: Based on the true story of a Comanche raid three hundred miles south of the United States border in Durango, Mexico, the screenplay fictionalized the actual events, filling the story with stereotypical western characters and situations. Jorge Stahl Jr. filmed it in CinemaScope and Deluxe color, near the area surrounding the town of Durango. Alfonso Sanchez Tello, who later worked with American filmmakers Don Siegel and Sam Peckinpah, was production manager. *Comanche* marked the first American screen appearance of Argentine-born actress Linda Cristal, who started her career in Mexican films. She was discovered by John Wayne, who asked her to be in his production of *The Alamo* (1960). Following *Comanche*, Cristal was put under contract to Universal Pictures, for whom she appeared in the 1958 made-in-Mexico feature *Last of the Fast Guns*, and opposite Tony Curtis in *The Perfect Furlough*. She is best known as strong-willed Victoria Cannon on the popular TV series *The High Chaparral*.

THE BEAST OF HOLLOW MOUNTAIN (UNITED ARTISTS, 1956)

Director: Ismael Rodríquez and Edward Nassour

Screenplay: Robert Hill, Jack Dewitt, from a story by Willis O'Brien

Producer: Edward and William Nassour

Cast: Guy Madison (Jimmy Ryan), Patricia Medina (Sarita), Carlos Rivas (Felipe Sanchez), Mario Navarro (Panchito), Pascual Garcia Pena (Pancho), Eduardo Noriega (Enrique Rios), Julio Villareal (Don Pedro), Lupe Carriles (Margarita)

Story: An American cowboy living in Mexico discovers that his cattle are being eaten by a prehistoric dinosaur.

Production: *The Beast of Hollow Mountain* (*La Bestia de la Montana*) was filmed in both English and Spanish versions. It was co-produced and co-directed by Ed Nassour and veteran Mexican director Ismael Rodríguez through Peliculas Rodriquez S.A. The movie was photographed in CinemaScope and Deluxe color by Jorge Stahl Jr., in and around Cuernavaca and Tepotzlan, with interiors at Estudios Churubusco. The "beast" of the story is actually a prehistoric dinosaur, a Tyrannosaurus Rex. The film was developed from a story idea by Willis O'Brien, the pioneering stop-motion animation and special effects master who brought *King Kong* (1933) and *Mighty Joe Young* (1949) to the screen. The Nassours developed Regalscope, a process of combining stop-motion with live-action footage. It was used only for this film and proved inferior to the processes developed by stop-motion animator Ray Harryhausen and others.

THE TIJUANA STORY (COLUMBIA PICTURES, 1957)

Director: Leslie Kardos

Screenplay: Louis Morheim

Producer: Sam Katzman

Cast: Rodlofo Acosta (Manuel Mesa), James Darren (Mitch), Jean Wiles (Liz), Robert Blake (Enrique Mesa)

Story: A crusading Mexican journalist fights a one-man war against a crime syndicate in the Mexican border town of Tijuana in the 1950s.

Production: This is a low-budget, black-and-white exploitation movie filmed mostly on the Columbia Ranch, with some exteriors shot on location in Tijuana. Veteran Mexican supporting character Rodolfo Acosta shines in a rare leading role. The film is based on real-life newspaperman Manuel Acosta Meza, a columnist for the *El Imparcial* newspaper, who exposed criminal corruption in Tijuana and was assassinated in front of his daughter in 1961. The perpetrators were never found. (The murder of investigative journalists—not only in Mexico but worldwide—has escalated at an alarming rate.) The movie portrays an early form of drug and human trafficking into the U.S. that predates the modern cartels. There is also a subplot concerning an American teenager who gets involved in drugs.

THE BLACK SCORPION (WARNER BROS., 1957)

Director: Edward Ludwig

Screenplay: Robert Blees, David Duncan, Paul Yawitz

Carlos Muzquiz, Carlos Rivas, Mara Corday, and Richard Denning in the filmed-in-Mexico science fiction film *The Black Scorpion* (1957).

Producer: Jack Dietz, Frank Melford

Cast: Richard Denning (Hank Scott), Mara Corday (Teresa Alvarez), Carlos Rivas (Arturo Ramos), Mario Navarro (Juanito), Carlos Muzquiz (Dr. Velazco), Pascual Garcia Pena (José De La Cruz)

Story: Violent volcanic eruptions lay waste a vast area of rural Mexico. Geologists Hank Scott and Arthur Ramos help out as best they can and meet rancher Teresa Alvarez. When giant scorpions emerge from the volcanic vents in the earth, the two geologists lower themselves into one of the deepest fissures to destroy the monsters hidden below.

Production: The finale takes place in a Mexico City stadium (Estadio Olimpico Universitario), where a giant scorpion battles guns, tanks, and helicopters. Stop-motion animation is by Willis O'Brien (*King Kong*, 1933), who struggled through most of the fifties to develop story ideas and have them made into motion pictures.

THE RIVER'S EDGE (20TH CENTURY-FOX, 1957)

Director: Alan Dwan

Screenplay: James Leicester, based on the novel by Harold Jacob Smith

Producer: Benedict Bogeaus

Cast: Ray Milland (Nardo Denning), Anthony Quinn (Ben Cameron), Debra Paget (Meg Cameron), Harry Carey Jr. (Chet)

Story: Nardo, a murderous thief with a suitcase full of money, makes his way to a cattle ranch where rancher Ben Cameron is forced to guide the bank robber across the wild ranchlands on foot into Mexico. Unbeknown to Cameron, his wife Meg was once Nardo's girlfriend.

Production: *The River's Edge* was filmed by Harold Lipstein in the widescreen CinemaScope process and in Deluxe color, on location in Cuernavaca, Morelos, and Amecameca. It is a mix of a contemporary Western noir, directed by Alan Dwan, whose career began in 1909 and ended with his retirement in 1961 at the age of sevent-six, with over four hundred films to his credit. For two-time Oscar-winning actor Anthony Quinn, this would be the fourth of nine films he would eventually make in Mexico. Debra Paget was in Durango previously for the Western *The White Feather* (1954). Ray Milland was a frequent visitor to Mexico, but this was his first film assignment in the country. Harry Carey Jr. would make many trips to Mexico, mainly to Durango, for various Western film roles. Dwan and editor/screenwriter James Leicester would reteam a year later for Benedict Bogeaus's production of *Enchanted Island*, also filmed in Mexico.

THE SUN ALSO RISES (20TH CENTURY-FOX, 1957)

Director: Henry King

Screenplay: Peter Viertel, based on the novel by Ernest Hemingway

Producer: Darryl F. Zanuck

Cast: Tyrone Power (Jake Barnes), Ava Gardner (Lady Brett Ashley), Mel Ferrer (Robert Cohen), Errol Flynn (Mike Campbell), Eddie Albert (Bill Gorton), Juliette Greco (Georgette), Robert Evans (Pedro Romero), Carlos Musquiz (Juanito)

Story: In 1922 Paris, a disillusioned American World War I veteran, Jake Barnes, who was left impotent by a war injury, falls in love with the freewheeling Lady Brett Ashley. Barnes's friends are Mike Campbell, a

bankrupt alcoholic nobleman; Bill Gorton, a promising young writer; and Robert Cohen, a former boxer. The four decide to vacation in Pamplona, Spain, for the fiestas and the running of the bulls. Their lives are changed by their individual interactions during the fiesta and after.

Production: *The Sun Also Rises* was written in 1926 by Ernest Hemingway. The San Fermin Festival in Pamplona, Spain, made famous by the running of the bulls, was highlighted in the novel. As part of the festival, which dates back to the Middle Ages, participants test their courage and physical endurance as they run with loose bulls through city streets and, finally, into a bullring, where an amateur bullfight climaxes the event. Scenes were shot in Paris and Biarritz, France, and Pamplona, Spain. Principal photography was centered in the city of Morelia, Mexico, doubling for Pamplona, because Spiros Skouras, head of production at 20th Century-Fox, wanted to better control costs.

Director Henry King was also a pilot who enjoyed scouting his own locations. King discovered Morelia, Mexico, while flying from Panama, where he had been filming location scenes for *Marie Galante* (1934). Morelia became the filming location for King's *Captain from Castille*, *The Bravados*, and *The Sun Also Rises*. King worked as a director for Darryl F. Zanuck at 20th Century-Fox throughout most of the thirties, forties, and fifties. After Zanuck left his executive post at Fox, *The Sun Also Rises* was his first independent production. An ambitious film with a great visual style, CinemaScope and Deluxe color, it took advantage of the landscape and locales. Power, Gardner, and Flynn were among the top stars of the era but were twenty or more years older than the characters of the original novel. Flynn, in a downward career spiral, was typecast as a man whose life centered around womanizing, alcoholism, and drug abuse. He promised director Henry King that he would not drink alcohol during the production, but quickly broke his promise. A prop man fashioned binoculars to a case that would accommodate a false bottom filled with alcohol; it is clearly visible in the film. Though inebriated, Flynn was a professional on set and knew his lines, infusing his role with an accuracy that brought him late-career accolades. In Pamplona, second-unit footage was filmed at a bullfight and during the running of the bulls. None of the principal actors were present. Because of his relationship with the Mexican authorities, King was allowed to paint the bullring in Morelia to match the color footage of the bullring in Pamplona. Pamplona is in the Basque country of Spain, and the people there tend to be light-skinned as opposed to the darker Mestizo population of Morelia, so there were some cultural and linguistic discrepancies. But, for the most part, the footage in Pamplona and the footage in Mexico intercuts seamlessly and worked for general audiences of the time. Interiors were shot at Estudios Churubusco.

Jorge Stahl Jr. worked with the credited cinematographer Leo Tovar; Manuel Topete was the sound recordist, Roberto Silva was the art director, and Luis Sanchez Tello was the production manager on the Mexican side. Carlos Muzquiz does a fine job with his small role as Juanito Montoya, Romero's manager. Robert Evans, who played the bullfighter Romero, abandoned his acting career shortly afterwards and became a studio executive and independent producer.

THE BRAVADOS (20TH CENTURY-FOX, 1958)
Director: Henry King
Screenplay: Phillip Yordan

Barry Coe and Gregory Peck in a scene from *The Bravados* **(1958), filmed on location in the Arroyo de Michoacán Valley.**

Producer: Herbert B. Swope Jr.

Cast: Gregory Peck (Jim Douglass), Joan Collins (Josefa Velarde), Henry Silva (Lujan), Lee Van Cleef (Alfonso Parral), Stephen Boyd (Bill Zachary), Albert Salmi (Ed Taylor), Alicia del Lago (Angela Lujan), Ada Carrasco (Mrs. Parral)

Story: Jim Douglass pursues the four men he believes murdered and raped his wife to the small border town of Rio Arriba, where they are awaiting hanging for an unrelated crime. They escape from jail, and Douglass, bent on revenge, tracks them down one by one and kills them. At the end it is revealed that he has killed the wrong men.

Production: Set on the United States/Mexico border, *The Bravados* was filmed in Mexico in Patzcuaro, Morelia, Uruapan, and San Jose Purua by four-time Academy Award–winning cinematographer Leon Shamroy, who captures the contrasting landscapes of rocky terrain, ominous forests, grassy plains, and waterfalls. *The Bravados* was director Henry King's third film in Mexico and is one of the first "adult" westerns of the fifties, dealing openly with rape, murder, and revenge. The film influenced Italian filmmaker Sergio Leone, who cast character actor Lee Van Cleef (Alfonso Parral in *The Bravados*) in *For a Few Dollars More* (1965) and *The Good, the Bad and the Ugly* (1966). In the latter film, Van Cleef brandishes a pocket watch with the picture of his wife and daughter much as Jim Douglass in *The Bravados* does before dispatching his victims. Leone did not film in Mexico but created his Old West Mexican settings in Spain. He used recurring shots of the lone gunmen riding into the Mexican border town composed of a long row of white adobe houses, as does Peck in *The Bravados*. Henry Silva adds dimension to his role as the Mexican Indian Lujan.

VILLA!! (20TH CENTURY-FOX, 1958)

Director: James B. Clark
Screenplay: Louis Vittes
Producer: Plato Skouras
Cast: Cesar Romero (Tomás Lopez), Brian Keith (Bill Harmon), Rudolfo Hoyos Jr. (Villa), Margia Dean (Julie), Carlos Muzquiz (Cabo), Mario Navarro (Pajarito), Rosenda Monteros (Mariana Villa), Enrigue Lucero (Tenorio)
Story: Pancho Villa and his bandits, including a newly joined gringo, hide out in the nearby mountains and steal gold from a train. Pancho falls for an American saloon singer and brings her to his hideout. The saloon singer turns out to be the gringo's former flame. Pancho returns to the hacienda where he grew up and murders the hacendado who raped his sister. Pancho meets Madero and becomes a leader of the armies of the north when he attacks a federales garrison.
Production: Filmed in Mexico, with a predominantly Mexican crew. Cinematography is by Alex Phillips. Rudolfo Hoyos Jr., who plays Villa, was the Mexican-born (1916) son of a famous opera singer, Rodolfo Hoyos. Hoyos Jr. was a successful supporting actor from the mid-fifties until his death in 1983, appearing in many Hollywood westerns. His most important film is the Oscar-winning *The Brave One*.

SIERRA BARON (20TH CENTURY-FOX, 1958)

Director: James B. Clark
Screenplay: Houston Branch
Producer: Plato Skouras
Cast: Brian Keith (Jack McCracken), Rick Jason (Miguel Delmente), Rita Gam (Felicia Delmonte), Pedro Galvan (Judson Jeffers), Fernando Wagner (Grandall), Carlos Muzquiz (Andrews), Enrigue Lucero (Anselmo)
Story: In the 1800s the encroachment of Anglo settlers into Spanish/Mexican California creates conflicts. Things come to a head when the son of a recently murdered Spanish land baron, Miguel Delmente, finds his loyalty divided while defending his land from Anglo Rufus Bynham and his new friend Jack McCracken.
Production: Filmed back-to-back with *Villa!!*, both of which shared lead actor Brian Keith and the Mexican crew. Alex Phillips photographed it in Deluxe color, outside of Mexico City, where a Western town had been built in a national park. Robert Lippert, producer of a number of low-budget features for 20th Century-Fox, oversaw the production.

LAST OF THE FAST GUNS (UNIVERSAL, 1958)

Director: George Sherman

Screenplay: David P. Harmon

Producer: Howard Christie

Cast: Jock Mahoney (Brad Ellison), Gilbert Roland (Miles Lang), Eduard Franz (Padre Jesus), Linda Cristal (Maria O'Reilly), Lorne Greene (O'Reilly), Eduardo Noriega (Cordoba)

Story: An American gunfighter in the 1880s is hired by a dying American millionaire to find his long-lost brother who disappeared in Mexico thirty years prior. In Mexico, the gunfighter overcomes obstacles to find the missing man, and ultimately reevaluates his violent lifestyle.

Production: Beautiful cinematography in CinemaScope and Technicolor by Alex Phillips and direction by George Sherman (1908–1991) make stunning use of the beautiful Mexican locations in Morelos and Cuernavaca. Sherman also filmed *Treasure of Pancho Villa* and *Comanche* in Mexico. He was a prolific director of action films, including those starring John Wayne, Gene Autry, and Roy Rogers in some of their early westerns at Republic; he later directed Wayne's *Big Jake*, in Durango. Luis Sanchez Tello was the Mexican production manager; Argentian Linda Cristal, who was discovered in Mexico City, had a role previously in Sherman's *Comanche* (1956) and in Wayne's 1959 production of *The Alamo*. She went onto star in John Ford's *Two Rode Together* and NBC-TV's *The High Chaparral*.

ENCHANTED ISLAND (WARNER BROS., 1958)

Director: Allan Dwan

Screenplay: James Leicester, Harold Jacob Smith, from the novel *Typee* by Herman Melville

Producer: Benedict Bogeaus

Cast: Dana Andrews (Abner "Ab" Bedford), Jane Powell (Fayaway), Don Dubbins (Tom), Ted de Corsia (Captain Vangs)

Story: Sailor jumps ship in the Pacific, swims to a tropical isle where he falls in love with a native girl, and soon discovers that *he* is the object of desire on this cannibal-inhabited island.

Production: This low-budget programmer movie was filmed in Technicolor, in Acapulco subbing for the South Pacific, by cinematographer Jorge Stahl, billed as George Stahl.

TEN DAYS TO TULARA (UNITED ARTISTS, 1958)

Director: George Sherman

Screenplay: Laurence Mascott

Producer: George Sherman

Cast: Sterling Hayden (Scotty McBride), Grace Raynor (Teresa), Rodolfo Hoyos (Cesar), Carlos Musquiz (Dario)

Story: Scotty McBride, an American pilot, is forced to help a gang of gold thieves who have kidnapped his son. Because he is flying the getaway plane, the police are after him as well as the bandits. When gunfire causes a fuel leak, the bandits parachute into the jungle before the plane runs out of fuel and crashes. Scotty must help them reach their destination on the Pacific Coast within ten days or his son will be killed.

Production: *Ten Days to Tulara* largely takes place and is shot on locations in Mexico by veteran cameraman Alex Phillips at Estudios Churubusco. George Sherman, who knew how to get the most out of low-budget black-and-white films, directed this efficient programmer. Mario Cisneros was the assistant director; Ramon Rodríguez was the art director; Pina Lozada and Carmen Palomino were key makeup artists; and Alberto Ferrer was the production manager.

THE WONDERFUL COUNTRY (UNITED ARTISTS, 1959)

Director: Robert Parrish

Screenplay: Robert Adrey, based on the novel by Tom Lea

Producer: Charles Erskine, Robert Mitchum

Cast: Robert Mitchum (Martin Brady), Julie London (Ellen Colton), Pedro Armendáriz (Cipriano Castro), Gary Merrill (Major Colton), Jack Oakie (Travis Hight), Satchel Paige (Tobe Sutton), Albert Dekker (Captain Rucker), Victor Mendoza (General Marcos Castro), Anthony Caruso (Santiago Santos)

Story: As a young boy, Martin Brady fled from the United States to Mexico after killing his father's murderer. As an adult, he is torn between two countries: in Mexico, he is considered a gringo; in the United States, he is taken for a Mexican. He returns to Texas to broker an arms deal for the Castro brothers, who rule a section of Northern Mexico. Brady encounters a United States Cavalry regiment, which is chasing renegade Apaches, and falls for the unhappy wife of the post commander. Brady has an accident and, while he is being treated, the arms are stolen. He must now face—and possibly kill—Gov. Cipriano Castro.

Production: *The Wonderful Country* is an interesting but underappreciated film that was considered just another western at the time of its release. It was based on a 1952 novel by celebrated Texas artist and novelist Tom Lea (*The Brave Bulls*). *The Wonderful Country* was filmed in and around Durango, Mexico, during 1958. It was one of the first films to showcase African American participation in the winning of the West, with the integral use of the 10th Cavalry. This all-black unit, known as the "Buffalo Soldiers," helped capture the Apache leader Geronimo. One of the Buffalo Soldiers is played by African American Major League and Negro League baseball legend Leroy "Satchel" Paige. Floyd Crosby and Alex Phillips shared cinematography credit. Lea made a present of a Revolution era sombrero to Mitchum who wears it in the film. The sombrero originally belonged to Lea's father who had been Mayor of El Paso, Texas, during that era. Mitchum served as executive producer of *The Wonderful Country* . Famed stuntman Chuck Roberson did the horse fall on the black stallion at the beginning of the film for Mitchum. Roberson, who owned the animal, had trained the horse to fall on cue for the cameras. Roberson was John Wayne's stunt double for almost thirty years and spent considerable time on the many Durango set locations.

BEYOND ALL LIMITS (ASTOR PICTURES CORP., 1959)

Director: Roberto Gavaldon

Screenplay: Ed Blum

Producer: Miguel Contreras

Cast: Maria Felix (Magdalena Gamboa), Jack Palance (Jim Gatsby), Pedro Armendáriz (Pepe Gamboa), Paul Stewart (Pendergrest)

Story: Sailor Jack Gatsby has a passionate affair with Magdalena Gamboa while her husband is serving a short prison sentence. Returning to the same port town five years later, he hopes to rekindle the affair. Jack learns that he has a young son and that Magdalena has led her husband, Pepe, to believe the child is his. Jack convinces Pepe to join him in an illegal fishing scheme that allows Jack to get close to Magdalena. Magdalena and Jack rekindle their passion while Pepe suspects betrayal; he soon learns that he is not the boy's father. The youngster does not realize what is happening until Pepe begins to lash out in anger.

Production: Filmed in both Spanish- and English-language, versions, the Spanish version was called *Flor De Mayo*. Locations included Topolobampo, Sinaloa, Mexico, and a small port town on the Gulf of California, across from La Paz in Baja California. The bay of Topolobampo, with its dramatic landscapes and sea views, was captured in Eastmancolor by cinematographer Gabriel Figueroa. Maria Felix was the reigning queen of Mexican cinema and this is her only English-language movie with Hollywood stars, even though it is technically a Mexican film production.

THE UNFORGIVEN (UNITED ARTISTS, 1960)

Director: John Huston

Screenplay: Ben Maddow, based on a novel by Alan Lemay

Producer: Ben Hecht, James Hill, Burt Lancaster

Cast: Burt Lancaster (Ben Zachary), Audrey Hepburn (Rachel), Audie Murphy (Cash), Lillian Gish (Matilda), John Saxon (Johnny Portugal), Carlos Rivas (Lost Bird), Doug McClure (Andy), Charles Bickford (Zeb Rawlins), Joseph Wiseman (Abe Kelsey)

Story: Rancher Ben Zachary returns from a cattle drive to discover that a drifter has been spreading rumors that his sister Rachel is a Kiowa Indian, taken from her people as a child. The gossip spreads, but Zachary's mother, Matilda, denies the story until she is forced to admit that motherly love overcame her prejudice when she lost her own child, took in baby Rachel, and raised her as her own. A neighboring Indian chief believes Rachel is his sister and comes to claim her. Rachel must choose sides, both family and the community must confront their racism, and Ben must confront his previous potentially incestuous love for Rachel, whom he now knows is not a relative.

Production: Filmed in Durango, *The Unforgiven* is based on a novel by Alan Lemay (*The Searchers*), which deals with racism and white/Indian conflict in pioneer Texas. Director Huston had disagreements with star Burt Lancaster on set over interpretations. Actress Audrey Hepburn was thrown from a horse during a location shoot in Durango and suffered severe injuries that sidelined her for several weeks. Cinematographer Franz Planer captured the desert vistas of Durango (representing the Texas plains) in Panavision and Technicolor. The film comes off as a strange western, mixing different elements—acting styles, tone, and story mood—that don't quite jell. The second-unit director was Emilio Fernández; the second-unit director of photography was Jorge Stahl.

THE YOUNG ONE (CONTINENTAL RELEASING, 1960)

Director: Luis Buñuel

Screenplay: Hugo Butler, from the story "Travelin' Man" by Peter Matthiessen

Producer: George P. Werker

Cast: Zachary Scott (Miller), Bernie Hamilton (Traver), Kay Meersman (Evelyn), Claudio Brook (Reverend Fleetwood)

Story: A jazz musician falsely accused of raping a white woman escapes a lynch mob by stealing a boat and making his way to a small island off the coast of South Carolina. There, he encounters the island's only inhabitants: a game warden and a young girl.

Production: Luis Buñuel's second (and final) English-language film made in Mexico, touched on race and sexuality in America during the turbulent civil rights movement of the 1960s. *The Young One* was photographed in black and white by Gabriel Figueroa, on location near Acapulco doubling for South Carolina. Retitled *White Trash* for its U.S. release, *The Young One* is a nearly forgotten Buñuel film that merits reevaluation. African American Bernie Hamilton worked sporadically in American films and played opposite Frank Sinatra in *The Devil at 4 O'Clock* (1961). He found more lasting recognition as the police captain on the American TV series *Starsky and Hutch* (1975–1979). Hamilton is the brother of famed American jazz musician Chico Hamilton. Hugo Butler, a blacklisted writer living in Mexico, co-wrote the screenplay with Buñel. Butler had previously co-scripted Buñel's Mexican-made production *The Adventures of Robinson Crusoe* (1952) under the pseudonym Philip Ansell Roll.

THE MAGNIFICENT SEVEN (UNITED ARTISTS 1960)

Director: John Sturges

Screenplay: William Roberts

Producer: John Sturges, Walter Mirisch

Cast: Yul Brynner (Chris), Steve McQueen (Vin), James Coburn (Britt), Horst Bucholz (Chico), Charles Bronson (Bernardo), Robert Vaughn (Lee), Brad Dexter (Harry), Eli Wallach (Calvera), Rosenda Monteros (Petra), Natividad Vacio (villager), Enrigue Lucero (villager)

Story: Seven American gunmen are hired by the inhabitants of a poor Mexican village to protect them from a band of savage bandits.

Production: Filmed just outside Cuernavaca, Mexico, where the entire village set was built at the foot of a mountain range. Interiors were filmed in Mexico City, at Estudios Churubusco.

The movie is a western remake of Akira Kurosawa's acclaimed Japanese film *The Seven Samurai* (1954). The idea was originally introduced by actor Anthony Quinn, who suggested it to rising star Yul Brynner on the set of DeMilles's *The Buccaneer* (1958). Brynner seemed an odd choice for a western at that time: he had made his name in 1956 as the bald king of Siam in his Oscar-winning performance in *The King and I*, and as the pharaoh in DeMille's *The Ten Commandments*. Nevertheless, he brought to the film an interesting portrayal of a samurai-like, black-clad gunfighter. *The Magnificent Seven* was directed by action-movie fixture John Sturges and featured a cast of rising young stars, including Steve McQueen, Charles Bronson, James Coburn, Robert Vaughn, Horst Bucholtz, and Brad Dexter.

The Magnificent Seven influenced Sergio Leone and a generation of future filmmakers. Considering its source material and cast, it can be considered the first international western. Previous Hollywood movies, such as *Vera Cruz* (1954), had portrayed Mexicans as incapable of defending themselves without the aid of Americans' ingenuity. Since the Mexican government took exception to this portrayal, *The Magificent Seven* had to overcome several hurdles before filming in Mexico was allowed. After much discussion, Jorge Ferretis, of the Mexican Film Bureau, greenlit the movie provided the following changes were made to the script: One of the eponymous Seven had to be a Mexican (ironically, this character, Chico, was played by German actor Horst Bucholtz); and that the impoverished villagers intend to buy guns to defend themselves, but act on Chris's suggestion that men are cheaper than guns and, therefore,

Eli Wallach, Yul Brynner, and James Coburn on the Mexican village set of *The Magnificent Seven* **(1960), constructed near Cuernavaca.**

they should hire the gunfighters instead. Mexican actors with featured roles in the film include Natividad Vacio, Enrique Lucero, Rosenda Monteros, and Roberto Contreras. Before he became an Oscar-nominated (*Chinatown*) cameraman, Texas-born John A. Alonzo began his career as a bit player (billed as John Alonso), playing one of Calvera's bandits. Francisco Chico Day, the unit production manager, had started his career at Paramount Pictures in the thirties as an assistant director; he was Gilbert Roland's brother. Although not a domestic box-office success upon its initial release, *The Magnificent Seven* eventually became an international hit, establishing the careers of many of its players. The film was followed by three sequels; it was remade as a CBS Television network series from 1998 to 2000. A new theatrical version of *The Magnificent Seven* (2016), directed by Antoine Fugua and starring Denzel Washington, is not set in a Mexican village but in a Northern California Western mining town.

PEPE (COLUMBIA PICTURES, PASO FILMS, 1960)

Director: George Sidney
Screenplay: Claude Bryon, Dorothy Kingsley
Producer: George Sidney
Cast: Cantinflas (Pepe), Dan Dailey (Ted Holt), Shirley Jones (Suzie Murphy), William Demarest (studio gateman), Ernie Kovacs (immigration inspector), Cameos: Bing Crosby, Frank Sinatra, Debbie Reynolds, Janet Leigh, Tony Curtis, Kim Novak, Dean Martin, Cesar Romero
Story: A Mexican farmhand makes his way to Hollywood in search of his beloved horse that has been sold to a movie producer.
Production: The production features thirty-eight American stars in cameo roles portraying themselves; Cantinflas encounters these stars while searching for his horse in Hollywood. *Pepe* was filmed on a lavish scale by veteran director George Sidney, and was nominated for seven Academy awards, winning none. The film is best remembered for the classic musical number "Tequila," in which Cantinflas dances with Debbie Reynolds and an animated Mexican bull. *Pepe* was filmed over six months with five weeks on location in Acapulco. Gunther Gerzo served as art director, with Ted Haworth. The film failed at the U.S. box office and Cantinflas never made another English-langage American film. However, he remained a potent box-office force in all the Spanish-speaking countries until his death.

127

THE LAST SUNSET (UNIVERSAL-INTERNATIONAL, 1961)

Director: Robert Aldrich

Screenplay: Dalton Trumbo

Producer: Eugene Frenke, Edward Lewis

Cast: Rock Hudson (Dan Stribling), Kirk Douglas (O'Malley), Dorothy Malone (Belle Breckenridge), Joseph Cotten (Breckinridge)

Story: O'Malley is an outlaw who escapes across the U.S. border into Mexico; Dan Stribling is the lawman who pursues him. O'Malley heads for a ranch owned by Breckinridge and his wife, who was once his lover. Breckinridge and his wife plead with O'Malley to lead a cattle drive from Mexico to Texas, and he agrees—until Stripling arrives and complicates matters. The two agree to a truce until they get the cattle into Texas, where they will settle their differences in mortal gunplay.

Production: Filmed in Durango, and produced by Kirk Douglas. Dalton Trumbo was the former blacklisted screenwriter who had been exonerated, due partly to Douglas's intervention. Despite that, Trumbo was not able to give the screenplay the attention it needed: he was already at work on two other scripts, Douglas's *Spartacus*, and Otto Preminger's *Exodus*. Even with the combined talents of Douglas, Trumbo, and director Robert Aldrich, *The Last Sunset* never quite satisfies, although it has a provocative storyline, with themes of incest, lost love, and redemption. It was Aldrich's third western, and the second filmed in Mexico.

GERONIMO (UNITED ARTISTS, 1962)

Director: Arnold Laven

Screenplay: Pat Fielder

Producer: Arnold Laven, Arthur Gardner, Jules V. Levy

Cast: Chuck Connors (Geronimo), Kamala Davi (Teela), Armando Silvestre (Natchez), Ross Martin (Magnus), Pat Conway (Kayard), Adam West (Delahay), Giantah (Luis Carrillo), Enid Janes (Huera), Claudio Brook (Henry), Emilio "El Indio" Fernández (Dr. Sanchez), Eduardo Noriega (Colonel Morales)

Story: The film follows the events leading to the capture of the feared Apache warrior Geronimo, who waged war against the United States in 1886.

Production: Filmed in Los Organos y la Hacienda Weiker in Durango. Chuck Connors, a former pro-baseball player who became a minor supporting actor, found stardom in the television series *The Rifleman* (1958–1963). The producers of that TV show also produced this film, which explains how the six-foot-six, blue-eyed Connors was improbably cast as an Apache. The script was sympathetic to Native Americans and largely dramatized from their point of view. Indian (East Indian) actress Kamala Davi was cast as Geronimo's wife, Teela. Many Native American supporting roles were filled by Mexican actors.

DIME WITH A HALO (METRO-GOLDWYN-MAYER, 1963)

Director: Boris Sagal

Screenplay: László Vadnay, Hans Wilhelm

Producer: László Vadnay

Cast: BarBara Luna (Juanita), Rafael Lopez (Chuy Perez), Rog-

Riding on horseback across Sierra de Los Organos, Zacatecas, Chuck Connors (*foreground*) portrays the title character in *Geronimo* (1962); behind him is Mario Navarro.

er Mobley (Jose), Manuel Padilla Jr. (Rafael), Larry Domasin (Cesar), Tony Maxwell (Domingo)

Story: Five Tijuana street urchins rob a church poor box and bet the money on a horserace, which they win. The older sister of one of the urchins wants to use the winnings to escape her life as a stripper in a sleazy bar.

Production: *Dime with a Halo* was filmed partly on location in Tijuana, at the MGM–Hal Roach studios back lot, and in Los Angeles locations doubling for Tijuana. This charming tale features a young cast of U.S. Latino actors. BarBara Luna, as the older sister Juanita, made her debut on Broadway as a child actress as part of the original cast of Rodgers and Hammerstein's *South Pacific* in 1949. She made her film debut opposite Frank Sinatra and Spencer Tracy in *The Devil at Four O'clock* (1961). Luna is one of the most respected and prolific actresses to have worked alternately in films, on stage, and on television. Her film credits include *Elmer Gantry* (1960) with Burt Lancaster and Shirley Jones; *Ship of Fools* (1965) with Lee Marvin and Vivien Leigh; *Firecreek* (1968) with James Stewart and Henry Fonda; and *Che* (1967) with Omar Sharif. She also essayed more than two hundred television roles on such popular programs as *Star Trek*, *The FBI*, and *The Wild Wild West*.

FUN IN ACAPULCO (PARAMOUNT, 1963)

Director: Richard Thorpe

Screenplay: Alan Weiss

Producer: Hal Wallis

Cast: Elvis Presley (Mike Brigand), Ursula Andress (Marguerite), Elsa Cardenas (Dolores), Larry Domasin (Raoul), Alejandro Rey (Moreno)

Story: Former circus aerialist Mike Brigand loses his job on a boat and, with the aid of an enterprising street urchin, finds employment at an Acapulco resort hotel as a lifeguard by day and singer by night. He vies for the attention of two girls with local lifeguard Moreno, who is also a champion sea cliff diver. (Sea cliff diving, considered one of the first "extreme sports," was a longstanding practice in Acapulco, although an official diving team was not formed until 1934.) Moreno challenges Mike to a face-off in which he is forced to confront his personal demons.

Production: *Fun in Acapulco* was filmed largely on soundstages at Paramount in Hollywood. Detailed interior and exterior sets were constructed to closely approximate locations that included the Acapulco Hilton (the present-day Emporium), El Mirador Hotel, La Perla Restaurant, and La Quebrada sea cliffs. A second-unit crew was sent to Acapulco to film exterior backgrounds and process plates with a photo double for Elvis Presley (1935–1977) for long-shots with Ursula Andress, Elsa Cardenas, and Larry Domasin

The legendary "King of Rock and Roll," with his good looks, raw talent, and camera presence, quickly grew into a favored movie attraction. Through a multi-million-dollar deal negotiated by his manager, Colonel Tom Parker, with Paramount producer Hal Wallis, Elvis became a worldwide number-one box-office star, generating millions of dollars in sales of tickets and soundtrack albums. The formula for his screen vehicles was simple: scenic locations, silly plot lines, plenty of Elvis songs, and lots of beautiful girls. He made thirty-seven movies (with slowly diminishing returns) in twelve years, while continuing to record Top-Ten songs and performing live for his legion of fans as a headliner on the Las Vegas strip.

Though not publicly known at the time, Colonel Tom Parker was actually a Dutch-born illegal immigrant to the U.S., who reinvented himself as a carnival barker and music promoter. He never became a naturalized American citizen, nor did he possess a passport. Parker had a Machiavellian control over Elvis and, since his lack of immigration status prevented him from leaving the continental United States, he never allowed Elvis to leave the country either. Consequently, Elvis did not go to Mexico for the location shoot of *Fun in Acapulco*. Adding more complications, a wealthy Mexican politician at the time of the film's production invited Elvis to sing at his daughter's birthday celebration. When Elvis declined the offer, the spiteful politician solicited an influential Mexican journalist to fabricate a newspaper account in which Elvis disparaged Mexican women and Mexican food. A minor public uproar resulted, but Elvis's Mexican fans could not be swayed. In the film, the hip-swinging singer warbled several songs in Spanish, including the traditional Mexican favorite "Guadalajara." Acapulco, already an established beach resort frequented by the Hollywood elite, became a popular foreign tourist destination because of the movie.

Swiss actress Ursula Andress, who plays Margurite, had made an impression on moviegoers in the first James Bond film, *Dr. No* (1962). Few who have seen it can ever forget (nor would they want to) the scene in which the eye-popping beauty with her curvaceous figure emerges from the sea in a white bikini. Eight-year-old Mexican-American child actor Larry Domasin plays the endearing street urchin Raoul, who takes Elvis under his wing. Longtime north-of-the-border Latino actors Salvador Baguez, Martin Garailaga, and Alberto Morin also have supporting roles. Mexican actress Elsa Cardenas plays Dolores Gomez, the lady matador. Argentine-born American actor Alejandro Rey (1930–1987), who plays Moreno, is best remembered for his role as the affable playboy Carlos on *The Flying Nun* television series (1967–1970) starring Sally Field.

KINGS OF THE SUN (UNITED ARTISTS, 1963)

Director: J. Lee Thompson
Screenplay: Elliott Arnold, James R. Webb
Producer: Walter Mirisch, Lewis J. Rachmill
Cast: Yul Brynner (Black Eagle), George Chakiris (King Balam), Shirley Ann Field (Ixchel), Richard Basehart (Ah Min), Brad Dexter (Ah Haleb), Leo Gordon (Hunac Ceel), Barry Morse (Ah Zok), Armando Silvestre (Isatai)
Story: Young Mayan king Balam and his people are forced to flee from their original homeland by a rival tribal king Ah Haleb. They seek safety in a far-off coastal plain, but the area's native tribes consider the newcomers to be intruders. An uneasy alliance is formed when the intruders capture their leader, Black Eagle, and he falls in love with a Mayan woman. Both King Balam and Black Eagle's people unite to fight off Ah Haleb's invading forces.
Production: *Kings of the Sun* was the first (and only) American theatrical fictionalization of the ancient Mayan civilization until Mel Gibson's *Apocalypto* (2006). It was shot entirely in Mexico on real and recreated locations in the Yucatan and at Chichen Itza.

OF LOVE AND DESIRE (20TH CENTURY-FOX, 1963)

Director: Richard Rush
Screenwriter: Laslo Gorog, Richard Rush

Producer: Victor Stoloff

Cast: Merle Oberon (Katherine Beckman), Steve Cochran (Steve Corey), John Agar (Gus Cole), Curt Jurgens (Paul Beckman), Eduardo Noriega (Mr. Dominguez), Rebecca Iturbide (Mrs. Renard), Elsa Cardenas (Mrs. Dominguez), Tony Carbajal (Dr. Renard)

Story: A rich, promiscuous widow seduces an American engineer on assignment in Mexico City.

Production: *Of Love and Desire* was filmed in Acapulco and Mexico City by cinematographer Alex Phillips. The film makes use of its scenic Mexican locations in this soap-operatic tale. Mario Cisneros was the assistant director; Roberto Silva, the art director; sound was by Mauel Topete. Merle Oberon (1911–1979), an Anglo-Indian star of Hollywood's golden age, began her career in British films. Among her most important film credits are *The Scarlet Pimpernel* (1934) co-starring Leslie Howard, and *Wuthering Heights* (1939), co-starring Laurence Olivier.

THE NIGHT OF THE IGUANA (METRO-GOLDWYN-MAYER, 1964)

Director: John Huston

Screenplay: Anthony Veiller, John Huston, based on the play by Tennessee Williams

Producer: Ray Stark, John Huston, Sandy Whitelaw

Cast: Richard Burton (Reverend Shannon), Ava Gardner (Maxine), Deborah Kerr (Hannah Jelkes), Sue Lyon (Charlotte), James Ward (Hank), Grayson Hall (Judith Fellowes), Cyril Delevanti (Nonno)

Story: A defrocked American minister, Lawrence Shannon, wallowing in alcohol and self pity, finds himself in a small rundown Mexican seaside hotel owned by the earthy and recently widowed Maxine Faulk. Shannon makes a living by working as a tour bus guide; he is assigned a group of middle-aged Baptist women tourists. He alienates the group leader, Judith Fellowes, when she catches him in a compromising position with her nubile ward, Charlotte. Threatened by Fellowes with the loss of his job, he commandeers the busload of tourists to Maxine's remote hotel. At that pivotal moment, the troubled Shannon fosters a redemptive relationship with spinster Hannah Jelks and her elderly father, Nonno. They are impoverished but proud artists who seek temporary shelter at the hotel. The bottle gets the better of him, and the alcohol-fueled Shannon acts as a catalyst that provokes the hotel guests to confront the ugly truths of their lives.

Production: In late 1962, John Huston received an offer from producer Ray Stark to direct a film version of Williams's 1961 play, *The Night of the Iguana*. "I thought it would make a wonderful motion picture, especially in Mexico," said Stark. "And John, of course, was the guru of Mexico. I just got him at a lucky time when he wanted to get back there." Huston explained, "The location is just like an actor. It gives something to the picture, you know, envelops it in an atmosphere." Though *Iguana* was originally set in Acapulco, Huston elected to shoot in Mismaloya Village, Jalisco, and Puerto Vallarta. He could not have picked more difficult and remote locations. There were no paved roads, no telephone lines, little plumbing, and spotty electricity in Mismaloya, which is on the coast, about eight kilometers from Puerto Vallarta. Paved roads were bulldozed into the town and an airstrip was constructed so that equipment, cast, and crew could move in and out of the location. Emilio "El Indio" Fernández has a small part as a bartender who refuses Charlotte a drink at the beach. Fidelmar Duran and Roberto Leyva are the maraca-strumming beach boys who satisfy Maxine's sexual urges.

Director John Huston checks a camera angle for a scene between Richard Burton and Ava Gardner on the Puerto Vallarta, Mismaloya, location of *The Night of the Iguana* **(1964).**

The Night of the Iguana was among the most publicized films of its time. This was due largely to the presence of soon-to-be-married Elizabeth Taylor and Richard Burton. Their celebrated and scandalous affair had begun during the production of the ill-fated epic *Cleopatra*, in which they co-starred as the Queen of the Nile and Marc Antony. Taylor showed up to the set in Puerto Vallarta with Burton while she was still married to singer Eddie Fisher; Burton was then wed to Sybil Williams. The location was swarmed with media from around the world for the entire seventy-two-day shooting schedule, from late September through December 1963. It turned Puerto Vallarta, a small, remote fishing village on Mexico's Pacific Coast into a world-class tourist destination.

Critically well received, *The Night of the Iguana* was nominated for four Academy Awards but won only one, for Best Costume Design (Black and White) for Dorothy Jeakins. Gabriel Figueroa received a nomination for Best Black-and-White Cinematography. "This is my first film with John Huston," Figueroa remarked to a Mexican newspaper reporter. "A great director that I have admired for so many pictures and for a long time and I always had an interest to work with him."

THE GLORY GUYS (UNITED ARTISTS, 1965)

Director: Arnold Laven

Screenplay: Sam Peckinpah, based on the novel *The Dice of God* by Hoffman Birney

Producer: Jules V. Levy, Arthur Gardner, Arnold Laven

Cast: Tom Tryon (Captain Demas Harrod), Harve Presnell (Sol Rogers), Senta Berger (Lou Woddard), James Caan (Dugan), Michael Andersen Jr. (Hale), Slim Pickens (Sergeant Gregory), Andrew Duggan (General McCabe)

Story: Captain Harrod and his scout, Sol Rogers, vie for the affections of a frontier woman as the captain readies his new recruits for duty. Harrod is at odds with his Indian-hating and glory-hungry commanding officer, General McCabe, who leads his men to death in a bloody massacre.

Production: Filmed in Durango, in Panavision and Deluxe color by Oscar-winning cinematographer James Wong Howe, who had been in Mexico thirty years earlier as principal cameraman on *Viva Villa!* and *The Brave Bulls*. Arnold Laven returned to Durango as director after the commercial success of his previous Durango location shoot for *Geronimo*. The second-unit work was entrusted to Rene Cardona and Jaime Contreras; the second-unit cameraman was Alex Phillips, who also worked early in his career on *Viva Villa!*

The Glory Guys is a loose retelling of the 1876 massacre of the Seventh Cavalry, under General George Armstrong Custer, at the Little Big Horn. Peckinpah had written the script seven years earlier that contains themes he explored in later films: a glory-hungry commander who risks his command; disparate men who must learn to work together; and a love triangle involving two strong-willed men and a woman on the frontier.

MAJOR DUNDEE (COLUMBIA PICTURES, 1965)

Director: Sam Peckinpah

Screenplay: Harry Julian Fink, Oscar Saul, Sam Peckinpah

Producer: Jerry Bresler

Cast: Charlton Heston (Major Amos Dundee), Richard Harris (Benjamin Tyreen), James Coburn (Samuel Potts), Michael Anderson Jr. (Tim Ryan), Jim Hutton (Lieutenant. Graham), Senta Berger (Teresa Santiago), Mario Adorf (Sergeant Gomez), Brock Peters (Aesop), Warren Oates (Q. W. Hadley), Ben Johnson (Sergeant Chillum), Michael Pate (Charriba), R. G. Armstrong (Reverend Dehistrom), L. Q. Jones (Arthur Hadley), Slim Pickens (Wiley), José Carlos Ruiz (Riago), Aurora Clavell (Melinche), Begonia Palacio (Linda), Enrique Lucero (Dr. Aguilar), Francisco Reyquera (old Apache)

Story: Major Amos Dundee is a military officer who has been demoted to prison duty on the New Mexico border in the closing days of the Civil War. When Apache Indians murder a white settler family, abduct three children, and kill a small detachment of Union troops, Dundee assembles a fighting force of white Union soldiers, black soldiers, cowboys, and Indian scouts. Unable to enlist enough regular Union troops because the Civil War is raging, Dundee is forced to impress Confederate prisoners of war, led by Benjamin Tyreen. Dundee and Tyreen had been friends before the war and now form an uneasy alliance. During their pursuit of the Apaches, Dundee and his men illegally cross into Mexico, where they run into occupying French soldiers. Dundee, in need of supplies, liberates a Mexican village from a French garrison. After the unsuccessful Apache ambush, Dundee and his men slay the Indians and rescue the stolen chil-

Two-time Oscar-winning cameraman James Wong Howe (*left*) on the Durango location of *The Glory Guys* (1965).

dren; they then must confront the French troops intent on preventing them from crossing the Rio Grande River into the United States.

Production: *Major Dundee* started shooting in Mexico without a completed script. At the last minute the studio also cut fifteen days from the original seventy-five-day shooting schedule. Peckinpah and producer Jerry Bresler could not control the ambitious production. Many distant and difficult locations were selected in remote, rural Mexico. There were well-documented fights between Peckinpah, who was determined to create a modern, graphic, ambiguous western, and Bresler, who wanted a traditional cavalry movie. In his *Senses of Cinema* Internet article on *Major Dundee*, Dana Polan writes, "Despite the fact that its title singles out one figure, the film is more epic and episodic than that, giving the United States a wide range of interesting characters and loading onto them a series of weighty issues." The director's self-destructive nature made matters worse and created tension with star Charlton Heston. The Best Actor Oscar-winning Heston (1923–2008) was one of the most popular American film stars of the fifties and sixties (*The Ten Commandments*, 1956; *Ben-Hur, 1959*; *El Cid*, 1961; *Planet of the Apes*, 1968). Six four, handsome, with a booming voice, he personified historic, heroic characters. Richard Harris (1930–2002) was an Irish actor who came to prominence in the early sixties with the role of a rugby player in the British film *This Sporting Life* (1963), earning an Academy Award nomination as Best Actor in the process. After *Major Dundee*, he returned to Durango to star in *A Man Called Horse* (1970) and its sequel, as well as the western *The Deadly Trackers*. Columbia threatened to fire Peckinpah, but Heston stood up for him and he was allowed to complete the film. The finished product was overlong, so it was edited down to a reasonable length by the studio, without Peckinpah's participation. Ultimately, *Major Dundee* was flawed and disjointed, even though it had moments of brilliance. Years later, Heston remarked that *Major Dundee* was a rehearsal for Peckinpah's masterwork, *The Wild Bunch*. Locations included Durango, Tehuixtla, Cuatla, and Vista Hermosa. The final charge against the French was filmed on the Rio Balsasneon, Chilpancingo, and La Marquesa, twenty-five miles south of Mexico City, as well as on locations farther south, in Tequesquitengo. Interiors were filmed at Estudios Churubusco.

VIVA MARIA! (UNITED ARTISTS, 1965)

Director: Louis Malle

Screenplay: Louis Malle, Jean-Claude Carrière

Producer: Óscar Dancigers

Cast: Brigitte Bardot (Maria O'Malley), Jeanne Moreau (Maria), George Hamilton (Florès), Paulette Dubost (Madame Diogène), Claudio Brook (The Great Rodolfo), Carlos Lopez Moctezuma (Rodríguez), Poldo Bendandi (Werther), Gregor von Rezzori (Diogène), Francisco Reiguera (Father Superior), Fernando Wagner (Maria's father)

Story: Maria O'Malley is the young daughter of an Irish Republic anarchist at the turn of the twentieth century. Working in tandem, they dynamite English military compounds in Ireland, London, Gibraltar, and its colonial empire in Central America. By 1907 Maria is grown and living with her father in Central America, presumably in British Honduras (Belize). While attempting to blow up a bridge, Maria's father is shot and killed by British soldiers; meanwhile, a determined Maria completes the act of terrorism on her own. She eludes capture and hides out with a traveling circus, where she meets another Maria, a singer and dancer in the troupe. Together, they develop an act, becoming—quite by accident—a striptease sensation. In their travels across the countryside, they are captured by a local landowner and inspired by a young revolutionary named Florès. When Florès is killed, the two Marias lead a peasant revolt, overthrowing the landowner, the dictator, and some evil churchmen.

Production: Filmed in Cuernavaca, Texcoco, and Morelos as the fictitious Central American country of San Miguel. *Viva Maria!* is the first of the female "buddy pictures" and features two of the French cinema's most popular and beautiful actresses of the sixties, Brigitte Bardot and Jeanne Moreau. The film is a satirical adventure-comedy from director Louis Malle that takes jabs at dictators, feudal landowners, imperialism, and the Catholic Church. *Viva Maria!* was filmed in Panavision and Eastmancolor in Mexico by French cinematographer Henri Decae.

JOHN WAYNE AND DURANGO, MEXICO, FILMS

THE SONS OF KATIE ELDER (PARAMOUNT, 1965)
Director: Henry Hathaway
Screenplay: William H. Wright, Alan Weiss, Harry Essex, based on a story by Talbot Jennings
Producer: Hal Wallis
Cast: John Wayne (John Elder), Dean Martin (Tom), Michael Anderson Jr. (Bud), Earl Holliman (Matt), Rodolfo Acosta (Bondie Adams), James Gregory (Morgan Hastings), Dennis Hopper (Dave Hastings), George Kennedy (Curley), Martha Hyer (Mary Gordon), Paul Fix (Sheriff Billy), Jeremy Slate (Ben Latta)
Story: Four sons return to the ranch they had left years earlier to attend their mother's funeral. They discover that their father had lost the ranch in a card game; after he was suspiciously murdered, their mother lived on the charity of neighbors. The sons are determined to find out who murdered their father and how a scheming landowner acquired their family property.
Production: Filmed in Durango, in the village of Chupaderos and at El Saltito waterfalls, *The Sons of Katie Elder* introduced John Wayne's older film persona of the latter part of his career. Wayne had been diagnosed with lung cancer in September of 1964 and immediately underwent a serious operation that removed his left lung and two ribs. He did not tell anyone of his life-threatening illness for fear it could halt his career and ruin his rugged image. The press reported that he had entered the hospital on September 17 to repair an old football injury to his shoulder. In January of 1965, three months after leaving the hospital on October 7, Wayne was on location in Durango. Not only was the rough-and-tumble actioner shot in the high desert at an altitude of 5,000 feet, but director Henry Hathaway (also a cancer survivor, and an old friend of Wayne's) tested the actor's physical endurance with a rigourous filming schedule, which included his jumping from a bridge and swimming across an icy river. Besides the inconvenience of encounters with the occasional desert rattlesnakes and the infamous native scorpions, several night exteriors had to be postponed because of frigid weather. Wayne made it through the filming, albiet in extreme pain and sometimes aided by an oxygen tank. In a brave career move that inspired millions of fans, he eventually admitted to the press that he had undergone cancer surgery. Wayne was co-starred with Dean Martin, with whom he was paired successfully in Howard Hawks's *Rio Bravo* (1959). Martin loved playing the cowboy, and

he and Wayne got along famously. Wayne housed many of the cast at the Mexican Courts Motel, located just outside of town. Lucien Ballard captured the spectacular Durango locations in Technicolor. He had worked previously in Mexico, as did director Henry Hathaway on *Garden of Evil* (1954), and would return for two other films: *5 Card Stud* (1968) and *Raid on Rommel* (1971). Interiors were shot at Estudios Churubusco.

THE WAR WAGON (UNIVERSAL STUDIOS, 1967)

Director: Burt Kennedy
Screenplay: Clair Huffaker, based on his novel *Badmen.*
Producer: Marvin Schwartz
Cast: John Wayne (Taw Jackson), Kirk Douglas (Lomax), Bruce Cabot (Pierce), Howard Keel (Levi Walking Bear), Robert Walker Jr. (Billy Hyatt), Keenan Wynn (Wes Fletcher), Emilio Fernández (Calita)
Story: Taw Jackson has spent three years in prison and has had his land stolen by Pierce. He teams up with an old nemesis, Lomax, in order to steal gold from Pierce's mining operations. The gold is transported in the seemingly impregnable War Wagon. Made of steel, the War Wagon sports a Gatling gun mounted on top, and is additionally guarded by thirty armed horsemen. Jackson brings together several cohorts with varying expertise to help him pull off the heist.
Production: Filmed from September to December 1966, in Zacatecas at Los Organos State Park (called Los Organos because the majestic rock wall formations resemble church organ spires). In Durango, it took art director Albert Sweeney only six weeks to build a western town comprised of twenty-seven buildings of wood and brick, complementing pre-existing structures.
The War Wagon is a fast-moving action film with top performances from Wayne and Douglas, who try to top each other in humorous exchanges. It was a huge box-office hit for Wayne and the second of his films to be shot in Durango, which had become a popular location due to his presence there.

THE UNDEFEATED (20TH CENTURY-FOX, 1969)

Director: Andrew V. McLaglen
Screenplay: James Lee Barrett
Producer: Robert L. Jacks
Cast: John Wayne (Colonel John Henry Thomas), Rock Hudson (Colonel James Langdon), Antonio Aguilar (General Rojas) Lee Meriwether (Margaret Langdon), Pedro Armendáriz Jr. (Escalante). Carlos Rivas (Diaz)
Story: In the aftermath of the American Civil War, former Union Col. John Henry Thomas leads his men into Mexico to sell wild horses to the unpopular government of Emperor Maximilian. Meanwhile, Col. James Langdon leads a wagon train of former Confederate soldiers and their families from Louisiana to a new life in Mexico City. Meeting on the trail, the groups form an uneasy alliance to fend off bandits. When the Confederates are captured by the Juaristas and held for ransom, Col. Thomas must rescue the beleaguered Southerners and fight off the French occupation forces under Maximilian who want to get their hands on the horses.
Production: *The Undefeated* was filmed by cinematographer William H. Clothier in Durango, in Zacatecas at Los Organos National Park, and in Louisiana from early February to mid-May of 1969. This marked the first (and only) pairing of John Wayne and Rock Hudson. Mexican singing idol and film star Antonio Aguilar plays Juarista General Rojas, and Pedro Amendariz Jr. makes a brief appearance as a bandit.

CHISUM (WARNER BROS., 1970)

Director: Andrew V. McLaglen

Screenplay: Andrew J. Fenady

Producer: Andrew J. Fenady, Michael Wayne

Cast: John Wayne (John Chisum), Forrest Tucker (Lawrence Murphy), Christopher George (Dan Nodeen), Ben Johnson (James Pepper), Geoffrey Duel (Billy the Kid), Glenn Corbett (Pat Garrett)

Story: In 1878 New Mexico, cattle baron John Chisum is determined to protect his land against a corrupt business magnate. An all-out range war explodes—involving Billy the Kid and, later, Pat Garrett—after Billy's benefactor, Henry Tunstall, is murdered.

Production: Filmed in Durango, from October to December 1969 at Rancho La Joya ("The Jewel"), which was purchased by John Wayne as a filming location. William H. Clothier's Panavision and Technicolor cinematography of Durango's landscapes display a late-summer, brownish hue. Michael Wayne, John's eldest son, produced all of his father's films in Durango through Batjac Productions, except for *The Sons of Katie Elder* (though Batjac was a production entity on the film) and *The Undefeated*.

RIO LOBO (NATIONAL GENERAL, 1970)

Director: Howard Hawks

Screenplay: Burton Wahl, based on a story by Leigh Brackett

Producer: Howard Hawks

Cast: John Wayne (Colonel Cord McNally), Jorge Rivero (Pierre Cardona), Jennifer O'Neil (Shasta Delaney), Christopher Mitchum (Tuscarora), Jack Elam (Phillips), Victor French (Ketchum), Susana Dosamantes (Maria Carmen), Sherry Lansing (Amelita)

Story: In the closing days of the American Civil War, a daring train heist of a Union gold shipment by Confederate rebels causes the death of a Union colonel, Cord McNally's fellow officer. McNally vows to find the Union traitor who alerted the rebels of the gold shipment. After the war, with the help of two ex-Confederates, his search for the traitor leads to a small Texas town controlled by a corrupt sheriff and a powerful rancher.

Production: Hawks and Wayne had wanted to shoot the entire film in Mexico, but the Durango Western town sets were being utilized for Michael Winner's *Lawman*; Old Tucson, in Arizona, was used instead. Legendary pioneering stuntman, stunt coordinator, and second-unit director Yakima Canutt supervised the imaginative train heist sequence shot in Cuernavaca, where a period narrow-gauge train was still in use. Mexican screen idol Jorge Rivero was cast in the hopes of attracting a younger, more international audience, something Wayne and Hawks had achieved with Montgomery Clift in *Red River*, Ricky Nelson in *Rio Bravo*, and, to certain extent, a young James Caan in *El Dorado*.

BIG JAKE (NATIONAL GENERAL, 1971)

Director: George Sherman

Screenplay: Harry Julian Fink, R. M. Fink

Producer: Michael A. Wayne

Cast: John Wayne (Jake McCandles), Maureen O'Hara (Martha McCandles), Richard Boone (John Fain), Patrick

Wayne (James McCandles), Chris Mitchum (Michael McCandles)

Story: At he turn of the twentieth century, in the last days of the Wild West, a group of vicious outlaws descends on the huge McCandles ranch, shooting the inhabitants and kidnapping six-year-old Jake McCandles. The kidnappers demand a million dollar ransom. Estranged from his family, aging Texas cattleman "Big Jake" McCandles is entrusted with the mission of going into Mexico, determined to pay the ransom and rescue his grandson.

Production: Filmed in Durango, with cinematography by William H. Clothier. Other scenes were shot in Los Organos (the ambush sequence), El Saltito (the waterfall), Las Huertas, La Punta, Lerdo de Tejaca, El Pueblito, and El Arenal. The McCandles ranch in *Big Jake* is the same ranch location used for *Chisum*. Veteran director George Sherman, who directed Wayne in several Three Mesquiteers B-westerns at Republic during the thirties, was hired by the actor to direct *Big Jake*. The movie reflected many of the changes occurring in westerns in the sixties and seventies. Directors like Sam Peckinpah and George Roy Hill, who added graphic violence, themes of aging heroes in a changing time, and light humor to the genre, had an impact that could no longer be ignored. Wayne was reunited briefly with his longtime leading lady Maureen O'Hara for *Big Jake*, but she was largely wasted in the role which amounted to a cameo, requiring only her screen presence. Ethan Wayne, Wayne's youngest son, who played his grandson Little Jake, recalled in an interview with the author, "He [Wayne] took me with him on all the locations when I was a little boy. On that picture [*Big Jake*], to be able to be there the entire time and also be involved in the production, has got to be one of my greatest memories."

THE TRAIN ROBBERS (WARNER BROS., 1973)

Director: Burt Kennedy

Screenplay: Burt Kennedy

Producer: Michael Wayne

Cast: John Wayne (Lane), Ann-Margret (Mrs. Lowe), Ben Johnson (Jesse), Rod Taylor (Grady), Christopher George (Calhoun), Ricardo Montalban (Pinkerton agent)

Story: Lane, an aging gunfighter, is hired by a widow to find a buried train with with a load of gold that was stolen by her late husband. She wants to return the gold to clear her family name. Lane enlists the aid of a group of fellow gunfighters to help him in his quest. Meanwhile, they are pursued by a band of unknown gunmen.

Production: Filmed from March to June of 1972 on Wayne's Rancho La Joya in Durango, *The Train Robbers* was also shot north of Durango at the sand dunes "Las Dunas De Bilbao," near Torreon, where a train lies wrecked in the desert sands (a location also seen in *The Wild Bunch*). Cinematography is by longtime Wayne collaborator William H. Clothier, who captured the desert landscaes in Panavision and Technicolor, under the direction of Burt Kennedy (who was also the screenwriter). A motif he frequently employed was a trek across the desert by a group of desperate men. This sometimes involved a woman, as in his screenplay for Boetticher's *Seven Men from Now* (1956). Movie reviewer Roger Ebert wrote in 1973: "I wonder if there's ever been a western as visually uncluttered as this one [*The Train Robbers*]. Most of the action takes place in the high desert around Durango, Mexico, and Kennedy goes for clean blue skies, sculpted white sand dunes and human figures arranged against the landscape in compositions so tasteful we're

Director Burt Kennedy *(right, wearing glasses)*, on location in Durango, Mexico, prepares to shoot a scene for *The Train Robbers* (1973), with cinematographer Bill Clothier *(right)*, John Wayne, Ann-Margret, Ben Johnson, and Rod Taylor.

reminded of Samurai dramas." Wayne, not wanting his old friend and co-star Ben Johnson to miss the Academy Awards ceremony, had his private plane fly Johnson from the Durango location to Los Angeles where he did win the Oscar as Best Supporting Actor for his role as "Sam The Lion" in *The Last Picture Show* (1971) and was present to accept it.

CAHILL U.S. MARSHALL (WARNER BROS., 1973)

Director: Andrew V. McLaglen
Screenplay: Harry Julian Fink, R. M. Fink
Producer: Michael Wayne
Cast: John Wayne (Cahill), George Kennedy (Fraser), Gary Grimes (Danny), Neville Brand (Lightfoot), Clay O'Brian (Billy Paul), Harry Carey Jr. (Hank)
Story: J. D. Cahill is a U.S. marshall who has spent most of his life tracking down outlaws, to the detriment of his relationship with his teenage sons. When his sons become involved in a bank robbery and a sheriff is shot, Cahill must go after his own progeny.
Production: Filmed in Durango in November of 1972 at Wayne's La Joya Ranch, among other sites. The working title of the film was "Wednesday Mornin'".

THE BANDITS/LOS BANDIDOS (LONE STAR, 1966)

Director: Alfredo Zacarias, Robert Conrad

Screenplay: Edward Di Lorenzo, Robert Conrad, Alfredo Zacarias

Producer: James M. George

Cast: Robert Conrad (Craig Barnett), Manuel Lopez Ochoa (Valdez), Roy Jensen (Josh Radner), Jan-Michael Vincent (Brown), Maria Dubal (Sra. Valdez), Pedro Armendariz Jr. (priest)

Story: Three Mexican bandits desert the French Army during the French Intervention in Mexico and disappear into the neighboring United States. When they save three American bandits from hanging, they all team up to surprise the French Army and steal hidden treasures from a monastery.

Production: This production was filmed in Mexico during the first-season hiatus of the television series *The Wild Wild West* (1965–1969), utilizing key personnel from the series, including its star Robert Conrad. Ted Voightlander was the cinematographer. This B-Western is competently made, but it has a style to it that classifies it as a hybrid Mexican–U. S. co-production. The violence in the film, the relationship among the bandits, and the climactic shootout in which the Gringo bandits are killed predates Sam Peckinpah's *The Wild Bunch* (1969) by three years. In the interim, Jan-Michael Vincent was signed by Universal Studios, for whom the handsome young actor made standout appearances on a number of television shows. Despite the appeal of Conrad and Vincent, as well as its Peckinpah-like motifs, *The Bandits* did not secure a U. S. release until 1979, thirteen years after it was made. The limited release went unnoticed at the box-office and was handled by a startup distributor, Lone Star International.

RAGE (COLUMBIA PICTURES, 1966)

Director: Gilberto Gazcón

Screenplay: Gilberto Gazcón

Producer: Gilberto Gazcón

Cast: Glenn Ford (Reuben), Stella Stevens (Perla), David Reynoso (Pancho), Armando Silvestre (Antonio)

Story: Drama about a backwater doctor who contracts rabies and then must race against time to save his own life.

Production: Filmed on location in Durango and Mexico City, *Rage* was a co-production between Columbia Pictures and Mexico's Cinematografica Jalisco, along with the Mexican National Film Bank. Principal photography lasted from December 1, 1965, through February 1, 1966. The gritty drama was made on a budget of $640,000, with Eastmancolor cinematography by Rosalio Solano.

HOUR OF THE GUN (UNITED ARTISTS, 1967)

Director: John Sturges

Screenplay: Edward Anhalt

Producer: John Sturges

Cast: James Garner (Wyatt Earp), Jason Robards Jr. (Doc Holliday), Robert Ryan (Ike Clanton), Jorge Russek (Latigo), Jon Voight (Curly Bill Brocius), Sam Melville (Morgan Earp), Charles Aidman (Horace Sullivan)

Story: Beginning with the infamous gunfight at the O. K. Corral, Wyatt Earp, his brothers, and Doc Holliday contend with Tombstone authorities and politics to resolve the situation with Ike Clanton. Earp, exceeding his authority, uses his badge in a series of violent encounters that ultimately end in a showdown with Clanton in Mexico.

Production: Filmed in Durango and nearby Torreon under the title "The Law and Tombstone," with cinematography by Lucien Ballard. The Mexican locations doubled for Tombstone and surrounding Arizona locales as well as Colorado and Mexico. Made ten years after Sturges's own *Gunfight at the O. K. Corral* (a more traditional western), *Hour of the Gun* told the purported truth behind the Earp-Clanton legend. Garner is cast against type as a grim Wyatt Earp; Jason Robards delivers a nuanced performance as Doc Holliday; and Robert Ryan, in one of his latter-career supporting roles, is excellent as Ike Clanton. *Hour of the Gun* marked Ryan's first film in Mexico (Durango and Torreon) since *The Tall Men*; he would return twice more. *Hour of the Gun* did not find favor with audiences, perhaps, even in the explosively candid 1960s, they were not ready to see their traditional western heroes tarnished. Oscar-winner Jon Voight (*Midnight Cowboy*, 1969) made his cinema debut here as one of Ike Clanton's henchmen. Jorje Russek (*The Wild Bunch*, 1969) is Latigo, another of Clanton's hired guns.

DAY OF THE EVIL GUN (METRO-GOLDWYN-MAYER, 1968)

Director: Jerry Thorpe

Screenplay: Charles Marquis Warren, Eric Bercovici

Producer: Jerry Thorpe

Cast: Glenn Ford (Lorne Warfield), Arthur Kennedy (Owen Fields), Dean Jagger (Jimmy Noble), Pilar Pellicer (Lydia), John Anderson (Captain Addis) Harry Dean Stanton (Sargent Parker), Paul Fix (Sheriff Kelso)

Story: Lorne Warfield returns home after a long absence to find his ranch burned to the ground and his wife and two daughters abducted by Apache Indians. He attempts to track the riding party through inhospitable country in hopes of rescuing them.

Production: *Day of the Evil Gun* is a minor, late-career Glenn Ford western shot in Durango on a modest budget. It is competently executed by prolific television director Jerry Thorpe and has a supporting cast of veteran character actors, including Paul Fix, John Anderson, Harry Dean Stanton, and Royal Dano. Mexican actress Pilar Pellicer has a key role in the film, as Lydia. She appeared in the Mexican film *Pedro Paramo* (1967) with John Gavin, and in the George Hamilton comedy spoof *Zorro: The Gay Blade* (1981). Actors Jorge Martinez de Hoyos, Jose Chavez, and Jaime Hernandez are also featured.

5 CARD STUD (PARAMOUNT, 1968)

Director: Henry Hathaway

Screenplay: Marguerite Roberts

Producer: Hal Wallis

Cast: Dean Martin (Van Morgan), Robert Mitchum (Reverend Jonathan Rudd), Inger Stevens (Lily Langford), Roddy McDowall (Nick Evers), Yaphet Kotto (Little George)

Story: A gambler is murdered on the night of an infamous poker game and all the players are suspects, including the sheriff. While the poker players are killed off one by one by an unknown assailant, a mysterious preacher arrives in town.

Production: Veteran director Henry Hathaway had previously filmed in Durango, for *The Sons of Katie Elder* with Dean Martin; he utilized many of the same crew and locations in this Hal Wallis production for Paramount. Exterior scenes for *5 Card Stud* were filmed in the rough cactus country around Durango, which doubled for the town of Ricon, Colorado. Paramount leased the town of Chupaderos, just outside of Durango, for filming. Interiors were shot at Estudios Churubusco. Two of Hollywood's biggest stars, Dean Martin and Robert Mitchum, were brought together for this film: Martin plays a smooth frontier gambler with a knack for attracting trouble and pretty women; Mitchum, as a self-ordained preacher, is reminiscent of his scary turn as a preacher in the classic thriller *Night of the Hunter* (1955).

THE SCALPHUNTERS (UNITED ARTISTS, 1968)

Director: Sydney Pollack

Screenplay: William Norton

Producer: Jules Levy, Arthur Gardner, Arnold Laven

Cast: Burt Lancaster (Joe Bass), Ossie Davis (Joseph Lee), Shelly Winters (Kate), Telly Savalas (Jim Howie), Armando Silvestre (Two Crows)

Story: Joe Bass is a fur trapper heading to a trading post after a successful hunting season when he runs into a band of Kiowa Indians, led by Two Crows. Outnumbered, he is forced to give up his furs and, in exchange, he is given an educated black runaway slave named Lee. Bass, vowing to track the band of Indians and retrieve his furs, forms an uneasy partnership with Lee. A gang of white men attack and massacre the Indians to collect the bounty on their scalps and, in the aftermath, acquire not only the furs but Lee. Lee is content to stay with the scalphunters since they are headed for Mexico, where slavery is illegal. Bass does everything he can to stop the gang and retrieve his furs while contending with Indians bent on avenging their fallen comrades.

Production: Filmed in Durango, this comedy-western, set in the Pre-Civil War American frontier, is a social commentary on the racial unrest and the civil rights movement of 1960s America. It also underlines feminist, social, and sexual mores of the time, as well as those of the western genre. Mexican actor Armando

Silvestre plays the Native American Kiowa warrior Two Crows; Mexican extras play other Native Americans. This was the third of six films made in Mexico by Burt Lancaster; others were: *Vera Cruz, The Unforgiven, Lawman, Cattle Annie and Little Britches*, and *The Little Treasure*. Ossie Davis (1917–2005), one of the most prominent African American actors and directors of the post–World War II era, was also a civil rights activist along with his wife, actress Ruby Dee. Director Sydney Pollack began as an assistant to frequent Lancaster collaborator, director John Frankenheimer. Pollack moved into directing and established a reputation for making successful mainstream movies with popular stars, including *They Shoot Horses, Don't They?* (1969) with Jane Fonda and Gig Young; *The Way We Were* (1972) with Robert Redord and Barbra Striesand; *Tootsie* (1982) with Dustin Hoffman; and his Oscar-winning Best Picture *Out of Africa* (1985) with Robert Redford and Meryl Streep, for which he won an Oscar for Best Director.

SOL MADRID (METRO-GOLDWYN-MAYER, 1968)

Director: Brian G. Hutton

Screenplay: David Karp, from the novel by Robert Wilder

Producer: Hall Bartlett

Cast: David McCallum (Sol Madrid), Ricardo Montalban (Jalisco), Stella Stevens (Stacey Woodward), Pat Hingle (Mitchell), Telly Savalas (Dietrich), Rip Torn (Villanova)

Story: An undercover government agent goes on the trail of heroin smugglers and their agents in 1960s Mexico.

Production: Filmed at MGM studios and in Acapulco, Mexico, this routine crime-drama is, in hindsight, about an early form of drug cartels. *Sol Madrid* feels like an undistinguished made-for-television movie. Lead actor David McCallum made this movie in Mexico while on hiatus from his co-starring role opposite Robert Vaughn on the phenomenally successful MGM television espionage series *The Man from U.N.C.L.E.* (1964–1968).

GUNS FOR SAN SEBASTIAN (METRO-GOLDWYN-MAYER, 1968)

Director: Henri Verneuil

Screenplay: Serge Gance, Miguel Morayta, Ennio De Concini; English-language screenplay by James R.Webb, based on the novel *A Wall for San Sebastian* by William Barby Faherty

Producer: Jacques Bar, Ernesto Enriquez

Cast: Anthony Quinn (Leon Alastray), Anjanette Comer (Kinia), Charles Bronson (Teclo), Silvia Pinal (Felicia), Sam Jaffe (Father Joseph)

Story: Historical adventure set in eighteenth century colonial Mexico. Leon Alastray is an outlaw who, mistaken for a priest, protects a peasant village against a violent tribe of Yaqui Indians.

Production: A French-American co-production filmed in San Miguel de Allende and the state of Durango. Working titles included "Wall for San Sebastian" and "Miracle of San Sebastian." Anthony Quinn utilized

El Saltito waterfalls in Durango provide the backdrop for a scene from *Guns for San Sebastian* **(1968), starring Anthony Quinn.**

his screen presence as the reluctantly heroic, lusty, brutish but capable outlaw who helps poor villagers fight off marauding Yaquis when government troops fail them. A patented Zorba-like performance from Quinn marked the actor's fourth Mexican film location in his country of birth. Mexican actress Silvia Pinal has a small role as Felicia, Leon's secret lover, who is married to a sympathetic aristocrat. Veteran supporting player Charles Bronson was on the verge of his ascent as an international star with his role in this film and in MGM's *The Dirty Dozen* (1967).

SHARK (CINEMATOGRAFICA CALDERON S. A. HERITAGE ENTERTAINMENT, 1969)

Director: Samuel Fuller

Screenplay: John Kingsbridge

Producer: José Luis Calderon, Mark Cooper

Cast: Burt Reynolds (Caine), Arthur Kennedy (Doc), Barry Sullivan (Mallare), Silvia Pinal (Anna), Enrigue Lucero (Batok), Manuel Alvarado (Latalla), Carlos Barry (Runt)

Story: A gunrunner finds his way to a Sudanese port on the Red Sea where he is recruited to assist in an undersea exploration. Later, he discovers that the scientists are out to recover stolen gold from a lost undersea shipwreck, in shark-infested waters.

Production: Filmed in Manzanillo, Colima, Mexico, subbing for the Sudan and the Red Sea, with cinematography by Raul Martinez Solares under the direction of iconoclastic American B-movie director/writer Samuel Fuller, *Shark* was originally titled "Caine," after its lead character. It suffered from its low budget, a tragedy during filming, and poor taste on the part of the producers: they expoited the death of a stuntman killed by a shark during filming to promote the movie. *Shark* was disowned by Fuller when the producers took the final cut from him and reedited the film for its release. The producers' edit was later re-released to theaters to capitalize both on the shark

craze caused by the blockbuster *Jaws* (1975) and the star ascendancy of its charismatic lead actor Burt Reynolds. He was a top box-office attraction for most of the seventies and eighties, with such hits as *Deliverance* (1972), *Smokey and The Bandit* (1977), *The Longest Yard* (1974), and *Cannonball Run* (1981). Reynolds would return to Mexico to star in Stanley Donen's *Lucky Lady* (1975). World-renowned Mexican actress Silvia Pinal, who starred in Buñuel's *Viridana* (1961), *Simon of the Desert* (1965), *and The Exterminating Angel* (1962), has the female lead of Anna in *Shark*. The role did not require much from the talented Pinal, who shared the screen with veteran American supporting players Arthur Kennedy and Barry Sullivan.

THE WILD BUNCH (WARNER BROS., 1969)

Director: Sam Peckinpah

Screenplay: Walon Green, Sam Peckinpah, based on a story by Walon Green and Roy N. Sickner

Producer: Phil Feldman

Cast: William Holden (Pike Bishop), Robert Ryan (Deke Thorton), Ernest Borgnine (Dutch), Warren Oates (Lyle), Ben Johnson (Tector), Emilo "El Indio" Fernández (Mapache), Jaime Sánchez (Angel), Jorge Russek (Lieutenant Zamora), Alfonso Arau (Herrera)

Story: In 1916, some American outlaws near the Mexican border look to make one last score. The outlaws are also trying to outrun their former ally, Deke, and his gang of bounty hunters.

Production: Filmed on various locations in Northern Mexico, especially in and around the small resort- and winemaking-town of Parras de la Fuente in the state of Coahuila, where the opening bank robbery sequence was filmed. The Hacienda Cienega del Carmen, an hour's drive outside of Parras, is the location of Mapache's hideout where—over the span of eleven days—the climactic sequence was shot.

The bridge collapse was filmed at Rio Nazas, south of Torreon. Locations for the train sequences where a rail spur south of La Goma, Torreon and the Durazno Arroyo Canyon. {AU: I'm unclear as to what that sentence means; please revise} An area behind the Rincon Del Montero hotel is where Angel's village was set. *The Wild Bunch* illustrates the quintessential American view of Mexico through the prism of Sam Peckinpah, as a place where gringos can play out their fantasies, a never-never land of sex, violence, and ultra machismo. In this brutal drama of violent men, the eponymous Bunch realize the conflicting strains of their harsh yet humane characters. After a violent bank robbery in a U.S. border town, they cross the Rio Grande into Mexico. The film then takes on a sudden tranquility in a brief pastoral interlude, when they visit the village of the Bunch's only Mexican member, Angel.

Peckinpah does not portray Mexico as a complete paradise. *Mapache* (English translation: raccoon) represents an early form of twentieth century dictators, with all the military trappings. He is evil incarnate. Mapache's automobile is the first the Bunch has ever seen. Later, that car is used to drag around the body of the tortured Angel. Surrounded by adoring children, German military advisers, whores, and sadistic killers,

Featured in the climactic death march in Sam Peckinpah's *The Wild Bunch* (1969) are Ben Johnson, Warren Oates, William Holden, and Ernest Borgnine. The location is the Hacienda Ciénega del Carmen, near Parras, Coahuila, Torreon.

Mapache delights in the destructive power of his machine gun. That four Americans kill what seems to be hundreds of Mexicans before meeting their own demise could be interpreted as a symbol of American superiority, except that Peckinpah has created a far more nuanced view, in which characters are neither as good—nor as bad—as they appear. Peckinpah presents Angel's village as a little paradise and their visit there helps to create a conscience in Pike Bishop and his band of outlaws. The sentimental vision of the entire Mexican village lining up to bid farewell to the Americanos (to the tune of the Mexican folk tune "La Golondrina") might be regarded as a projection of benign American imperialism. But, as it turns out, the village does not need the protection of the Bunch; they are using the Americanos to advance their revolution and are perfectly capable of careful planning and execution. This is well illustrated by their swift action when retrieving the rifles promised to them by Angel. The villagers do not ask the Bunch (as in *The Magnificent Seven*) to do their fighting for them—all they want are the tools needed. The village elder states, "In Mexico, señor, these are the years of sadness, but if we had rifles like these . . ."

A classic western, *The Wild Bunch* is unjustly remembered more for its intense slow-motion blood baths and less for its textured acting and feeling of authenticity. It is still relevant: there is a ferocity and edge to it that makes contemporary films seem timid in comparison. *The Wild Bunch* is director Sam Peckinpah's masterpiece, a story of men living beyond their time, of mixed loyalties, and of Mexico as a place of salvation and redemption. Interestingly, at the time of its original release the film's violent content and revisionist look at the Old West and its heroes generated negative critical reviews and commentary.

Three-time Oscar-nominated composer Jerry Fielding, in his score for *The Wild Bunch*, evokes the setting by integrating popular Mexican folk tunes of the nineteenth and twentieth centuries. Oscar winner William Holden was a major star for more than four decades (*Golden Boy*, 1939; *Sunset Blvd.*, 1950; *Stalag 17*, 1953; *The Bridge on the River Kwai*, 1957; *Network*, 1976; *SOB*, 1981), but although he made his fair share of westerns, he was not strongly associated with the genre when he made *The Wild Bunch*. Robert Ryan was a leading man and supporting player who rose to prominence in the post–World War II era at RKO. He had previously been in Durango for his co-starring role opposite Clark Gable in *The Tall Men* and in John Sturges's *Hour of the Gun*. Oscar-winning Best Actor Ernest Borgnine (*Marty*, 1955) worked in Mexico previously in a small supporting role in Robert Aldrich's *Vera Cruz* and later returned to Durango for the minor films *The Revengers* (a blatant ripoff of *The Wild Bunch*) that starred William Holden, and *The Devil's Rain*. Character actor Warren Oates worked previously with Peckinpah in *Ride the High Country* and *Major Dundee* and later returned to Mexico in a leading role for Peckinpah's *Bring me the Head of Alfredo Garcia* and in Jack Nicholson's *Goin' South*. Screen veteran Ben Johnson (*She Wore a Yellow Ribbon*, 1949); *Mighty Joe Young* (1949), *Wagon Master*, 1950; *Shane*, 1953; *One-Eyed Jacks*, 1961) was also a stuntman and champion rodeo rider. He won an Oscar as Best Supporting Actor for his role as Sam, who runs the last remaining movie house in town, in Peter Bogdanovich's *The Last Picture Show* (1971). Johnson returned to Mexico to co-star with John Wayne in *The Train Robbers*. Puerto Rican actor Jaime Sánchez plays Angel, the youngest member of the Bunch, and the only Mexican. Sánchez is primarily remembered today as Angel, but he had a promising film career for most of the sixties, with strong supporting roles in Sidney Lumet's *The Pawn Broker* (1964) opposite Rod Steiger, Frank Perry's *David and Lisa* (1962), and Cornel Wilde's *Beach Red* (1967). He continues to work on stage and in minor film roles.

BUTCH CASSIDY AND THE SUNDANCE KID (20TH CENTURY-FOX 1969)

Director: George Roy Hill

Screenplay: William Goldman

Producer: John Foreman

Cast: Paul Newman (Butch Cassidy), Robert Redford (Sundance Kid), Katharine Ross (Etta Place), Strother Martin (Percy Garris), Cloris Leachman (Agnes)

Story: Infamous turn-of-the-twentieth-century outlaws Butch Cassidy and the Sundance Kid rob the wrong Union Pacific railroad train and find themselves chased by a relentless posse sent by the railroad magnate. After

Paul Newman and Robert Redford as the titular characters in *Butch Cassidy and the Sundance Kid* **(1969), with Tlayaca-pan, Morelos, standing in for Bolivia.**

eluding the posse through the American Southwest, Butch and Sundance decide to go to South America to find new frontiers and avoid the long arm of the law. They head south to Bolivia—and to their destiny—as legends.

Production: The Bolivia sequences were filmed near Taxco, Guerrero, Morelos, and Cuernavaca, Mexico. The climactic gun battle was filmed in Tlayacapan, about thirty miles south of Cuernavaca. The town square was transformed into a festive marketplace where the Bolivian army makes its lethal attack. "The actual historical location where Butch and Sundance shot it out with the Bolivian Cavalry was a much more confined location than the one we actually picked," said director George Roy Hill. "You can't follow the script closely when you come to an action situation like this. You have to invent your activities to take advantage of the locations you've got. In this case, in order to give our guys some cover on their dash across the courtyard, we turned this little square into a marketplace and we put these stalls all around the sides so we could give Paul [Newman] and Bob [Redford] somewhere to go for cover."

Following the exploits of two nineteenth century bank robbers who find it increasingly difficult to stay ahead of the law, the film revitalized the western, even as it mourned its passing. The adventures of the real-life Butch and Sundance had fascinated writer William Goldman. The studio intended the two leading roles for Paul Newman and Steve McQueen, but McQueen balked at Newman's getting top billing. Director Hill then suggested Robert Redford, who was not yet a major star. Redford's onscreen chemistry with Newman was powerful. Newman, used to playing brooding loners (*Cat on a Hot Tin Roof*, 1958; *The Hustler*, 1961; *Hud*, 1963), proved he could handle comedy; Redford's easy charm and dashing good looks immediately made him a star. The film's tone—elegiac and comic, modern and traditional—confused some critics but resonated with audiences, who made it the top-grossing film of the year. It went on to win four Oscars, for Conrad Hall's burnished cinematography, Burt Bacharach's score and song "Raindrops Keep Fallin' on my Head," and Goldman's screenplay. With this box-office success, Hill moved to the top ranks of Hollywood directors. He reunited with Redford and Newman for another phenomenally successful buddy film, *The Sting* (1973), which won the Best Picture Academy Award.

THE BIG CUBE (WARNER BROS.-SEVEN ARTS, 1969)

Director: Tito Davison

Screenplay: William Douglas Lansford

Producer: Lindsley Parsons

Cast: Lana Turner (Adriana Roman), George Chakiris (Johnny Allen), Richard Egan (Frederick Lansdale), Victor Junco (Delacroix), Norma Herrera (Stella), Pedro Galvan (university dean)

Story: Soap opera–style cautionary story of an unloved, spoiled, rich girl who gets involved with drugs during the late 1960s hippie/flower child movement. A young medical student makes LSD, a hallucinatory mind-expanding drug, and shares it with his friends. The accidental death of a fellow student who takes the drugs lead to the drug maker's expulsion from school. He then plots to marry a rich girl, which leads to a murder plot.

Production: Lana Turner was a blonde beauty American actress and sex symbol of the 1940s. Known as the "sweater girl" (because of the tight, revealing sweater she wore in her screen debut, *They Won't Forget*, in 1937), she was put under contract to MGM, where she was groomed for stardom. As she grew more mature, she played powerful matriarchs in films of varying quality, from *Peyton Place* (1957) for which she received an Oscar nomination, *Imitation of Life* (1959), and *Portrait in Black* (1960). *The Big Cube* was photographed by Gabriel Figueroa from a screenplay by Mexican-American William Douglas Lansford that originated with a story by writer/director Tito Davison. In one drug-related sequence, Figueroa photographed a kaleidoscope of melting faces and skulls to indicate the LSD experience; another sequence features the appearance of a devil and an ocean transforming into sky. Wardrobe was by Oscar-winning costumer William Travilla, best known for his designs for Marilyn Monroe. George Chakiris, a Greek-American actor, had won a Best Supporting actor Oscar for his role as the tough Puerto Rican gang leader Bernardo in *West Side Story* (1961).

Richard Harris, as Morgan, and Manu Tupou, as Yellow Hand, with Mexican extras as Sioux villagers, in Elliott Silver-stein's *A Man Called Horse* **(1970), filmed in Durango.**

A MAN CALLED HORSE (NATIONAL GENERAL, 1970)

Director: Elliot Silverstein

Screenplay: Jack de Witt, based on a short story by Dorothy Jackson

Producer: Sandy Howard

Cast: Richard Harris (John Morgan), Corinna Tsopei (Running Dear), Dame Judith Anderson (Buffalo Cow Head), James Gammon (Ed), Manu Tupou (Chief Yellow Hand)

Story: While on a hunting trip to the wilderness of America in the early nineteenth century, an English lord named John Morgan is captured by Sioux Indians. Until he wins their respect, Morgan is treated like an animal. He proves himself with displays of courage and endurance and is transformed by the experience, assimilating into their culture and becoming a valued member of their tribe.

Production: Filmed in Durango, near Rio Chico and in Rancho Canoas, near Navios, by cameramen Robert

Hauser and Gabriel Torres, *A Man Called Horse* reflects the counter-culture ideals of the late sixties and early seventies. Hippies, as they called themselves, believed that established society was corrupt and sought to create a utopian world through "free love," returning to nature, and using mind-expanding drugs (the latter depicted in visually arresting hallucinatory sequences).

As was common in Hollywood at that time, the film does not feature Native Americans in leading roles. Instead, the leads include an Irishman (Richard Harris), and portraying members of the Sioux: a Greek (Corinna Tsopei), a Fijian (Manu Tupou), and a Brit (Dame Judith Anderson). Mexicans in supporting roles portray the other Native Americans. Iron Eyes Cody (who claimed to be Native American but was of Italian descent, born Espara De Corti in Guyedan, Louisiana) played a small role and served as technical advisor. The popular film spawned two sequels: *The Return of a Man Called Horse* (1976, filmed in Durango) and *Triumph of a Man Called Horse* (1983).

SOLDIER BLUE (AVCO EMBASSY, 1970)

Director: Ralph Nelson

Screenplay: John Gay, based on the novel *Arrow in the Sun* by Theodore Van Olsen

Producer: Gabriel Katzka, Harold Loeb

Cast: Candice Bergen (Cresta Marybelle Lee), Peter Strauss (Private Honus Gent), Jorge Rivero (Spotted Wolf), Donald Pleasence (Isaac Cumber), Bob Carraway (Lieutenant John Mcnair), Mort Mills (Sergeant O'Hearn), Jorge Russek (Running Fox), Marco Antonio Arzate (Kiowa Brave), Aurora Clavell (Indian woman)

Story: Setting out to meet her fiancé, Lt. John McNair, a white woman named Cresta Marybelle Lee is kidnapped by the Cheyennes. She is held captive for two years and becomes Chief Spotted Wolf's wife. After he sets her free, Cresta is traveling with Pvt. Honus Gent and a United States Cavalry unit when the group is ambushed by Cheyenne. Only she and Honus survive. They stay alive in the wilderness by relying on each other's strengths. Making their way back to Fort Reunion, they encounter Cumber, a gunrunner who has spent a lifetime on the frontier and can smell Indians and gold a hundred miles off. Cumber takes them both prisoner and plans to turn them over to the Indians. Cresta and Honus manage to escape, but Cumber seriously wounds Gent. As Cresta nurses him back to health, she falls for the young soldier. When she later discovers an army plan to attack a Cheyenne village, Cresta warns Spotted Wolf of the advancing cavalry. When the chief displays a white flag, a Custer-like Col. Iverson and his men ignore the attempts at peace and slaughter the Indians. Honus tries to stop an artilleryman during the battle and is arrested, tried, and sent to prison. Spotted Wolf is murdered, and Cresta chooses to remain with the Cheyenne.

Production: Magnificent Western landscapes duplicating the story's Colorado Territory were captured by cinematographer Robert B. Hauser in the green slopes and mountainous area called Tres Marias, near San Miguel, between Cuernavaca and Mexico City. Two separate camps were constructed: a Cheyenne village, consisting of forty-five teepees, and a cavalry encampment. The cavalry extras were members of the Mexican Army. Mexican leading man Jorge Rivero played the Cheyenne chief, Spotted Wolf, in his American film debut. Rivero's agent submitted him for the role even though it wasn't the lead, because his client wanted to break into Hollywood films . *Soldier Blue*, along with *A Man Called Horse*, could be considered revisionist westerns of the 1970s, a period which deconstructed American history and myths. *Soldier Blue* referenced

the era's women's rights movement in the strong and capable character of Cresta. There are also references to changing times and distrust in government interventions, both directly related to the ongoing war in Vietnam. The controversial, graphically violent ending in which the U.S. Cavalry brutally rapes, dismembers, and kills residents of a peaceful Cheyenne village, was the polar opposite of John Ford's romantic image. Although the film is based on an actual 1864 slaughter of Indians at Sand Creek, Colorado, many felt it alluded to the March 16, 1968 M⊠ Lai Massacre, the slaying of innocent South Vietnamese women and children by U.S. troops. *Soldier Blue* was not well received by audiences in the United States and had limited success upon its release.

CATCH-22 (PARAMOUNT, 1970)

Director: Mike Nichols

Screenplay: Buck Henry, from the novel by Joseph Heller

Producer: John Calley, Martin Ransohoff

Cast: Alan Arkin (Captain Yossarian), Martin Balsam (Colonel Cathcart), Richard Benjamin (Major Danby), Jon Voight (Minderbinder), Martin Sheen (Dobbs), Art Garfunkle (Nately), Bob Balaban (Orr)

Story: United States Army Air Force bombardier Capt. Yossarian is stationed in Italy during World War II. Having flown and survived many dangerous missions, Yossarian is trying to be declared insane so he can be grounded, permanently. The problem is that he and everyone around him are involved in the insane act of war and to recognize this insanity proves that he is really sane, an example of the bureaucratic absurdity of Catch-22.

Production: Filmed on location in Guaymas, Sonora, on the northwest coast of Mexico, with the Bahia De San Carlos doubling for the Italian Mediterranean. An airstrip runway, military base, and part of an Italian village were constructed on the location. The movie opens with the sun rising over the commanding two-horned Tetas de Cabras (Goat Tits Hill) in the Sonoran desert mountain range San Carlos, Guaymas, Sonora. The closing scene showcases San Carlos Bay and the mountains of the Sonoran desert. A small air force of still-functioning World War II bombers was used in the film. Flight scenes required complicated and time-consuming preparation to shoot takeoff and landing maneuvers.

Catch-22 was based on Joseph Heller's popular 1961 best-selling novel, which dealt with the irrationality of war in a satirical and comical manner. The film version was highly anticipated and was produced with the most formidable talents of the day. Yet, contemporary audiences rejected the film and, despite its pedigree, it has nearly been forgotten.

TWO MULES FOR SISTER SARA (UNIVERSAL PICTURES, 1970)

Director: Don Siegel

Screenplay: Albert Maltz, from a story by Budd Boetticher

Producer: Martin Rackin, Caroll Case

Cast: Clint Eastwood (Hogan), Shirley MacLaine (Sister Sara), Manolo Fabregas (Colonel Beltran), Alberto Morin, (Colonel Le Claire) Armando Silvestre (1st American), Ada Carrasco (Juan's mother), José Chavez (Horacio)

Story: In 1866 Mexico, an American mercenary working for the Juaristas against Maximillian's French forces rescues a nun from being raped by bandidos. The mercenary and the nun form an unlikely partnership, hoping to reach the Juarista forces planning to liberate a town from a French garrison. Hogan finds the nun to be strong-willed, ill-tempered, and foul-mouthed, all of which makes sense when he later discovers that she is actually a prostitute. Her familiarity with the French officers and their barracks, along with Hogan's expertise with dynamite, will help the Juaristas gain the upper hand in the assault on Maximiillian's soldiers.

Production: *Two Mules for Sister Sara* is an American production filmed in Mexico. It was based on an original story idea by Budd Boetticher. The director/writer had originally hoped to make the film with John Wayne and Mexican actress Silvia Pinal. When Boetticher had money troubles while financing a documentary on famed bullfighter Carlos Aruzza, he sold the story to Universal Studios. Universal signed then-rising star Clint Eastwood to do *Two Mules for Sister Sara* as part of a multi-picture contract. The formerly blacklisted writer Albert Maltz was hired to rewrite the script, and Universal tapped action director Donald Siegel to make the film in Mexico. The idea for a Mexican co-star was abandoned and Elizabeth Taylor was courted instead. Due to other commitments, Taylor was not available. Shirley MacLaine, who at the time was starring in a major Universal adaptation of the stage musical *Sweet Charity*, was cast as Sister Sara. Eastwood's character is essentially the same "Man with No Name" he played in Sergio Leone's Dollar trilogy that catapulted him to international stardom following his role as cowboy Rowdy Yates on TV's *Rawhide* (1959–1966). Though the Dollar films were made from 1964–1966, and were international hits in Europe, the Italian/German productions were not released in the U.S. until 1967. To further the association between this film and Leone's, the same composer, Ennio Morricone, was hired to write the score. *Two Mules for Sister Sara* marked the second collaboration of Eastwood and his mentor/director Donald Siegel. They had worked previously on *Coogan's Bluff* (1968), and later went on to make Eastwood's career-defining *Dirty Harry* (1971), among other films.

On location in Cuatla, Morelos, Gabriel Figueroa captured the landscapes and atmosphere which comprised the stunning opening title sequences. Eastwood was so pleased with the cameraman's work that he requested Figueroa for his next film, *Kelly's Heroes* (1970), which would be made in Yugoslavia for director Brian Hutton. Manolo Fábregas is excellent in the last third of the movie as the Juarista Colonel Beltran.

Clint Eastwood and Shirley MacLaine in Don Siegel's *Two Mules for Sister Sara* **(1970), filmed in Cuautla, Morelos.**

RAID ON ROMMEL (UNIVERSAL, 1971)

Director: Henry Hathaway

Screenplay: Richard Bluel

Producer: Harry Tatelman

Cast: Richard Burton (Captain Foster), John Colicos (MacKenzie), Clinton Greyn (Tarkington), Wolfgang Preiss (Rommel)

Story: Foster, a British captain, is slated to lead a commando unit through the Sahara Desert to attack German-occupied Tobruk, Libya, but a mistake strands him with a medical unit led by a Quaker. Foster must complete his mission at all costs, with only an untrained troop under his command.

Production: Filmed in San Felipe, Baja California, Mexico, standing in for the North African desert, *Raid on Rommel* utilized extensive stock footage, as well as equipment and wardrobe from Universal's big-budget production *Tobruk* (1967) starring Rock Hudson, George Peppard, and Nigel Green. The earlier film had the same major plot involving a group of commandos sent on a mission to the Libyan port city of Tobruk during World War II. *Tobruk* was filmed in Spain, Yuma, Arizona, and Universal Studios in Hollywood, and bombed at the box office. *Raid on Rommel* was supposed to recoup *Tobruk*'s losses and made considerable use of recycled footage. Burton had previously played a British officer in North Africa in the much-superior film *The Desert Rats*, which featured James Mason as Field Marshall Rommel, and was also directed by Henry Hathaway. Other movies filmed—or partially filmed—in the San Felipe area are *The Fast and the Furious* (2001), *Resident Evil 3* (2007), and *Jarhead* (2005).

LAWMAN (UNITED ARTISTS, 1971)

Director: Michael Winner

Screenplay: Gerald Wilson

Producer: Michael Winner

Cast: Burt Lancaster (Jarod Maddox), Robert Ryan (Cotton), Lee J. Cobb (Vincent Bronson), Sheree North (Laura Shelby), Joseph Wiseman (Lucas), Robert Duvall (Vernon Adams), Richard Jordan (Crowe)

Story: Marshall Jared Maddox goes after the drunken cowhands who shot up his town and killed one of the residents. He follows their trail to the nearby town of Sabbath, where the troublemakers work for a powerful rancher. Bent on arresting the cowhands and bringing them to justice, Maddox must contend with the rancher and his corrupt sheriff, resulting in a series of violent confrontations.

Production: A gritty and grim western filmed in Durango by English director Michael Winner, *Lawman* features a superb ensemble cast of veteran actors, many of whom were associated with the western genre, including Burt Lancaster, Robert Ryan, Lee J. Cobb, Robert Duvall, Sheree North, and Joseph Wiseman. Director/producer Howard Hawks wanted to shoot *Rio Lobo* in Durango, but the Western town set was

The village of Chupaderos, Durango, Mexico, was used as an Old West town set for countless Westerns, including *Lawman* (1971), with Burt Lancaster and Robert Duvall.

secured earlier by Winner for *Lawman*; Hawks was forced to shoot his film primarily at Old Tucson Studios in Arizona.

SOMETHING BIG (NATIONAL GENERAL, 1971)

Director: Andrew V. McLaglen

Screenplay: James Lee Barrett

Producer: James Lee Barrett, Andrew V. McLaglen, Harry Bernsen

Cast: Dean Martin (Joe Baker), Brian Keith (Colonel Morgan), Honor Blackman (Anna), Ben Johnson (Jesse Bookbinder), Carol White (Dover), Albert Salmi (Jonny Cobb), José Angel Espinoza (Emilio Estevez), Denver Pyle (Junior Frisbee), Enrique Lucero (Indian spy), Lupe Amador (village woman)

Story: Small-time outlaw Joe Baker wants to leave his mark by doing something big on the eve of Army Calvary Col. Morgan's retirement. He hatches a plot to steal a Gatling gun, then confronts a Mexican bandit who is sitting on a cache of buried gold, south of the border.

Production: Filmed in Durango. *Something Big* is a comedy-western that is rife with politically incorrect western stereotypes, including Mexican bandits, bandidos, and drunken Indians. Even worse, it is not funny. At the climax of the film, Dean Martin's character, outlaw Joe Baker, uses a Gatling gun to mow down an army of bandidos at their stronghold in a Mexican village. How that sequence got by the Mexican government film censors is a mystery.

THE REVENGERS (CINEMA CENTER FILMS CBS, 1971)

Director: Daniel Mann

Screenplay: Wendell Mayes, from a story by Stephen W. Carabatsos

Producer: Martin Rackin

Cast: William Holden (John Benedict), Ernest Borgnine (Hoop), Woody Strode (Job), Roger Hanin (Quiberon), Reinhard Kolldehoff (Zweig), Jorge Luke (Chamaco), Jorge Martínez de Hoyos (Cholo), Susan Hayward (Edith O'Reilly)

Story: A rancher seeks revenge when his family is killed by marauding Indians led by white comancheros. He enlists the aid of a disparate group of convicts in his mission to find and kill those responsible.

Production: This film is a blatant ripoff of story elements from *The Wild Bunch* (1969), *The Dirty Dozen* (1967), *The Wages of Fear* (1953), *The Searchers* (1956), and many other movies. *The Revengers* even goes so far as to waste the talents of *The Wild Bunch*'s William Holden and Ernest Borgnine in order to capitalize on the previous film's success. This bloody western was clearly made with the world market in mind with its international cast that featured French, German, and Mexican actors. It was Oscar-winning Best Actress (*I Want To Live*, 1958) Susan Hayward's last film appearance before she died of cancer. She had been in Mexico eighteen years earlier to work on *Garden of Evil* (1954) opposite Gary Cooper. Filmed in Durango, Parras, and Torreon, Mexico, *The Revengers* utilized many of the locations used in *The Wild Bunch*, including the sand dunes (Las Dunas de Bilbao), and the rope bridge leading to an abandoned mining town at Puente de Juela, in Durango. The river used to portray the Rio Grande and the prison set were in the same canyon arroyo where Holden's Pike Bishop has his confrontation with Lt. Herrera (Alfonso Arau) in *The Wild Bunch*. Expert camerawork of the above-mentioned locations by Gabriel Torres contributed to the rugged texture of this violent film.

BUCK AND THE PREACHER (COLUMBIA PICTURES, 1972)

Director: Sidney Poitier

Screenplay: Ernest Kinoy

Producer: Joel Glickman, Sidney Poitier, Harry Belafonte, Joel Wallerstein

Cast: Sidney Poitier (Buck), Ruby Dee (Ruth), Harry Belafonte (Preacher), Cameron Mitchell (Deshay), Enrique Lucero (Indian chief)

Story: After the Civil War, Buck, a former Union Cavalry sergeant, is hired as a scout by a group of black settlers. Among those traveling across Kansas to the new territories in Colorado are Buck's wife and a con artist preacher. A group of racist bounty hunters pursue them, determined to return the ex-slaves to a life of sharecropping in Louisiana.

Production: Filmed in Durango, Mexico; the final scene was shot in Marysville, California, *Buck and the Preacher* is the first major studio film made by an African American director. Sidney Poitier (1926–   ) took over direction of the film from the original director, Joseph Sargent, whose work proved unacceptable to the approach Poitier had in mind. Alex Phillips Jr. was the cinematographer. Black extra players were recruited from an expatriate community in Guadalajara; Cubans and Brazilians living in Mexico City were hired as well. Mexican actor Enrique Lucero plays an Indian chief sympathetic to Buck and the freed slaves' predicament, but is unwilling to risk the lives of his people to help them.

Sidney Poitier was the first African American to win the Best Actor Oscar (*Lilies of the Field*, 1963). In 1967, he starred in three major box-office and critically acclaimed films, the Oscar-winning *In the Heat of the Night*; *Guess Who's Coming to Dinner*; and *To Sir, with Love*. Poitier used his star power, the growing influence of the African American urban film audience, and the civil rights–era social climate to make this western about the African American frontier experience. He enlisted world-famous calypso recording artist, actor, and social activist Harry Belafonte to co-star as a Bible-thumping con artist. The screen chemistry between Poitier and Belafonte in this Western buddy movie is much like Newman and Redford in *Butch Cassidy and The Sundance Kid*. (They teamed again for another Poitier-directed film, *Uptown Saturday Night*, in 1974). The story is fictional, but is based on the experiences of freed slaves leaving the South and the varied obstacles they faced trying to make new lives for themselves in the West. Cameron Mitchell (1918–1994) plays the head bounty hunter, Deshay; he had previously worked in Durango when he co-starred in *The Tall Men* and *Garden of Evil* (both 1954) opposite Clark Gable. Early in his career, Poitier also co-starred with Clark Gable, in the Civil War drama *Band of Angels* (1957). Mitchell was a veteran of the stage and screen who was first signed by MGM and, later, secured a long-term contract with 20th Century-Fox. He co-starred with Marilyn Monroe, John Wayne, Doris Day, and James Cagney. He also worked for directors Elia Kazan and John Ford. Mitchell is best known for his role as Buck Cannon on *The High Chaparral*.

THE WRATH OF GOD (METRO-GOLDWYN-MAYER, 1972)

Director: Ralph Nelson

Screenplay: Ralph Nelson, based on the novel *The Wrath of God* by James Graham

Producer: Peter Katz, Ralph Nelson

Cast: Robert Mitchum (Father Oliver Van Horne), Ken Hutchinson (Emmett Keogh), Victor Buono (Jennings), Frank Langella (Tomas De La Plata), Rita Hayworth (Señora De La Plata) Enrigue Lucero (Nacho) Jorge Russek (Cordero)

Story: A gunrunning priest gets caught up with a former Irish revolutionary in a war-torn fictional Latin American country.

Production: Filmed in Guanajuato, Mexico, with interiors at Estudios Churubusco. The setting of the film is not specified, but the presence of Aymara Indians indicates Bolivia. Cinematography was by Alex Philips Jr. It was the seventh movie that Robert Mitchum filmed in Mexico, and the last major theatrical feature role for Rita Hayworth: sadly, it amounted to little more than a cameo. Hayworth and Mitchum had worked together previously in *Fire Down Below* (1957).

THE DEADLY TRACKERS (WARNER BROS., 1973)

Director: Barry Shear

Screenwriter: Lukas Heller, based on the story "Riata" by Samuel Fuller

Producer: Edward Rosen, Fouad Said, David Oliver

Cast: Richard Harris (Kilpatrick), Rod Taylor (Frank Brand), Al Lettieri (Gutierrez),William Smith (schoolboy), Neville Brand (Choo Choo), Pedro Armendáriz Jr. (Herrera), Isela Vega (Maria)

Story: A pacifist sheriff in an Old West border town has his faith tested when a group of outlaws rob the town bank and murder innocent citizens, including his wife and child. He decides to go it alone across the border into Mexico after the perpetrators.

Production: The film began production in Spain as "Riata," in October of 1972, under the direction of original writer/director Samuel Fuller, with Richard Harris as Sheriff Sean Kilpatrick, Bo Hopkins as Frank Brand, and Alfonso Arau as the Mexican lawman Gutierrez. Both Hopkins and Arau had gained attention with their roles in *The Wild Bunch*. After five weeks of filming, the production was shut down and Samuel Fuller was fired. Cinemobile Film Guarantor Fouad Said picked up the film rights and worked out a co-production deal with Mexico City's National Film Bank and Estudios Churubusco, along with Warner Bros. Lukas Heller was hired to rewrite the original script. Barry Shear, a director schooled in television with feature credits (*Wild in the Streets*, 1968; *Across 110th St.*, 1972), replaced Fuller. Harris was retained as star, but Rod Taylor replaced Hopkins, and Al Lettieri replaced Arau. *The Deadly Trackers* was shot on location in Durango, beginning in May of 1973, with interiors at Estudios Churubusco. A violent film with irredeemable characters, *The Deadly Trackers* is a distasteful hybrid of an American/Mexican western, panned by audiences and critics alike. None of the footage shot by Fuller was used in the final film, but chunks of Jerry Fielding's music score from *The Wild Bunch*, which was owned by Warner Bros., were recycled for the movie. Cinematographer Gabriel Torres shot the similarly themed western *The Revengers* (1972); he worked frequently as a director of photography for Universal Studios Television on series episodes filmed in Mexico, including *Columbo*, *McCloud*, and *The Virginian*. In Mexico, Torres also shot forty-eight episodes of the TV series *Tarzan* (1966–1968).

PAT GARRETT AND BILLY THE KID (METRO-GOLDWYN-MAYER, 1973)

Director: Sam Peckinpah

Screenplay: Rudy Wurtlitzer

Producer: Gordon Carroll

Cast: James Coburn (Pat Garrett), Kris Kristofferson (Billy the Kid), Bob Dylan (Alias), Katy Jurado (Mrs. Baker), Slim Pickens (Sheriff Baker), Barry Sullivan (Chisum), Jason Robards (Governor Lew Wallace), L. Q. Jones (Black Harris), R. G. Armstrong (Ollinger), Rita Coolidge (Maria), Emilio Fernández (Paco), Jorge Russek (Silva)

Story: Wealthy landowners and business interests hire aging lawman Pat Garerett to hunt down and kill his old friend, the outlaw—Billy the Kid.

Production: Even though Sam Peckinpah wanted originally to film in New Mexico, MGM insisted on Durango to control costs. Durango was then at the height of its popularity as an economical and scenic filming location for American westerns. *Pat Garrett and Billy the Kid* has a few memorable sequences and a good lead performance by James Coburn. An episodic film, the disconnected scenes seem to simply exist rather than move the story to its inevitable conclusion. This may be the result of the movie being taken way from Peckinpah and recut by others at the studio for release. Katy Jurado, Emilio Fernández, and Jorge Russek appear briefly.

JORY (AVCO-EMBASSY, 1973)

Director: Jorge Fons

Screenplay: Gerald Herman, Robert Irving, based on the novel by Milton R. Bass

Producer: Howard Minsky, Leopoldo Silva, Gerald Herman

Cast: Robby Benson (Jory Walden), John Marley (Roy Starr), Claudio Brook (Ethan Walden), Patricia Aspillaga (Carmelita), Carlos Cortes (Logan), Brad Dexter (Jack), Ted Markland (Corporal Evans)

Story: After Jory's father is murdered in a bar fight, the fifteen-year-old orphan joins a cattle drive. The trail boss becomes a surrogate father to the boy.

Production: This Mexican-American co-production was filmed in Durango under the direction of Jorge Fons, whose later credits include *Rojo Amanecer* (1990) and *Midaq Alley* (1995). Cinematography is by Jorje Stahl Jr.

BRING ME THE HEAD OF ALFREDO GARCIA (UNITED ARTISTS, 1974)

Director: Sam Peckinpah

Screenplay: Gordon Dawson, Sam Peckinpah, from a story by Frank Kowalski

Producer: Martin Baum

Cast: Warren Oates (Bennie), Isela Vega (Elita), Gig Young (Quill), Robert Webber (Sappensly), Emilio Fernández (El Jefe), Kris Kristofferson (Biker)

Warren Oates (holding machete) and Isela Vega in Sam Peckinpah's *Bring Me the Head of Alfredo Garcia* **(1974).**

Story: A pregnant Mexican girl is sunning herself by a river when she is seized and coerced by her landowner father to identify the man who made her pregnant. He offers a reward to anyone who can bring him the head of the man, revealed to be Alfredo Garcia. Two American henchmen find Bennie, a piano player in a Mexican dive bar, who agrees to locate Garcia. Bennie's prostitute girlfriend, Elita, informs Bennie that Garcia was a customer of hers and that he was recently killed in a car accident. Bennie is determined to find the grave, dig up the corpse, decapitate it, and present the head for the reward money. But nothing is as easy as it seems. Bennie and Elita go on the road across Mexico to find the body and are soon enmeshed in a bloody quest that turns to vengeance.

Production: Filmed in Mexico City, in the El Camino Real Hotel and the Tlaquepaque Bar in Garabaldi, *Bring Me the Head of Alfredo Garcia* is a nightmarish crime-drama about unscrupulous, deeply ambitious failures scheming to make a living in an unforgiving world. In Cholula is the site of the historic Hacienda de San Juan, which was used as El Jefe's abode. With the exception of a few key people, the entire crew was Mexican. The cinematographer was Mexico's Alex Phillips Jr. The scenario was based on a story idea given to Sam Peckinpah in 1970 by his longtime friend Frank Kowalski. Peckinpah and Kowalski worked on a twenty-page treatment and hired Walter Kelly to write the script. He wrote the first half before Peckinpah fired him. Peckinpah went to producer Martin Baum, who had a production deal with United Artists, and hired writer Gordon Dawson. James Coburn and Peter Falk turned down the finished script and then Peckinpah offered it to veteran character actor Warren Oates (1928–1982). Without reading the script, Oates accepted the role on the strength of his longtime relationship with Peckinpah. Their career association began with Oates in supporting roles in Peckinpah's *Ride the High Country*, followed by *Major Dundee* and *The Wild Bunch*. In *Alfredo Garcia*, Oates turns in a virtuoso performance, fearlessly delving into human desperation similar in quality to Bogart's Fred C. Dobbs in *The Treasure of the Sierra Madre*. Huston's film clearly influenced Peckinpah: Gig Young's character, Henchman Sapensky, is the name Dobbs gives when asked to identify himself in the bar scene. Peckinpah wrapped *Alfredo Garcia* a few days before Christmas and was allowed final cut on the film. Veteran Mexican film actor/director Emilio Fernández played El Jefe. Mexican actress Isela Vega brought a sexy, sensual but earthy quality to Elita. The film opened in August of 1974 to bad reviews, and audiences stayed way. A difficult film to watch, it contains a strange mixture of a contemporary western set against a background of gothic horror with Shakespearean touches. It is perhaps Peckinpah's most personal film and the one in which he was allowed to fully express himself without major studio interference.

ONCE UPON A SCOUNDREL (WARNER BROS., 1974)

Director: George Schaeffer

Screenplay: Alford Van Ronkel

Producer: James S. Elliott, Donald E. Leon

Cast: Zero Mostel (Carlos de Refugio), Priscilla Garcia (Alicia), A Martinez (Luis), Katy Jurado (Delfina), Leon Singer

Story: A wealthy Mexican landowner falls for a young girl who is already promised to a young man. The landowner has the young man imprisoned, but the villagers have other plans in store for the rich landowner.

Production: Filmed in Cuernavaca and at Estudios Churubusco, with cinematography by Gabriel Figueroa, this small but lushly photographed comedy stars Zero Mostel, who was blacklisted in Hollywood during the fifties, carved out a substantial Broadway theatrical career, had a film comeback in 1968 (in Mel Brooks's *The Producers*), and remained active onscreen until his death in 1977. Though an excellent actor, Mostel's portrayal (and those of the villagers) might seem quaint and stereotypical to the modern viewer. George Schaefer (1920–1997) made his multi-award-winning reputation as a television and Broadway director of classic dramas.

THE DEVIL'S RAIN (WARNER BROS., 1975)

Director: Jim Cullen, Michael Glick

Screenplay: Gabe Essoe, James Ashton, Gerald Hopman

Producer: Sandy Howard

Cast: Ernest Borgnine (Jonathan Corbis), Ida Lupino (Mrs. Preston), Eddie Albert (Dr. Sam Richards), William Shatner (Mark Preston), Keenan Wynn (Sheriff Owens), Tom Skeritt (Tom Preston), John Travolta (Danny), Claudio Brook (Preacher), Tony Cortes (first captor)

Story: Devil worshippers inhabit a small Southwestern town. Mark Preston must save his family from Corbis, an emissary of Satan, and his followers.

Production: Alex Phillips Jr. was the cinematographer, and Mario Cisneros was an assistant director on this horror movie filmed in Durango, Mexico. *The Devil's Rain* is notable for its special effects ending and for featuring future superstar John Travolta, almost unrecognizable in makeup as a devil worshipper in one of his first film roles, and for hiring Anton and Diane LeVey, founders of the Church of Satan and his wife, in acting roles alongside Hollywood cinema notables. The movie was shot from January 24 to March 24, 1975.

LUCKY LADY (20TH CENTURY-FOX, 1975)

Director: Stanley Donen

Screenplay: Wilard Hyuck, Gloria Katz

Producer: Michael Gruskoff

Cast: Burt Reynolds (Walker), Liza Minnelli (Claire), Gene Hackman (Kibby), Robby Benson (Billy)

Story: During Prohibition in the late twenties, three inept American drifters decide to smuggle booze by boat along the coast, from Mexico to Southern California.

Production: Filmed in Guaymas, doubling for Baja Mexico and San Diego Bay circa 1920s, the movie's budget escalated from $10 million to $22 million over a 250-day shooting schedule. Filming was complicated by constant script changes. More than two-thirds of *Lucky Lady* takes place on the water, which also caused numerous production delays. Full-sized, refitted period boats were utilized for water action scenes. The art department dressed parts of Guaymas to resemble a Prohibition-era town, complete with signs, furnishings, and contemporary cars. Emilio Fernández has a bit part as Ybarra, and Roger Cudney is a hotel clerk. Locals were not enamored of the predominantly American, British, and Mexican cast and crew which nearly took over their town thanks to the prolonged and disruptive shooting schedule. Guaymas had earlier hosted another lengthy big-budget, all-star production, *Catch-22*.

THE GREAT SCOUT & CATHOUSE THURSDAY (AMERICAN INTERNATIONAL PICTURES, 1976)

Director: Don Taylor

Screenplay: Richard Shapiro

Producer: Jules Buck, David Korda

Cast: Lee Marvin (Sam), Oliver Reed (Joe Knox), Strother Martin (Billy), Kay Lenz (Thursday), Robert Culp (Jack Colby), Elizabeth Ashley (Nancy Sue), Sylvia Miles (Mike)

Story: Sam and Joe Knox try to claim their share of a gold strike from a crooked politician who was once their partner. Along the way they are joined by Cathouse Thursday and an assortment of characters.

Production: This offbeat comedy-western was filmed in Durango by cinematographer Alex Phillips Jr. One of the first big-budget, all-star, mainstream productions from the usually low-budget teen-oriented American International Pictures, it was produced late in the company's history, shortly before its demise. Ana Verdugo, C. C. Charity, Luz Maria Pena, Leticia Robles, and Phaedra play prostitutes. `

SWASHBUCKLER (UNIVERSAL STUDIOS, 1976)

Director: James Goldstone

Screenplay: Jeffery Bloom, from a story by Paul Wheeler

Producer: Jennings Lang, Elliott Kastner

Cast: Robert Shaw (Ned Lynch), James Earl Jones (Nick Debrett), Genevieve Bujold (Jane Barnet), Peter Boyle (Lord Durant), Beau Bridges (Major Folly), Pepe Serna (street entertainer)

Story: A pirate and a noblewoman join forces to overthrow the evil vice-governor of Jamaica, who has imprisoned her father and mother.

Production: Although it has its moments, Universal's lavish attempt to recapture the fun and spirit of Hollywood's action-adventure genre did not draw much audience or critical enthusiasm in the mid-seventies. British actor Robert Shaw, as Ned Lynch, had the required athleticism and charisma; he was just coming into his own after important supporting roles in the Oscar-winning Best Picture *The Sting* and the phenomenal blockbuster success of *Jaws*. African American actor James Earl Jones, nominated for a Best Actor Oscar for his portrayal of Jack Johnson in *The Great White Hope* (a role he created on the Broadway stage), co-starred as buccaneer Nick Debrett. Veteran character actor Pepe Serna's film credits include *Day of the Locust* (1975), *Car Wash* (1976), *Scarface* (1983), and *Downsizing* (2017).Filmed on location in Mexico, the fortress was a sixteenth century sugar mill near Cuernavaca in Villa Hermosa, which was founded by Conquistador Hernan Cortes. Other locations include Los Arcos (the partially submerged caves along the Puerto Vallarta coast) and a restored Spanish colonial hacienda used as the governor's mansion. Additional scenes were filmed at Universal Studios. Veteran cinematographer Philip Lathrop captured the Mexican Pacific Coast locations in widescreen Panavision and Technicolor.

DOMINO PRINCIPLE (AVCO-EMBASSY, 1977)

Director: Stanley Kramer

Screenplay: Adam Kennedy, from his novel

Producer: Stanley Kramer

Cast: Gene Hackman (Roy Tucker), Candice Bergen (Elle Tucker), Mickey Rooney (Spivente), Richard Widmark (Tagge), Edward Albert (Ross Pine)

Story: Vietnam veteran Roy Tucker is serving time in prison for murder when he is approached by a representative of a secret operative organization who enlists him as an assassin for political murders in exchange for his freedom.

Production: In this inept political thriller, Puerto Vallarta doubled for the Central American country of Costa Rica. *The Domino Principle* opened to mostly negative reviews and no audience interest; it quickly disappeared from theater screens. Producer/director Stanley Kramer (1913–2001) was known for his "message films," which entertainingly dealt with American society and its problems: *High Noon* (1952, civil liberties), *The Defiant Ones* (1958, race relations), *On the Beach* (1959, nuclear war), *Inherit the Wind* (1960, religious bigotry), *Judgment at Nuremberg* (1961, the Holocaust), and *Guess Who's Coming to Dinner* (1967, interratial marriage).

SORCERER (PARAMOUNT/UNIVERSAL, 1977)

Director: William Friedkin

Screenplay: Walon Green

Producer: William Friedkin

Cast: Roy Scheider (Jackie Scanlon/"Dominguez"), Bruno Cremer (Victor Manzon/"Serrano"), Francisco Rabal (Nilo), Amidou (Kassem/"Martinez"), Ramon Bieri (Corlette)

Story: A collection of desperados flee to an impoverished South American village. Desperate for money, they sign up for a suicidal mission, driving trucks carrying nitroglycerin over two hundred miles of mountainous jungle terrain, to stop an oil well fire.

Production: *Sorcerer* is an interpretation, or a remake, of *The Wages of Fear*, H. G. Clouzot's classic 1953 French film, based on the 1952 novel by Georges Anaud. *Sorcerer* was produced with the participation of two major studios, Paramount and Universal, which shared the production costs of an estimated $17 million. It was produced and directed by William Friedkin, on the heels of his two phenomenally successful films, *The French Connection* (1971) and *The Exorcist* (1973). Walon Green (*The Wild Bunch*) wrote the screenplay. At a Directors Guild presentation in 2015, Friedkin said about *Sorcerer*, "It was the most difficult film I've ever made, in every way." Friedkin further explained that the title *Sorcerer* came from a name he observed on one of the oil trucks, and that "fate is the evil sorcerer or wizard in our lives." The movie was partly shot in the Dominican Republic at the insistence of Paramount head Charlie Bludhorn, who had financial interests there. Most of the scenes of the Nicaraguan hellhole of Porvenir were filmed in the Dominican Republic. After $1 million was spent to construct a bridge across a river for a critical scene in the movie, the rainy season ended and the the river underneath the bridge dried up. (This was long before the advent of Computer Generated Imagery, better known as CGI.) The location, therefore, was moved to Mexico. The memorable bridge sequence is an action set piece that was filmed over a three-week period at the Papaloapan River, south of Veracruz, near Tuxtepec. The river had to be dammed to keep the water level consistent, and wind and rain effects were added to the scene while filming. The Zocalo, or city center, of the port city of Veracruz was used for the opening scene in which Francisco Rabal, as a hit man, kills his intended victim. Central Mexico was also used for shots of the trucks journeying to the oil refinery. Other locations included Elizabeth (NJ), Paris, Jerusalem, and Farmington (NM). The film is visually compelling, well executed, and uniformly good, but there are no charismatic stars, nor are the deeply flawed main characters in any way heroic; they are, instead, a terrorist, a hit man, a swindler who abandons his wife, and a mobster. Roy Scheider (*Jaws*, 1975*; All That Jazz*, 1979) gives a good performance as a man descending into madness.

WHO'LL STOP THE RAIN (UNITED ARTISTS, 1978)

Director: Karel Reisz

Screenplay: Judith Rascoe, Robert Stone, based on the novel *Dog Soldiers* by Robert Stone

Producer: Herb Jaffe, Gabriel Katzka

Cast: Nick Nolte (Hicks), Tuesday Weld (Marge), Michael Moriarty (Converse), Richard Masur (Danskin), José Carlos Ruiz (Galindez), Anthony Zerbe (Anthiel), Joaquin Martinez (Angel)

Story: In 1971, Ray Hicks, a merchant seaman and U.S. Marine Vietnam veteran, is asked by his friend Converse, a journalist covering the Vietnam War, to smuggle heroin into the U.S. Hicks delivers the drug to his friend's wife Marge's bookstore in Berkeley, California, but two corrupt federal agents, hoping to steal the heroin, break in and ransack the house and attack Marge. Hicks intervenes and disables the crooked cops, then goes on the run with Marge. Fearing for their lives, Hicks and Marge hole up at a mountaintop hippie commune, where they are forced into a violent confrontation.

Production: Areas of Durango double for the New Mexico mountain commune and Vietnam in the film; other locations included Berkeley and San Francisco. Cameraman Richard H. Kline began his career in 1941 and earned Academy Award nominations for his cinematography on the lavish musical *Camelot* (1967) and the 1976 remake of *King Kong*. The assistant director was Jesus Marin.

THE CHILDREN OF SANCHEZ (LONE STAR INTERNATIONAL, 1978)

Director: Hall Bartlett

Screenplay: Cesare Zavatini, Hall Bartlett

Producer: Hall Bartlett

Cast: Anthony Quinn (Jesus Sanchez), Dolores del Rio (Paquita), Lupita Ferrer (Consuelo Sanchez), Stathis

Giallelis (Roberto Sanchez), Lucia Mendez (Marta Sanchez)

Story: Living in a Mexico City slum, Sanchez family patriarch Jesus Sanchez struggles to abide by tradition. His eldest daughter, however, decides to break with custom, adversely affecting the family's dynamics and their dreams of attaining a better life.

Production: *The Children of Sanchez* was based on the Oscar Lewis anthropological study of a Mexican family, published in 1961. Screenwriter-turned-producer Abby Mann bought the film rights in 1962 and wrote the screenplay in hopes of producing a movie starring Anthony Quinn. However, the Mexican government objected to its national image as portrayed in the book and vetoed location filming. The rights reverted to Lewis and, in 1971, producer/director Hall Bartlett secured the rights from the author. He hired screenwriter Cesare Zavatini (who had written many Italian neo-realist films for directors such as Vittorio De Sica) to write a screenplay, and sought Anthony Quinn for the role of Jesus Sanchez. Bartlett finalized a production deal in March of 1976 with the National Film Bank of Mexico and the Corporacion Nacional Cinemtographica (CONACINE), which were looking to make their mark with international co-productions. Luis Bekris was the production manager, and Jesus Marin was the assistant director. The finished film had a very limited release and met with an indifferent critical and commercial response. *The Children of Sanchez* is long, depressing, and suffers from Bartlett's pedestrian direction. Quinn's performance overpowers the rest of the impressive cast (Dolores del Rio, Katy Jurado, Lucia Mendez, Lupita Ferrer), who are also hindered by an uninspired script. Famed cameraman Gabriel Figueroa filmed *Children of Sanchez* in and around Mexico City locales, with interiors shot at Estudios Churubusco. The memorable score was by noted American jazz trumpeter Chuck Magione.

GOIN' SOUTH (PARAMOUNT, 1978)

Director: Jack Nicholson

Screenplay: John Heran Shaner, Al Ramus, Charles Shyer, Alan Mandel

Producer: Harry Gittes, Harold Schneider

Cast: Jack Nicholson (Henry Moon), Mary Steenburgen (Julia Tate), Christopher Lloyd (Towfield), John Belushi (Deputy Hector), Danny DeVito (Hog)

Story: In 1866, down in Longhorn, Texas, outlaw Henry Moon is about to be hanged when he is spared by a local ordinance allowing a single woman of property to marry a condemned man (able-bodied men are scarce in this part of the West). Julia marries Henry and puts him to work at her mine. Henry plans to escape the marriage and the mine at the first opportunity. Then Henry and Julia unexpectedly discover gold, and the mine is threatened by railroad and banking interests. Henry and Julia must learn to live together and find love.

Production: This light romantic comedy-western was filmed in Durango by Oscar-winning cinematographer Nestor Almendros (1978's *Days of Heaven*). Famed comedian John Belushi (*Saturday Night Live*) made his film debut as Mexican deputy Hector. Actress Mary Steenburgen also made her film debut here. Nicholson had previously appeared in a number of low-budget features for producer Roger Corman; he also worked as Corman's collaborator. In 1976, he won the first of his three Academy Awards as Best Actor, this one for *One Flew Over the Cuckoo's Nest* (1975). An amusing scene at the beginning of *Goin' South* is a sendup of a classic western movie cliché—the American outlaw who escapes a pursuing posse by crossing into Mexico. Once he is on the other side, Henry Moon figures he has escaped the law and taunts the posse. Unfortunately for Moon, the posse rides into Mexico, causing his horse to faint and Moon to be captured.

10 (ORION PICTURES 1979)

Director: Blake Edwards

Screenplay: Blake Edwards

Producer: Blake Edwards

Cast: Dudley Moore (George Webber) Bo Derek (Jenny Miles), Julie Andrews (Samantha)

Story: A middle-aged American composer with a troubled marriage and career obsesses over a beautiful, young bride and pursues her to the Mexican resort, where she and her husband are honeymooning.

Production: *10* was filmed at Las Hadas Hotel in Manzanillo, located in the small Mexican state of Colima on the Pacific Coast, between Puerto Vallarta and Acapulco. The memorable scene where George first spots Jenny in her swimsuit and daydreams of her running on the beach was shot at the nearby Santiago Bay beach La Audiencia. The romantic-comedy was a major box-office hit and turned Bo Derek into a sex symbol of the late seventies and early eighties. Derek's beaded cornrow hairstyle in *10*, a longtime chic coiffure among African American women, spiked a fashion trend. The film was nominated for two Academy Awards, both for composer Henry Mancini in the Best Music Original Score and Best Original Song category.

BORDER COP [ORIGINAL TITLE: THE BORDER A. K. A. BLOOD BARRIER] (HEMDALE, 1979)

Director: Christopher Leitch

Screenplay: Michael Billin

Producer: Donald Langdon

Cast: Telly Savalas (Frank Cooper), Eddie Albert (Moffat), Danny De La Paz (Benny Romero), Michael V. Gazzo (Chico Suarez), Cecilia Camacho (Leina)

Story: U. S. Border Patrol Agent Frank Cooper battles a crime boss who smuggles illegal alien labor across the border from Mexico into the United States.

Production: The exteriors for *Border Cop* were filmed in Durango, doubling for the U.S./Mexico border area. The perfunctory cinematography was by Gabriel Figueroa, in the final stretch of his legendary career. Telly

Savalas (1924–1994) had acted previously in Durango as a supporting actor in *The Scalphunters* (1968) starring Burt Lancaster who, coincidentally, was in Durango at the same time filming *Cattle Annie and Little Britches* (1981). Savalas, who had long been a character actor, became a breakout television star in his Emmy Award–winning role as Theo Kojak, the tough, charismatic, lollypop-sucking New York City police detective in *Kojak* (1973–1978). His popularity resulted in his being cast in starring roles in several modest-budgeted feature films. Danny De La Paz was a young Mexican-American actor whose credits include *Boulevard Nights* (1979), *Cuba* (1979), *and Barbarosa* (1982). Cecilia Camacho continues to work in Mexican films and telenovelas.

HERBIE GOES BANANAS (WALT DISNEY PRODUCTIONS, 1980)

Director: Vincent McEveety

Screenplay: Don Tait, based on a character created by Gordon Buford

Producer: Ron Miller

Cast: Cloris Leachman (Aunt Louise), Joaquin Garay III (Paco), Stephen Burn (Pete), Charles Martin Smith (D. J.), Harvey Korman (Captain Blythe), Richard Jaeckel (Shepard), Ruben Moreno (store owner), Alma Beltran (General's wife), Aurora coria (General's daughter)

Story: Pete and his mechanic D. J. are in Puerto Vallarta to pick up the prize-winning Volkswagen Herbie in order to compete in the Brazil Grande Premio race. They encounter a little street urchin who steals their wallets and, soon after, the wallets of three nefarious characters. The wallets get mixed up and one of the them holds the photo of the location of a lost Incan city with hidden gold. The nefarious characters try to retrieve the wallet, but Paco eludes them by hiding inside Herbie. Escapades ensue.

Production: *Herbie Goes Bananas* is the fourth and final theatrical feature film in the popular franchise that included *The Love Bug* (1969), *Herbie Rides Again* (1974), and *Herbie Goes to Monte Carlo* (1977). The central character of Herbie, the magical Volkswagen Bug, endeared itself to family audiences, making box-office gold for the Walt Disney Studios. *Herbie Goes Bananas* was filmed in Puerto Vallarta, Guadalajara, Tijuana, and Baja California Norte. Anuar Badin was the unit production manager in Mexico, and Mario Cisneros was second-unit director. A comic highlight is a sequence where Herbie is cornered in a bullring and has to fight a bull on his way out.

CABO BLANCO (AVCO- EMBASSY, 1980)

Director: J. Lee Thompson

Screenplay: Mort Fine, Milton Gelman

Producer: Lance Hool, Paul A. Joseph, Alan Conrad Hool

Cast: Charles Bronson (Giff Hoyt), Dominique Sanda (Marie Claire), Jason Robards (Beckdorff), Fernando Rey (Police Captain Torredo), Simon MacCorkindale (Lewis Clarkson), Gilbert Roland (Dr. Rudolfo Ramirez)

Story: Intrigue involves an American bar owner who helps a woman find a missing fortune amid former

Nazis in a post–World War II South American port town.

Production: Based on the actual sinking of a Nazi ship off the coast of Argentina during World War II; the ship, bound for South America, was laden with stolen European art treasures. *Cabo Blanco* was one of the first attempts at international filmmaking by the Mexico City–based producers Lance and Conrad Hool. Charles Bronson plays the central character, Giff Hoyt, an enigmatic man seeking solace from the outside world. Bronson's tough-guy presence fueled his rise from supporting actor in major film productions such as *The Magnificent Seven*, *The Great Escape*, and *The Dirty Dozen* to leading roles in European hits, including *Rider on the Rain* (1970); he achieved huge U.S. box-office success with his starring role in *Death Wish* (1974). British director J. Lee Thompson (*Guns of Navarone*, 1961) was contracted to direct, and Fernando Rey, a veteran of over a hundred Spanish Films, and two-time Academy Award winner Jason Robards joined the cast along with British actor Simon MacCorkingdale, screen veteran Camila Sparv, and French actress Dominique Sanda. Filming began in January 1979 with a combined Mexican, English, and American cast and crew. The director of photography was Alex Phillips Jr. Future Oscar-winning cinematographer Guillermo Navarro (*Pan's Labyrinth*) was a production assistant. Though set in Cabo Blanco, Peru, the movie was filmed on the central west coast of Mexico, in Barra de Navidad, Jalisco, a tiny fishing village with a blue-green bay and lagoon that has since seen extensive tourism development.

When it was released in the U.S. in 1981, *Cabo Blanco* was unfavorably viewed as a poor imitation of the Humphrey Bogart classic *Casablanca* (1942).

CATTLE ANNIE AND LITTLE BRITCHES (UNIVERSAL, 1981)

Director: Lamont Johnson

Screenplay: David Eyre and Robert Ward, based on the novel by Robert Ward

Producer: Rupert Hitzing, Alan King

Cast: Amanda Plummer (Annie), Diane Lane (Jenny), Burt Lancaster (Bill Doolan), Rod Steiger (Sheriff Tilghman), John Savage (Newcomb), Scott Glenn (Bill Dalton), Roger Cudney (Capps), Mike Moroff (Deputy), Buck Taylor (Dynamite Dick)

Story: Two teenage orphan girls travel west, from Oklahoma, to find and join the real-life outlaws of the popular dime novels of the late 19th century. When they finally meet their idols, they find them past their prime and doggedly pursued by a determined sheriff. Realizing by the girls' disappointment that their outlaw days are all but over, they plan one last big heist. Nothing goes as planned until the girls concoct a jail break.

Production: *Cattle Annie and Little Britches* was filmed in Durango in 1979, but was not released theatrically until 1981, when it played briefly in New York City and in the American Southwest, performing minimally at the box office. Mario Cisneros served as assistant director; the color cinematography was by British cameraman David Pizer. Locations included Calle Howard, a complete Old West town set, Chupaderos, Canyon

Delgado, Los Organos State park in Zacatecas, the dry lake bed of Miguel Hidalgo, the wooded region of Vista Diablo, and the El Saltito waterfalls.

Over the years, this little-seen film has gained something of a cult status due to its feminist twist, its memorable performances by both newcomers (twenty-three-year-old Amanda Plummer and fifteen-year-old Diane Lane) and veterans (Rod Steiger and Burt Lancaster), and its light tone and direction by Lamont Johnson. This was the fifth Mexican location film for Burt Lancaster (1913–1994), who would go on to make a final film in the country, *The Little Treasure* (1985). Rod Steiger (1925–2002), a New York Method actor and member of the Actors Studio, won an Academy Award as Best Actor for his convincing portrayal of the bigoted, Southern small-town sheriff of *In The Heat of The Night* (1967). He had previously been nominated for his roles in *The Pawnbroker* (1964) and in *On The Waterfront* (1954). John Savage would go on to receive acclaim for his performance in Michael Cimino's Oscar-winning Best Picture *The Deer Hunter* (1979).

CAVEMAN (UNITED ARTISTS, 1981)

Director: Carl Gottlieb

Screenplay: Rudy de Luca, Carl Gottlieb

Producer: David Foster, Larry Turman

Cast: Ringo Starr (Atouk), Dennis Quaid (Lar), Barbara Bach (Lana), Shelley Long (Tala), Miguel Angel Fuentes (Grot)

Story: Atouk, smallest and weakest of his caveman tribe, has been kicked out of the cave by the boyfriend of his heart's desire, Lana. Forced to wander in the wilderness, he meets an assortment of characters and becomes their leader. Atouk returns to his cave, wins Lana's love, and regains a place in the cave society.

Production: Filmed in Durango, Puerto Vallarta, and at Estudios Churubusco. All of the cave dwellers, both featured players and extras, were Mexican. Alan Hume, the English director of photography, has extensive credits, including *For Your Eyes Only* (1981), *Star Wars VI: Return of the Jedi* (1983), and *Octopussy* (1983).

Ringo Starr, of course, was the drummer for the legendary rock group The Beatles. He first ventured into movies with the Beatles films *A Hard Day's Night* (1964) and *Help!* (1965). He made his solo film debut with the brilliant English actor/comedian Peter Sellers in *The Magic Christian* (1969). While on location during the making of *Caveman*, as told to the author by a hotel manager, Ringo walked into a music store across the street from his hotel in Durango and began to bang away on a set of drums. The owner, not recognizing the former Beatle, asked him to refrain from playing the drums unless he planned on buying them. As Ringo was leaving the store, the owner remarked that he "should really buy the drum set because he is a lousy drummer and needs lessons and practice." *Caveman* has a hilarious scene in which a T-Rex has a drug-induced stupor after eating hallucinatory berries. The cheesy special effects make the dinosaurs more cartoon-like than realistic. Since FX technology at the time was capable of much more, this was likely done intentionally, for comedic effect. Never mind that, historically, man and dinosaurs did not exist at the same time, forget that the film features a Beatle as a silly leading man, guys in the audience could still enjoy watching women in skimpy outfits, especially actress/model Barbara Bach (*The Spy Who Loved Me*, 1977; *Force 10 From Navarone*, 1978). She and co-star Ringo Starr met on the Durango location of *Caveman* in February of 1980. They fell in love and were married in April of 1981. Ringo and Barbara are still married as of this writing. In December 2017, Ringo Starr was knighted by Queen Elizabeth.

HIGH RISK (AMERICAN CINEMA, 1981)

Director: Stewart Raffill

Screenplay: Stewart Raffill

Producer: Anuar Badin , Luigi Cingolani, Gerald Green, John Daly

Cast: James Brolin (Stone), Chick Vennera (Tony), Bruce Davison (Dan), Anthony Quinn (Mariano), James Coburn (Serrano), Cleavon Little (Rockney), Eduardo Noriega (General), Lindsay Wagner (Olivia)

Story: A group of American working-class friends use a weekend fishing trip as a guise to fly to Colombia, South America, to pull a heist on an American-born drug lord. After they steal $5 million they must make their way out of the jungle while evading the pursuing army and local bandits.

Production: *High Risk* is an entertaining action-adventure, funny and tongue-in-cheek, with a top-notch cast of veteran Oscar winners (Anthony Quinn, Ernest Borgnine, and James Coburn) and young performers (James Brolin, Cleavon Little, Bruce Davison, and Chick Vennera). The British/Mexican/American co-production was shot in Mexico by cinematographer Alex Phillips Jr. It had a limited U.S. release by a small distribution company called American Cinema and was overlooked in the wake of higher profile major studio efforts. Similar in style and tone to *Romancing the Stone* (1984), it presents a "What could go wrong?" situation which parallels a situation most effectively used in John Boorman's *Deliverance* (1972). Stewart Raffill (*The Philadelphia Experiment*, 1984; *The Adventures of the Wilderness Family*, 1975), who directed and wrote *High Risk*, says in the film's press notes, "There's a lot of fun and light moments in *High Risk*. . . . There's humor but the bullets and the dangers are real. Our heroes are not really competent enough to do what they do. They are working-class guys who gamble their all on a chance of making it rich. They are simply doing what we all would like to do, have an adventure that would make our dreams a reality."

ZORRO, THE GAY BLADE (20TH CENTURY-FOX, 1981)

Director: Peter Medak

Screenplay: Hal Dresner, based on a character created by Johnston M. McCulley

Producer: George Hamilton, C. O. Erickson

Cast: George Hamilton (Don Diego Vega/Bunny Wigglesworth), Ron Leibman (Estefam), Brenda Vaccaro

(Florinda), Paco (Donovan Scott), Lauren Hutton (Charlotte Taylor Wilson), Eduardo Noriega (Don Francisco), Jorge Russek (Don Fernando)

Story: The dashing caballero Don Diego De La Vega is actually the heroic Zorro, defender of the people of Old California. When he breaks his leg, he must relinquish his role. His weak-willed, effeminate twin brother Ramon, now known as Bunny Wigglesworth, ably takes up the banner of fighting injustice—with some outrageous variations.

Production: Filmed at Estudios Churubusco in Mexico City, and in Cuernavaca, Morelos.

Cinematography is by Oscar-nominated Dallas, Texas-born John A. Alonzo (*Chinatown*, 1974). Early in his career, before turning to camera work; Alonzo came to Mexico as an actor/stuntman in the 1960 western classic *The Magnificent Seven*, playing one of Calvera's gang of outlaws.

George Hamilton, a young MGM leading man of the early sixties, revived his failing career in 1979 with a hit comedy, *Love at First Bite*, in which he spoofed Count Dracula. Hamilton's charming, tongue-in-cheek portrayal of the King of Vampires found favor with critics and audiences alike. He hoped to achieve the same level of success with *Zorro, The Gay Blade*. Most of the comedy stemmed from the homosexual Bunny Wigglesworth character and the spoofing of the swashbuckling—or, in this case "Swishbuckling"—film genre. Hamilton received independent film financing from Melvin Simon, a multi-millionaire real estate developer who promoted the then-new concept of shopping malls across America.

MISSING (UNIVERSAL, 1982)

Director: Costa-Gavras

Screenplay: Costa-Gavras, Donald E. Stewart, from a book by Thomas Hauser

Producer: Edward Lewis, Sean Daniel

Cast: Jack Lemmon (Ed Horman), Sissy Spacek (Beth), John Shea (Charles Horman)

Story: While in the resort town of Vina del Mar, American journalist and activist Charlie Horman seems to have found out a little too much about American involvement in the political coup in Chile. His inquisitiveness and a journal put him at odds with the new Chilean regime, with

Costa Gavras directs a scene on location in Mexico City doubling for Chile for the film *Missing*.

176

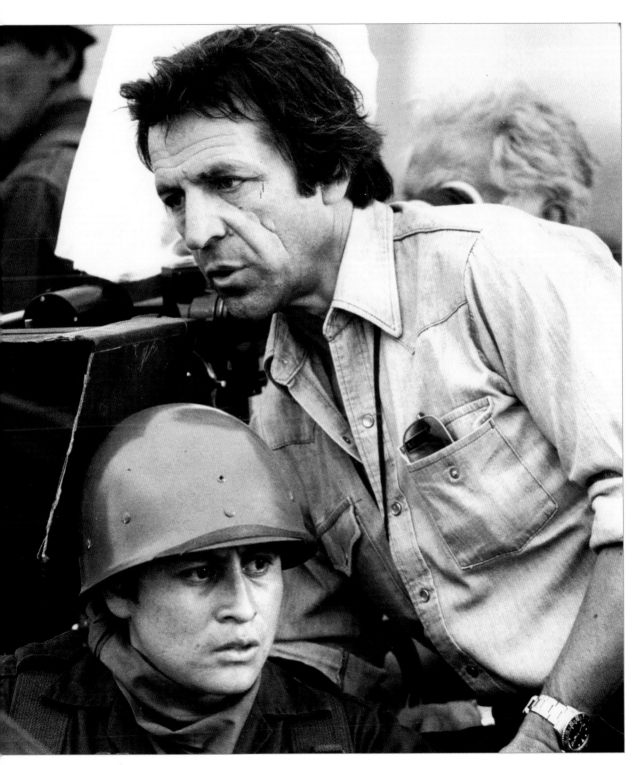

their repressive and brutal tactics of subjugation. Soldiers and police arrest Charlie at home while his wife, Beth, spends a nightmarish night evading soldiers, arrest, and possible death under government-imposed martial law. Upon reaching home, she finds Charlie missing and the place ransacked. Neighbors tell Beth her husband was taken away by military police. When neither Chilean nor American officials will give her answers, she reluctantly asks for help from Ed, Charlie's conservative father, who travels to Chile to find out what has happened to his son. At odds with his daughter-in-law over their political differences, the politically naïve Ed slowly recognizes and unravels the truth about the unspoken conspiracy between the United States and Chile's repressive dictatorship, which led to the murder of thousands of innocent Chilean civilians—and his son.

Production: The controversial film was critical of the United States government's role in the Chilean coup of Augustine Pinochet in 1973. Filmed in Mexico City, doubling for Chile, *Missing* was inspired by the disappearance of American activist and journalist Charles Horman, who was found dead after the coup in Chile. Costa-Gavras is a Greek/French filmmaker best known for political thrillers such as *Z* (1969), which won him the Best Foreign Language Oscar in 1970; this was followed by *State of Siege* in 1973. *Missing* was Costa-Gavras's first English-language film with American stars, including the versatile Jack Lemmon and Sissy Spacek. Because audiences identified with Lemmon's screen personification of the average American, his search for his missing son became personal and emotionally packed. *Missing* won an Academy Award for Best Adapted Screenplay; it also received nominations for Best Picture, Best Actor, and Best Actress. Harry Kopoian was the local industry contact and played a bit role; Emily Gamboa was the production office coordinator; and Anna Roth is credited as a second-unit assistant director.

UNDER FIRE (ORION, 1983)

Director: Roger Spottiswoode

Screenplay: Ron Shelton, Clayton Frohman

Producer: Jonathan T. Taplin

Cast: Nick Nolte (Russell Price), Gene Hackman (Alex Crizie), Joanna Cassidy (Claire), Ed Harris (Oates), Alma Martinez (Isela)

Story: Set in Nicaragua, Central America, in 1979. After decades under unpopular dictators, civil war has broken out against President Somoza. Russell Price is a leading photojournalist, whose pictures have been featured on the cover of *Time* magazine, among others. At first, Price is determined to stay neutral; as he says, "I don't take sides, I take pictures." But soon, events around him demand a greater commitment from him and his reporter friends Claire and Alex, who are involved in a love triangle. Alex sees this assignment as a stepping-stone for a network news anchor. Price is manipulated into a situation he cannot control.

Production: This political drama was made four years after the Nicaraguan Revolution, during which the

Gene Hackman, Nick Nolte, and Alma Martinez in a scene from *Under Fire* (2016), with Mexico doubling for Nicaragua.

Sandanista National Liberation Front (named for Augusto Sandino, a freedom fighter in 1930 who resisted the U.S. occupation of his country) deposed Anastasio Somoza's government. By 1983, the time of the film's release, the Sandanista government had become the enemy of American interests in the country. *Under Fire* was filmed in Chiapas and Oaxaca, Mexico, convincingly doubling for Nicaragua. Director Roger Spottiswoode turned a town into a most believable Nicarauguan war zone where bodies lie dead in the street. Alma Martinez plays Isela Cruz, a rebel leader who is also a translator for the American journalists. Rene Enriguez plays Somoza, and Jenny Gago plays Miss Panama, with Eloy Phil Casados as Pedro, Enrique Lucero as a prison priest, and Jorge Zepeda as Rafael, the rebel leader. Anna Roth, from Mexico, was associate producer, and Edward Teets was executive producer as well as unit production manager. Roger Spottiswoode had worked as an editor previously for Sam Peckinpah before turning to directing. *Under Fire* was photographed by famed Stanley Kubrick cameraman John Alcott, whose credits include *2001: A Space Odyssey* (1968), *A Clockwork Orange* (1971), and *The Shining* (1980) and who won an Academy Award for his work on *Barry Lyndon* (1975).

BEYOND THE LIMIT/A.K.A. THE HONORARY CONSUL (PARAMOUNT, 1983)

Director: John Mackenzie

Screenplay: Christopher Hampton

Producer: Norma Heymas

Cast: Michael Caine (Charlie Fortner), Richard Gere (Dr. Eduard Plarr), Bob Hoskins (Colonel Perez), Joaquim De Almeida (Leon), Elpidia Carrillo (Clara), A Martinez (Aquino), Jorge Russek (Señor Escobar), Erica Carlsen (Señora Escobar)

Story: A young, half-British/half-Paraguayan doctor returns to Argentina and beds his former lover, who is now the wife of the alcoholic British consul. The doctor aids some rebels in the hopes of having his father, a political prisoner, freed; meanwhile, he uses his friendship with the consul to pry vital information from him. The rebel plans go awry, and his betrayal of the consul's friendship puts everyone's lives at risk.

Production: Based on the 1973 novel *The Honorary Consul* by Graham Greene (*The Fugitive*), Michael Caine turns in a superlative performance as the boozing has-been British consul, reminiscent of *Under The Volcano*'s British Consul Fermin. Richard Gere plays the idealistic doctor, and the alluring Elpidia Carrillo turns in a strong performance as the native woman. Filmed in Coatzacoalcos, Veracruz, Mexico City, and Distrito Federal, Mexico, and at Shepperton Studios, England. *New York Times*' Vincent Canby stated in his September 30, 1983, review: "The best thing about 'Beyond the Limit' is the physical production, the movie locations; it was shot on or near Mexico's Gulf Coast [and] looks absolutely Argentine."

EL NORTE (ISLAND ALIVE, 1983)

Director: Gregory Nava

Screenplay: Gregory Nava, Anna Thomas

Producer: Anna Thomas

Cast: Zaide Silvia Gutierrez (Rosa), David Villapando (Enrique), Ernesto Gomez Cruz (Arturo), Lupe Ontiveros (Nacha), Enrique Castillo (Jorge), Tony Plana (Carlos), Mike Gomez (Jaime)

Story: After their village is destroyed, a Guatemalan brother and sister escape the violence of their homeland. Their grueling journey takes them through Mexico to the United States, where they hope to become undocumented workers in Los Angeles.

Production: A simple, yet emotionally evocative, independent film, *El Norte* was financed by PBS's *American Playhouse* and a British production entity. The movie was partly filmed in Chiapas, Mexico's southernmost state, which borders Guatemala, Morelos, and Mexico City D. F. (Distrito Federal) doubling for Guatemala. Other locations include the border city of Tijuana, San Diego, and Los Angeles. James Glennon was the cinematographer. Gregory Nava and Anna Thomas were nominated for an Academy Award for Best Original

Screenplay in 1984, the first independent film to be so honored. Nava and Thomas were also nominated for Best Screenplay Written Directly for the Screen, by the Writers Guild of America (WGA). Nava won the Grand Prix de Ameriques at the Montreal World Film Festival (1984) and is well known for his work on the multiple-award-winning movies *My Family/Mi Familia* (1995), *Selena* (1997), and *Frida* (2002).

UNDER THE VOLCANO (UNIVERSAL, 1984)

Director: John Huston

Screenplay: Guy Gallo, from the novel by Malcolm Lowery

Producer: Michael Fitzgerald

Cast: Albert Finney (Geoffrey Firmin). Jaqueline Bissett (Yvonne), Ignacio Lopez Tarso (Dr. Virgil), Emilio Fernández (Diosdado)

Story: Alcoholic ex-British consul drinks himself senseless. Set against the backdrop of the Day of the Dead festival in Mexico in 1938 on the eve of World War II.

Production: Filmed in Cuernavaca, Mexico, in the town of Yautepec. Icons of the Mexican film industry worked on the film with Huston, including cinematographer Gabriel Figueroa, production designer Gunther Gerzo, actor/director Emilio "El Indio" Fernández, and actress Katy Jurado. Albert Finney was nominated for an Academy Award for his performance. In *"Under The Volcano*: Before the Stillness," an essay for the Criterion Collection, Christian Vivani writes: "These two films [*The Night of the Iguana* and *Under the Volcano*] together with *The Treasure of the Sierra Madre* constitutes a Mexican trilogy for Huston. All concern characters in exile searching for a new beginning. Here at the border with the United States, Mexico offers the fantasy of an imaginary geography where Hustonian 'misfits' wander between adventure (*Sierra Madre*) and sex (*Night of the Iguana*), before accepting death (*Under the Volcano*)."

DUNE (UNIVERSAL, 1984)

Director: David Lynch

Screenplay: David Lynch, based on the novel by Frank Herbert

Producer: Raffaella DeLaurentiis

Cast: Kyle Maclachlan (Paul Atreides), José Ferrer (Padishah, Emperor Shaddam IV), Max Von Sydow (Dr. Kynes), Linda Hunt (Shadout Mapes), Sting (Feyd Rautha), Patrick Stewart (Gurney)

Story: An intergalactic warrior is seen as a messia able to save the harsh desert planet Arrakis (also known as Dune) and the universe from evil forces. Giant worms and an underground human population inhabit the planet, which is the only source for "Spice," a mind-expanding substance which allows for astral projection.

Production: Principal photography began in Mexico City in March 1983. Prior to that, *Dune* had been in preproduction in Mexico for six months. The size and scope of the huge production necessitated that director David

Lynch and producer Rafaela DeLaurentiis spend almost a year and a half in Mexico working on the production. Filming took place at the sound stages of Estudios Churubusco, where Dune's enormous sets occupied the entire studio. Other locations included the Tlaxcala desert, Las Aguilas, and the Samalayuca Dune Fields. Estadio Azteca was used as a landing field in the movie. As a result of the Volcano Iztaccíhuatl's eruption, five thousand years ago, Las Aguilas is a lava bed which houses a present-day trash dump. It became one of the locations for the arid, dusty Arrakis. For weeks prior to filming, a cleanup crew combed the site, removing the debris of generations, sterilizing it, and, finally, sifting for broken glass. The lava dust rose in small puffs as technicians and actors walked through the location. Dyed Fuller's earth was added to enhance the scorched appearance. Over a two-week period, temperatures in the Samalayuca Dune Fields rose to 120 degrees, creating an arduous filming environment. At one point, four different film units worked simultaneously to complete the bloated production, which cost an estimated $40 million to make. It bombed at the box office.

John Huston (*center*) and the principal cast of *Under the Volcano* (1984) in Cuernavaca, Mexico.

Star Arnold Schwarzenegger and director Richard Fleischer at the Nevada de Toluca location of *Conan the Destroyer* **(1984).**

CONAN: THE DESTROYER (UNIVERSAL, 1984)

Director: Richard Fleischer

Screenplay: Stanley Mann, based on the Conan stories by Robert E. Howard

Producer: Raffaella DeLaurentiis, Dino De Laurentiis

Cast: Arnold Schwarzenegger (Conan), Grace Jones (Zula), Wilt Chamberlain (Bombatta), Olivia d'Abo (Princess Jennha), Mako (Akiro)

Story: Conan and his companions aid the niece of a treacherous queen on a perilous journey to find a magic gemstone and solve the mystery of an ancient race. In exchange, the queen pledges that she will bring Conan's true love, Valeria, back from the dead.

Production: *Conan the Destroyer* is the sequel to the sword-and-sorcery film *Conan the Barbarian*, which was filmed in Spain and written and directed by John Milius, from the Robert E. Howard novels. *Conan the Barbarian* helped launch the career of bodybuilder-turned-action-star Arnold Schwarzenegger, who reprised his role for the sequel. *Conan the Destroyer* was directed by Richard Fleischer (*20,000 Leagues Under the Sea*, 1954; *The Vikings*, 1958), and stunningly filmed by legendary Oscar-winning British cinematographer Jack Cardiff (*The Red Shoes*, 1948) at Estudios Churubusco, with locations at Pachuca, the extinct volcano at the Nevada de Toluca, and the desert near Ciudad Juarez. A devaluation of the Mexican peso allowed De Laurentiis to produce two movies for the price of one, so *Conan the Destroyer* was filmed with the extra crew and locations being used simultaneously on *Dune*. American basketball star Wilt Chamberlin plays Bombaata, eunich offi-

Kathleen Turner and Michael Douglas in *Romancing the Stone* **(1984).**

cer of the queen's guard. To accommodate his six-foot-seven-inch frame, a special bed had to be constructed for the Mexico City hotel where he stayed during filming.

ROMANCING THE STONE (20TH CENTURY-FOX, 1984)

Director: Robert Zemeckis
Screenplay: Diane R. Thomas
Producer: Michael Douglas
Cast: Michael Douglas (Jack Holt), Kathleen Turner (Joan Wilder), Danny de Vito (Ralph), Manuel Ojeda (Zolo), Zack Norman (Ira), Alfonso Arau (Juan)
Story: Celebrated romance novelist Joan Wilder lives in a fantasy world, but when her sister is kidnapped in Colombia, South America, and the only way to save her is to take a treasure map to her captors, reality becomes stranger than fiction. Arriving at the airport, Wilder is misguided from her destination of the seaside city of Cartagena and thrown into a jungle full of gunfire, mudslides, and poisonous snakes. Her only hope lies with Jack Colton, a rugged wanderer straight out of her novels. Together, they will have to outwit the bandits and survive the jungle if they are to save her sister and find the secret to "El Corazon."
Production: Though set in Colombia, the film was shot in Durango, Chihuahua, Oaxaca, Jalapa, Veracruz, and the port city of Vera Cruz, the latter of which include the fortress of San Juan Ulloa. In Durango, stuntman Terry Leonard doubled for actor Michael Douglas in an incredible dive from a car as it went over

the eighty-foot El Saltito waterfall. *Romancing the Stone* was a big hit with critics and audiences alike. It was a combination Harlequin Romance and action-adventure film, in which he heroine is at the center of the story. The chemistry between Kathleen Turner and Michael Douglas was undeniable and helped to establish Douglas as a leading man. Danny de Vito and Alfonso Arau ably assist them in comic roles. Michael Douglas also served as producer. Director Robert Zemeckis went on to tremendous success with *Back to the Future* (1985) and *Who Framed Roger Rabbit* (1988), among others. *Romancing the Stone* spawned a sequel in 1986 called *Jewel of the Nile*, which was also successful; that film took place in the Middle Eastern deserts.

"I like the idea of shooting something like it in the jungle down in Mexico," said Michael Douglas in an electronic Press Kit Interview. "You form a bond on pictures like that in a foreign country that doesn't exist in a normal kind of film when you go home at night or go to your hotel room."

AGAINST ALL ODDS (COLUMBIA PICTURES, 1984)

Director: Taylor Hackford

Screenplay: Eric Hughes, Daniel Mainwaring

Producer: William S. Gilmore, Taylor Hackford

Cast: Jeff Bridges (Terry Brogan), Rachel Ward (Jessie Wyler), James Woods (Jake Wise), Richard Widmark (Ben Caxton), Jane Greer (Mrs. Wyler), Alex Karras (Hank Sully)

Story: A man with criminal ties hires an aging American football star to find his girlfriend who has run away to Mexico. The football player locates her and proceeds to falls in love with her. The resulting complications lead to murder and deceit.

Production: *Against All Odds* is a remake of the 1947 noir thriller *Out of the Past*, which starred Robert Mitchum, Jane Greer, and Kirk Douglas. Jane Greer makes an appearance in *Against All Odds* playing Mrs. Wyler. Though some of the action takes place in Mexico in the original film, most of the location work was done at the RKO backlot in Hollywood. In the original, Mitchum finds the gangster's girlfriend, who passionately assures him that she never stole forty-thousand dollars from the gangster, never ever. Mitchum replies, "Baby, I don't care," and kisses her. The remake couldn't have the inimitable Mitchum, but it does have Mexican locations: the Mayan Temples of Tulum perched on a rocky cliff overlooking a spectacular Caribbean beach, Islas Mujeres, and the Mayan ruins of Chichen Itza in the Yucatan. *Against All Odds* was producer/director Taylor Hackford's first film following his hit *An Officer and a Gentleman* in 1982. Hackford steered clear of Latino stereotypes but also avoided having any major Mexican characters in the movie. The Mexican locations serve simply as a backdrop, and the American characters have little interaction with the Mexican populace. A murder sequence, which takes place inside the temple ruins at Tulum, was expressly forbidden by the Mexican government censors. The interior of the temple, therefore, was constructed on a sound stage at Columbia studios, temporarily housed at the Warner Bros. lot in Burbank. It is ironic since the ancient temple was the scene of so much bloodletting in its time, but the Mexican government was more concerned about the environmental damage a film company might inflict on the ancient interior than the murder sequence itself.

THE EVIL THAT MEN DO (TRI-STAR/ITC, 1984)

Director: J. Lee Thompson

Screenplay: John Crowther, David Lee Henry

Jeff Bridges and Rachel Ward face danger at the Chichen Itza ruins in Taylor Hackford's *Against All Odds* (1984).

Producer: Pancho Kohner, Lance Hool
Cast: Charles Bronson (Holland), Theresa Saldana (Rhiana), José Ferrer (Lomelin), Rene Enriquez (Max Ortiz), Ernesto Gomez Cruz (café owner)
Story: Former assassin Holland travels to a Central American country in order to kill Nazi war criminal Clement Molloch, who had tortured and killed Holland's friend, dissident journalist Jorje Hidalgo.
Production: *The Evil That Men Do* was filmed in Mexico over six weeks, from mid-March to May of 1983, on locations in Puerto Vallarta and Guadalajara. The film's co-producer Lance Hool was born in Mexico City and worked his way up through the Mexican film industry. He has numerous U.S. box-office hits to his credit; in 2000, he was nominated for the NCLR Alma Award as Outstanding Director for *One Man's Hero* (1999). J. Lee Thompson was nearly seventy when he made *The Evil That Men Do*; it was his forty-first film and his fifth with Bronson. Thompson is best known for his direction of *The Guns of Navarone* (1961) and the original *Cape Fear* (1962) with Gregory Peck and Robert Mitchum.

MISSING IN ACTION 2 (CANNON FILMS, 1985)
Director: Lance Hool
Screenplay: Steve Bing, Larry Levinson, Arthur Silver

Producer: Yoram Globus, Menahem Golan

Cast: Chuck Norris (Colonel James Braddock), Soon Tek Oh (Colonel Yin)

Story: Suffering, forgotten American prisoners of war in Vietnam are led to escape and freedom by Col. Braddock.

Production: Directed by Mexican-born Lance Hool and filmed on location in Jalapa Veracruz and St. Kitts doubling for the jungles of South East Asia. *Missing in Action 2* stars martial arts champion Chuck Norris. This prequel to *Missing in Action* (1984) was one of numerous worldwide box-office hits for the American Norris, who became an international action film star to rival Stallone, Bronson, and Eastwood in the late seventies and eighties.

LITTLE TREASURE (TRISTAR, 1985)

Director: Alan Sharp

Screenplay: Alan Sharp

Producer: Herb Jaffe

Cast: Burt Lancaster (Delbert), Margot Kidder (Margo), Ted Danson (Eugene), Enrique Lucero (priest).

Story: A prostitute arrives in a little town in Mexico to visit her ailing father. He soon dies, but not before telling her of a stolen treasure buried years earlier.

Production: Filmed in Durango by cinematographer Alex Phillips Jr.; Ramiro Jaloma was the first assistant director; José Luis Ortega was the second assistant.

REMO WILLIAMS: THE ADVENTURE BEGINS (ORION, 1985)

Director: Guy Hamilton

Screenplay: Christopher Wood, based on The Destroyer book series by Warren Murphy and Richard Sapir

Producer: Larry Spiegel, Judy Goldstein

Cast: Fred Ward (Remo), Joel Grey (Master Chiun), Wilford Brimley (Smith), J. A. Preston (MacCleary), Kate Mulgrew (Major Fleming), Patrick Kilpatrick (Stone)

Story: Remo, a New York City police officer, near death, is saved and given a new face through plastic surgery. He is recruited by a secret United States government agency as an assassin under the tutelage of the Korean Master Chiun. After training, Remo is sent on a mission to terminate a millionaire arms dealer with ties to the United States government.

Production: A duplicate of the top half of the Statue of Liberty was constructed on a hillside on the outskirts of Mexico City, where close-up shots would match scenes filmed on location in New York Harbor. When local Mexican residents found similarities between Lady Liberty and the Mexican religious icon the Virgin of Guadalupe, the hillside set became the object of local worshippers. Newly formed Orion Pictures hoped that *Remo* would become a hit franchise, but the film met with a poor reception. In a way, *Remo Williams: The Adventure Begins* was a few years ahead of its time. Based on a series of cult novels—a precursor to graphic novels—it is best considered alongside the post-millennial rash of comic book films such as *Spider-Man* (2002), *Sin City* (2005), *The Dark Knight* (2008), and *Guardians of the Galaxy* (2014). Adapted from The Destroyer pulp novels by Warren Murphy and Richard Sapir, the movie is basically an origin story introducing the main characters and storyline. It was hoped that British director Guy Hamilton, who was responsible for the James Bond breakout international hit *Goldfinger* (1964), might make a similar success of

Remo Williams. There are excellent action sequences atop the Statue of Liberty and the area around El Popo Volcano, just outside of Mexico City, which doubled for the forests of the United States Pacific Northwest. Cinematography was by Andrew Laszlo.

THE FALCON AND THE SNOWMAN (ORION PICTURES, 1985)

Director: John Schlesinger

Screenplay: Steven Zaillian, based on the book by Robert Lindsey

Producer: Gabriel Katzka, John Schlesinger

Cast: Timothy Hutton (Christopher Boyce), Sean Penn (Andrew Dalton Lee), Pat Hingle (Mr. Boyce), Lori Singer (Lana)

Story: When his conscience conflicts with his faith, Christopher Boyce drops out of the seminary and returns home. His childhood friend Andrew Dalton, on probation for possession of narcotics with intent to sell, travels between Mexico and his family home in California, dealing drugs. Needing a job, Boyce is recommended by his father, a retired FBI agent, for a position at RTX Credit. Boyce is promoted from the mailroom to the aerospace division that operates surveillance satellites, which the company manufactures and maintains for the CIA. Working in a communications vault, Boyce discovers a cable revealing that the CIA has infiltrated a labor union in Australia in an effort to affect the political leadership of the country. Upset that the United States is mired in covert actions with no connection to national security, Boyce presents Dalton with a business proposition. Dalton travels to Mexico City, where he makes contact with the Soviet embassy clerk. Soon, he's selling military secrets to the USSR; he is also snorting heroin and becomes

(*Left to right*): **Sean Penn, Timothy Hutton, director John Schlesinger, and script supervisor Ana Maria Quintana at Teotihuacan for** *The Falcon and the Snowman* **(1985).**

erratic as a courier. Boyce settles down with a girl, intending to quit his job and return to school, but Dalton threatens to expose him if he dissolves their partnership. Boyce arrives in Mexico to terminate the operation personally, but the Soviets advise him that quitting won't be easy.

Production: Filmed in 1983 in Mexico City and at Estudios Churubusco. This marked the first produced screenplay for writer Steve Zaillian, who went on to win an Oscar for *Schindler's List* (1993). *The Falcon and the Snowman* was directed by Oscar-winning filmmaker John Schlesinger (*Midnight Cowboy*, 1969; *The Day of the Locust*, 1975; *Marathon Man*, 1976) and starred Sean Penn and Timothy Hutton. At the age of twenty, Hutton became the youngest male actor to receive a Best Supporting Actor Oscar for his perfrormance in Robert Redford's *Ordinary People* (1980); Sean Penn went on to win two Best Actor Oscars for his perfrormances in *Mystic River* (2003) and *Milk* (2008).

VOLUNTEERS (TRI-STAR, 1985)

Director: Nicholas Meyer
Screenplay: David Isaacs, Keith Critchlow, Ken Levine
Producer: Richard Shepard, Walter F. Parkes, Theodore Parvin
Cast: Tom Hanks (Lawrence Bourne III), Rita Wilson (Beth Wexler), John Candy (Tom Tuttle), Tim Thomerson (John Reynolds)
Story: A wealthy young man escapes problems at home by joining the Peace Corps in the sixties. In Thailand, he and a fellow volunteer, Tom Tuttle, are entrusted with helping to build a bridge for the locals. They must contend with a drugged-out CIA agent, a communist military leader, and a local drug lord and his henchmen.
Production: Filmed in Catemaco and Tuxtepec, Mexico, doubling for Thailand, *Volunteers* marked the second teaming of John Candy and Tom Hanks following their success in *Splash* (1983). Hanks met his future wife Ruta Wison on this film.

RAMBO: FIRST BLOOD PART II (TRI STAR PICTURES, 1985)

Director: George P. Cosmatos
Screenplay: Sylvester Stallone, James Cameron
Producer: Mario Kassar, Andrew Vajna
Cast: Sylvester Stallone (John Rambo), Richard Crenna (Colonel Trautman), Charles Napier (Murdock), Julia Nickson (Co)
Story: Recovering in prison from events in Oregon, Rambo is visited by his mentor, Col. Trautman, who asks him to go back to Vietnam to find missing prisoners of war. He locates one prisoner, but is told many more are being held. Deserted at a rendezvous point, Rambo, with the help of a Vietnamese woman, discovers the prison camp, frees the POWs, and fights his way out of the jungle.
Production: *First Blood Part II* (a follow-up to *First Blood*, released in 1982) was filmed in and around Acapulco, doubling for Vietnam and South East Asia locations. One of the principal settings is a Vietnamese prison camp hidden deep in the jungle. The sprawling camp was built in the middle of the jungle, about a mile inland from the small village of Kilometer Twenty One (the town was named after the highway location). Construction began in late July 1984, with bulldozers clearing a road out of the dense vegetation for the expansive prison set as well as a production base camp to house large tents for catering, wardrobe facilities, equipment trucks, dressing rooms for

Tom Hanks and John Candy portray American Peace Corps buddies in *Volunteers* (1985), with Catemaco, Veracruz, standing in for South East Asia.

the cast and crew, and a landing field for the helicopters used in the film. Another location was a tropical lagoon, some twelve miles from Acapulco in Pie de La Cuesta, a narrow strip of coast bordered by the ocean on one side and the bay on the other. Here, with jungle and mountains as a backdrop, a key river chase sequence was shot involving a pirate sampan and a PBR river patrol boat pursuing Rambo and a Vietnamese agent as they attempt to escape from the prison camp. A waterfall location, high in the mountains overlooking Acapulco, required the daily helicopter transport of the cast and crew. A Mexican military base was used for the Thailand sequences, and the Acapulco Convention center, with its large interior, was used as a sound stage. Legendary Oscar-winning British cinematographer Jack Cardiff (*Black Narcissus*, 1947; *The Red Shoes*, 1948) captured the dense jungle images in striking color. Filming in the intensely hot and humid tropical interior was an arduous experience for director George P. Cosmatos (*Tombstone*, 1993) and the international cast and crew of American, Asian, Italian, English, and Mexican personnel. Co-screenwriter James Cameron would later write, produce, and direct the Academy Award–winning *Titanic* (1997), which was filmed in Rosarito, Baja, California. Lead actor Sylvester Stallone is most closely identified with two screen roles, boxer Rocky Balboa in the Oscar winning *Rocky* which catapulted him to movie stardom and the six sequels that followed (1976–2015) and the role of John Rambo, an emotionally scarred Vietnam war veteran in four *Rambo* films from 1982–2008, of which this is the sequel.

POWER (LORIMAR, 1986)

Director: Sidney Lumet

Screenplay: David Himmelstein

Producer: Reene Schisgal, Mark Tarlov

Cast: Richard Gere (Pete St. John), Julie Christie (Ellen Freeman), Gene Hackman (Wilfred Buckley), Kate Capshaw (Sydney Beckerman), Denzel Washington (Billings), Omar Torres (Roberto Cepeda)

Story: High-powered political media consultant has four clients of dubious backgrounds whom he will see elected to office through the manipulation of the media and public opinion.

Production: The subplot, with Roberto Cepeda running for the presidency of an unnamed Latin country, is truncated and goes unresolved in the film. The scenes consisting of a political rally in a Latin American city square where a terrorist bombing is recorded by the medial consultant's camera crew, were shot on location in Durango. An intended follow-up to Sidney Lumet's Academy Award–winning *Network* (1976), written by Paddy Chaefsky, this highly anticipated, all-star film was mired by a flawed script. Vincent Canby, in his *New York Times* review of January 31, 1986 wrote, "'Power' is a well-meaning, witless, insufferably smug movie . . . [which] anesthetizes legitimate outrage at some of the things going on in our society."

FIREWALKER (CANNON FILMS, 1986)

Director: J. Lee Thompson

Screenplay: Robert Gosnell

Producer: Menaheim Golan, Yoram Globus

Cast: Chuck Norris (Max Donigan), Louis Gossett Jr. (Leo Porter), Melody Anderson (Patricia Goodwyne), Alvaro Carcano (Willie), Will Sampson (Tall Eagle), Sonny Landham (El Coyote), Zaide Silvia Gutierrez (Indian girl)

Story: Two American adventurers help a beautiful blonde archeologist with a treasure map find a lost Aztec city. They are soon competing with others, including El Coyote and the Firewalker, who will employ any means to stop the trio. After surmounting obstacles along the way, the explorers discover the temple with the gold. Unfortunately for them, the Firewalker wants to retain the power of his ancestors and stop them from securing the booty. In the end, they overcome all hurdles and return home with the riches.

Production: Filmed in Durango and Puerto Vallarta with interiors at Estudios Churubusco doubling for nondescript Central American locales and the fictional town of San Miguel. The director of photography was Alex Phillips Jr. *Firewalker* is an action-adventure buddy film with martial arts star Chuck Norris and Best Supporting Actor Oscar winner (*An Officer and a Gentleman*, 1982) Louis Gossett Jr. *Firewalker* is entertaining fare but is derivative of several popular movies and genres of the era, including *Raiders of the Lost Ark* (1981) and *Romancing the Stone* (1984).

LET'S GET HARRY (TRISTAR, 1986)

Director: Stuart Rosenberg (billed as Alan Smithee)

Screenplay: Charles Robert Carner, based on a story by Samuel Fuller and Mark Feldberg

Cast: Mark Harmon (Harry Burck), Robert Duvall (Norman Shrike), Gary Busey (Jack), Thomas F. Wilson (Bob), Elpidia Carrillo (Veronica), Ben Johnson (Burck Sr.), Glenn Frey (Spence)

Story: An American engineer is kidnapped and held for ransom in Colombia, South America, by an extremist drug lord. When the American government is unable and unwilling to negotiate or mount a rescue, his brother and a group of friends enlist an ex-mercenary to train them for a covert rescue mission in the jungles of Colombia.

Production: *Let's Get Harry* is an action-adventure filmed in Vera Cruz, Mexico, doubling for the South American jungles of Colombia. Despite its cast of rising young stars, a veteran performer (Robert Duvall), and a strong premise, the film is muddled, haphazardly edited and executed. There are plenty of explosions and action but very little in between. Director Rosenberg took his name off the film when it was reedited with additional footage shot without his consent, so it bears the commonly used anonymous directorial credit Alan Smithee. Cinematography is by James A. Contner. Critics and audiences panned the film when it was released, and it was quickly forgotten.

MIRACLES (ORION PICTURES, 1986)

Director: Jim Kouf
Screenplay: Jim Kouf
Producer: Stephen Goldlatt
Cast: Tom Conti (Roger), Teri Garr (Jean), Paul Rodriguez (Juan), Jorge Russek (Judge), Zaide Silvia Gutierrez (Kin's wife), Jorge Reynoso (Kin)
Story: A doctor and his recently divorced wife find themselves with an inept jewel thief who takes them on an extraordinary adventure in which they are marooned, left for dead, and hijacked in Mexico.
Production: This comedy (with well-executed action sequences) was filmed at Estudios Churubusco and in and around Mexico City. Paul Rodriguez is an actor/standup comedian, born in Mexico but raised in Los Angeles, with credits in such films as *D. C. Cab* (1983), *Born in East L.A.* (1987), *Tortilla Soup* (2001) and *Bloodwork* (2002). Zaida Silvia Gutierrez starred in Gregory Nava's *El Norte* (1983).

SALVADOR (ORION, 1986)

Director: Oliver Stone
Screenplay: Oliver Stone, Richard Boyle
Producer: Gerald Green, Oliver Stone
Cast: James Woods (Richard Boyle), Jim Belushi (Dr. Rock), Michael Murphy (Ambassador Kelly), Elpidia Carrillo (Maria), Tony Plana (Major Max), John Savage (Cassady), Cindy Gibb (Caty Moore)
Story: In 1980, men, women, and children are being brutally killed in a bloody civil war in El Salvador. It's a horrific setting, but a perfect one for Richard Boyle, a sleazy war photojournalist whose career needs a jump-start. Armed with his camera, Boyle heads for the front lines to capture atrocious but valuable images of pain and horror. But with each picture he takes, he catches a tragic side of humanity that ignites his long-buried sense of compassion. He unexpectedly discovers something that will change him forever: his soul.
Production: Filmed in Morelos, Guerrero, and Acapulco, *Salvador* was a difficult film to shoot. Within only seven shooting weeks, the filmmakers had to manage several military tanks, horses, airplanes, helicopters, ninety-three speaking roles, and more than a thousand extras.

In the early eighties, American journalist Richard Boyle risked his life to report on the chaos of war-torn El Salvador. He and other reporters strove to reveal the irony behind that country's continual flow of mil-

Writer/director Oliver Stone *(far right)* **directs James Woods and Elpidia Carrillo in the Mexico-based political drama** *Salvador/Questa è la Vita* **(2006).**

itary aid from the United States. While the El Salvadoran government took an anti-communist stance, its regime used brutally repressive tactics against dissidents and rebels reminiscent of the communist regimes they opposed. In December 1984, Boyle gave Oliver Stone an unpublished book of his experiences in El Salvador. Stone was immediately inspired by the work. Both Stone and Boyle had served in Vietnam, Stone as a soldier and Boyle as a photojournalist. Stone agreed to go to El Salvador with Boyle. Though he was both disturbed and fascinated by what he saw in the ravaged country, Stone decided that the film should be about the experiences of the journalist. "I didn't want to make a message movie about El Salvador," he said, "I wanted to do a movie about a correspondent." *Salvador* would receive stunning reviews and two Oscar nominations, one for Stone and Boyle's screenplay and one for Woods's acting. James Woods became interested in the role of Richard Boyle because of its contradictory nature. "He goes back to El Salvador just to make some money," Woods said. "But then he gets swept up on a personal level and becomes truly interested in finding the truth." Jim Belushi (billed as James Belushi) portrays real-life San Francisco disc jockey Dr. Rock. "My character is ignorant of Central American issues [as is] most of the American general public," Belushi explained. "So I am the touchstone for the audience at the beginning of the movie. My character discovers El Salvador just as the audience does." The film portrayed many real-life events, including the murder of a group of American nuns and the assassination of Salvadoran Archbishop Romero, who had spoken out against the government. Oliver Stone became a two-time Oscar winning writer/director and one of the most

important and controversial filmmakers of his generation. Onscreen, he tackled some of the most important events and issues of recent history, including the Vietnam War (*Platoon, Born on the Fourth of July*, both
1986), United States President John F. Kennedy's assasination (*JFK*, 1991), self-destructive rock stars (*The
Doors*, 1991) and the rise and fall of an American president (*Nixon*, 1995). Stone's early work included an
Academy Award for Best Adapted Screenplay for *Midnight Express* (1978). He also wrote the screenplayfor the
enduring cult hit *Scarface* (1983), directed by Brian De Palma.

PREDATOR (20TH CENTURY FOX, 1987)

Director: John McTiernan
Screenplay: Jim Thomas, John Thomas
Producer: Lawrence Gordon, Joel Silver
Cast: Arnold Schwarzennegger (Dutch), Carl Weathers (Dillon), Elpidia Carrillo (Anna), Bill Duke (Mac),
Jesse Ventura (Blain), Sonny Landham (Billy), Richard Chaves (Poncho)
Story: A covert American commando unit on a mission is dropped off in a Central American jungle where
they become the targets of a deadly extra-terrestrial.
Production: Filmed in Puerto Vallarta, Jalisco, in a jungle area called "El Eden"; the final sequences of the film
were shot in Palengue, Chiapas, Mexico. The crew consisted of Americans, Australians, and Mexicans who worked
on the Mexican portion of the shoot for twelve weeks. Interiors were shot at 20th Century Fox Studios in Hollywood. *Predator* could be considered the perfect action film in that it places a group of capable men, led by a strong,
no-nonsense hero, on a dangerous mission in a deadly territory. They succeed with the mission but then are
picked off by an unknown force. Director John McTiernan rose to prominence with *Predator* and followed with
the 1988 hit action movie *Die Hard*, which catapulted Bruce Willis to stardom, and *The Hunt for Red October* (1990)
starring Sean Connery and Alec Baldwin. McTiernan would return to Mexico for the adventure-comedy *Medicine
Man*, also a Connery vehicle. Arnold Schwarzenegger had already established himself with the sword-and-sorcery
Conan films, and cemented his worldwide box-office clout with *The Terminator* (1984). Mexican actress Elpidia
Carrillo plays Anna, a prisoner-turned-survivor who is the first to become aware of the Predator. Carl Weathers,
who played Dillon, became a star with his breakout role in *Rocky* (1976) and its two sequels as Rocky's fierce oppo-
nent Apollo Creed. The success of *Predator* spawned four sequels, each with diminishing returns, *Predator 2* (1990),
Alien vs. Predator (2004*), Alien vs. Predator: Requiem* (2007), and *Predators* (2010).

BORN IN EAST L. A. (UNIVERSAL PICTURES, 1987)

Director: Cheech Marin
Screenplay: Cheech Marin
Producer: Peter Macgregor-Scott
Cast: Cheech Marin (Rudy), Paul Rodriquez (Javier), Daniel Stern (Jimmy), Kamala Lopez (Dolores),
Jam-Michael Vincent (McCalister), Lupe Ontiveros (Rudy's Mother) Urbani Lucero (Rudy's Sister), Tony
Plana (Feo), Alma Martinez (Gloria), Sal Lopez (What's Happening Boys), Del Zamora (What's Happening
Boys), Jason Scott Lee (What's Happening Boys), Dyana Ortelli (mother with orange).
Story: Rudy Robles, an American of Mexican descent, is picked up by the U. S. immigration authorities in

Carl Weathers (left) and Arnold Schwarzenegger (*right*) in a scene from *Predator* (1987), filmed near Puerto Vallarta and in Palenque, Chiapas.

a factory raid in Los Angeles. His family is out of town and his wallet was left at home. Deported to Mexico with no proof of citizenship or identification, he must figure out a way to get across the border and back to East Los Angeles.

Production: Filming took place over six weeks in Tijuana, Baja California Norte, and in the San Ysidro/ Tijuana border area, as well as in East Los Angeles locations. With its themes of immigration and social and ethnic identity on both sides of the border, *Born in East L. A.* is still relevant. *Born in East L. A.* also marked the theatrical directing debut of Cheech Marin, one-half of the comedy duo Cheech and Chong, the counter-culture pot-smoking comedy team of the seventies and eighties. Inspired by a true-life incident that was reported in the *Los Angeles Times, Born in East L. A.* was written by Marin as a social comedy. He chose to parody the hit Bruce Springsteen song "Born in the USA," with his own lyrics. East Los Angeles has been home to the nation's largest Mexican-American community for several generations. Among the many comic highlights is a sequence in which seemingly hundreds of undocumented immigrants converge on a hillside. They run down the hill and cross the border into the U. S. from Mexico (with Neil Diamond's "Coming to America" on the soundtrack), overwhelming and evading the border guards.

HOT PURSUIT (PARAMOUNT, 1987)

Director: Steven Lisberger

Screenplay: Steven Lisberger, Steven Carabatsos

Producer: Pierre David, Theodore R. Parvin

Cast: John Cusack (Dan Bartlett), Robert Loggia (Mac Maclaren), Jerry Stiller (Victor Honeywell), Wendy Gazelle (Lori Greenberg), Ben Stiller (Chris Honeywell)

Story: High school student Dan Bartlett plans to vacation in the Caribbean with his girlfriend and her wealthy family. These plans are stalled when he must take a final chemistry exam. Though he fails the test, a sympathetic teacher gives him a passing grade. He takes a flight out to join them but misses them at every turn, leading to a series of escapades involving zany characters and situations.

Production: This fast-moving comedy-adventure is highlighted by its location photography in Ixtapa, Guerrero, Mexico, doubling for Jamaica and other Caribbean locales. John Cusack was then a young actor on the rise after such hit movies as John Hughes's *Sixteen Candles* (1984) and Rob Reiner's *Stand By Me* (1986). *Hot Pursuit* also features one of the first screen appearances of actor Ben Stiller, who co-stars with his famous father, Jerry Stiller.

GABY: A TRUE STORY (TRI-STAR, 1987)

Director: Luis Mandoki

Screenplay: Michael James Love, Martin Salinas, developed by Luis Mandoki (as told to him by Gabriela Brimmer)

Producer: Pinchas Perry, Luis Mandoki

Cast: Liv Ullman (Sari), Norma Aleandro (Florencia), Robert Loggia (Michel), Robert Beltran (Luis) Rachel Levin (Gaby)

Story: Biography of Gabriela Brimmer, the daughter of Jewish refugees from Nazi Germany, who settles in Mexico. She overcomes crippling cerebral palsy with the help of a devoted Mexican nanny.

Production: *Gaby: A True Story* was a critically accalimed Mexican/American co-production, filmed entirely in and around Mexico City D. F. and Cuernavaca, Morelos. Argentinean actress Norma Aleandro was nominated for a Best Supporting Actress Oscar for her role as the Mexican nanny Florencia. Future Oscar-winning director Alfonso Cuaron was the second-unit director on this film; future Oscar-winning cinematographer Emmanuel Lubezki was the second assistant director. Director Luis Mandoki, notable for his work in both Mexico and the United States, has directed such Hollywood films as *Message in a Bottle* (1999) with Kevin Costner and Paul Newman; *White Palace* (1990) with James Spader and Susan Sarandon; *When a Man Loves a Woman* (1994) with Andy Garcia and Meg Ryan; and *Angel Eyes* (2001) with Jennifer Lopez. Mandoki continues to make films in Mexico.

BUSTER (MGM, 1988)

Director: David Green

Screenplay: Colin Schindler

Producer: Norma Heyman

Cast: Phil Collins (Buster), Julie Watkins (June), Larry Lamb (Bruce), Stephanie Lawrence (Franny), Anthony Quayle (Sir James McDowell), Evangelina Sosa (Maria), Francisco Morales (Mexican doctor).

Story: The story of one of the lesser-known culprits of the British Great Train Robbery that took place in

England in 1963. Ronnie "Buster" Edwards makes his way to Mexico after the robbery to escape the law but returns to England to face arrest, conviction, and prison because he misses his wife back in England.

Production: The Mexico scenes were filmed on location in Acapulco, Guerrero, Mexico, and at Estudios Churubusco in Mexico City. *Buster* marked the film acting debut of rock/pop star Phil Collins, whose contributed songs to the period film's soundtrack reached Billboard's Top 100 charts. The focus of this British production is not on the heist but on the heartwarming and realistic relationship between Buster and Jean. Batan Silva was second assistant to Mario Cisneros, the assistant director for the Mexico unit.

THE PENITENT (CINEWORLD ENTERPRISES, 1988)

Director: Cliff Osmond

Screenplay: Cliff Osmond

Producer: Michael Fitzgerald

Cast: Raul Julia (Ramon Guerola), Julie Carmen (Corina), Armand Assante (Juan Mateo), Rona Freed (Celia Guerola), Lucy Reina (Margarita), Eduardo Lopez Rojas (mayor)

Story: In a small village in New Mexico, preparations for the yearly ritual reenactment of the Crucifixion are taking place. A member of the "Penitentes," a local Catholic sect, must be chosen to play the role of Jesus. Against this backdrop tensions arise between a jealous husband, his wife, and a friend.

Production: Filmed on location in San Miguel de Allende and Pozos, *The Penitent* is vague as to the location of the village in the story. Los Hermanos Penitentes, a Catholic lay society, has existed for four hundred years and is characterized by the practice of self-flagellation and other physical punishment as penance for sins. In this film, Juan is crucified and left tied to a cross for a day, to live or die. Cliff Osmond, a favorite character actor of film director Billy Wilder, wrote the script and, with actor Armand Assante, raised funds to make the film independently. Julie Carmen is best known for her role in John Cassavetes's *Gloria* (1980), *The Milagro Beanfield War* (1988), and *Fright Night 2* (1989). *The Penitent* was controversial and received a limited release in 1988 due to its subject matter. It features an early film appearance by future Oscar-nominee Demian Bichir, as Roberto. Michael Fitzgerald was the executive producer of John Huston's *Under the Volcano*, also shot in Mexico with a largely Mexican crew. Fitzgerald also utilized Huston's assistant director, Tom Shaw, who had previously worked in Mexico on *Volcano* and *The Night of the Iguana*.

FIST FIGHTER (TAURUS FILMS, 1989)

Director: Frank Zuniga

Screenplay: Carlos Vassalo

Producer: Jorge Rivero

Cast: Jorge Rivero (C. J. Thunderbird), Edward Albert (Harry Moses), Brenda Bakke (Ellen), Mike Connors (Billy Vance), Simon Andreu (Moreno)

Story: C. J. Thunderbird is an ex-boxer who works the dangerous and illegal bare-knuckle boxing circuit in Mexico. As he seeks vengeance for the death of a friend a devious promoter attempts to thwart his efforts.

Production: This action-adventure film was shot in Durango and in and around Mexico City. Director Frank Zuniga, born in Gallup, New Mexico, got his start working on *Walt Disney's Wonderful World of Color* TV series during the 1970s and went on to direct the theatrical features *Heart Beaker* (1983), *The Golden Seal* (1983), among others.

HONEY, I SHRUNK THE KIDS (DISNEY, 1989)

Director: Joe Johnston

Screenplay: Ed Naha, Tom Schulman

Producer: Penny Finkleman Cox

Cast: Rick Moranis (Wayne Szalinski), Matt Frewer (Big Russ Thompson), Marcia Strassman (Diane Szalinski), Kristine Sutherland (Mae Thompson), Thomas Wilson Brown (Little Russ Thompson), Jared Rushton (Ron Thompson)

Story: A preoccupied inventor can't seem to get his electro-magnetic shrinking machine to work. When he accidentally shrinks his kids down to a quarter-inch tall and tosses them out with the trash, the real fun begins. Now, the kids face incredible dangers as they try to make their way home through the jungle of their own backyard. They must evade hurricane sprinklers, dive-bombing bees, lawn mowers, and more.

Production: Filmed at Estudios Churubusco under the working title "The Teenie Weenies," *Honey, I Shrunk the Kids* employed full-size sets that were built to scale and a modern American Midwestern street exterior that was built on the Estudios Churubusco backlot.

LICENSE TO KILL (UNITED ARTISTS, 1989)

Director: John Glen

Screenplay: Richard Maibaum, Michael Wilson

Producer: Albert R. Broccoli, Barbara Broccoli

Cast: Timothy Dalton (James Bond), Robert Davi (Franz Sanchez), David Hedison (Felix Leiter), Pedro Armendáriz Jr. (Presidente Hector Lopez), Benicio Del Toro (Dario), Talisa Soto (Lupe Lamora)

Story: James Bond must protect his maimed friend, CIA agent Felix Leiter, and avenge the death of Leiter's wife at the hands of the notorious drug lord Franz Sanchez.

Production: The nineteenth entry in the James Bond series, *License to Kill* went into production in July of 1988 at Estudios Churubusco, where it took over seven of eight sound stages. Veracruz, Durango, and Temaoya were used to portray the fictional South American country of Isthmus, which resembles Panama. A second-unit crew filmed underwater scenes near Islas Mujeres in Cancun; the climactic truck stunts were filmed over seven weeks in the deserts near the border town of Mexicali. A luxurious home in Acapulco doubled for Sanchez's lair. Principal photography ended on November 18. Mexican actor Pedro Armendáriz Jr. plays Presidente Hector Lopez of Isthmus; his father was the famed international Mexican film star Pedro Armendáriz, who played Kerim Bey in the second James Bond film, *From Russia with Love* (1963), opposite Sean Connery. Locations in Mexico City included the main post office (which was used as the bank) and the ornate Casino Espanol was, in fact, a social club founded by Spanish expatriates. At the time of the filming, gambling was illegal in Mexico, so no actual casinos existed. Actor Benicio Del Toro made his film debut in a small role.

OLD GRINGO (COLUMBIA PICTURES, 1989)

Director: Luis Puenzo

Screenplay: Aida Bortnik, Luis Puenzo, from the novel by Carlos Fuentes

Producer: Jane Fonda, Lois Bonfiglio

(*Left to right*): **Gregory Peck, Jimmy Smits, and Jane Fonda, director Luis Puenzo, and novelist Carlos Fuentes on location at Hacienda Venta de Cruz for** *Old Gringo* **(1989).**

Cast: Jane Fonda (Harriet Winslow), Gregory Peck (Ambrose "Old Gringo" Bierce), Jimmy Smits (General Tomas Arroyo), Patrico Contreras (Colonel Frutos Garcia), Jenny Gago (La Garduna), Pedro Armendáriz Jr. (Pancho Villa)

Story: In 1913, American spinster Harriet Winslow leaves her comfortable life in Baltimore to become a teacher for the wealthy Miranda family in Mexico. She arrives just as Pancho Villa's forces are gaining a foothold in Chihuahua. General Thomas Arroyo kidnaps her to gain access to the Miranda hacienda, now held by government troops. Ambrose Bierce, an elderly American writer, has also crossed the border into Mexico, hoping to live out his last days in the passion of the Revolution. He befriends Arroyo and helps him during a crucial battle, during which he meets Harriet. The three characters become involved in a strange romantic triangle.

Production: *Old Gringo* is based on the novel by celebrated Mexican novelist Carlos Fuentes (1928–2012). It is a fictional tale inspired by the real-life disappearance in Mexico of famed American journalist Ambrose Bierce

(1842-1914) during the Mexican Revolution. Two-time Academy Award–winning actress Jane Fonda, daughter of screen actor Henry Fonda (1905-1982), was at the height of her star power when she took an interest in the novel and obtained the film rights. Produced by Fonda Films, she developed *Old Gringo* with the intention of playing the female lead, Harriet Winslow, an American spinster school teacher who travels to Mexico and becomes romantically involved with the elder Bierce and a young Mexican general. Fonda was given the production go-ahead by the new chairman of Columbia Pictures, Academy award–winning English producer David Putnam (*Chariots of Fire*, 1981). Luis Puenzo, Argentine director of 1986's Oscar-winning Best Foreign Language Film, *The Official Story*, directed and co-wrote *Old Gringo*. The cinematography was by Felix Monti; production design was by Bruno Rubeo, husband of Mexican production designer Mayes Rubeo. Jimmy Smits alternated between leading roles in feature films (*My Family/Mi Familia* (1995), *Price of Glory* (2000), *Star Wars: Episode II* (2005), and television (*L.A. Law*, for which he won an Emmy, and *N.Y.P.D. Blue*).

Filmed on location in Mexico with a cast of thousands, *Old Gringo* was produced on a lavish budget with big battle scenes, some of which attain the level of a David Lean epic, visually sweeping the viewer into the time period and turbulent action of the Mexican Revolution. Locations include Zacatecas, Durango, Hacienda de Santa Maria Regla, Hidalgo, Zempoala, and Estudios Churubusco, where the lavish interior sets of the Hacienda were constructed. Burt Lancaster was initially cast to play Old Gringo, but due to a heart condition he was deemed uninsurable. He was replaced by Gregory Peck, who was making his only return to Mexico since filming *The Bravados* in 1958. The Mexican crew welcomed him back with much love and affection. Peck, an Oscar-winning (*To Kill a Mockingbird*, 1962) Hollywood legend, was courteous to everyone and was the consummate professional on set. *Old Gringo* was his last major film role.

FATMAN AND LITTLE BOY (PARAMOUNT, 1989)

Director: Roland Joffe
Screenplay: Bruce Robinson, Roland Joffe
Producer: Tony Garnett
Cast: Paul Newman (General Groves), Dwight Schultz (Oppenheimer), Laura Dern (Kathleen Robinson), Bonnie Bedelia (Kitty Oppenheimer), John Cusack (Robert Merriman)
Story: In 1942, at the beginning of America's involvement in World War II, the United States government brings together some of the greatest scientists in the world at a secret and remote facility in Los Alamos, New Mexico, to develop the atomic bomb before Nazi Germany does. The mission, known as the Manhattan Project, is led by scientist J. Robert Oppenheimer and overseen by U.S. Army General Groves. *Fatman* and *Little Boy* are the code names given to the bombs dropped over Hiroshima and Nagasaki, Japan, in August of 1945, which forced the Japanese to surrender and brought about the end of World War II. However, the awesome destructive power of the atom bomb made some of the scientists regret their participation.
Production: Filmed in Torreon, Coahuila, Estudios Churubusco, and San Francisco, California. In Durango, an exact reproduction of the Los Alamos National Laboratory was constructed. The Oscar-winning director of photography was Vilmos Zsigmond (*Close Encounters of the Third Kind*, 1977; *The Deer Hunter*, 1978). Popular American film star Paul Newman (1925–2008) had been in Durango previously for the filming of the Bolivia sequences of *Butch Cassidy and The Sundance Kid* (1969).

ROMERO (FOUR SQUARE, 1989)

Director: John Duigan
Screenplay: John Sacret Young
Producer: Ellwood Keiser
Cast: Raul Julia (Archbishop Romero), Richard Jordan (Father Grande), Ana Alicia (Arista Zelada), Eddie Velez (Lieutenant Columa), Alejandro Bracho (Father Osuna), Tony Plana (Father Morantes), Claudio Brook (Bishop Flores)
Story: Based on true events in El Salvador in the 1970s, *Romero* chronicles the transformation of Oscar Romero from an apolitical, complacent priest to a committed leader of the Salvadoran people. Romero, as archbishop of El Salvador, speaks against the repression caused by a military junta, which leads to his assassination while conducting Mass in 1980.
Production: *Romero* was filmed in and around Cuernavaca, Mexico, doubling for the Central American country of El Salvador. It is a plodding but well-intentioned film, independently financed by members of the United States Catholic Church, through Paulist Productions. Under Father Ellwood Keiser, Paulist Productions produced *Insight*, a long-running syndicated dramatic television series which featured many top Hollywood stars and gave young, inexperienced actors an opportunity to appear on the small screen. Famed Puerto Rican Broadway stage and screen actor Raul Julia (1940–1994), best known for his performances in *Kiss of the Spider Woman* (1985) and *The Addams Family* (1991), gives a moving portrayal of Archbishop Romero. Future Oscar winner Alfonso Cuaron served as an assistant director.

REVENGE (COLUMBIA PICTURES, 1990)

Director: Tony Scott
Screenplay: Jeff Fiskin, Jim Harrison, based on the short story by Jim Harrison
Producer: Ray Stark, Stanley Rubin, Hunt Lowry
Cast: Kevin Costner (Cochran), Anthony Quinn (Tiburon Mendez), Madelyn Stowe (Miryea), Miguel Ferrer (Amador), Tomas Milian (Cesar), John Lequizamo (Ignacio), Claudio Brook (Barone), Sally Kirkland (Rock Star), James Gammon (Texan), Joaquin Martinez (Mauro)
Story: Jay Cochran, a United States Navy pilot, retires after twelve years of service and decides to accept an invitation to visit an old friend in Mexico. Jay and Tiburon "Tibey" Mendez became friends years earlier when Jay saved Tibey's life on a hunting trip. Tibey, a wealthy and powerful crime lord who is well connected politically and surrounded by heavily armed bodyguards, has a beautiful younger wife named Miryea. When Cochran and Miryea meet, their mutual attraction is instantaneous and they begin a passionate affair. Tibey quickly realizes what is going on. When he catches the couple in flagrente delicto, he viciously beats up Cochran, leaving him for dead in the desert; as for Miryea, he slashes her face and sends her to live in a brothel. A Mexican traveler finds Cochran and nurses him back to health. After recovering, Cochran leaves to find Mireya and take vengeance on Tiburon.
Production: Filmed in Durango, Cuernavaca, and Puerto Vallarta, with interiors at Estudios Churubusco, *Revenge* has breathtaking camera work by Jeffrey Kimball, who captures the Mexican countryside, from the small villages, opulent estates, tropical resort areas, and desert vistas with such expertise that Mexico itself becomes a central character. It is based on the novella by Jim Harrison, who wrote the screenplay with Jeff Fiskin. John

Huston was going to direct *Revenge* but fell into a disagreement with producer Ray Stark, with whom he had worked successfully on *The Night of the Iguana*. Tony Scott directed this character-driven story of romance and revenge, peppered with hard action. Despite the quality of the film, the downbeat ending, in which the girl dies, kept audiences away. Kevin Costner was a rising star with such hits to his credit as *No Way Out* (1987), *Bull Durham* (1988), and *Field of Dreams* (1989). While filming *Revenge*, he was in the early stages of preparation for his directorial debut, *Dances with Wolves* (1991). Due to financial reasons, Costner and his producer, Jim Wilson, once considered filming *Dances with Wolves* in Durango, but opted instead for authenticity, shooting the epic western on location in South Dakota, with Native American and First Nation actors. Costner has remained one of the leading American actors of his generation with a quiet authority and unassuming masculinity. *Revenge* co-star Anthony Quinn said during the shoot that Costner reminded him of his friend Gary Cooper.

Director Tony Scott had a fascination with Mexico, so much so that he returned for *Man on Fire* (2004) and an unrealized project based on Clifford Irving's 1984 fictional adventure novel *Tom Mix and Pancho Villa*, which depicted the exploits of former soldier and 1920s cowboy film star and the hero of the Mexican Revolution.

TOTAL RECALL (TRI-STAR, 1990)
Director: Paul Verhoeven
Screenplay: Ronald Shusett, based on the short story by Philip K. Dick
Producer: Ronald Shusett, Buzz Feitshans
Cast: Arnold Schwarzenegger (Douglas Quaid), Sharon Stone (Lori), Rachel Ticotin (Melina), Ronny Cox (Cohaagen), Michael Ironside (Richter)
Story: In the year 2084, a construction worker is haunted by a recurring dream about a trip to Mars with a mysterious woman. Hoping to find answers, he goes on a mind-bending journey through the virtual technology of Rekall, without having to physically leave the planet. Then things go terribly wrong. Someone who knows the truth about his dream wants to kill him at any cost.
Production: This wildly imaginative science fiction tale (which would go on to win an Academy Award for its visual effects) was filmed on the sound stages of Estudios Churubusco. It was Arnold Schwarzenegger's third film in Mexico; the first was *Conan the Destroyer* (1984), followed by *Predator* (1987). Schwarzenegger returned to Mexico once again, this time for *Collateral Damage* (2002).

THE TAKING OF BEVERLY HILLS (ORION, 1991)
Director: Sidney J. Furie
Screenplay: Rick Nstkin, David Fuller, David J. Burke
Producer: Graham Henderson
Cast: Ken Wahl (Boomer Hayes), Matt Frewer (Kelvin), Robert Davi (Robert Masterson), Harley Jane Kozak (Laura Sage), Branscombe Richmond (Benitez)
Story: A famous football quarterback, at a party in a luxurious Beverly Hills mansion, battles ex-cops who execute a toxic spill to cover up a raid on Beverly Hills banks and homes after residents are evacuated and the city is closed off.
Production: Filmed in Mexico City at Estudios Churubusco, where a section of Beverly Hills' Rodeo Drive was recre-

ated and destroyed, *The Taking of Beverly Hills* received a limited U.S. release due to the bankruptcy of distributor Orion Pictures and was compared unfavorably with the similar but vastly superior film *Die Hard* starring Bruce Willis.

PURE LUCK (UNIVERSAL PICTURES, 1991)

Director: Nadia Tass

Screenplay: Herschel Weingrod, Timothy Harris

Producer: Sean Daniel, Lance Hool, Conrad Hool

Cast: Martin Short (Proctor), Danny Glover (Campanella), Sheila Kelley (Valerie), Sam Wanamaker (Highsmeith), Jorge Russek (Inspector Segura), Jorge Luke (Pilot), Rodrigo Puebla (Fernando)

Story: A detective and a bookkeeper are tasked with locating a millionaire's daughter who is missing in Mexico. Since the young woman suffers from the same accident-prone condition as the bookkeeper, a psychologist is convinced that this shared disorder will put them on a similar trail to her whereabouts.

Production: American remake of a French comedy *La Chevre* starring Gerard Depardieu and Pierre Richard. This less funny (and less successful) version was filmed in Acapulco, Guerrero, and Mexico City.

RUBY CAIRO [A.K.A. DECEPTION] (MIRAMAX, 1992)

Director: Graeme Clifford

Screenplay: Robert Dillon, Michael Thomas

Producer: Lloyd Phillips, Hiroshi Sugawara

Cast: Andie MacDowell (Bessie Faro), Liam Neeson (Fergus Lamb), Viggo Mortensen (John Faro)

Story: When businessman John Faro dies in a plane crash in Mexico, his widow, Bessie, travels to her husband's air cargo terminal in Veracruz. While settling his business affairs, Bessie discovers untold bank accounts with large sums of cash scattered across the globe. With the help of Fergus Lamb, she goes on a quest to unravel the mystery behind the money and his presumed death.

Production: *Ruby Cairo/Deception* is something of a relationship/mystery/travelogue that was shot on location in Veracruz, Berlin, Athens, and Cairo. Actress and model Andie MacDowell had made her film debut in *Greystoke: The Legend of Tarzan, Lord of the Apes* (1984) and achieved critical acclaim for her role in Steven Sodenbergh's *sex, lies, and videotape* (1989). Irish actor Liam Neeson achieved stardom as Oskar Schindler in Steven Spielberg's Academy Award–winning Holocaust drama *Schindler's List* (1993).

MEDICINE MAN (HOLLYWOOD PICTURES, 1992)

Director: John McTiernan

Screenplay: Tom Schulman

Producer: Andrew Vajna, Donna Dubrow

Cast: Sean Connery (Dr. Robert Campbell), Lorraine Bracco (Dr. Rae Crane), José Wilker (Dr. Miguel Ornega), Elias Montero Da Silva (Palala), Angelo Barra Moreira (Medicine Man) José Lavat (government man), Edinei Maria Serria Dos Santos (Kalana)

Story: Deep in the forbidding Amazon rain forest, a brilliant but eccentric biochemist has discovered a cure for cancer. After six years in the jungles of Brazil, Dr. Robert Campbell is on the verge of astonishing the world with a major medical breakthrough, but then loses the formula and must rediscover it. Making matters worse, the pharmaceutical corporation sponsoring his research has sent another biochemist, Dr. Rae Crane, to investigate the reclusive genius. A hardheaded female scientist is the last thing Campbell wants around his camp, but Crane refuses to leave and is soon caught up in the quest to find the rare antidote. In a race against time and the coming destruction of the rain forest, the pair embarks on a mission to save the precious plant.

Production: A strange mixture of comedy and adventure, *Medicine Man* reflects serious themes of the vanishing rainforest, a cancer cure, changing modern-day gender roles, and professional relationships. Filming began in March 1991 in the jungles of Catemaco, Veracruz, Mexico, doubling for the Amazon in Brazil. Brazilian actors filled the principal native roles, and local Mexican talent was utilized in minor parts and as extras. Emily Gamboa was the production coordinator on the film. Sean Connery's leading lady, Lorraine Bracco, attained notice in Martin Scorseses's *Goodfellas*, but never achieved big-screen prominence; she later found recognition on cable television with her role as the psychiatrist on the acclaimed HBO series *The Sopranos*.

FREE WILLY (WARNER BROS., 1993)

Director: Simon Wincer

Screenplay: Keith A. Walker, Corey Biechman

Producer: Lauren Shuler-Donner, Jennie Lew Tugend

Cast: Jason James Richter (Jesse), Michael Madsen (Glen Greenwood), Jayne Atkinson (Annie Greenwood), Lori Petty (Rae), Michael Ironside (Dial)

Story: Jesse, an orphaned street boy, does service time in an aquarium as restitution for vandalism. While there, he develops a relationship with Willy, a captive Orca killer whale. The aquarium's trainers are unable to train the Orca, but after befriending him, Jesse manages to do so. A foster family takes the boy in and he enlists the aid of the trainers to save Willy when the aquarium owner plans to kill the whale to collect the insurance money.

Production: Though most of the film was shot in Astoria, Oregon, it was partly filmed at Estudios Churubusco. All of the scenes of the Oceanic Park, in which you see the real whale in action, were filmed at Reyno Aventura theme park in Tlaplan, Mexico City. Since then, the theme park has been refurbished as Six Flags, Mexico. *Free Willy* was a surprise hit at the box office and was followed by two theatrical sequels and a made-for-video sequel.

CLEAR AND PRESENT DANGER (PARAMOUNT, 1994)

Director: Phillip Noyce

Screenplay: Donald Stewart, Steve Zailian, John Milius, from the novel by Tom Clancy

Producer: Mace Neufield

Cast: Harrison Ford (Jack Ryan), James Earl Jones (Admiral Greer), Anne Archer (Cathy Ryan), Willem Dafoe (John Clark), Harris Yulin (James Cutter), Joachim Almeida (Cortez), Miguel Sandoval (Ernesto Escobedo)

Story: When his mentor Admiral Greer becomes gravely ill, Jack Ryan is appointed acting CIA deputy director of the Central Intelligence Agency. His first assignment is to investigate the murder of one of the president's friends, a prominent United States businessman with secret ties to Colombian drug cartels. Unbeknown to Ryan, the CIA has already launched a clandestine operation led by a deadly field operative in retaliation against the Colombian drug lords. Caught in the crossfire, Ryan takes matters into his own hands, risking his career and life for the only cause he still believes in—the truth.

Production: Filmed in Mexico, a Colombian Street was built on a soccer field in a stadium outside of Mexico City for an attempted assassination sequence, after Mexico City officials denied access because of the pyrotechnic action involved. Built from the ground up, their set offered complete control for filming. The assasination sequence, including stunt action, took three weeks to rehearse and film. A real hilltop mansion near Jalapa, Veracruz, was blown up and totally destroyed for the film cameras. *Clear and Present Danger* is the third film in the popular Jack Ryan movie franchise, based on the popular novels by Tom Clancy, following *The Hunt for Red October* (1990) and *Patriot Games* (1992). In the first film, Jack Ryan was played by a young Alec Baldwin, and in the latter two by Harrison Ford (*Star Wars*, 1977; *Raiders of the Lost Ark*, 1981). Ford is said to have enjoyed working in Mexico and with the Mexican crews. Anna Roth was the Mexican production manager; Australian cameraman Donald McAlpine was the cinematographer.

WAGONS EAST (TRI STAR PICTURES, 1994)

Director: Peter Markle

Screenplay: Matthew Carlson, story by Jerry Abrahamson

Producer: Gary Goodman, Barry Rosen, Robert Newmyer, Jeffrey Silver

Cast: John Candy (James Harlow), Richard Lewis (Phil Taylor), Robert Picardo (Ed Wheeler), Ed Lauter (John Slade), Rodney A. Grant (Little Feather), Russell Means (Chief)

Story: An inept and drunken scout is hired to lead a wagon train of settlers from the Western frontier back to Eastern civilization.

Production: Filmed in Durango, Mexico, *Wagons East* was meant to be a comedic satire of the western film genre. Star John Candy died of a heart attack in his room on location in Durango just before filming was completed; a photo double was used to complete certain scenes. Candy was a popular comedic actor best known for *Splash*, 1984; *Planes, Trains & Automobiles* (1987); *Uncle Buck* (1989); *Only the Lonely*, 1991). He had worked previously in Jalapa, Veracruz, in *Volunteers* (1985).

DESPERADO (COLUMBIA PICTURES, 1995)

Director: Robert Rodriquez

Screenplay: Robert Rodriguez

Producer: Robert Rodriguez, Carlos Gallardo, Bill Borden, Elizabeth Avellan

Cast: Antonio Banderas (El Mariachi), Salma Hayek (Carolina), Joaquim de Almeida (Bucho), Cheech Marin (short bartender), Danny Trejo (Navajas), Quentin Tarantino (pick-up guy)

Story: El Mariachi is a mysterious, gun-slinging, guitar-toting stranger who walks into a Mexican town to rid it of an assortment of bad guys, especially the drug lord who ruined his life. He is joined in this endeavor by the beautiful and most capable Carolina.

Production: Filmed in the Mexican border town of Ciudad Acuna (Acuna City) in the Mexican state of Coahuilla, just the other side of the Rio Grande, and the city of Del Rio, Texas, *Desperado* is the big-budget studio remake of *El Mariachi*, the $7,000 16mm independent film which rocked the Sundance Film Festival and launched the career of filmmaker Robert Rodriguez. *Desperado* was first conceived as a sequel but was turned into something

Director Robert Rodríguez and Antonio Banderas.

much more as the story and budget were developed with Columbia Pictures. The original actor, Carlos Gallardo, was replaced by Spanish leading man Antonio Banderas, who was gaining prominence in English-language cinema. Despite studio protests, Rodriquez cast then-unknown Mexican actress Salma Hayek as Carolina. The film catapulted Banderas and Hayek to international prominence. Cinematography was by Guillermo Navarro, the production design was by Cecilia Monteil, and the costume designer was Graciela Mazón. The influence of the *mariachi* as a gun-toting symbol lies in the Mexican *charro* tradition, which Rodriguez, a Texas-born director of Mexican descent, morphed into a Sergio Leone–like "Man with No Name" anti-hero.

MY FAMILY/MI FAMILIA (NEW LINE CINEMA, 1995)

Director: Gregory Nava
Screenplay: Gregory Nava, Anna Thomas
Producer: Laura Greenlee, Anna Thomas, Nancy De Los Santos, Francis Ford Coppola
Cast: Jimmy Smits (Jimmy), Edward James Olmos (Paco), Esai Morales (Chucho), Jenny Gago (Maria), Enrique Castillo (Memo "Bill"), Elpidia Carrillo (Isabel), Lupe Ontiveros (Irene), Jacob Vargas (young José) Maria Canals (young Irene), Scott Bakula (David Ronconi), Mary Steenburgen (Gloria), Jennifer Lopez (young Maria)

Story: Multi-generational saga of the Sanchez family, beginning with their arrival from Mexico to Los Angeles in the thirties.

Production: Produced by Francis Ford Coppola (*The Godfather,* 1972), who saw similarities between this story and his own Italian-American immigrant experience. Though largely filmed in Los Angeles, the early scenes in Mexico were filmed on location in and around Pátzcuaro Michoacán. Jimmy Smits dominates the latter portion of the film with his performance as the adult Jimmy Sanchez, the son who is most affected by witnessing the tragic death of his older brother, played by Esai Morales. *My Family/Mi Familia* features one of the first screen roles for Jennifer Lopez, who plays the young Maria in the early sequences. After her work in this film under the guidance of director Gregory Nava, Lopez played Mexican-American singer Selena Quintanilla in the biopic *Selena* (1997), which catapulted her to stardom. American-born Mexican actor Eduardo Lopez Rojas was brought to Hollywood from Mexico by Nava to play José, the patriarch of the Sanchez family. Leon Singer, also from Mexico, played Los Angeles oldtimer El Californio.

ROMEO + JULIET (MIRAMAX COMPANY, 1996)

Director: Baz Luhrmann

Screenplay: Craig Pearce, Baz Luhrmann

Producer: Baz Luhrmann, Gabriella Martinelli

Cast: Leonardo Di Caprio (Romeo), Claire Danes (Juliet), John Leguizamo (Tybalt), Brian Dennehy (Ted Montaque), Paul Sorvino (Fulgencio Capulet)

Story: Shakespeare's immortal tragedy of two young star-crossed lovers from rival families, set in a gritty, urban, modern environment.

Production: Art direction transformed Mexico City and Veracruz into contemporary Verona for this production, directed by Baz Luhrmann (*Strictly Ballroom*, 1992; *Moulin Rouge!*, 2001; *The Great Gatsby*, 2013). The cityscapes are not identifiable but some of the architecture has a pseudo-Latin flavor that sets the tone for the film. The exterior of the historic Chapultepec Castle in Mexico City was transformed into an opulent mansion. A giant statue of Jesus Christ was matted into the Mexico City La Reforma that looms large in the film. The opening sequence, establishing the families and gang rivalries, was filmed on one of the busiest streets in downtown Mexico City, where an abandoned gas station set was built. Interior sets were constructed at Estudios Churubusco. The carnival-like Sycamore Beach of the story was fabricated on a deserted beach in Veracruz. The effects of an approaching hurricane that hit on the last day of filming in Veracruz can be seen in the film; the storm damaged all the sets. Veteran Australian cinematographer Donald McAlpine (*Predator*, 1987; *Medicine Man*, 1992; *Clear and Present Danger*, 1994) lensed the film. The scene in the church which is seemingly lit by hundreds of candles, shows the influence of the late Mexican cinematographer Gabriel Figueroa. The location used for this scene was the Immaculate Heart of Mary Catholic Church, in the Del Valle neighborhood.

Shakespeare's tragedy was repurposed and retold for contemporary audiences in much the same way as *West Side Story* (1961), becoming a landmark production for audiences of that era. Leonardo Di Caprio, as Romeo, was only a year away from attaining major stardom in *Titanic* (1997). Claire Danes, who essayed the role of Juliet, continued a successful acting career, starring in such films as *Little Women* (1994), *The Mod*

Squad (1999), *Terminator 2* (2003), and *Stardust* (2007). Danes has won three Emmy awards for her leading roles in the television series *My So-Called Life* (1994–1995) and *Homeland* (2011–). John Lequizamo, who plays Tybalt, Juliet's cousin and Romeo's sworn enemy, has had a successful career as an actor, comedian, writer, and producer on the Broadway stage, on the big screen, and in television He also appeared in Luhrmann's *Moulin Rouge!* (2001).

TITANIC (20TH CENTURY FOX/PARAMOUNT, 1997)

Director: James Cameron

Screenplay: James Cameron

Producer: James Cameron, Jon Landau

Cast: Leonardo DiCaprio (Jack Dawson), Kate Winslet (Rose DeWitt Bukater), Billy Zane (Cal Hockley), Kathy Bates (Molly Brown), Frances Fisher (Ruth DeWiit Bukater), Jonathan Hyde (Bruce Ismay), Victor Garber (Thomas Andrews), David Warner (Spicer Lovejoy), Bill Paxton (Brock Lovett), Gloria Stuart (old Rose)

Story: The 1912 sinking of the luxury liner RMS *Titanic*, one of the most famous maritime disasters in history, provides the backdrop for the personal drama of two young people from different classes who fall in love on the fateful voyage. American Jack Dawson wins a ticket on RMS *Titanic* during a dockside card game. Aboard the ship, he spots lovely society girl Rose Bukater. She is engaged to be married in Philadelphia to the wealthy Cal Hockley, whom she does not love. Feeling trapped, she contemplates suicide on the ship's bow, but is rescued by Jack. Jack is invited to dine with Rose and Cal, but the elites humiliate him. Jack brings Rose down to the immigrant third-class accommodations, where she revels in the freedom and joy of life she finds there. Rose learns that Jack is an artist and asks him to draw her nude—except for the blue diamond necklace given to her by Cal. Cal finds the drawing and has Jack incarcerated by the ship's authorities. When the *Titanic* hits an iceberg, Rose must find Jack—and elude Cal—as the ship sinks.

Production: Produced at a cost of $200 million, *Titanic* was the most expensive film made up to that time. It took the combined efforts of two major Hollywood studios, 20th Century Fox and Paramount Pictures, to produce this film. It went on to win eleven Academy Awards, including Best Picture and Best Director. Fox leased forty acres of oceanfront property in Rosarito, Mexico, and built a $10 million production facility. The coastal location provided a constant horizon necessary for shipboard scenes. Construction crews built two huge water tanks. One was ninety feet deep and over eight hundred feet wide, so a *Titanic* replica could slowly sink into seventeen million gallons of water fed directly from the Pacific Ocean. The second tank was thirty feet deep; it contained three million gallons of water and housed the elegant first-class dining salon and the three-story Grand Staircase. Maneuverable reproductions of portions of the exterior of the *Titanic*, and lavish interior sets, were also built on nearby sound stages. Most of the passengers on the ship were played by nine hundred Mexican extras, recruited from Baja, California, and as far south as Mexico City. Extras spent weeks in full period costumes portraying the victims and survivors of the sea disaster, falling into the water from the decks and floating in the water tank, as the ship sunk repeatedly for the cameras. Hundreds of Mexican technicians, craftsmen, and laborers contributed to the movie. Cameron's assistant director was Sebastian Silva, whose team included Joaquin Silva, A. Hugo Gutierrez, and Giselle Gurza.

Kate Winslet and Leonardo Di Caprio receive instructions from director James Cameron on the set of the Oscar-winning classic *Titanic* (1997), filmed entirely in Mexico at the Baja Studios.

I STILL KNOW WHAT YOU DID LAST SUMMER (COLUMBIA PICTURES, 1998)

Director: Danny Cannon

Screenplay: Lois Duncan, Trey Calloway

Producer: William S. Beasley, Neal Moritz

Cast: Jennifer Love Hewitt (Julia), Freddie Prinze Jr. (Ray Bronson), Brandy Norwood (Karla Wilson)

Story: Recovering from the traumatic events of the previous summer, during which she lost several friends to a madman, Julia and an entourage decide to vacation at a beach resort in the Bahamas. There, her past catches up to her.

Production: *I Still Know What You Did Last Summer* was a sequel to the hit teen/slasher thriller *I Know What You Did Last Summer* (1997). Needing a resort over which the production company could exercise complete control, a location was found two-and-a-half hours south of Puerto Vallarta, known as the abandoned El Tecuan Resort. Badly damaged by an earthquake, it proved to be a great location. With the help of American and Mexican construction crews under the supervision of the art department, the site was refurbished. (El Tamarindo Beach in Jalisco was also utilized.) The Mexican mountains, rock formations jutting out of the ocean, and glimpses of Spanish architecture are no match for the mostly flat Bahamian Island landscapes. Jose Ludlow headed the Mexican unit; Arturo del Rio was the second assistant director; Ricardo del Rio served as the Mexican unit production manager.

Director Martin Campbell discusses an upcoming scene with Anthony Hopkins and Antonio Banderas on the Hacienda Santa Maria Regla set of *The Mask of Zorro* (1998).

THE MASK OF ZORRO (SONY, 1998)

Director: Martin Campbell

Screenplay: Ted Elliott, Randall Johnson, John Eckow, based on a character created by Johnston M. McCulley

Producer: Doug Claybourne, David Foster

Cast: Antonio Banderas (Murietta/Zorro), Catherine Zeta Jones (Elena), Anthony Hopkins (Don Diego de la Vega/Zorro), Stuart Wilson (Don Raphael Montero), Pedro Armendáriz (Don Pedro)

Story: In 1821, Don Diego de la Vega is Zorro, the defender of the downtrodden against Don Rafael Montero, the cruel governor of Alta-California. Zorro is captured, his wife accidentally killed, and his infant daughter abducted. Imprisoned for twenty years, De la Vega escapes when he learns that Montero has returned with his now-grown daughter, Elena. De la Vega encounters a young thief, Alejandro Murietta, who has his own score to settle with Montero. After a few false starts, De la Vega grooms him to take up the mantle as the new Zorro.

Production: *Zorro* is the Spanish word for *Fox*, and the black-clad masked man is one of the most popular and recognizable fictional characters in the Spanish-speaking world, having been featured in books, movies, and on television. American writer Johnston M. McCulley created Zorro in 1919 in a serialized novel called *The Curse of Capistrano*. Zorro is the secret identity of Don Diego de la Vega, a masked, sword-wielding Californio nobleman who fought injustice in Old Spanish California. Silent screen star Douglas Fairbanks purchased the rights to the story and adapted it into the hit film *The Mark of Zorro* in 1920. The black costume associated with the character stems from this adaptation. 20th Century-Fox made a sound remake in 1940 with leading man Tyrone Power that was stylishly directed by Rouben Mamoulian. In 1958, Walt Disney introduced Zorro to a new generation of admirers with a popular television series.

There was much anticipation when it was announced in 1997 that Tri-Star Pictures and Amblin Entertainment were producing the first major Zorro film in nearly fifty years. Martin Campbell, who had previously directed the hit James Bond entry *GoldenEye* (1995), was tapped to direct the film, which was to be shot in Mexico. The story is an original one, in which Alejandro Murietta (Spanish-born heartthrob Antonio Banderas) succeeds the aging Zorro (Academy Award–winning British actor Sir Anthony Hopkins), who seeks vengeance for the death of his wife, his imprisonment, and the abduction of his daughter Elena (Welsh-born actress Catherine Zeta Jones).

The Mask of Zorro was filmed on location, from January through May of 1997, with Central Mexico doubling for Old California, An elaborate town plaza set was built at the San Blas Hacienda outside the city of Tlaxcala; Hacienda El Mortero was filmed in the village of Tetlapayac, in the state of Hidalgo; Mortero's gold mine was shot in an abandoned quarry outside of the town of De Atotonilco de Tula in Hidalgo; the Talamanca prison scenes were filmed in Santa Maria Regla, outside the town of Pachuca, also in the state of Hidalgo. Coastal scenes were shot in and around the beaches of Guaymas, in the state of Sonora. Interiors were filmed at Estudios Churubusco in Mexico City. The production designer was Cecilia Monteil; the costume designer was Graciela Mazon. Steven Spielberg served as one of the executive producers.

BEFORE NIGHT FALLS (FINE LINE FEATURES, 1999)

Director: Julian Schnabel
Screenplay: Cunningham O'Keefe, Lazaro Gomez Carriles, Julian Schnabel
Producer: John Killik
Cast: Javier Bardem (Reinaldo Arenas), Olivier Martinez (Lazaro), Johnny Depp (Bon Bon/Lieutenant Victor), Sean Penn (Cuco Sanchez)
Story: The life of openly gay Cuban rebel poet and novelist Reinaldo Arenas, from his early life in Cuba through the Cuban revolution and his exile to the United States.
Production: *Before Night Falls* filmed for sixty days in Mexico in 1999 in such locations as Veracruz and Merida doubling for Cuba between the years 1943 and 1990. Julian Schnabel made his reputation with his feature directorial debut, *Basquiat*, in 1996. He credits production designer Salvador Parra and cinematographers Xavier Perez Grobet and Guillermo Rosas for helping achieve the natural, realistic, and poetic look of the film. Most of the crew and cast were Mexican. Spanish-born actor Javier Bardem received Golden Globe and Oscar nominations as Best Actor for his portrayal.

DEEP BLUE SEA (WARNER BROS., 1999)

Director: Renny Harlin

Screenplay: Duncan Kennedy, Donna Powers, Wayne Powers

Producer: Bruce Berman, Akiva Goldstein, Tony Budwing

Cast: Thomas Jane (Carter Blake), Safford Burrows (Susan McAlester), Samuel Jackson (Russell Franklin), Jaqueline McKenzie (Janice Higgins), L L Cool J (Preacher)

Story: Scientists conducting experiments to genetically alter the brains of live sharks for Alzheimer's research in an underwater sea facility find themselves attacked by these sea creatures that have somehow become smarter and deadlier than humans.

Production: *Deep Blue Sea* was a $60 million science fiction/action/horror film that was filmed at Fox Baja Studios in Rosarito, Baja, California. It is a self-contained complete production facility that features some of the world's largest stages and filming tanks originally constructed for James Cameron's *Titanic* (1997). The twenty-eight-foot Mako sharks seen in the film, more than twice their normal size, were made up of a combination of practical Animatronics and CGI effects. Anna Roth was the production supervisor; Rafael Cuervo, the unit manager.

ONE MAN'S HERO (ORION PICTURES, 1999)

Director: Lance Hool

Screenplay: Mary M. Patton, Milton S. Gelman

Producer: Lance Hool, Conrad Hool

Cast: Tom Berenger (Sergeant John Riley), Daniela Romo (Marta), Joaquin DeAlmeida (Cortina), Patrick Bergen (General Winfield Scott), Rodolfo de Anda (General Campeche), Roger Cudney (Colonel Harvey)

Story: In 1846, a group of Irish-Catholic immigrants desert after enduring cruelly discriminatory treatment from the mostly Protestant U.S. Army. After fleeing to Mexico, they are persuaded by a local insurrectionist to join the Mexican Army, where they are easily accepted by fellow Catholics. Field-decorated Sgt. Joe Riley feels torn between loyalty to the adopted United States, his troops, and his newfound country, which is engulfed in a war with the United States. Riley also finds himself falling in love with Marta, the insurrectionist's lover.

Production: The focus of this historical epic is the St. Patrick's Battalion of mostly Irish-Catholic immigrants who fought for Mexico during the United States–Mexican War of 1846–1848. Known as "San Patricios," they are considered heroes in Mexico; in the United States they are considered traitors. A complex, little-known piece of history that dealt with United States expansionism, the United States gained not only Texas but New Mexico, California, Utah, and Arizona under the 1848 Treaty of Guadalupe, which ended the war.

Locations for *One Man's Hero* included Sierra De Los Organos, Sombrerete, Zacatecas, and Durango. Cinematography is by Brazilian cinematographer Jao Fernandes. The film was produced and directed by Mexican-born Lance Hool. It was to be released by Orion Pictures in 1998, but Orion went bankrupt and was purchased by MGM; the film was shelved for a year and then received a limited theatrical release. Critical and audience response was mixed. *One Man's Hero* is oddly similar in tone and production value to a film made in 2013—also in Durango—called *For Greater Glory* (*La Cristiada*) about the Cristeros religious conflict of 1925–1929.

ORIGINAL SIN (METRO-GOLDWYN-MAYER, 2001)

Director: Michael Cristofer

Screenplay: Michael Cristofer

Producer: Denis Di Novi, Kate Guinzburg, Carol Lees

Cast: Antonio Banderas (Luis Antonio Vargas), Angelina Jolie (Julia Russell), Thomas Jane (Walter Downs), Pedro Armendáriz Jr.(Jorge Cortes)

Story: A tale of passion, obsession, eroticism, and murder in 1930s Cuba, where people are not what they seem to be. Julia Russell, a mysterious American woman, arrives in Havana to marry Luis Antonio Varga. She believes he is a clerk at a coffee factory, but soon learns that he is the well-to-do owner. Believing her to be a plain Jane from her photograph, Luis is surprised by Julia's beauty and sensuality.

Production: *Original Sin* was directed by Pulitzer Prize– and Directors Guild of America Award–winner Michael Cristofer, who had directed Angelina Jolie's breakout role as super model Gia Carangi in the 1998 HBO film *Gia*. Antonio Banderas first made his mark in his native Spain in such films as Pedro Almodovar's *Women on the Verge of a Nervous Breakdown* (1988) and *Tie Me Up! Tie Me Down!* (1989) before making his Hollywood debut in *The Mambo Kings* (1992). He became a star through his work in *The Mask of Zorro* (1998), *Evita* (1996), and *Desperado* (1995), among others. Following *Original Sin*, Banderas made three other movies in Mexico, including *The Legend of Zorro* (2005), *Once Upon a Time in Mexico* (2003), and *And Starring Pancho Villa as Himself* (2003).

According to the production notes, the political situation between the United States and Cuba made it impossible to film there since there has been no economic or political relationship with the island nation since the 1960s. After scouting several countries in the Caribbean and Latin America, the filmmakers found exactly what they were looking for in Mexico. Since Cuba and Mexico were both claimed and colonized by Spain in the sixteenth century, the production, through painstaking location scouting, found architectural structures and physical landscapes in the latter country which strongly resemble the former. Interiors were shot at Estudios Churubusco and locations in Mexico City, including the Casino Espanol, which served as an elegant Havana Hotel, with a colorful Caribbean carnival spilling out into the street. The ex Hacienda Santa Monica, was built in 1770 in the suburb of Tlainepantla and served as a coffee warehouse, offices, and café. Among other locations were Puebla, the town of Campeche in the Yucatan state, an abandoned hacienda on a former sugar plantation in the tiny village of Oacalco (about thirty minutes outside of Cuernavaca in the state of Morelos), as well as a former train station and depot in Cuatla. Rodrigo Prieto (*Amores Perros*, 2000) was the cinematographer. He had previously won two Ariel Awards for *Sobrenatural* (*All of Them Witches*), in 1996, and *Un Embrujo* (*Under a Spell*), in 1998.

BLOW (NEW LINE CINEMA, 2001)

Director: Ted Demme

Screenplay: David McKenna, Nick Cassavetes, based on Bruce Porter's 1993 book, *Blow: How a Small-Town Boy Made $100 Million with the Medellin Cocaine Cartel and Lost It All*

Producer: Joel Stillerman

Cast: Johnny Depp (George Jung), Penelope Cruz (Mirtha), Ray Liotta (Fred), Rachel Griffith (Ermine), Jordi Molla (Diego Delgado), Cliff Curtis (Pablo Escobar), Miguel Sandoval (Olivares), Julia Vera (Clara Blanco), Bert Rosario (Panama banker), Tony Perez (banker)

Story: In the 1970s, George Jung, a California hippie, eventually follows a path that leads him to become an innovative drug trafficker of cocaine to America. He is eventually hunted down and caught by the FBI.

Production: According to the press notes, *Blow* was shot on Southern California locations and in Mexico. Mexican locations in the state of Morelos and Acapulco, Guerrero, served to also represent Colombia. René Villarreal was the first assistant director; Jose Ludlow was the line producer. Johnny Depp stars as Yung; his sexy Columbian wife who becomes addicted to the cocaine which supports the family business, is played by Spanish actress Penelope Cruz.

PEARL HARBOR (BUENA VISTA, 2001)

Director: Michael Bay

Screenwriter: Randall Wallace

Producer: Jerry Bruckheimer

Cast: Ben Affleck (Rafe), Josh Harnett (Danny), Kate Beckinsale (Evelyn), Cuba Gooding Jr. (Dorie Miller), Jon Voight (Franklin Delano Roosevelt), Alec Baldwin (General James H. Doolittle)

Story: Epic war drama about two young pilots and a beautiful nurse who are caught up in the events of the 1941 surprise attack by the Empire of Japan on Pearl Harbor, Hawaii, on Sunday December 7, 1941.

Production: *Pearl Harbor* was filmed in Hawaii and Southern California locations, and at Baja Studios in Rosarito, Baja California Norte. In June of 2000, two weeks were spent at the facility, filming underwater scenes. The largest tank was used to reenact the capsizing of the battleship USS *Oklahoma* and the sinking of the USS *Arizona*; the smaller tanks were used for the English Channel scenes.

THE MEXICAN (DREAMWORKS PICTURES, 2001)

Director: Gore Verbinski

Screenplay: J. H. Wyman

Producer: Lawrence Bender, John Baldecchi

Cast: Brad Pitt (Jerry) Julia Roberts (Samantha), James Gandolfini (Winston Baldry), Bob Balaban (Bernie Nayman), Richard Coca (Car Thief #1), Pedro Armendáriz Jr. (Mexican policeman), Castulo Guerra (Joe), Salvador Sanchez (Gunsmith), Ernesto Gomez Cruz (Tropillo), Daniel Zacapa (Mexican bartender), Angelina Palaez (mother)

Story: Not only is Jerry and Samantha's relationship in trouble, Jerry's unethical activities have landed him in trouble with the mob. As a last-ditch effort to redeem himself, Jerry must retrieve a cursed but valuable nineteenth-century pistol from Mexico, where he encounters an unfriendly landscape littered with numerous unsavory characters. Samantha finds herself on a journey of her own with hitman Winston that also leads her to Mexico and Jerry. The "Mexican" of the title refers to the gun with a storied past.

Production: Filmed in the historical town of Real de Catorce, which is located in the north central highlands of Mexico near San Luis Potosi, and nestled in the surrounding mountains at an elevation of 8,000 feet, the once-thriving silver-mining town is only accessible via a fifteen-and-a-half-mile cobblestone road which ends at the Ogarrio Tunnel, a one-lane former mine shaft. For two months prior to production, a team of technicians and contractors upgraded the town's infrastructure to supply the motion picture company's modern electrical, plumbing, and telecommunications needs. The production designer was Cecilia Montiel, and the art director was Diego Sandoval. In the production notes, Verbinski commented: "We had a lot of Mexican actors out of Mexico City but the Mexican crew is the best I ever worked with and I would go back there to shoot another movie." Because of the star power of Brad Pitt and Julia Roberts, the small town of fifteen hundred residents was besieged by worldwide paparazzi and received considerable media attention.

FRIDA (MIRAMAX, 2002)

Director: Julie Taymor
Screenplay: Clancy Sigal, Diane Lake, Gregory Nava, Anna Thomas
Producer: Salma Hayek, Liz Speed, Roberto Sneider, Nancy Hardin, Jay Polstein, Lindsey Flickinger
Cast: Salma Hayek (Frida Kahlo), Alfred Molina (Diego Rivera)
Story: A biography of Mexican artist Frida Kahlo, centering on her passionate relationship with fellow Mexican artist Diego Rivera. Kahlo was virtually unknown outside of Mexico until the mid-1980's, when she and her art were discovered by a new international generation. Decades after her death in 1954, Kahlo became the world's most coveted female painter, a cult figure and symbol of the feminist movement.
Production: *Frida* was filmed entirely on location in Mexico City, Puebla, and San Luis Potosi from April to July 2001. Mexico's rich, diverse architecture also enabled the production to find suitable locales to double for Paris and New York in the thirties and forties. To recreate the Mexico City suburb of Coyoacan in the twenties, cast and crew traveled to Puebla, about eighty miles east of Mexico City, for the first week of filming. Nestled in the Sierra Madre foothills, this four hundred-year-old city boasts stunning colonial Renaissance and neo-classical architecture in its historic center. Since the real Frida Kahlo house (The Casa Azul) is now a busy museum, the production team built a replica of the house and its courtyard on Stage 4 at Estudios Churubusco, where portions of several murals were also recreated. Actual locations in Mexico City included: the Ministry of Education building, where one of Rivera's murals is located; the San Angel studio, La Casa Azul, where Diego and Frida lived and worked (now a museum dedicated to their work); and the pyramids of Teotihuacan, where filming required special permission from then-President Vicente Fox. It took seven years for Salma Hayek's production company, Ventanarosa, to bring *Frida* to the big screen. Hayek first established herself as a bankable lead actress in movies like *Desperado* (1995) and *From Dusk Till Dawn* (1996) before she could take on the challenges of *Frida*. She chose experimental Tony Award–winning director Julie Taymor (*The Lion King*) to direct. As Taymor stated in the film's press notes: "This is a huge passionate love story, not just about Frida, told against a canvas of Mexico during an exciting, largely unknown time in that country's history . . . it was a volatile time with a strong sense of intellectual and political commitment." Adrian Grunberg was the first assistant director; Mexican director and journalist Diego Lopez Rivera, the grandson of Lupe Marin and Diego Rivera, served as historical consultant; and director of photography was Mexican-born Rodrigo Prieto. Production designer Felipe Fernández and art director Bernardo Trujillo collaborated with Hayek and Taymor. For both Fernández and Trujillo, working on *Frida* was a labor of love and a source of pride in their culture.

Frida premiered at the Venice Film Festival in August 2002. Salma Hayek was nominated for an Academy Award as Best Actress. Other nominations included Best Art Direction, Best Costume Design, Best Makeup, and Best Original Song "Burn It Blue," by Elliot Goldenthal and Julie Taymor; it won for Best Makeup and

Filmed in and around Mexico City and Puebla, *Frida* (2002) was nominated for six Academy Awards, including one for Salma Hayek as Best Actress.

Best Original Score. Score composer Elliot Goldenthal augmented the studio orchestra with a small group of Mexican musicians playing traditional instruments. Born in Brooklyn, New York, and a graduate of the Manhattan School of Music, Goldenthal (who also studied under Aaron Copeland) gained his expertise of Mexican music forms during his thirty years of travels to the country.

COLLATERAL DAMAGE (WARNER BROS., 2002)

Director: Andrew Davis

Screenplay: David Griffiths, Peter Griffiths

Producer: David Foster, Steven Reuther

Cast: Arnold Schwarzenegger (Gordy), John Leguizamo (Felix Ramirez) Cliff Curtis (Claudio), Elias Koteas (Peter Brandt, John Turturro (Sean Armstrong), Miguel Sandoval (Joe Phipps), Tyler Posey (Mauro) Raymond Cruz (Junior)

Story: When a terrorist explosion kills his family in Los Angeles, firefighter Gordy Brewer follows those responsible to Colombia on his quest for revenge.

Production: Filmed in Jalapa, Veracruz, and at Estudios Churubusco in Mexico City, *Collateral Damage* has well-staged action sequences and excellent use of Veracruz locations standing in for Colombia. This is Arnold Schwarzenegger's fourth film in Mexico following *Conan The Destroyer* (1984), *Predator* (1987), *and Total Recall* (1990). New Zealand born Maori actor Cliff Curtis (*Once Were Warriors*, 1994, *Colombiana*, 2011) plays lead villain Claudio "The Wolf " Perini. Actor/comedian/writer John Leguizamo makes an early screen appearance in a supporting role. The film relies heavily on the image of the lone American mowing down faceless Latinos in their home country. Coming on the heels of the tragedy of September 11, this violent film met with a cool reception at the box office from audiences who were still reeling from real life events. Today it can be viewed as a typical big budget action-adventure entertainment vehicle for star Arnold Schwarzenegger.

ONCE UPON A TIME IN MEXICO (COLUMBIA PICTURES, 2003)

Director: Robert Rodriguez

Screenplay: Robert Rodriguez

Producer: Carlos Gallardo, Robert Rodriguez, Elizabeth Avellan

Cast: Antonio Banderas (El Mariachi), Salma Hayek (Carolina), Johnny Depp (Agent Sands), Willem Dafoe (Barillo), Cheech Marin (Belini), Pedro Armendáriz Jr. (El Presidente), Mickey Rourke (Billy), Eva Mendes (Ajedrez), Enrique Iglesias (Lorenzo), Ruben Blades (Jorge FBI), Danny Trejo (Cucuy)

Story: American CIA agent Sands hires hitman El Mariachi to save the President of Mexico from an assassin hired by a drug cartel leader. Meanwhile, a vengeful El Mariachi also hunts the corrupt general who caused his wife's death. Chaos and bloodletting ensue.

Production: Filmed in San Miguel De Allende, Guanajuato, Mexico, this is the third entry in Robert Rodriguez's "Mexican Trilogy": *Once Upon a Time in Mexico* follows *El Mariachi* (1992) and *Desperado* (1995). Graciela Mazón created the costumes.

MASTER AND COMMANDER: THE FAR SIDE OF THE WORLD (20TH CENTURY FOX, 2003)

Director: Peter Weir

Screenplay: Peter Weir, John Collee, from the novels by Patrick O'Brian

Producer: Samuel Goldwyn Jr., Duncan Henderson, Peter Weir

Cast: Russell Crowe (Captain Lucky Jack Aubrey), Paul Bettany (Dr. Stephen Maturin), James D'Arcy (Lietenant Pullings), Edward Woodall (Lieutenant Mowett), Chris Larkin (Captain Howard), Billy Boyd (Barrett Bonden)

Story: During the Napoleonic Wars (1803–1814) between England and France, Lucky Jack Aubrey, captain of the HMS *Surprise*, is ordered to seize and destroy the HMS *Acheron*, somewhere along the coast of South America. Outmanned, he still must complete his mission. When an initial foray with the *Acheron* almost ends in disaster for Aubrey and his crew, he repairs the ship and chases the *Acheron* from Brazil, around treacherous Cape Horn, to a life-or-death battle near the Galapagos Islands.

Production: Filmed at Fox Studios in Rosarito, Baja California, *Master and Commander* was nominated for nine Academy Awards, including Best Picture and Best Director. It won for Russell Boyd's cinematography.

MAN ON FIRE (20TH CENTURY FOX, 2004)

Director: Tony Scott

Screenplay: Brian Heigeland, from the novel by A. J. Quinnell

Producer: Lucas Foster, Arnon Milchan, Tony Scott

Cast: Denzel Washington (Creasy), Radha Mitchell (Lisa Ramos), Dakota Fanning (Lupita), Christopher Walken (Rayburn), Marc Anthony (Mr. Ramos), Giancarlo Giannini (Manzano), Rachel Ticotin (Mariana), Gustavo Sanchez Parra (Daniel Sanchez), Jesus Ochoa (Victor Fuentes), Carmen Salinas (Guardian Three)

Story: Mexico City is the kidnapping capital of the world. Disillusioned and alcoholic former Special Forces operative Creasy asks his old friend in Mexico to land him a job. He arranges for Creasy to work for a wealthy Mexican businessman and his family as the bodyguard for their daughter Pita, with whom he develops an unlikely friendship. Things take a violent turn when Pita is kidnapped by a criminal gang in a shootout that leaves Creasy for dead. While recovering from his near-fatal wounds, he vows to exact revenge on the perpetrators and, hopefully, bring Pita back alive.

Production: *Man on Fire* is based on the novel by A. J. Quinnell; it revolves around the world of executive protection and the reality of international kidnappings. The original story was written and set in Italy during the 1970s, and a low-budget film of it, starring Scott Glenn, was made in 1987. By the time the 2004 remake went into production, Italy had solved its kidnapping situation, while Mexico currently ranked third among countries with major kidnappings. "We made a decision to switch the locale to a place where it was really happening, and Mexico City was chosen for its immediacy and for its film infrastructure that goes back to the 1930s," remarked executive producer Lance Hool in the production notes. Conrad Hool served as co-producer; Brian Helgeland, who won an Academy Award for his script for *L. A. Confidential* (1997), wrote the screenplay.

Man on Fire was the first Hollywood film to be shot almost entirely on location in contemporary Mexico City in more than forty years. Production began on April 7, 2003, following months of preparation. Locations included a spacious Spanish-style villa located in the wealthy Lomas De Chapultepec section that served as the Ramos family compound; the neighborhoods of La Condess, Colonia Roma, and the quaint San Angel district; the world-famous Garibaldi Square where hundreds of mariachi bands gather nightly; and the newly restored postal building in the historic center that was turned into a bank. The city's fash-

Mexico City's Mayor Marcelo Ebrard, actors Denzel Washington and Dakota Fanning, director Tony Scott and producer Lucas Foster at the Lomas de Chapultepec mansion location of *Man on Fire* (2004).

ionable Zona Rosa district proved too crowded and unmanageable to film a harrowing action sequence, so the town plaza of Puebla, a colonial city founded by Spanish explorers in 1531, located ninety miles from Mexico City, doubled for the location. Mextepec, a timeless village thirty miles outside of Puebla, with its sweeping landscape of agricultural lands, isolated bridges and volcano looming in the background, became the setting for the finale.

Given Tony Scott's extensive research into Mexico and the social and political conditions that led to its ranking as third in the world in kidnappings, it's not surprising that the country itself, as well as its capital, Mexico City, play important roles in *Man on Fire*. He captures Mexico City's pollution, traffic, and the cacophony that bombard its citizens. "I wanted to make the city a major character," says Scott. "It has a rich cultural history and is full of visual contrasts and architectural richness. It is sensual and beautiful and, at the same time, it's dark and dangerous." To give *Man on Fire* a taught, claustrophobic, reality-based feel, the production filmed mostly on location throughout Mexico City. Shooting in the oldest, largest, and most traffic-congested city in North America was a constant challenge. More than fifty vehicles were needed to thread cast, crew, and equipment through the narrow, crowded streets. In addition, general strikes were an almost daily fact of life, and the filmmakers had to wade through Mexico City's labyrinthine bureaucracy of seventeen mini-states, each with its own municipality and governor. "But it was all worth it," says producer Lucas Foster, "because audiences will see a contemporary Mexico of extremes, brimming with light, color and extraordinary people."

"Extremes" might also describe Tony Scott's and director of photography Paul Cameron's use of light, color, exposures, and film processes to reflect Crease's emotional and psychological upheaval during and after the kidnapping. Academy Award–winning actor Denzel Washington (*Training Day*, 2001) stars as Creasy, the former covert operative-turned-bodyguard. He began his successful collaboration with Tony Scott on *Crimson Tide* (1995)

and continued with *Man on Fire*, *Déjà Vu* (2006), and *Unstoppable* (2010). He is ably supported by Oscar winner Christopher Walken (Best Supporting Actor for *The Deer Hunter*, 1978), Australian actress Radha Mitchell, former eighties leading man Mickey Rourke, salsa singer-turned-actor Marc Anthony, Italian film idol Giancarlo Gianini as a Mexican policeman, and Rachel Ticotin as a journalist. Eleven-year-old Dakota Fanning, who caught moviegoers' attention in *I Am Sam* (2001), is Pita.

TROY (WARNER BROS., 2004)

Director: Wolfgang Petersen

Screenplay: David Beniof, from *The Iliad* by Homer

Producer: Wolfgang Petersen, Diana Rathburn, Colin Wilson

Cast: Brad Pitt (Achilles) Eric Bana (Hector), Orlando Bloom (Paris), Diane Kruger (Helen), Peter O'Toole (Priam)

Story: Achilles, Greece's greatest warrior, serves in the army of King Agamemnon. When Prince Paris of Troy visits Greece, he falls in love with Queen Helen, and they steal away back to Troy. Her husband, King Mennaleus of Sparta, joins with his brother Agamemnon in gathering the armies of Greece to attack the walled city of Troy across the Aegean Sea and retrieve Helen. Achilles and his men arrive first and seize the landing beach and temple before Agamemnon and his troops can establish a beachhead. Agamemnon hurts Achilles's pride by not recognizing his victory, even after he discovers that Achilles had captured Hector, the brother of Paris. Achilles falls in love with a temple virgin and vows to return to Greece when his cousin, pretending to be Achilles, is slain in battle by Hector. Achilles vows revenge. After he kills Hector in a monumental fight at the foot of Troy's gate, Achilles and his men hide inside a statue of a forty-foot-tall wooden horse, left as a prize for the Trojans. The Trojans bring the horse within the city walls and, after nightfall, the Greeks slip out, open the city gates, and the full force of the army invades, sacking, looting, and burning Troy.

Production: *Troy* was filmed in London, Malta, and Los Cabos, Baja Mexico on a grand scale. Sweeping visuals and stunning set design (aided by computer-generated imagery) give power to this story. According to producer Diane Rathburn, "There was no expanse of beach big enough for our computer graphics expert to put a thousand ships or enough underdeveloped land to stage a battle involving 75,000 troops." Morocco was first considered as a location, but political instability in the region ruled that out. A suitable stretch of

Brad Pitt and Director Wolfgang Petersen on the Cabos San Lucas set of *Troy* (2004).

broad, underdeveloped beach was found in Los Cabos, Mexico, at the southernmost tip of the Baja Peninsula, one hundred miles from the United States border. For cinematic purposes, the beach believably stands in for the Aegean Sea. Crewmembers were hired from Mexico City. Two filming units worked simultaneously six days a week to capture the necessary action. Two hundred and thirty laborers were utilized to build two working, full-sized Greek ships, the magnificent Temple of Apollo, and the imposing wall surrounding the city of Troy. Five hundred Mexican extras and three hundred Bulgarian extras were hired to comprise the Greek and Trojan armies. These numbers would be multiplied onscreen through the use of CGI and other special effects. Four weeks prior to filming, the extras underwent rigorous training so they could execute precision movements of an ancient army utilizing swords, arrows, and spears while outfitted in full armor. Massive battle scenes in full combat are choreographed and magnificently staged. Filming took place on the unshaded beach in the middle of the summer and the temperatures often soared above one hundred degrees, so a compound was constructed to offer support services for the entire company. Production in Mexico began on July 11 and continued until September 21 when, with only two weeks of filming remaining, Hurricane Marty struck the southern tip of Baja. The sets suffered major damage, including the collapse of the middle two-thirds section of the wall of Troy. The final scene (the monumental fight of kings, between Achilles and Hector) was delayed while the walls of Troy and other sets were rebuilt; these were not completed until December.

CLUB DREAD (20TH CENTURY FOX, 2004)

Director: Jay Chandrasekhar (as Broken Lizard)

Screenplay: Jay Chandrasekhar, Kevin Heffernan, Steve Lemme, Paul Soter, Erik Stolhanske (billed individually as Broken Lizard)

Producer: Conrad Hool, Lance Hool, Richard Perello

Cast: Bill Paxton (Coconut Pete), Erik Stolhanske (Sam), Brittany Daniel (Jenny), Steve Lemme (Juan), Jay Chandrasekhar (Putnam), Paul Soter (Dave)

Story: A tropical island pleasure resort, run by former rock star Coconut Pete, is a nonstop party for the young guests until the festivities are interrupted when guests start turning up dead. It is up to a group of resort staff members and guests to try and find out who is behind these murders before they become victims themselves.

Production: The movie was filmed north of Manzanillo, Mexico. The filmmakers created Coconut Pete's Pleasure Island Resort, set in Costa Rica, at the luxurious Tamarindo Resort. The cast and crew were housed at the resort in which they were filming. Members of Broken Lizard, a successful comedy troupe, have continued to make their own brand of comedy films, *Beerfest* (2006), *The Slammin' Salmon* (2009), and producing multi-media content. *Club Dread* is a horror-comedy that doesn't always succeed in bringing the two genres together, but there are laughs, sexy women, and zany characters in this tequila-soaked 24/7 party resort.

THE LEGEND OF ZORRO (COLUMBIA PICTURES, 2005)

Director: Martin Campbell

Screenplay: Alex Kurtzman, Roberto Orci, Ted Elliott, Terry Rossio, based on a character created by Johnston M. McCulley

Producer: Laurie MacDonald, Walter F. Parkes, Lloyd Phillips

Cast: Antonio Banderas (Zorro), Catherine Zeta Jones (Elena), Rufus Sewell (Armand), Adrian Alonso (Joaquin), Nick Chitlund (Jacob McGivens), Julio Oscar Mechoso (Fray Felipe)

Story: Zorro must save California from unscrupulous individuals who are trying to take over the territory before it becomes the thirty-first state in the union. Through all of this, Zorro attempts to balance his home life with his fight against injustice and be a role model for his young son. Elena separates from him and is recruited by the United States government for a secret mission, of which Zorro is unaware, until they find themselves fighting the same enemy.

Production: Set in Old California but filmed in San Luis Potosi and San Miguel De Allende Mexico, with the primary location site being Hacienda Gogorron, *The Legend of Zorro* is a big, overblown production with vistas which are too populated for the time period and with extravagant haciendas that would not have existed in 1850s California. Interiors were shot and constructed at Estudios Churubusco in Mexico City. Mexican actors featured in the cast are Raul Mendez as Ferroq, Gustavo Sanchez Parra as Cortez, Giovanna Zacarias as Blanca, and Pedro Armendáriz Jr. as the governor of California. Armendáriz appeared in *The Mask of Zorro* in the role of Don Pedro. For this sequel, Cecilia Montiel returned as production designer, and Graciela Mazón returned as costume designer.

MATADOR (MIRAMAX, 2005)

Director: Richard Shepard

Screenplay: Richard Shepard

Producer: Pierce Brosnan, Beau St. Clair

Cast: Pierce Brosnan (Julian Noble), Greg Kinnear (Danny Wright), Hope Davis (Carolyn "Bean" Wright), Phillip Baker Hall (Mr. Randy)

Story: International hit man Julian Noble and struggling salesman Danny Wright (Greg Kinnear) form an unexpected bond during a chance meeting in a luxurious Mexico City bar. Six months later, Julian, the self-proclaimed "facilitator of fatalities," turns up at the Wrights' doorstep, desperate for help. Danny and his wife are both horrified but intrigued enough to oblige. Together, the two men set out for the most critical kill of Julian's career—and Danny's unexpected repayment of a favor owed to Julian.

Production: Filmed entirely in Mexico City, *Matador* incorporates imaginative uses of locations in and around the city, including El Camino Real Hotel and Plaza Mexico bullring. Mexico City is portrayed as a vibrant, exciting, colorful, modern metropolis. It also doubles in the film for Budapest, Sydney, Denver, and the Philippines.

BABEL (PARAMOUNT, 2006)

Director: Alejandro Gonzalez Iñárritu

Screenplay: Guillermo Arriaga

Producer: Jon Kilik, Steve Golin

Cast: Brad Pitt (Richard Jones), Cate Blanchett (Susan), Gael Garcia Bernal (Santiago), Adriana Barraza (Amelia), Rinko Kikuchi (Chicko Wataya), Koji Yashuko (Yasujiro Wataya)

Story: Armed with a Winchester rifle, two Moroccan boys set out to look after their family's herd of goats. In the silent echoes of the desert, they decide to test the rifle but the bullet goes farther than they thought it would. In an instant, the lives of four separate groups of strangers on three different continents collide, caught up in the rising tide of mishaps that escalate beyond anyone's control. The characters include a vacationing American couple; a rebellious, deaf Japanese teenager and her father; and a Mexican nanny who, without permission, takes two American children across the border.

Production: Filmed in Morocco, Mexico, California, and Tokyo, Japan. The Mexico sequences were shot in Tijuana, in the northern town of El Carrizo, standing in for Los Lobos Hamlet. Key sequences were shot along the border, between Mexico and California. *Babel* was nominated for seven Academy Awards in 2007, including Best Picture, Best Director, and Best Supporting Actress for Adriana Barraza in recognition of her portrayal as the well-meaning Mexican nanny. The film received but one Oscar, for Best Music Score by Gustavo Santaolalla.

BANDIDAS (20TH CENTURY FOX, 2006)

Director: Joachim Renning, Espen Sandberg

Screenplay: Luc Besson, Robert Mark Kamen

Producer: Luc Besson, Ariel Zeitoun

Cast: Salma Hayek (Sarah Sandoval), Penelope Cruz (Maria Alvarez), Steve Zahn (Quentin), Ismael "East" Carlo (Don Diego), Dwight Yoakam (Tyler Jackson), Sam Shepard (Bill Buck), Gary Carlos Cervantes (Pedro), Ernest Gomez Cruz (Brujo)

Story: Sara Sandoval is the daughter of a wealthy Mexican rancher, while Maria Alvarez is the daughter of a poor Mexican farmer. The women, who seem to have nothing in common except their Mexican heritage, are thrown together by fate. With Quentin, a New York detective, they battle a land grab by the Texas representative of a New York bank.

Production: Filmed in Durango, Real De Catorce, and at Estudios Churubusco in Mexico City, *Bandidas* was produced by Luc Besson with the combined talents of a French, American, and Mexican cast and crew. *Bandidas* is a female buddy film in the guise of an action-comedy, with two of the most beautiful and talented actresses of world cinema, Spanish-born Penelope Cruz and Mexican-born Salma Hayek.

NACHO LIBRE (PARAMOUNT, 2006)

Director: Jared Hess

Screenplay: Jerusha Hess, Jared Hess, Mike White

Producer: Jack Black, Mike White, Julia Pistor

Cast: Jack Black (Ignacio/Nacho), Ana Maria Reguerra (Sister Encarnación), Héctor Jiménez (Steven/Esqueleto), Darius A. Rose (Chancho), Richard Montoya (Guillermo), Cesar Gonzales "Silver King" (Ramses), Moises Arias (Juan Pablo)

Story: Ignacio, an orphan raised in a Mexican monastery, grows up to be a cook. When he learns that the monastery lacks money to buy proper food for the oprhans in its charge, Ignacio decides to follow his life-long dream of becoming a masked wrestler, hoping to win cash prizes in the ring to raise funds for the monastary. The arrival of a beautiful young nun, Sister Encarnación, spurs him to action and he partners with an agile street thief to form an unlikely tag team.

Production: Filmed in Oaxaca, Mexico, the final scene was filmed in the ancient Zapotec ruins of Monte Alban, an archeological site in the southern part of the state of Oaxaca. *Nacho Libre* is based on the true story of Fray Tormenta (a.k.a. Reverend Sergio Gutiérrez Benítez), a real-life Mexican priest who had a twenty-three-year career as a masked wrestler. It is the first American film that explores the world of Mexican masked wrestlers, or *Luchadores*. It captures the cultural spirit of this uniquely Mexican popular cultural entertainment phenomenon. Director Jared Hess was earlier celebrated when his quirky 2004 comedy *Napoleon Dynamite* became a critical and box-office hit. Director of photography is Xavier Perez Grobet.

APOCALYPTO (TOUCHSTONE, 2006)

Director: Mel Gibson

Screenplay: Mel Gibson, Farhad Sarfinia

Producer: Mel Gibson, Farhad Sarfinia, Bruce Davey

Cast: Rudy Youngblood (Jaquar Paw), Raoul Trujillo (Zero Wolf), Rudolfo Palacios (Snake Ink), Gerardo Taracena (Middle Eye), Fernando Hernandez (High Priest), Dalia Hernandez (Seven), Jonathan Brewer (Blunted), Carlos Ramos (Monkey Jaw)

Story: In the Kingdom of the Mayans before the Spanish Conquest, hunter Jaguar Paw and his villagers enjoy a tranquil existence until a warring tribe destroys their hamlet and takes prisoners to sell as slaves or be sacrificed to the gods. At the seat of the Mayan Kingdom, Jaguar Paw, slated for sacrifice, beats tremendous odds and escapes his impending death. He struggles to return home to his pregnant wife and child, all the while being pursued by relentless captors through a savage jungle.

Production: Filmed in the state of Veracruz, Mexico, at such locations as Catemaco, San Andrés Tuxtla, and Paso De Ovejas, Academy Award–winning actor/director Mel Gibson's *Apocalypto* brilliantly captures the fascinating period of the Mayan Empire. Most of the $45 million budget went into creating this lost world. The company spent six months on location in the jungles near Catemaco, and an area of flat terrain where the Mayan city set was constructed outside Veracruz, a bustling port city with modern hotel accommoda-

Oscar-winning director Mel Gibson on the Vista de Salto de Eyipantla, Catemaco, Veracruz, location of *Apocalypto* (2006).

tions for the cast and crew. The waterfall scene was shot at Salto de Eyipantla, near San Andrés Tuxtla. Academy Award–winning cinematographer Dean Semler (*Dances with Wolves*, 1990) utilized up to four cameras to capture the action. Production designer Tom Sanders, costume designer Mayes Rubeo, makeup artist Aldo Signoretti, and makeup designer Vittorio Sodano worked together to create the looks of the main characters as well as the hundreds of extras depicting various levels of Mayan society. Nearly every element of the film was handmade by hundreds of craftsmen and artists throughout Mexico. Costume designer Rubeo, a native of Mexico City, assembled a team of fifty-two people who crafted individual pieces for each character. Rubeo tried to use materials indigenous to the Mayans, procuring patterned fabric from present-day Mayan communities in Chiapas, such as San Cristobalde las Casa, and in Oaxaca, famous for elaborate hand-loomed cotton goods. There was not sufficient indigenious fabric to costume seven hundred extras, so reproducible cloth was used. A master dyer from Mexico City hand-dyed the fabrics to match the colors that the ancient Mayans obtained from animal, mineral, and plant sources. Casting director Carla Hool helped Gibson find authentically indigenous actors to tell this story. Native American actors from the United States and Canada interpreted many leading roles, while local talent filled supplemental spots. Most of the actors were unknowns with limited experience, but Gibson worked with them extensively. A major challenge was the dialogue language, Yucatec Mayan, which is spoken only in the Yucatan region of Mexico and Central America and rarely heard elsewhere. A local Mayan language expert was utilized by the production to teach the actors a semblance of the language for onscreen purposes. Cameraman Dean Semler captured the pristine natural environments of the rivers, the rain, and the lush green jungle, all of which makes *Apocalypto* visually stunning. The Mayan city sequences bring stand-out production elements together to entrance viewers of this absorbing action-adventure.

THE AIR I BREATHE (THINKFILM PATHÉ, 2007)

Director: Jicho Lee

Screenplay: Jicho Lee, Bob DeRosa

Producer: Emilio Diez Barroso, Darlene Caamano Loquet, Paul Schiff

Cast: Brendan Fraser (Pleasure), Sarah Michelle Gellar (Sorrow), Andy Garcia (Fingers), Kevin Bacon (Love), Forest Whitaker (Happiness), Cecilia Suarez (Allison)

Story: Characters are unnamed but interconnected in four vignettes, based on a Chinese proverb about human emotions.

Production: *The Air I Breathe* is an independent film shot in and around Mexico City, although the location is never identified as such. An extraordinary cast of leading contemporary actors shine under the helm of first-time Korean/American director/writer Jicho Lee. This modest budget but ambitious and thought-provoking movie ultimately does not work as a whole; it needed the surer hand of a more experienced director. *The Air I Breathe* opened in one theater in New York before quickly disappearing.

TRADE (LIONSGATE, 2007)

Director: Marco Kreuzpainte

Screenplay: José Rivera

Producer: Roland Emmerich, Rosilyn Heller

Cast: Kevin Kline (Ray Sheridan), Cesar Ramos (Jorge), Pauline Gaitan (Adriana), Kate del Castillo (Laura), Marco Perez (Manuel) Alicja Bachleda (Veronica)

Story: Jorje's young teenage sister Adriana is kidnapped off the streets of Mexico City and sold into a sex-slave ring. From the barrios of Mexico City and the treacherous Rio Grande border, to a secret international sex-slave ring and the final climactic confrontation in a stash house in suburban New Jersey, American investigator Ray, and Mexican street urchin Jorge, forge a close bond as they give desperate chase to young Adriana's kidnappers in the hope of rescuing her.

Production: *Trade* began filming in Mexico City on November 28, 2005, in La Merced. The exterior of an old government building stood in for a snow-covered Poland in the winter. Snow was duplicated using sea salt, which worked effectively on camera. Except for a border crossing at El Paso, Juarez, the rest of the film was shot in and around Albuquerque, New Mexico, with second-unit exteriors in New Jersey. Cinematographer Daniel Gottschalk decided to shoot this movie almost exclusively with hand-held cameras. The film is based on a *New York Times Magazine* cover story written by Peter Landesman, who spent five months in Mexico City researching the story on the child sex trade crime network in the United States, Mexico, and Europe. The film was executive produced by Roland Emmerich (*Independence Day*, 1996; *The Patriot*, 2000); the initial idea was brought to him by his partner, Rosilyn Heller, who commissioned the script from José Rivera (*The Motorcycle Diaries*, 2004). Carla Hool was the casting director, and Emmerich—then busy with other film commitments—hired Marco Kreuzpaintner to direct.

BEVERLY HILLS CHIHUAHUA (WALT DISNEY PICTURES, 2008)

Director: Raja Gosnell

Screenplay: Ana Lisa La Bianco, Jeffrey Bushell

Producer: David Hoberman, Jeb Jacobs, Todd Lieberman

Cast: Drew Barrymore (Chloe), Jamie Lee Curtis (Viv), Piper Perabo (Rachel), Andy Garcia (Delgado), George Lopez (Papi), Edward James Olmos (El Diablo), Placido Domingo (Monte)

Story: Chloe, a pampered Beverly Hills-raised Chihuahua, is left in the care of her owner's irresponsible niece, who takes her to Mexico on a weekend trip. Chloe wanders away from the hotel and is dognapped. She eludes her captors and tries to make her way back home.

Production: Live-action film featuring dogs being voiced by well-known actors. Shooting locations included Guadalajara, Las Palmas Jalisco, Nuevo Vallarta, Nayarit, Hermosillo, Sonora, and Estudios Churubusco. The unit manager was Arturo del Rio; the second assistant director in Mexico was Renan Bendersky.

CHE (IFC FILMS, 2008)

Director: Steven Sodenbergh

Screenplay: Part One (*The Argentine*) by Peter Buchman, based on Guevara's *Reminiscences of the Cuban Revolutionary War*; Part Two (*Guerilla*) by Benjamin A. van der Veen

Producer: Laura Bickford, Benicio Del Toro, Steven Soderbergh

Cast: Benicio Del Toro (Che), Demian Bichir (Fidel Castro) Julia Ormond (Lisa Howard), Santiago Cabrera

(Camilo Cienfuegos), Victor Rasuk (Rogelio Acevedo), Catalina Sandino Moreno (Aleida March)

Story: *Che* is Oscar winning director (*Traffic* 2000) Steven Soderbergh's ambitious biographical film on iconic Argentinean Marxist hero of the Cuban Revolution, Ernesto "Che" Guevara. The four hour twenty-one minute film was edited into two parts for subsequent exhibition after its debut at Cannes to mixed reviews. Part One (The Argentine) crosscuts scenes between a recreated 1964 Guevara interview with a journalist during an official visit to New York and events in the Cuban Revolution (1953–1959). These include Guevara's first meeting in Mexico City with an exiled Fidel Castro, organizing and recruiting a rebel army across the Cuban countryside, survival in the rugged jungles of the Sierra Madres, and the armed revolt in Santa Clara that led to the overthrow of Cuban dictator Batista in Havana. Part Two (Guerilla) centered on the export of revolution to Bolivia and Che's capture and death.

Production: Part One was filmed on a thirty-nine day schedule in New York, Puerto Rico, and Campeche, Mexico, in 2007. Anna Roth was the line producer for the sequences filmed in Campeche, Mexico, doubling for Santa Clara, Cuba. Future Oscar nominee Demian Bichir first gained critical attention for his role as Fidel Castro. Though not the usual linear Biopic, *Che* is long, plodding, and demanded endurance in its one-sitting theatrical release. The film is better served in the home video or streaming format. The enigmatic Che is given a nuanced flesh and blood portrayal by Puerto Rican born actor Benicio Del Toro who won a Best Supporting actor Oscar in 2000 for his role as a conflicted Mexican policeman in Soderbergh's *Traffic*. Though segments of *Traffic* were set in Mexico they were actually filmed in Nogales, San Diego, and Tijuana.

VANTAGE POINT (20TH CENTURY FOX, 2008)

Director: Pete Travis

Screenplay: Barry L. Levy

Producer: Neal H. Moritz

Cast: Dennis Quaid (Thomas Barnes), Matthew Fox (Kent Taylor), Forest Whitaker (Howard Lewis), Sigourney Weaver (Rex), William Hurt (President Ashton), Zoe Saldana (Angie Jones), Eduardo Noriega (Enrique), Edgar Ramirez (Javier)

Story: During a historic counter-terrorism summit in Spain, the president of the United States is struck down by an assassin's bullet. Eight strangers have a perfect view of the kill, but what did they really see? As the minutes leading up to the fatal shots are replayed through the point of view of each witness, the reality behind the assassination takes form. But just when you think you know the answer, the shattering final truth is revealed.

Production: Mexico City substitutes for Salamanca, Spain. The challenge for production designer Brigitte Broch (who, with Catherine Martin, shared the Academy Award for Best Art Direction on 2001's *Moulin Rouge!*) was to build an exact duplicate of Salamanca's Plaza Mayor in Mexico City, which the production team would then blow up. Location scouts found an ideal place in the southern part of Mexico City, in an abandoned four-story mall. It housed the construction, carpentry, metal, and plastic shops; next to it was a pit, where the actual Plaza was built. The set had total security, privacy, and offered complete control for filming purposes.

FAST AND THE FURIOUS 4 (UNIVERSAL PICTURES, 2009)

Director: Justin Lin

Screenwriter: Chris Morgan

Producer: Neal H. Moritz, Vin Diesel, Michael Fotrell

Cast: Vin Diesel (Dominic Toretto), Paul Walker (Brian O'Conner), Michelle Rodriguez (Letty Ortiz), Jordana Brewster (Mia Toretto), Gal Gadot (Gisele Yashar), Don Omar (Rico Santos), Tego Calderon (Tego), John Ortiz (Arturo Braga), Laz Alonso (Fenix Calderon)

Story: *The Fast and the Furious*'s main characters are reunited when it is believed that Letty has been murdered. Dominic returns to Los Angeles to find the perpetrator; at the same time, Brian, who is now an FBI agent, is on the hunt for drug dealer Arturo Braga. Both Dominic and Brian find themselves investigating clues that lead them on the path of the same suspect and, ultimately, to Mexico.

Production: Principal photography for the Mexico scenes in *Fast and the Furious 4* was shot in and around Los Angeles's Canyon Country and Antelope Valley. Cast and crew left Los Angeles and relocated to the small Mexican border town of Magdalena de Kino in Sonora for one week of filming within the city limits. This is the fourth entry in the action-packed franchise, which was first introduced in 2001. As of this writing, the series is on its eighth installment, *Fate of the Furious* (2017), despite the untimely passing of series regular Paul Walker (1973–2013). It has become Universal Pictures' top moneymaking series of all time.

DRAGONBALL: EVOLUTION (20TH CENTURY FOX, 2009)

Director: James Wong

Screenplay: Ben Ramsay, based on characters created by Akira Toriyama

Producer: Tim Van Rellim, Stephen Chow

Cast: Justin Chatwin (Goku), James Marsters (Lord Piccolo), Chow Yun Fat (Roshi), Emmy Rossum (Bulma), Jamie Chung (ChiChi) Ernie Hudson (Sifu Norris)

Story: On a futuristic parallel earth, the young warrior Goku discovers he has extraordinary powers that require advanced knowledge. He must collect the seven powerful Dragon Balls that give super powers before evil warload Piccalo finds them and controls, or destroys, the universe.

Production: Filmed in Durango, Mexico, doubling for a futuristic parallel earth with Far East influences, *Dragonball: Evolution* is based on the popular Dragonball Japanese anime and video game. José Ludlow was the Mexican production manager.

COLOMBIANA (TRI STAR, 2011)

Director: Olivier Megaton

Screenplay: Luc Besson, Robert Mark Kamin

Producer: Luc Besson, Ariel Zeitoun

Cast: Zoe Saldana (Cataleya), Jordi Molla (Marco), Lennie James (Agent Ross), Michael Vartan (Danny Delany), Cliff Curtis (Emilio Restrepo), Jesse Borrego (Fabio) Ofelia Medina (Mama)

Story: Eleven-year-old Cataleya, who lives in Bogota, Colombia, witnesses the murders of her mother and father; they are killed by members of the Colombian cartels, under the orders of Don Julio. Cateleya barely escapes with her own life. She makes her way to the United States, where, in Chicago, she locates her only living relative, a mobster uncle. She asks her uncle to teach her to be a hired assassin. Fifteen years later, she exacts her revenge.

Production: Filmed in Mexico City, Miami, New Orleans, Chicago, and Paris. According to the film's press notes, director Megaton commandeered a small Paris-based crew, which traveled to the many locations and coordinated with larger local crews. Mexico City doubled for Bogota, Colombia. Unit managers in Mexico were Hector Villegas and Alejandra Santan, the line producer was Mariano Carranco, and the third assistant director was Santiago Limon.

GET THE GRINGO (AIRBORNE PRODUCTIONS, 2012)

Director: Adrien Grunberg

Screenplay: Stacy Perskie, Adrian Grunberg, Mel Gibson

Producer: Bruce Davey, Mel Gibson, Stacey Perskie

Cast: Mel Gibson (Driver), Kevin Hernandez (Kid), Daniel Gimenez Cacho (Javi), Jesus Ochoa (Caracas)

Story: An American career criminal pulls the heist of a lifetime, but his getaway plans go south (of the border) when a high-speed car chase lands him in a tough Mexican prison. There, he learns to survive with the help of a ten-year-old boy.

Production: *Get the Gringo* was filmed over nine weeks in Veracruz, Mexico, with Mexico City doubling for San Diego. The mostly Mexican cast and crew had worked previously on Gibson's *Apocalypto*. Mexican assistant director Adrien Grunberg made his feature film debut as director and co-writer of this character-driven action film. Stacey Perskie, who co-wrote the screenplay and served as co-producer, was an assistant to Gibson on *Apocalypto* and to director Tony Scott on *Man on Fire*. The film was not released theatrically in the United States but instead went straight-to-video due to Gibson's higly publicized drunk-driving arrest, during which he made numerous anti-Semitic statements. The prison in *Get the Gringo* was modeled after a real prison in Tijuana. "El Pueblito" and the Veracruz location became available when an actual prison was being vacated.

LIMITLESS (20TH CENTURY FOX, 2011)

Director: Neil Burger

Screenwriter: Leslie Dixon, based on a novel by Alan Glynn

Producer: Ryan Kavanaugh, Scott Kroopf

Cast: Bradley Cooper (Eddie Morra), Robert De Niro (Carl Van Loon), Abbie Cornish (Lindy)

Story: A struggling writer takes an experimental drug which allows him to reach his full brain potential, transforming him and taking his life to unprecedented success—and dangerous consequences.

Production: Select sequences of this science-fiction thriller were filmed in and around Puerto Vallarta, Mexico: a Maserati speeding by the Malecon, cliff diving on the Marietas islands, a resort area in Punto Mita, and the Casa China Blanca Villa residence. Line producer in Mexico was Ricardo del Rio; cinematography was by Jo Willems.

FOR GREATER GLORY (NEW LAND FILMS, 2013)

Director: Dean Wright

Screenplay: Dean Wright, James Michael Love

Producer: Pablo José Barroso

Cast: Andy Garcia (Enrique Gorostieta Vlarde), Eva Longoria (Tulita), Peter O'Toole (Father Christopher), Bruce Greenwood (Ambassador Morrow), Oscar Isaac (Victoriano Ramirez), Catalina Sandino Moreno (Adriana), Ruben Blades (President Plutarco Calles), Eduardo Verastequi (Anacleto Gonzalez Flores)

Story: A chronicle of the little-known Cristeros War (1925–1929), which began as a rebellion against the Mexican government's attempt to secularize the country and limit the freedom of worship for Catholics in the years following the Mexican Revolution. An impassioned group of men and women decides to risk all for family, faith, and the future of their country. General Gorostieta is a retired military man who, at first, believes he has no stake in the fight. But as he and his wife watch Mexico fall into a violent civil war, he soon becomes the rebellion's most inspiring and self-sacrificing leader. He begins to see the cost of religious persecution on his fellow countrymen and transforms a ragtag band into a heroic force. Those he meets during the war, youthful idealists, feisty renegades, and most of all, a remarkable boy named José, reveal to him how courage and faith are forged even when justice seems lost. Due to the influence of the Catholic Church, the anticlerical provisions of the 1917 Mexican Revolutionary Constitution went unenforced until the regime of Presidente Plutarco Elias Calles. The resulting war was so bloody in its persecution of the Mexican Catholic Church and the rebels that the United States government had to intervene diplomatically in order to protect its intersts in the country.

Production: Filmed in Durango and Zacatecas, Mexico, by cinematographer Eduardo Martinez Solares, this handsome English-language production was directed by American visual effects specialist Dean Wright, with a largely Latino cast and a Mexican crew. Salvador Parra was the production designer. *For Greater Glory* was the most expensive Mexican film made up to that time, but this well-made epic about a mostly forgotten chapter in Mexican history found little audience interest, even in Mexico.

ALL IS LOST (LIONSGATE (U. S., 2013; INTERNATIONAL, FILMNATION ENTERTAINMENT, 2014)

Director: J. C. Sandor

Screenplay: J.C. Sandor

Producer: Neal Dodson, Anna Gerber

Cast: Robert Redford (Sailor)

Story: A lone man struggles to survive against the sea and its elements after his sailboat is struck by a floating cargo container in the middle of the Indian Ocean.

Production: *All Is Lost* was filmed on a $9 million budget at the Baja Film studios in Rosarito Beach, Baja California Norte, where the three huge water tanks built for *Titanic* were utilized. The world's largest water tank sits right on the ocean and has an infinity edge horizon line. The tanks mimic being out at sea, but are in a controlled environment. Seven weeks of preparation went into the thirty-day shoot in Mexico by director J. C. Shandor. The line producer was Luisa Gomez da Silva. The studio also provides nearby access to the technical and artistic expertise of both Mexico and the U. S. Robert Redford, the only person on screen for the entire running time, was praised by critics for his solo performance. During a press conference at the completion of *All is Lost*, Redford remarked, "When I get back to the U. S., I can easily recommend to my filmmaking colleagues the facilities and locations at the Baja Studios."

ELYSIUM (TRISTAR, 2013)

Director: Neil Blomkamp

Screenplay: Neil Blomkamp

Producer: Bill Block, Neil Blomkamp, Simon Kinberg

Cast: Matt Damon (Max), Jodie Foster (Delacourt), Sharito Copley (Kruger), Alice Braga (Frey), Diego Luna (Julio), José Pablo Carrillo (Sandro)

Story: In the year 2054, two classes of human beings exist: the rich, who live on a perfect space station called Elysium; and the poor, who inhabit a devastated and overcrowded planet Earth. Max is an ex-con who lives in Los Angeles and constructs robots, which act as guardians. When he is exposed to lethal amounts of radiation, he travels to Elysium for medical care. There, he encounters President Delacorte, a woman who will stop at nothing to keep distraught Earth inhabitants from accessing the pristine space station.

Production: *Elysium* was filmed in Vancouver, British Columbia, Canada; the scenes which take place on earth in the shattered Los Angeles in 2054 were filmed in Mexico City. Mexican actor Diego Luna plays Julio, a rebel helping Matt Damon's Max travel to Elysiu. Luna has appeared in such Hollywood films as *Open Range* (2003), *The Terminal* (2004), *Milk* (2008), and *Contraband* (2012); he made his directorial debut with the feature film *Chavez* (2013). In an interview with Naibe Reynoso of Fox New Latino on August 6, 2013, Luna stated, "In fact, *Elysium*'s writer and director Neil Blomkamp said he was inspired to write the movie after spending a day in Tijuana, Mexico." In an another interview, this one with *Se Fija Online* magazine's Angela Ortiz, Luna said, "The production quality you get in Mexico now is so vast. They are very impressive and professional. And not only because U.S. film companies are coming to film there, it's because Mexico is producing more than sixty films per year."

CESAR CHAVEZ (LIONSGATE/PANTELION FILMS, 2014)

Director: Diego Luna

Screenplay: Keir Pearson, Timothy J. Sexton

Producer: Pablo Cruz, John Malkovich

Cast: Michael Pena (Cesar Chavez), America Ferrera (Helen Chavez), Rosario Dawson (Dolores Huerta), Yancey Arias (Gilbert Padilla), Jacob Vargas (Richard Chavez), John Malkovich (Bogdanovitch)

Story: Chronicling the birth of a modern American movement led by famed Mexican American civil rights leader and labor organizer Cesar Chavez, the film focuses on the Delano grape strike of the 1960s. Torn between his duties as a husband and father and his commitment to bringing dignity and justice to others, Chavez embraces non-violence as he battles greed and prejudice in the struggle for the rights of farm workers.

Production: Directed by Mexican actor Diego Luna, who along with Gael Garcia Bernal and producer Pablo Cruz, formed Canana Films in Mexico City in 2005. *Cesar Chavez* was filmed in Hermosillo, Sonora Mexico, whose surrounding vinyards were used to replicate the fields surrounding Delano, California, in the sixties. It was released through Lionsgate Films in association with Pantelion/Televisa Cine, a Canana presentation in association with participant Imagenation Abu Dhabi and Mr. Mudd, with the support of El gobierno del Estado de Sonora, Mexico. Xavier Clave was the first assistant director, and Arturo Sampson was the unit manager.

SPECTRE (SONY/METRO-GOLDWYN-MAYER, 2015)

Director: Sam Mendes

Screenplay: John Logan, based on characters created by Ian Fleming

Producer: Michael G. Wilson, Barbara Broccoli

Cast: Daniel Craig (James Bond), Christoph Waltz (Oberhauser), Monica Bellucci (Lucia Sciarra), Ralph Fiennes (M), Dave Bautista (Mr. Hinx), Stephanie Sigman (Estrella)

Story: A cryptic message from James Bond's past sends him on a rogue mission to Mexico City and Rome to uncover a sinister organization. While M battles political forces to keep the secret service alive, Bond discovers a criminal organization bent on worldwide dominance of surveilance systems masterminded by a criminal organization, SPECTRE.

Production: *Spectre* opens with an extended sequence that cranes down over a massive parade of people dressed in skeleton costumes before closing in on a masked James Bond. The camera follows him into a hotel, an elevator, and then a bedroom. He flings Estrella (Stephanie Sigman) onto a bed, changes swiftly into a perfectly tailored suit, and climbs out the window to walk along the roof of a separate building. Gun in hand, he performs an assassination while the ghoulish parade continues below. Set during Mexico City's Day of the Dead, the sequence introduces a longer pre-credit action set piece, complete with crashing buildings and a hand-to-hand encounter in an out-of-control helicopter over the skies of Mexico's City Center. The Mexican government offered the Bond filmmakers a reported $14 million worth of production incentives to film part of the twenty-fourth installment in the lucrative James Bond franchise in Mexico. According to hacked Sony emails, reported by Tax Analysts.com and other global media, the Mexican government asked the producers to modify the script and cast a known Mexican actress as a Bond Girl. As reported, the incentives were to present Mexico in a positive light and offset images of drug violence and corruption. It is unprecedented that a modern government could require such extensive, but nominal, creative changes to a film production in exchange for monetary compensation. The producers were anxious to reduce the cost, which was approaching $300 million. The script changes included: substituting an international ambassador for a Mexican government official, one with an international ambassador as an assassin's target; trading Mexican police with a special law-enforcement group; having Bond pursue the assassin Sciarra through the streets of Mexico during a Day of the Dead parade; and highlighting an aerial view of the modern Mexico City skyline. The opening sequence of the film takes place in Mexico on November 2, the date Mexicans pay respect to deceased relatives and friends, adorning altars with skeletons, marigolds, and other death-related decorations. Producer Michael G. Wilson, at a Mexico City press conference on March 15, 2015, was reported in the Mexico City press as saying, "Mexico's Day of the Dead traditions will be seen in the film or at least a Bond version where everything is magnified." He added, "The writers thought the Day of the Dead would be an excellent background in the opening sequence, very colorful and mysterious. You can only do that in Mexico, there is no other place that offers that but Mexico." Two sound stages at Estudios Churubusco were utilized, with more than eighty professionals working in makeup, hair, and wardrobe departments. Most of the filming took place between March 19 and April 1, 2015, on actual downtown Mexico City locations, with more than fifteen hundred extras. The locations included Plaza Tolsa, nearby streets Xicotencate, Donceles and Tacuba, the interior of the historic Chamber of Senators, and the Zocalo square facing the ornate

The Mexico City Day of the Dead parade is the backdrop for the opening sequence of *Spectre* (2015), featuring Stephanie Sigman as Estrella, and Daniel Craig as James Bond—agent 007.

National Palace. Hoyte van Hoytema (*Interstellar*, 2014) was the cinematographer on *Spectre*. Mexican actress Stephanie Sigman (*Miss Bala*, 2011) is the first-ever Mexican Bond Girl in her role as Estrella. In previous Bond films, Nicaraguan-born actress Barbara Carrera was a Bond Girl in *Never Say Never Again* (1983), as was Puerto Rican actress Talisa Soto in the Mexican location–filmed *License to Kill* (1989). *Spectre* is the fourth James Bond entry to be shot whole, or in part, in Mexico, but the first in which Mexico plays itself on film. In an occasion where life imitates art, in November 2016, Mexico City held its first Day of the Dead parade spectacle, complete with floats, giant skeletons, marionettes, and more than a hundred costumed participants, inspired by the opening sequence of *Spectre*. The Day of the Dead is not traditionally observed with a parade anywhere in Mexico. "When this movie hit the big screen and was seen by millions and millions of people in sixty-seven countries, that started to create expectations that we would have something," said Lourdes Berho, CEO of the governments Mexico Tourism Board in an Associated Press story that appeared in *The Hollywood Reporter* on November 1, 2016. *Spectre* is the fourth entry in which Daniel Craig plays James Bond, following his 007 predecessors Pierce Brosnan, Timothy Dalton, Roger Moore, George Lazenby, and Sean Connery.

SICARIO (LIONSGATE FILMS, 2016)

Director: Denis Villeneuve
Screenplay: Taylor Sheridan
Producer: Basil Iwanyk, Thad Luckinbill, Trent Luckinbill
Cast: Benicio Del Toro (Alejandro), Josh Brolin (Matt Garver), Emily Blunt (Kate Mercer), Daniel Kaluuya (Reggie), Julio Cesar Cedillo (Fausto Alarcon), Raoul Trujillo (Rafael), Bernardino Saracino (Manuel Diaz)
Story: *Sicario* is the story of Kate Mercer, an idealistic FBI agent who is enlisted by a mixed U.S. law-enforcement task force to aid in the escalating war against drugs at the U.S./Mexico border. As Alejandro says in the film, "There are no good guys or bad guys in this world, only packs of wolves competing for territory and dominance."
Production: The title of the film and the word *Sicario* means "hired assassin" in Spanish. Ciudad Juarez, Mexico, lies just across the Rio Grande from El Paso, Texas, the once-booming border town which, in recent years, has become a violent place as a result of the drug wars and rampant crime. The actual location for the story—Ciudad, Juarez, Mexico—proved too dangerous, so most of the filming took place in Albuquerque, New Mexico, El Paso, Texas, and Veracruz doubling for Juarez. Overhead shots of Juarez and the surrounding terrain were used in the film. A reproduction of a section of The Bridge of the Americas that spans El Paso and Ciudad Juarez was constructed

in New Mexico. The line producer for the Mexico locations unit was Stacy Perskie; the first assistant director was Clave. Eleven-time Oscar-nominated cinematographer Roger Deakins remarked in the film's press notes: "We played with wide shots that allow the action to unfold without multiple cuts and we used vibrant, clean colors. The overall look is of naturalism. For me, the mood of *Sicario* comes from the characters and from Benicia's Del Toro's character in particular, Alejandro, a man who wears the story of the drug wars on his face and in body language."

Film critic Peter Travers wrote in his *Rolling Stone* review of September 17, 2005: "In film terms, *Sicario* is sensational, the most gripping and tension-packed spin through America's covert war on drugs since Steven Soderberg's *Traffic* fifteen years ago. French-Canadian director Denis Villeneuve (*Prisoner, Incendies*) working from a script by *Sons of Anarchy* actor Taylor Sheridan is out to shatter your nerves and does he ever."

DESIERTO (FOCUS FEATURES, 2016)

Director: Jonas Cuaron
Screenplay: Jonas Cuaron, Mateo Garcia
Producer: Alfonso Cuaron, Carlos Cuaron, Jonas Cuaron
Cast: Gael Garcia Bernal (Moises), Jeffrey Dean Morgan (Sam), Alondra Hidalgo (Adela)
Story: An undocumented Mexican immigrant crossing the desert on foot from Mexico into the United States finds himself hunted in the harsh desert environment by an American vigilante gunman.
Production: Filmed in the Baja deserts in and around Mexicali, Puerto Penasco, Catavina, and Alta Sonora.

GRINGO (AMAZON, 2018)

Director: Nash Edgerton
Screenplay: Anthony Tambala, Matthew Stone
Producer: Rebecca Yeldham
Cast: David Oyelowo (Harold Soyrnka), Charlize Theron (Elaine Markinson), Yul Vasquez (Diego Catano)
Story: An American pharmaceutical executive goes to Mexico and ends up crossing the line from citizen to criminal when he fakes his own kidnapping.
Production: *Gringo* is an unfunny action comedy with stock characters and offensive Latin stereotypes. It was filmed in Veracruz, Mexico City, and Chicago.

SICARIO: DAY OF THE SOLDADO (SONY PICTURES 2018)

Director: Stefano Sollima
Screenplay: Taylor Sheridan, based on characters created by Sheridan.
Producer: Basil Iwanyk, Edward L. McDonnell, Molly Smith, Thad Luckinbill and Trent Luckinbill
Cast: Benicio Del Toro (Alejandro), Josh Brolin (Matt Graver), Isabela Moner (Isabela Reyes) Manuel Garcia- Rulfo (Gallo), Elijah Rodriguez (Miguel Hernandez), Catherine Keener (Cynthia Foard), Matthew Modine (James Riley)
Story: CIA agent Matt Graver recruits the mysterious Alejandro to incite a war between the rival drug cartels and stop terrorist infiltration of the U.S. facilitated by human trafficking.
Production: *Sicario: Day of The Soldado* (soldier) is a sequel to the highly regarded *Sicario* (2015). It was filmed around Albuquerque, New Mexico, doubling for the U. S. / Mexico border with two weeks of location film-

ing in Mexico City in such locales as the historic downtown district, the modern high rise Santa Fe area, Coyoacan, and the Reforma Hotel. A CIA Deputy's statement to Graver, "Your objective is to start a war between the Mexican cartels, not with the Mexican government" serves as a diplomatic disclaimer between the two countries for the fictional film. Cinematographer Darius Wolzki also lensed *The Mexican* (2001).

MISS BALA (SONY PICTURES, 2019)

Director: Catherine Hardwicke
Screenplay: Gareth Dunnet Alcocer, based on the original script by Gerardo Naranjo and Mauricio Katz
Producer: Pablo Cruz, Kevin Misher, Andy Berman
Cast: Gina Rodriquez (Gloria), Matt Lauria (Brian), Ismael Cruz Cordova (Lino), Christina Rodlo (Suzu), Ricardo Abarca (Pablo)
Story: A beauty pageant contestant in Tijuana witnesses a violent incident and is drawn into the world of a powerful drug cartel. When she goes missing, her friend finds herself a pawn in a dangerous game involving the CIA, the DEA, and a charismatic drug lord.
Production: This is an English-language remake of the Mexican film *Miss Bala*, which was nominated for an Academy Award for Best Foreign Film in 2011; it was shot on location in Tijuana by cinematographer Patrick Murgia. Gina Rodriquez is best known as the Golden Globe–winning star of the television series *Jane the Virgin* (2014–   ). Christina Rodlo is a Mexican actress known for her work on the Spanish-language series *El Vato/The Dude* (2016–2017). Costuming by Graciela Mazon; stunts coordinated by Hugo Aguilera and Julian Brico; the casting director was Carla Hool.

GODZILLA: KING OF THE MONSTERS (WARNER BROS., 2019)

Director: Michael Dougherty
Screenplay: Max Borenstein, Michael Dougherty, Zach Shields
Producer: Alex Garcia
Cast: Bobby Brown (Madison Russell), Vera Farmiga (Dr. Emma Russell), Kyle Chandler (Mark Russell), Ken Watanabe (Dr. Ishiro Serizawa), Sally Hawkins (Vivienne Graham), Anthony Ramos (Corporal Martinez)
Story: The heroic efforts of the Crypto Zoological Agency are on display as its members face off against a gargantuan battery of monsters.
Production: *Godzilla: King of the Monsters* was filmed in Mexico city for a week in August of 2017 at the Plaza Santa Domingo in the city's historic center, near the Zocalo. The fuselage of a supposedly downed airliner was placed in the center of the plaza. More than seven thousand extras were used over a three-day shoot. The script called for a city with a volcano where Godzilla would meet his adversaries. Ciudad Antigua, in Guatemala, was first considered but proved visually unsuitable, resulting in Mexico City being used instead. Mexico City has an architectural richness difficult to find anywhere else in the world. Pre-Hispanic ruins, colonial buildings, and contemporary skyscrapers blend to form a unique urban landscape, with Popocatepetl Volcano in the background. Godzilla and the other monsters will be recreated through the use of CGI. Irene Munoz, Mexico City's director of tourism and promotion, stated at a Mexico City press conference at the beginning of production: "The immediate economic benefit of the production to the city is significant as well as the long-term promotional value to Mexican tourism generated by the film's worldwide exhibition."

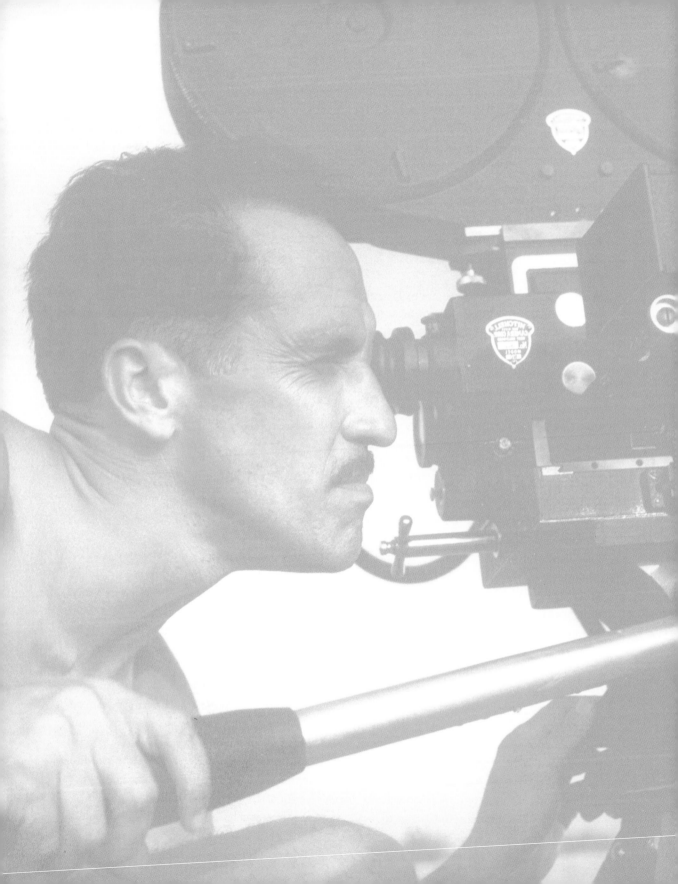

CHAPTER 8

CROSSING BORDERS

The following is not meant to be a comprehensive listing but an overview of the most notable and recognized border-crossing talents in cinema.

ART ACORD (1890–1931)
ACTOR

Art Acord was born in Oklahoma and was a real-life cowboy who became both a stuntman and actor in silent movies. Acord starred in many silent westerns between 1910 and 1929, most of which are lost. He developed

At Universal City Studios in July 1925 (left to right): Alicia Calles; Art Acord, Western star; Jose Sedgewick Sr., Borachano; Fred Humes, Western star, Harrison E. Moore; Mrs. Plutarco Elias Calles, wife of the president of Mexico; Mrs. Chacon; and F. D. Chacon.

a fan following in Mexico and along the border states where his movies were shown frequently because of lower rental costs. To capitalize on his international fame, Acord and his wife went on a personal appearance tour of South America in 1922. After his Hollywood heyday, he settled in Mexico where he was still somewhat of a celebrity and made appearances at rodeos. In 1931, he died under suspicious circumstances in a hotel in Chihuahua. Although Mexican police officially listed his death (by cyanide poisoning) as a suicide, it was suspected that he had been murdered by a Mexican politician who had caught Acord having an affair with his wife.

RODOLFO ACOSTA (1920–1974)
ACTOR

Mexican actor Rodolfo Acosta achieved his greatest success in Hollywood westerns, usually as a bad hombre, a bandit, or an Indian warrior. His most notable role in Mexican cinema was in Emilio Fernández's *Salon Mexico* (1949), which resulted in Acosta winning the Best Supporting Actor Ariel Award. While under contract to Universal Pictures he was cast in *Wings of the Hawk* (1953), *Hondo* (1953), *A Life in the Balance* (1955), *Bandido* (1956), *One-Eyed Jacks* (1961), *How the West Was Won* (1962), and *The Sons of Katie Elder* (1965), to name just a few. He also guest starred on many popular TV western series and is perhaps best known for his regular supporting role as Vaquero in the worldwide hit series *The High Chaparral* (1967-1971). Acosta was born in Chihuahua, Mexico, and at three years of age his family moved to California. He studied at Los Angeles City College and graduated from UCLA. Offered a scholarship to Bellas Artes in Mexico City, he studied for three years, until World War II broke out. Acosta, who spoke seven languages, returned to the U.S. and served in U.S. Naval Intelligence. After the war ended, he returned to Mexico and began working in the film industry. Through his friendship with Emilio Fernández he was introduced to John Ford, who was filming *The Fugitive* (1947) in Mexico. In that film Acosta landed his first (uncredited) screen role, that of a policeman.

ALFONSO ARAU (1932–)
ACTOR/DIRECTOR/WRITER/PRODUCER

Alfonso Arau began his acting career in the Mexican film industry in the fifties, but is perhaps best known for his memorable portrayal of Lt. Herrera in *The Wild Bunch* (1969) and as the bandit leader El Guapo in the comedy-western *The Three Amigos* (1986). His other U.S. film credits include *Run, Cougar, Run* (1972), *Posse* (1975), *Romancing the Stone* (1984), and *Walker* (1987). He was also seen in Jodorowsky's Mexican-made cult western *El Topo* (1970). Arau directed a number of films in Mexico, including the acclaimed *Like Water for Chocolate/Como Agua Para Chocolate* (1990), based on the novel by his then-wife, Laura Esquivel. This success led to Arau directing Keanu Reeves and Anthony Quinn in *A Walk in the Clouds* (1995) and Woody Allen in *Picking Up the Pieces* (2000). Among his other credits are the Mexican feature *Zapata* (2004) starring Alejandro Fernández, and a cable television version of *The Magnificent Ambersons* (2002).

SERGIO ARAU (1951–)
DIRECTOR

Arau, the son of Mexican director Alfonso Arau, is a cartoonist, musician, writer, and director. With Yareli Arizmendi, he co-wrote and helmed the satirical film *A Day Without a Mexican* (1998), produced by Isaac Artenstein.

PEDRO ARMENDÁRIZ (1913–1963)
ACTOR

Tall, handsome, with dark mestizo features and expressive piercing eyes, Pedro Armendáriz was the most important leading actor during the golden age of Mexican motion pictures. He starred in some of the most significant films of the era, usually as a leading man; in Hollywood, he only played supporting roles, such as outlaws, soldiers, or Native Americans. He was born in Mexico, the son of a Mexican father and an American mother, but grew up in Texas and graduated from California Polytechnic State University. He entered the Mexican film industry in 1935 and made forty-two Spanish-language films, including *Maria Candelaria* (1943), *Bugambilia* (1944), Enamorada (1946), *The Pearl* (1947), *Flor Silvestre* (1942), *El Bruto* (1952), and *La Cucaracha* (1960). In Hollywood, he co-starred with John Wayne in *Three Godfathers* (1948), *Fort Apache* (1948), and *The Conqueror* (1956). His other films include John Huston's *We Were Strangers* (1949) and *The Wonderful Country* (1959). His last—and perhaps best known—role is as Kerim Bey, in the second James Bond film, *From Russia with Love* (1963). He took ill while making the film and was diagnosed with terminal cancer. In his Los Angeles hospital room, Armendáriz took his own life, by gunshot.

PEDRO ARMENDÁRIZ JR. (1940–2011)
ACTOR

Like his father, Pedro Armendáriz, he was a prolific actor in films, television series, telenovelas, and on the stage. He caught the acting bug while spending time with his father on many of his film sets. After receiving a degree in architecture from the Universidad Iberoamericana, Pedro decided to pursue acting, making his screen debut in *Outside the Law* (1966). One of his first film roles was as a young priest in *Guns for San Sebastian* (1968). Armendáriz, who was bi-lingual, worked extensively in Hollywood movies shot in Mexico, including *The Undefeated* (1968), *Chisum* (1970), *Earthquake* (1974), *The Magnificent Seven Ride* (1972), *License to Kill* (1989), *Old Gringo* (1989), *Tombstone* (1993), *Amistad* (1997), *The Mask of Zorro* (1997), *The Mexican* (2001), *Once Upon a Time in Mexico* (2002), and *Casa de Mi Padre* (2012, released posthumously). He won two Ariel Awards, for *Mina* (1977) and *La Ley de Herodes/Herod's Law* (1999). Just before his untimely passing, the charaismatic and beloved actor starred as Tevye in a Mexico City stage and touring production of *Fiddler on the Roof*.

GUILLERMO ARRIAGA (1958–   )
SCREENWRITER/NOVELIST/DIRECTOR

Arriaga, a native of Mexico City, is recognized for his screenplays for *Amores Perros* (2000), *21 Grams* (2003), and *Babel* (2006), all of which were directed by Alejandro Gonzalez Iñárritu. Arriaga wrote the screenplay for *The Three Burials of Melquiades Estrads* (2005) and *The Burning Plain* (2008), the latter of which he also directed.

ANUAR BADIN (19??–   )
PRODUCTION MANAGER

Badin was the Mexican production manager on *Conan the Destroyer* (1984), *Dune* (1984), *Rambo: First Blood II* (1985), *Salvador* (1986), and *Total Recall* (1990).

LUCIEN BALLARD (1908–1988)
CINEMATOGRAPHER

Ballard, an American cinematographer, is best known for the clean, elegant, visual style he brought to outdoor photography on westerns. His credits include six movies shot in Mexico, among the best known of which is Sam Peckinpah's *The Wild Bunch* (1969). In his July 4, 1969, review of *True Grit* (1969), which Ballard also shot, Vincent Canby of the *New York Times* wrote: "Anyone interested in what good cinematography means can compare Ballard's totally different contributions to 'The Wild Bunch' and 'True Grit.' In 'The Wild Bunch,' the camera work is hard and bleak and largely unsentimental. The images of 'True Grit' are as romantic and autumnal as its landscapes which in the course of the story turn with the seasons from the colors of autumn to the white of winter." Ballard's other Mexican credits are *Seven Cities of Gold* (1955), *White Feather* (1955), *The Magnificent Matador* (1955), *The Sons of Katie Elder* (1965), and Hour of the Gun (1967).

ADRIANA BARRAZA (1956–   )
ACTRESS

Born in Toluca, Mexico City, Barraza gained worldwide attention for her role in *Amores Perros* (2001). She was nominated for an Academy Award (as well as a Golden Globe) for Best Supporting Actress in *Babel* (2006) directed by Alejandro Gonzalez Iñárritu. Since then, her credits have included *Cake* (2014), *Thor* (2011), and *From Prada to Nada* (2011).

ALFONSO BEDOYA (1904–1957)
ACTOR

Alfonso Bedoya was a Mexican character actor who started his career in Mexican films and made his American film debut with his portrayal of the bandit Gold Hat in John Huston's *The Treasure of the Sierra Madre* (1948). Bedoya's lines of dialogue in his thick Mexican accent are now a part of Hollywood hi**Story:** "Badges? We ain't got no badges! We don't need no badges. I don't have to show you any stinkin' badges!"

DEMIAN BICHIR (1963–   )
ACTOR

Demian Bichir was born in Mexico City to a family in the entertainment industry: he has two brothers who are also actors. For many years he appeared in Mexican films, telenovelas, and on the stage before earning an Oscar nomination as Best Actor for his lead performance as an undocumented immigrant in the feature film *A Better Life* (2011). He also gained attention for his portrayal of Fidel Castro in Steven Soderburg's *Che* (2008). Since then, Bichir has been a lawyer in Oliver Stone's *Savages* (2012), Sandra Bullock's boss in *The Heat* (2013), and a Mexican outlaw in Quentin Tarantino's *The Hateful Eight* (2015). On the Showtime series *Weed* (2005–2012), he had a recurring role as the mayor of Tijuana. He also starred for two seasons as Detective Marco Ruiz on the FX series *The Bridge* (2013–2014), set in El Paso/Juarez.

LONKA BECKER (1910-1997)
CLAUDIA BECKER (1945–2009)

SANDRA LEON BECKER (19??-   )
CASTING DIRECTORS

Lonka Becker was born in France and came to Mexico with her husband. She was an actress, an agent, and one of the first professional casting directors for films in Mexico. Upon her retirement, she was succeeded by her daughter, Claudia Becker, who got her start as a casting director for Sam Peckinpah's *Bring Me the Head of Alfredo Garcia* (1974). She quickly became the go-to person for casting local talent in Mexico on Hollywood film productions, such as *Romancing The Stone* (1984), *Salvador* (1986), *License To Kill* (1989) *Old Gringo* (1989), *Total Recall* (1990) *Romeo + Juliet* (1996), and *Frida* (2002). Claudia's daughter, Sandra Leon Becker, presently runs the Mexico City–based casting agency.

GAEL GARCIA BERNAL (1978-   )
ACTOR/PRODUCER

Gael Garcia Bernal was born in Guadalajara to parents who are both actors. Gael first gained attention with his role in Alejandro Gonzalez Iñárritu's *Amores Perros* (2000), and in Alfonso Cuaron's *Y Tu Mama Tambien* (2001). He played the young Che Guevara in the celebrated film *The Motorcycle Diaries* (2004) and starred in Almodovar's *Bad Education* (2004). Among his recent film credits are Iñárritu's *Babel* (2006), the comedy *Casa De Mi Padre* (2012), and Jon Stewart's *Rosewater* (2014), wherein he plays an imprisoned Iranian journalist. Bernal has produced and starred in films under his Canana Films banner with associate Diego Luna.

BRIGETTE BROCH (1943-   )
ART DIRECTOR/PRODUCTION DESIGNER

Brigette Broch is a German-born production designer who has made Mexico her home for more than fifty years. She won an Academy Award (shared with Catherine Martin) for Best Set Decoration on Moulin Rouge! (2001). Broch also received an Oscar nomination for her work on *Romeo + Juliet* (1996). Her other credits include Guillermo del Toro's *Cronos* (1993), Iñárritu's *Amores Perros* (2000), *21 Grams* (2003), *Babel* (2006), and *Biutiful* (2010).

HUGO BUTLER (1914–1968)
SCREENWRITER

Canadian-born Hugo Butler worked for MGM on a number of notable films and received an Academy Award nomination for co-writing the screenplay for *Edison, the Man* (1940). In 1951, the House Un-American Activities Committee subpoenaed him. He moved his family from Los Angeles to Mexico and became another expatriot writer blacklisted by Hollywood during the communist witch hunts of the fifties. In Mexico, he continued writing under a pseudonym for Luis Buñuel's *The Adventures of Robinson Crusoe* (1954) and *The Young One* (1960). Butler also wrote and directed *Los Peguenos Gigantes* (*The Little Giants* 1960), the true-life story of the impoverished Mexican Little League team that overcame incredible odds and rose to win the international Little League championship in Pennsylvania. The Writers Guild of America later restored his writing credits on a number of films.

EUGENIO CABALLERO (1972-)
ART DIRECTOR

Born in Mexico City, Eugenio Caballero won an Academy Award in 2007 for Best Art Direction for Guillermo del Toro's *Pan's Labyrinth*.

ELSA CARDENAS (1935–)
ACTRESS

Elsa Cardenas began her film career in 1954 with roles in two Spanish-language films, *Madalena* and *El Joven Juarez*. Her portrayal of a mother in the Oscar-winning Hollywood film *The Brave One* in 1956 led to her being cast in George Stevens's *Giant*, released that same year. Her long career encompasses more than one hundred films and TV series. All of Cardenas's scenes with Elvis Presley in *Fun in Acapulco* (1963) were filmed at Paramount Studios. Elvis was unable to travel to the Mexican locations because his manager, Col. Tom Parker, was actually an illegal alien from Holland and could not leave the United States. As a result, process shots of Cardenas, Swiss actress Ursula Andress, and a photo-double of Elvis were made on location in Acapulco by a second unit. Cardenas also appeared in *The Wild Bunch* (1969).

CANTINFLAS/MARIO MORENO REYES (1911–1993)
COMEDIAN/ACTOR/ PRODUCER/WRITER

Cantinflas was Mexico's greatest and most beloved comedy film star. Sporting a comically broken mustache, he adopted the persona of a poor Mexican barrio dweller (a "Pelado" /Penniless) wearing old trousers held up with a rope, a beattered felt hat, a handkerchief tied around his neck, and a ragged coat. His talent was so considerable that Charlie Chaplin called him "the world's best comedian, next to me." One of Cantinflas's noted techniques was using the Spanish language to the point of confusion and incomprehensibility, not unlike a Hispanic version of Groucho Marx. Reyes's story is that of someone who started performing out of necessity in tent shows and theatres and then, through trial and error, creating a character with whom the downtrodden could identify. He made his film debut in 1941 with *Ahi Esta el Detalle* (*It's All in the Details*) and made over fifty-five films; his last, *El Barrendero* (*The Sweeper*), was released in 1982. In addition to performing, he produced many of his films and had a hand in the creative and business ends, making him one of Mexico's most successful performers in all Spanish-speaking countries. He was also a labor activist who helped to establish the Mexican Screen Actor's Guild (ANDA) and engaged in the fight for better working conditions for those in the industry. In 1956, he made a splash in Hollywood with his role as Phileas Fogg's man servant Passepartout in the Academy Award–winning Best Picture *Around the World in 80 Days*. However, *Pepe* (1960), an all-star extravaganza which he co-produced with Columbia Pictures, did not receive a warm reception with U.S. audiences; as a result, he never made another Hollywood film.

ELPIDIA CARRILLO (1961–)
ACTRESS

Born in Santa Elena, Michoacan, and occasionally credited as Elpedia, she made her American film debut opposite Jack Nicholson in Tony Richardson's *The Border* (1982). Elpidia is perhaps best known for her role as Anna, the Central American refugee taken hostage by commandoes in *Predator* (1987). She exemplifies the strong, resilient, indigenous Latina in a number of Hollywood films, including *Salvador* (1986), *My Family/Mi Familia* (1995), *Bread and Roses* (2000), *Mother and Child* (2005), and *Seven Pounds* (2008)..

WILLIAM H. CLOTHIER (1903–1996)
CINEMATOGRAPHER

Clothier spent the late 1930s as first cameraman in the fledgling Mexican and Spanish film industry. He shot newsreels of the Spanish Civil War for Paramount Pictures until he was jailed by the Spanish authorities and deported to the United States. When Clothier was sent to Mexico on an errand, he wound up taking over camera duties on a Mexican film. That film's director, Raphael J. Seville, hired Clothier to work with him on *El Ciento Trece* in 1937, for which Clothier served as director of photography. He served in that capacity on twenty-two John Wayne films, beginning in 1955 with *Blood Alley*; he filmed all but one of the westerns Wayne filmed in Durango, Mexico. He worked with John Ford on *The Horse Soldiers* (1959), *The Man Who Shot Liberty Valence* (1962), and *Cheyenne Autumn* (1964), as well as directors Andrew V. McLaglen and Burt Kennedy. He was nominated for two Academy Awards.

LINDA CRISTAL (1934–   )
ACTRESS

Cristal, a dark-haired, beautiful Argentine actress, began her career in Mexican films. While under contract to Universal-International in 1958, she co-starred in *The Perfect Furlough* opposite Tony Curtis, and *Last of the Fast Guns*, which was shot in Mexico. She was handpicked by John Wayne to be his leading lady in *The Alamo* (1960), and followed this with John Ford's *Two Rode Together* (1961) opposite James Stewart and Richard Widmark. She guest-starred on many popular television series of the era, including *Rawhide* starring Clint Eastwood. She is perhaps best known today for her role as strong-willed Victoria Cannon on *The High Chaparral* television series (1967–1971).

PABLO CRUZ (1984–   )
PRODUCER

In 2005, Pablo Cruz, along with actors Diego Luna and Gael Carcia Bernal, formed Canana, a film and television production company based in Mexico City and Los Angeles. Under the Canana banner he has produced such films as *Chavez* (2014), *Miss Bala* (2011), *Abel* (2014), and *Sin Nombre* (2009). He is currently producing episodes of AMC's series *Fear the Walking Dead* out of the Baja Studios facilities in Rosarito, Baja Mexico, where he brings together some of the best artists and technicians from Mexico and the United States.

ALFONSO CUARON (1961–   )
DIRECTOR/SCREENWRITER/PRODUCER

Academy Award winner Alfonso Cuaron was born in Mexico City and studied at the Universidad Nacional Autonoma de Mexico. His first feature-length film was *Solo Con Tu Pareja* (1991), a dark, Spanish-language comedy about AIDS, written with his brother Carlos. Pproduced by IMCINE (Instituto Mexicano de Cinematografia), it brought him to the attention of Hollywood when it was screened at the Toronto Film Festival. In 1995, Cuaron directed his first Hollywood movie, *A Little Princess*, staring Julianne Moore and Robert DeNiro. After returning to Mexico in 2001, he filmed *Y Tu Mama Tambien*, a Spanish-language road comedy with political overtones; this went on to become an international hit with audiences and critics alike. In 2004, Cuaron directed the third film in the popular Harry Potter series, *Harry Potter and the Prisoner of Azkaban*. He followed this with the science-fiction thriller *Children of Men* (2006). Cuaron won two Academy Awards for directing and editing another science-fiction film, *Gravity* (2013) starring Sandra Bullock and George Clooney. Co-written with his son Jonas Cuaron, *Gravity* won a total of seven Oscars.

ROGER CUDNEY (1937–)
ACTOR

Cudney, an Ohio-born actor, has had a long career in Mexican films and television, dating back to the 1970s. Fully conversant in English and Spanish, he has primarily played gringos, both good and bad, but occasionally had roles as Mexicans. He often works in Hollywood films shot in Mexico, including *Remo Williams: The Adventure Begins* (1985), *The Mask of Zorro* (1998), *Old Gringo* (1989), *Total Recall* (1990), and *Cantinflas* (2014).

ARTURO DE CÓRDOVA (1908–1973)
ACTOR

Arturo de Córdova was a popular leading man and heartthrob in Mexican cinema who was put under contract by Paramount Pictures in the 1940s. He appeared in such films as *For Whom the Bells Toll* (1943) and *Frenchmen's Creek* (1944), in which he played the lead opposite Joan Fontaine, and starred opposite Dorothy Lamour in the award-winning *A Medal for Benny* (1945), based on the John Steinbeck story. Perhaps because of the all-American heroes being presented during the war years, De Cordova did not catch on with American audiences despite the all-out effort of the Paramount Pictures publicity department. In 1948, he returned to Mexico, where he had maintained his popularity.

BEATRICE DE ALBA (1964–)
MAKEUP AND HAIR STYLIST

De Alba won an Academy Award (shared with John E. Jackson) for Best Makeup and Hair for the Salma Hayek starrer *Frida* (2002). Among her other credits are *Bandidas* (2005), *The Curious Case of Benjamin Button* (2008), *Into the Wild* (2009). *The Twilight Saga: Part I* (2011), and *The Hunger Games: Catching Fire* (2013).

KATE DEL CASTILLO (1971–)
ACTRESS

The daughter of Mexican actor Eric del Castillo, Kate del Castillo has appeared in several American films while continuing her successful career in Mexico and Spain. She starred in the Fox Searchlight release *Under the Same Moon* (2007), appeared as the "other woman" in the suspense-thriller *No Good Deed* (2014), and co-starred in Patricia Riggen's *The 33* (2015). On television, she has guest-starred on *American Family, CSI Miami*, and the *Dallas* reboot. She recently received acclaim for starring in one of the highest rated telenovelas in American and Mexican Television history, *The Queen of the South* (2011).

DOLORES DEL RIO (1905–1983)
ACTRESS

Dolores del Rio was one of the most beautiful actresses to have graced the silver screen during the twentieth century. Born in Durango, Mexico, del Rio was discovered by American film director Edwin Carewe, who brought her to Hollywood. She quickly attained stardom in a series of well-received films: *Joanna* (1925), *What Price Glory* (1926), *The Loves of Carmen* (1927), and *Ramona* (1928). Although she attained stardom in the twenties and thirties, when sound came in she was typecast as an exotic type, with limited opportunities for expanding her talents. In 1942, she returned to Mexico, where she was able to play a wide variety of leading roles. Her biggest sound-era smash in Hollywood was *Flying Down to Rio* (1933), but although she was the star, the film is best remembered for introducing the dance team of Fred Astaire and Ginger Rogers. Among del Rio's other popular hits was *Bird of Paradise* (1932), in which she starred as the native girl Luana who sacrifices herself to a volcano. During a remarkable career spanning over fifty years, Dolores del Rio made an indelible mark in silent and sound films, television and the stage.

GUILLERMO DEL TORO (1964–)
DIRECTOR/SCREENWRITER/PRODUCER

Guillermo del Toro's fantasy-romance *The Shape of Water* (2017) won two Academy Awards, for Best Picture and Best Director, at the 90th Oscar Awards ceremony, held on March 4, 2018.

Del Toro was born in Guadalajara, Jalisco, Mexico. A movie fan since his youth, he was fascinated by the horror genre, especially the work of such directors as James Whale, George A. Romero, and Alfred Hitchcock. Del Toro learned the art of film makeup and appliances and started his own makeup-effects company in Mexico. He first rose to prominence with *Cronos* (1993), which won the Jury Prize at the Cannes Film Festival, which put him on the world map. His first Hollywood film was *Mimic* (1997) starring Mira Sorvino. He directed *The Devil's Backbone* (2011) in Spain for Pedro Almodovar, and in Hollywood the comic-book vampire action movie *Blade II* (2002) starring Wesley Snipes. His next film, *Pan's Labyrinth* (2006), won several Academy Awards. Since then, his work has included the *Hellboy* (2004) and *Pacific Rim* (2013) film and video game franchises, as well as the animated 3D feature *The Book of Life* (2014), directed by Mexican Jorge Gutierrez.

EUGENIO DERBEZ (1963–)
ACTOR/PRODUCER/WRITER/DIRECTOR

The most popular contemporary Mexican television comedian, Eugenio Derbez starred in, wrote, produced, and directed the most successful Spanish- and English-language independent film released in the United States to date, the 2013 comedy *Instructions Not Included/No se acceptan devoluciones* (literally: *Returns Not Accepted*). The film was, likewise, a tremendous hit in Mexico, where it was produced. Derbez followed with the box-office hit comedies *How to Be a Latin Lover* (2017), in which he stars with Salma Hayek, Raquel Welch, and Rob Lowe and *Overboard* (2018) with Anna Faris.. Derbez has appeared in *Under the Same Moon* (2007) and provided his vocal talents for the animated film *The Book of Life* (2014).

LAURON "JACK" DRAPER (1892–1962)
CINEMATOGRAPHER

Born in Spencer, Indiana, Draper is regarded as one of the Mexican film industry's top cameramen. He worked as a cinematographer in silent and early sound films in Hollywood prior to beginning his career in Mexico in 1933. His more than one hundred film credits include Fernando de Fuentes's ¡*Vámonos Con Pancho Villa!* (1935), *Janitzio* (1934), and *Ahi Esta El detalle* (1940), the latter of which marked Cantinflas's first onscreen appearance. Among Draper's Hollywood films shot in Mexico are *Tarzan and the Mermaids* (1948), *Mystery in Mexico* (1948), *The Bullfighter and the Lady* (1951), *Plunder of the Sun* (1953), and *Robbers Roost* (1955).

JESUS "CHUCHO" DURAN GALVAN (1935–2010)
SPECIAL EFFECTS

Jesus "Chucho" Duran worked his way up through the Mexican film industry to become the leading special effects man in Mexico, ultimately heading his own company, F/X Duran. He worked on most of the major American movies shot in Mexico from the mid-fifties until his death in 2010. Among Duran's many feature credits are *Che: Part One*, *Apocalypto*, *The Legend of Zorro*, *Man on Fire*, *Original Sin*, *Wagons East*, *Predator*, *Revenge*, *Old Gringo*, and *Missing*. In 1957, Duran developed a close working relationship with director Henry King during the making of *The Sun Also Rises*. He also established a bond with one of the film's stars, Errol Flynn, who, upon completion of the film, invited him for a week of fun in Havana. Duran soon after worked with Flynn again, on *The Big Boodle* (1957) co-starring Pedro Armendáriz. Filmed in 1956 entirely on location in Havana, Cuba, *The Big Boodle* utilized a largely Mexican crew. In 2008, Duran received recognition for his contributions to the Mexican film industry when he was presented with its highest honor, the Ariel Award, for his fifty-year career.

ESTHER FERNÁNDEZ (1920–1999)
ACTRESS

A leading lady of the thirties and forties, Esther Fernández started her acting career at the age of thirteen. She starred with Tito Guizar in *Alla En El Rancho Grande* (1936), the first international Mexican film hit. Fernández appeared in one Hollywood film, Paramount Pictures' *Two Years before the Mast* (1946), opposite Alan Ladd.

NORMAN FOSTER (1903–1976)
DIRECTOR

Foster began his film career as an actor before gravitating toward directing. His first venture was so successful that he was put under contract to 20th Century-Fox, where he directed many entries of the Charlie Chan and Mr. Moto series. Foster is perhaps best known for directing Walt Disney's live-action films in the fifties and sixties, including *Davy Crockett, King of the Wild Frontier* (1955) and the *Zorro* TV series starring Guy Williams. Foster went to Mexico for several years and directed five Spanish-language films, including a 1943 remake of *Santa* (1931), which featured a young actor named Ricardo Montalban. Foster's other Mexican film credits are *La Fuga* (1943), *La Hora De La Verdad* (1944), *El Ahijado de La Muerte* (1946), and *Cancion De La Sirena* (1948). Previously, he had spent time in Mexico filming the "My Friend Benito" segment of Orson Welles's unfinished Good Neighbor policy documentary "It's All True." He also received directing credit, though he was supervised by Welles, on *Journey Into Fear*.

ROBERTO GAVALDON (1909–1986)
DIRECTOR

Gavaldon was one of Mexico's leading directors during the forties through the early sixties. The director's best-known film is the Day of the Dead fable *Macario* (1960), photographed by Gabriel Figueroa. *Macario* was nominated for Best Foreign Language Film by the Academy of Motion Picture Arts and Sciences and was screened at the Cannes Film Festival. Gavaldon directed *The Littlest Outlaw* (1955) for Walt Disney, and *Beyond All Limits* (1959), a Mexican-American co-production starring Pedro Armendáriz and Jack Palance.

XAVIER PEREZ GROBET (1964–)
CINEMATOGRAPHER
Grobet was born In Mexico City and came to U.S. attention with his work on *Before Night Falls* (2000). He followed this with *In the Time of the Butterflies* (2001) for Salma Hayek's Ventanrosa Productions and Showtime. His feature credits include *Tortilla Soup* (2000), *Nacho Libre* (2006), *Mother and Child* (2009), *What to Expect When You're Expecting* (2009), and *The Backup Plan* (2010). Among his Mexican film credits are *Santitos* (1997) and *Sexo, Pudor Y Lagrimas* (1999).

TITO GUIZAR (1908–1999)
SINGER/MUSICIAN/ACTOR
Born in Guadalajara, Mexico, Guizar was an established recording and concert artist in New York, with his own radio program in Mexico in the 1930s. In 1936, he stepped before the film cameras dressed like a *charro*, playing his guitar and singing. The film, *Alla en el Rancho Grande /Out There on the Ranch*, became the first international hit of the Mexican cinema and made Tito Guizar a household name. He was put under contract to Paramount Pictures, where he appeared with Bob Hope in *The Big Broadcast of 1938*, and in a western, *The Llano Kid* (1939). He also appeared with his American singing cowboy counterpart Roy Rogers in *On the Old Spanish Trail* (1947) and *The Gay Ranchero* (1948). Guizar spent the next seven decades starring in films, recording songs, and performing in concert halls all over the world, bringing Mexican music and its composers to international acclaim. In the last years of his life he acted in several Mexican soap operas with the Mexican singer Thalia. He died in 1999, at the age of ninety-one, in San Antonio, Texas.

SALMA HAYEK (1966–)
ACTRESS/PRODUCER/DIRECTOR
Beautiful, petite Salma Hayek, born in the oil town of Coatzacoalcos, was nominated for an Academy Award as Best Actress for her role as legendary Mexican painter Freda Kahlo in her production of *Frida* (2002). She first came to the attention of Mexican audiences in the title role of *Teresa* (1989-1991), a Mexican soap opera, after which she relocated to Los Angeles to pursue a movie career. She landed small roles in *Mi Vida Loca* (1993), *Road Racers* (1994), and *El Callejon de los Milagros* (1995), as well as a role in the short-lived American TV series *The Sinbad Show* (1993-94). In 1994, director Robert Rodriguez, after seeing her on a talk show, cast her as Carolina in *Desperado* (1995), opposite Antonio Banderas. She soon received more offers and landed a role as a snake dancer in Rodríguez's *From Dusk Till Dawn* (1996) opposite George Clooney and Quentin Tarantino. In 1997, she starred in four movies, *Fools Rush In* with Mathew Perry, *Breaking Up* opposite Russell Crowe, and *The Wild Wild West* opposite Will Smith. She produced—but did not appear in—the Mexican film *No One Writes to the Colonel* (1999); she produced and starred in the critically acclaimed Showtime movie *In the Time of the Butterflies* (2001); and she made her directorial debut, also for Showtime,

with *The Maldonado Miracle* (2003). That same year she reprised her role as Carolina in the final entry in the Desperado trilogy, *Once Upon a Time in Mexico*, for Robert Rodriguez. Among Hayek's other credits are starring roles in *After the Sunset* (2004) with Pierce Brosnan, and *Ask the Dust* (2006) with Colin Farrell. In Durango, she teamed with Penelope Cruz for the Luc Besson action-comedy *Bandidas* (2006). For the ABC television network, Hayek executive produced the Emmy Award–winning comedy series *Ugly Betty* (2006–2010), on which she made several guest appearances. Most recently she co-starred in the hit comedy *Grown Ups* (2010) opposite Adam Sandler, and its sequel *Grownups 2* (2013). Hayek received critical accolades for her role in *Beatriz at Dinner* (2017).

RODOLFO HOYOS JR. (1916–1983)
ACTOR

The Mexican-born son of famed opera singer Rodolfo Hoyos was a successful character actor in many American westerns, usually playing a Latino character. His most important film is the Oscar-winning *The Brave One* (1956). He played the title role in *Villa!!* (1958).

CARLA HOOL (19??–   )
CASTING DIRECTOR

Carla Hool has cast more than forty-five film and TV projects in the U. S. and Mexico, as well as in South America and Europe. Her film credits include *The 33* (2013), *A Better Life* (2011), *Vantage Point* (2008), *Apocalypto* (2006), *Nacho Libre* (2006), *Bandidas* (2006), and *The Matador* (2005). Hool served as voice casting director for the Oscar-winning animated feature *Coco* (2017). She is the daughter of film producer Conrad Hool.

LANCE HOOL (1944–   )
PRODUCER/DIRECTOR

Born and raised in Mexico City in a family environment of international politics and art, Lance Hool represents six generations of the entertainment industry. Legendary director Howard Hawks shot one of his earliest films, *Viva Villa!* on the Mexico City ranch owned by Hool's grandfather. Many years later, Lance Hool worked with Howard Hawks on his last film, *Rio Lobo* (1970) starring John Wayne. After working as an actor in such films as Ralph Nelson's *Soldier Blue* (1971), Hool set his sights on the production end of the business. From 1977 to 1980, he ran the U.S. operations of Pelmex, the Mexican national film distribution company. Over the past four decades, he has produced twenty-five major motion pictures, two of which reached the coveted number-one status at the box office: *Missing in Action* (1984) and *Man on Fire* (2004), both released by 20th Century Fox. While on location in New Mexico for the made-for-TV movie *The Tracker* (1988), Lance, his brother Conrad, and his son Jason were so inspired by the natural beauty and strong sense of community in Santa Fe that they created Santa Fe Studios, a state-of-the-art production facility, complete with sound stages.

CONRAD HOOL (1947–   )
PRODUCER/PRODUCTION MANAGER

Born in Mexico City, Conrad Hool entered the film industry as an assistant director. He has held the position of unit production manager and co-producer on a number of feature films, such as *Pure Luck* (1991),

McHale's Navy (1997), *Crocodile Dundee in Los Angeles* (2001), *Man on Fire* (2004), *and Club Dread* (2004).

ALEJANDRO GONZALES IÑÁRRITU (1963–)
DIRECTOR/SCREENWRITER/PRODUCER

The innovative and individualisic filmmaker Alejandro Gonzalez Iñárritu was born in Mexico City, D.F. He became the first Mexican director to be nominated for an Academy Award as Best Director (*Babel*, 2006), the first to win the Best Director Award at Cannes, and the Directors Guild of America award. His other credits include *Amores Perros* (2000), *Biutiful* (2000), and *21 Grams* (2003). Iñárritu won the Best Director Academy Award for *Birdman* (2014), which also won for Best Picture. He won the Best Director Academy Award for the second consecutive time for *The Revenant* (2015) starring Best Actor winner Leonardo Di Caprio.

KATY JURADO (1925–2002)
ACTRESS

Dark, almond-eyed, Gauadalajara-born Katy Jurado entered Mexican films in 1943 in *Internado Para Senoritas*, for which she won an Ariel Award. Thirteen starring roles followed, including Luis Buñuel's *El Bruto* (1953). She made her American film debut as Chelo in Budd Boetticher's *The Bullfighter and the Lady* (1951). When casting for *High Noon* (1952), producer Stanley Kramer and director Fred Zinnemann contacted Jurado and asked if she would agree to a screen test for the part of Helen Ramirez, Sheriff Will Kane's fiery ex-girlfriend. She refused, saying that if they wanted to see her work and how she looked onscreen, all they had to do was to go to downtown L.A. to the Spanish-language movie houses and watch one of her films currently playing there. They did, and she got the part. She did not speak a word of English at the time, but when she arrived in Los Angeles, veteran actor Antonio Moreno worked with her on the script and she learned her lines phonetically. For her dynamic performance, she received two Golden Globe awards, one for Best Supporting Actress and one for Most Promising Newcomer. Two years later, she received an Academy Award nomination in the Best Supporting Actress category for *Broken Lance* (1954) opposite Spencer Tracy. Jurado's extensive film credits also include *Arrowhead* (1953) with Charlton Heston, *Man from Del Rio* (1956) with Anthony Quinn, *Barabbas* (1961), *Stay Away Joe* (1968) with Elvis Presley, *One-Eyed Jacks* (1961) with Marlon Brando, *A Covenant With Death* (1967), Peckinpah's *Pat Garrett and Billy The Kid* (1973), and John Huston's *Under The Volcano* (1984), as well as many guest appearances on American television.

CHARLES L. KIMBALL (1897–1986)
EDITOR

Kimball was employed at RKO studios beginning in 1932. In 1934, he began to specialize as a film editor on films shot in Mexico. His credits include *The Torch* (1950), *Comanche* (1956), and *The Big Boodle* (1957). It was filmed with a largely Mexican crew in Havana, Cuba, just before the Castro revolution.

EMMANUEL LUBEZKI (1964–)
CINEMATOGRAPHER

Mexican-born Lubezki won the Academy Award for Best Cinematography three years in a row for his work on Alfonso Cuaron's *Gravity* in 2013, again in 2014 for Iñárritu's *Birdman*, and in 2015 for *The Revenant*. Lubezki's credits also include *Como Agua Para Chocolate* (1992), *Miroslava* (1993), *Reality Bites* (1994), *A Walk in the Clouds* (1995), *The Birdcage* (1996), *Sleepy Hollow* (1999), *Ali* (2001), *Y Tu Mama Tambien* (2001), and *Children of Men* (2006).

JOSE LUDLOW (19??–)
PRODUCER

Mexican-born Ludlow received a BA in Film and Television at University of Southern California, and an MFA from the American Film Institute. Jose has produced (or line produced) more than fifteen feature films, including *Blow* (2001), *Love in the Time of Cholera* (2007), *The Air I Breathe* (2008), *Dragon Ball: Evolution* (2009), and *The Chronicles of Narnia: The Voyage of the* Dawn Treader (2010).

JORGE LUKE (1942–2012)
ACTOR

Mexico City-born Jorge Luke appeared in such Hollywood films as *Ulzana's Raid* (1972), in which he portrayed an Indian scout; *Clear and Present Danger* (1994) with Harrison Ford; and Oliver Stone's *Salvador* (1996).

DIEGO LUNA (1979–)
ACTOR/DIRECTOR/PRODUCER

Diego Luna was recognized by Hollywood for his role in *Y Tu Mama Tambien* (2001) and has gone on to make an impact as an actor, director, and producer in both American and Mexican films. He appeared with Kevin Costner in the western *Open Range* (2003), *Milk* (2008) opposite Sean Penn, the science-fiction adventure *Elysium* (2013) with Matt Damon, and *Casa De Mi Padre* (2012) with Will Ferrell. Luna made his English-language directing debut with *Chavez* (2014). He starred in the stand-alone Star Wars film saga *Rogue One* (2016).

MARIA ELENA MARQUES (1926–2008)
ACTRESS

Maria Elena Marques starred in RKO's *The Pearl* with Pedro Armendáriz, and in MGM's Technicolor production of *Across the Wide Missouri* (1951) opposite Clark Gable and Ricardo Montalban. Her final American film was a B-western, *Ambush at Tomahawk Gap* (1953), in a thankless role as a Navajo Indian. She continued to work as an actress in the Mexican film industry and, later, television.

ANA MARTIN (1946–)
ACTRESS

Ana Martin was briefly under contract to MGM in the early sixties and appeared opposite Robert Taylor in the western *Return of the Gunfighter* (1967). The young actress returned to Mexico and has maintained her career, working exclusively in Mexican films and telenovelas. She co-starred with Salma Hayek, in the Mexican-made Showtime film *In the Time of the Butterflies* (2001).

GRACIELA MAZÓN (19??–)
COSTUME DESIGNER

Mexican-born Graciela Mazón created the costumes for *The Mask of Zorro* (1998) and its sequel, *The Legend of Zorro* (2005), as well as *Nacho Libre* (2006), *Desperado* (1995), and *From Dusk Till Dawn* (1996).

OFELIA MEDINA (1950–)
ACTRESS

This Merida, Yucatan, native is known for both her film and stage work. Most notably, she appeared with Richard Dreyfuss in *The Big Fix* (1978), *Before Night Falls* (2000) starring Javier Bardem and Johnny Depp, and her portrayal of Frida Kahlo in Paul Leduc's Spanish-language film *Frida* (1984).

ROSENDA MONTEROS (1935-)
ACTRESS

Rosenda Monteros was born in Veracruz and is best known for her role as Petra, the village girl, in *The Magnificent Seven* (1960). Her other film credits include *The White Orchid* (1954), *Nazarin* (1959), *She* (1965), and *Tiare Tahiti* (1965).

SARITA MONTIEL (1928–2013)
ACTRESS/SINGER

Also known as Sara Montiel, she was one of the biggest cinema and recording stars in Spain and Mexico. Montiel began her film career in her native Spain in 1944. Five years and fourteen films later, she landed a contract with the Mexican film industry, enjoying enjoyed tremendous success. By the time Hollywood came calling, she had appeared in thirty Spanish and Mexican films. She was formally introduced to American moviegoers with the deceptive onscreen credit "Introducing Sarita Montiel" with the role of Papayas, a beautiful Mexican señorita who capture's Gary Cooper's heart in *Vera Cruz* (1954), which was shot in Mexico. She portrayed yet another beautiful señorita, this time opposite renowned opera tenor–turned–film actor Mario Lanza in *Serenade* (1955). Her last American film appearance was as Yellow Moccasin, a Native American woman, in *Run of the Arrow* (1957), She would later say that in Spanish and Mexican movies she would be cast in any role but in Hollywood she could only play Mexican Spitfires and Yellow Mocccasins. Still, Montiel continued her screen trajectory with one box-office success after another. She retired from films in 1974, but continued recording and touring worldwide. She starred in her own television variety show in Spain, and in a miniseries.

RICARDO MONTALBAN (1920–2003)
ACTOR

Ricardo Montalban was born in Mexico City, the son of Spanish-born parents, and raised in Torreon. Ricardo's older brother Carlos was a journalist, actor, and voice-over artist who found success in Los Angeles. Ricardo followed Carlos there, enrolling in Fairfax High School. He starred in many films in Mexico throughout the 1940s, after which he landed a contract at MGM and returned to the United States. After securing small parts in several Broadway productions (one with Tallulah Bankhead), Montalban became a heartthrob in Mexican films, His first major American film appearance came in 1947 opposite Esther Williams in the MGM musical *Fiesta*. In 1949, he had his first starring role in *Border Incident*, and co-starred in the war drama *Battleground*, directed by William Wellman. Montalban founded the Latino Arts Advocacy organization NOSOTROS in Hollywood, which helped to improve the image of Latinos in movies and television, as well as providing a training ground for the performing arts. He won an Emmy Award for his portrayal of a Native-American chief in the miniseries *How the West Was Won* (1978) and a Tony Award nomination for his performance opposite the legendary Lena Horne in the Broadway musical *Jamaica*. He is perhaps best known to moviegoers as Khan, Captain Kirk's nemesis in the film *Star Trek II: The Wrath of Khan* (1982), a role he originated on the *Star Trek* (1966–1969) television series. On television, despite hundreds of guest appearances on most of the major television series, Montalban is remembered for his starring role as the mysterious Mr. Roarke on the popular series *Fantasy Island* (1978–1984). Ricardo Montalban died at the age of eighty-eight and was buried alongside his wife of sixty-three years.

GUILLERMO NAVARRO (1955–)
CINEMATOGRAPHER

Born in Mexico City, Guillermo Navarro has worked with many of the major directors of his generation, including Guillermo del Toro, Quentin Tarantino, and Robert Rodriguez. Navarro won the 2007 Academy Award for Best Cinematography for *Pan's Labyrinth* (2006). Among his many other credits are *Cabeza De Vaca* (1991), *Cronos* (1992), *Desperado/El Mariachi* (1994), *From Dusk Till Dawn* (1996), *Jackie Brown* (1997), *Spy Kids* (2000), *Hellboy* (2004), *Night at the Museum* (2006), *Pacific Rim* (2011), and *Night at the Museum: Secret of the Tombs* (2014). The cinematographer has recently begun directing American episodic television series.

RAMON NOVARRO (1899–1968)
ACTOR

The first Mexican screen superstar, Novarro was born José Ramon Gil Samaniego in Durango, Mexico, and was a cousin to Dolores del Rio. His family immigrated to the United States to escape the ravages of the Mexican Revolution. He rose from bit player to become a major draw for MGM, starring in that studio's first epic, *Ben-Hur: A Tale of the Christ* (1925). Following the death of Rudolph Valentino, Novarro became Hollywood's new Latin Lover, co-starring opposite Greta Garbo, Joan Crawford, and Norma Shearer, the top female stars of the day. Offscreen, Novarro was involved with Photoplay journalist Herbert Howe. Openly gay (at least within the close confines of the industry), Novarro made the transition to talkies and was given some opportunities to sing onscreen. MGM failed to renew his contract in 1935, prompting the multi-talented actor to pursue playwrighting, musical theater, and radio. After being out of the public eye for a number of years, he made something of a comeback by appearing sporadically on television in character roles. His life ended tragically in 1968 when he was beaten to death by two male hustlers he had hired.

ROCIO ORTEGA
ANIMAL TRAINER

Rocio Ortega provides all types of domestic and exotic animals for motion pictures, television shows, and commercials in Mexico. A former champion rodeo rider, she followed in her father's footsteps by joining the film industry, supplying and transporting trained horses, livestock, and wranglers to and from sets. Ortega operates from her ranch, located on the outskirts of Mexico City. Her many film credits over a three-decade-long career include *Master and Commander: The Far Side of The World* (2003), *And Starring Pancho Villa as Himself* (2003), *Old Gringo* (1989), and *Old Gringo* (2018).

ANDREA PALMA (1903–1987)
ACTRESS

Born in Durango, Mexico, Andrea Palma was a cousin to both Ramon Novarro and Dolores del Rio. Prior to her moving to Hollywood, Palma was a milliner in Mexico City. Through her Hollywood connections, she became a stand-in and designer for Marlene Dietrich and appeared in bit parts in such films as *Girl of the Rio* (1932) starring her cousin Dolores del Rio; all the while she continued to earn her living designing and making hats. When Palma was offered the lead role in a Mexican film, *La Mujer del Puerto/ The Woman of the Port* (1934), she accepted; her role of the prostitute Rosario made her a star. Palma patterned herself after Dietrich, which served her well: she is regarded as the Mexican screen's first diva. For the rest of her career Palma remained in Mexico, appearing in films, on television, and on the stage. She has a strong supporting role in the Mexico-filmed Hollywood production of *Tarzan and the Mermaids* (1948).

PINA PELLICER (1938–1964)
ACTRESS

Pellicer was a young, pretty, petite Mexican actress who appeared in only three films, the most notable of which is *Macario* (1960). She co-starred with Marlon Brando and Katy Jurado in the only film Brando directed, *One-Eyed Jacks* (1961). The emotionally troubled actress committed suicide in December 1964.

STACY PERSKIE (19??–   )
PRODUCER

Stacy Perskie, also credited as Persky, began as a production assiatant on *Titanic* (1997). He also worked on *Man on Fire* (2004), *Apocalypto* (2006), and wrote and produced the Mel Gibson-starring feature film *Get the Gringo* (2012). He is also credited with providing Mexican production services to such films as *Elysium* (2013) *Spectre* (2015). *Sicario* (2015) and its sequel *Sicario: Day of the Soldado* (2018).

ALEX PHILLIPS (1900–1977)
CINEMATOGRAPHER

Alex Phillips was born Alexander Peleplock in Russia. After immigrating to Canada, he changed his last name to Phillips, and eventually landed in Hollywood. He worked as a bit player in silent films, and then became a cameraman in 1919. With this new skill, he relocated to Mexico, where he worked on the early sound films, beginning with the first, *Santa* (1931). From the thirties through the seventies he was director of photography on 202 Mexican films for such directors as Raphael J. Sevilla, Roberto Gavaldon, Julio Bracho, Emilio Fernández, and Arturo Ripstein.

ALEX PHILLIPS JR. (1935–2007)
CINEMATOGRAPHER

The son of Alex Phillips Sr. and Alicia Bolanos was born in Mexico City. The younger Phillips learned his profession by working as an assistant on many of his father's film assignments. His first Mexican film was *Yanco* (1960) for director Servando Gonzalez. He was also the cameraman on Robert DeNiro's *Sam's Song* (1969), Sam Peckinpah's *Bring Me the Head of Alfredo Garcia* (1974), and was handpicked by Sidney Poitier for the actor's debut feature as a director, *Buck and the Preacher* (1971). Phillips's biggest hit was the 1984 adventure-comedy *Romancing the Stone*, directed by Robert Zemeckis and starring Michael Douglas and Kathleen Turner. In Mexico, his best known work is *Canoa: A Shameful Memory* (1976), directed by Felipe Cazals.

RODRIGO PRIETO (1965–   )
CINEMATOGRAPHER

A native of Mexico City, Rodrigo Prieto has worked with Spike Lee, Ang Lee, Pedro Almodovar, Ben Affleck, Julie Taymor, Curtis Hanson, Martin Scorsese, and Alejandro Gonzalez Iñárritu. Prieto was nominated for an Oscar in 2006 for *Brokeback Mountain* and was the cinematographer on 2013's Academy Award–winning Best Picture, *Argo*. His other credits include 8 Mile (2002), *Frida* (2002), *The Homesman* (2014), and *The Wolf of Wall Street* (2014). Prior to coming to Hollywood, Prieto shot nine feature films in Mexico, the last being *Amores Perros* (2000). Since then, he has collaborated with Iñárritu on *21 Grams* (2003) and *Babel* (2006).

DAVID REYNOSO (1929–1994)
ACTOR

This burly Mexican actor appeared as a character lead in many Mexican films. His American cinema credits include *Rage* (1966) starring Glenn Ford, and *Stick* (1985) starring Burt Reynolds.

CARLOS RIQUELME (1914–1990)
ACTOR

Carlos Riquelme was a noted Mexican actor whose only major American film appearance was in *The Milagro Beanfield War* (1988) directed by Robert Redford.

CARLOS RIVAS (1928–2002)
ACTOR

Though born in Texas, Rivas appeared in many Mexican and international productions, including *The King and I* (1956), *The Deerslayer* (1957), *The Black Scorpion* (1957), *The Big Boodle* (1957), *The Unforgiven* (1960), and *True Grit* (1969). Tall, handsome, and bilingual, Rivas worked in episodic television well into the nineties, making an appearance in director Allison Anders's street drama *Mi Vida Loca* (1993).

ISMAEL RODRÍGUEZ (1917–2004)
DIRECTOR

Ismael followed his older brothers back to Mexico when they took their synchronized sound system and helped to start the Mexican film industry with *Santa* (1931). He labored in various capacities in the Mexican film industry and began his career as a director in 1942 with *Que Lindo Es Michoacan*. He directed Mexican singing idol

Pedro Infante in sixteen films and was one of the leading directors of Mexico's Golden Age of Cinema.

GILBERT ROLAND (1905–1994)
ACTOR

Gilbert Roland's career spanned more than six decades, from the silent screen to sound, color, widescreen CinemaScope, and television. He was born Luis Antonio Dámaso Alonso in Ciudad Juarez, Chihuahua, Mexico, one of six children. When Pancho Villa expelled all Spaniards from Northern Mexico during the Spanish Revolution, his family fled to El Paso, Texas. At the age of fourteen, he left home and made his way to Los Angeles. He started as an extra in movies alongside future star Clark Gable. Gilbert Roland (his adopted stage name) was picked for a leading role in the Clara Bow feature *The Plastic Age* (1925), followed by a star-making role in *Camille* (1926). Roland easily made the transition from silent to sound movies, and even worked in Hollywood-produced Spanish-language films. Among his more notable credits are *Last Train from Madrid* (1937), *Juarez* (1939), *We Were Strangers* (1949), *Bullfighter and the Lady* (1951), *The Miracle of Our Lady of Fatima* (1952), *The Bad and the Beautiful* (1952), *The Big Circus* (1959), *Islands in the Stream* (1977), and his final film, *Barbarossa* (1982).

GUILLERMO "MEMO" ROSAS (19??–   )
CINEMATOGRAPHER

Veteran cinematographer, camera operator, and second-unit director of photography, Rosas's credits include the Academy Award–nominated film *Before Night Falls* (2000). Based in Mexico, he has worked with the industry's leading directors, including James Cameron (*Titanic*, 1997), Peter Weir (*Master and Commander: The Far Side of the World*, 2003), and Tony Scott (*Man on Fire*, 2004).

PATRICIA RIGGEN (1970–   )
DIRECTOR

Riggen is the only Mexican-born female director in the Directors Guild of America. Born in Guadalajara, she worked odd jobs in the local film industry before making her feature directorial debut with *Under the Same Moon/ Bajo La Misma Luna* (2007), which was a box-office hit in both the U.S. and Mexico. The movie focuses on a young woman who is working illegally in Los Angeles. Meanwhile, her nine-year-old son lives with his ailing grandmother. Upon her death, he is left alone and makes the arduous trek through Mexico and across the border to reunite with his mother. Riggen directed a 2011 Disney Channel movie *Lemonade Mouth*, and *Girl in Progress*, a 2012 Eva Mendez vehicle for Televisa/Lionsgate Pantelion Films. *The 33* (2015), the moving story of the trapped Chilean miners who were rescued with the help of several international agencies and the faith based film *Miracles from Heaven* (2016) are Riggen's latest directorial credits.

ANNA ROTH (19??–   )
PRODUCER, PRODUCTION MANAGER, PRODUCTION SUPERVISOR

Roth has worked on more than forty Hollywood movie productions filmed in Mexico in the capacity of production manager and production supervisor. Among her many film credits are *Missing* (1982), *Under Fire* (1983), *Old Gringo* (1989), *Predator* (1987), *Clear and Present Danger* (1994), *Titanic* (1997), *Traffic* (200), *Man On*

Fire (2004), and *Apocalypto* (2006). Born in Poland, Roth emigrated to Mexico with her family at age eleven, attended high school there and graduated from the Universidad Nacional Autonoma de Mexico. She began her career in the Mexican film industry as a production assistant on the films *10* (1978) and *Zorro, The Gay Blade* (1981). In recent years she has produced a number of Mexican films including *Por La Libre* (2000), *Innocent Voices* (2004), and *Las Paredes Hablan* (2012) and *Deseo* (2013).

MAYES C. RUBEO (1963–   )
COSTUME DESIGNER

For Mel Gibson's *Apocalypto* (2006), Mayes C. Rubeo created the richly detailed costumes worn by members of the Mayan society. She also created the costumes for the Na-Vi, a species of ten-foot-tall (3.0 m.), blue-skinned, sapient humanoids, in James Cameron's blockbuster *Avatar* (2009). Her other credits include *Dragonball: Evolution* (2009), *John Carter* (2012), and *World War Z* (2013).

JORGE RUSSEK (1932–1998)
ACTOR

Jorge Russek was born in Senora and began his career in the Mexican film industry in 1958. Usually cast as a heavy in American films, his credits include *The Wild Bunch* (1969), *Hour of the Gun* (1967), *Soldier Blue* (1970), *and License to Kill* (1989).

GLORIA SCHOEMANN (1910–2006)
EDITOR

Born in Mexico City, Gloria Schoemann was a pioneering editor in the Mexican film industry, amassing over two hundred credits during her five-decade-long career. For Emilio "El Indio" Fernandez alone she worked on twenty-three films; twenty-four were made in collaboration with Gabriel Figueroa. Her credits include *Maria Candelaria* (1944), *La Perla/The Pearl* (1947), *Maclovia* (1947), *Rio Escondido* (1948), *Enamorada* (1948), *Beyond All Limits* (1959), *Macario* (1960), and *Patrullero 777* (1978).

ARMANDO SILVESTRE (1926–   )
ACTOR

Armando Silvestre was born in San Diego, California. A handsome, muscular man, he began his career as an actor in 1947. He played in countless Mexican films, as well as American western movies and television shows, usually as Native Americans, Mexican bandits, or policemen. His film credits include *Geronimo* (1962), *Kings of the Sun* (1963), *Smoky* (1966), *The Scalphunters* (1968), and *Two Mules for Sister Sara* (1970). He has also worked extensively on American episodic series, including *The F. B. I.* (1965–1974), *Mannix* (1967–1975), *Police Woman* (1974–1978), and the miniseries *On Wings of Eagles* (1986).

JORGE STAHL (1886–1979)
CINEMATOGRAPHER/DIRECTOR/PRODUCER

Born in Puebla, Mexico, Jorge Stahl is one of the true pioneers of the Mexican film industry. He was eighteen when he bought a film projector and several short films at the Louisiana Purchase Exposition, held in St. Louis, Missouri, in 1904; he took these back to Mexico where he screened them for his fellow countrymen. In 1905, he—along with his brothers Carlos and Alfonso—started a film exhibition business in Mexico, renting films to theatres, hotels, and dance halls. They soon acquired a camera and began making their own short films of local sites and events. In time, they formed a full-fledged production company, processing, editing distributing, and exhibiting motion pictures. The chaos and turmoil of the Mexican Revolution put a temporary halt to their business, but, in 1931, they initiated the Estudios Cinematograficos Mexico Films, where they did the postproduction work on *Santa,* the first Mexican sound film.

JORGE STAHL JR. (1921–2003)
CINEMATOGRAPHER

Born in Mexico City, the son of Jorge Stahl became a respected cameraman and director in Mexican cinema. He later shared cinematography credit with Milton R. Krasner on 20th Century-Fox's *Garden of Evil* (1954) starring Gary Cooper. Among his many credits for Mexican-made movies are *Comanche* (1956) and *Enchanted Island* (1958), *The Beast of Hollow Mountain* (1956), *The Sun Also Rise* (1957), *Jory* (1973), and *Missing in Action 2* (1985).

MIROSLAVA STERN (1925–1955)
ACTRESS

This Czech-born actress immigrated to Mexico in the thirties, where her beauty and talent made her a cinema sensation. She had important roles in two Hollywood films, *The Brave Bulls* (1950) opposite Anthony Quinn and Mel Ferrer, and the western *Saddle Tramp* (1955) co-starring Joel McCrea. That same year she appeared in Luis Buñuel' *The Criminal Life of Archibald De La Cruz.* She committed suicide, aged thirty, in 1955, in Mexico City.

GABRIEL TORRES (1929–   )
CINEMATOGRAPHER

Mexican-born cinematographer Gabriel Torres photographed *The Revengers* (1972) starring William Holden, and *The Deadly Trackers* (1973) starring Richard Harris and Rod Taylor. For American television, he was the principal cameraman on forty-eight episodes of *Tarzan* (1966–1968) TV series, which was shot in Mexico. He also photographed episodes of the American television series *Columbo* and *McCloud,* which were filmed on location in Mexico.

LUPITA TOVAR (1910–2016)
ACTRESS

Discovered by American film director Robert Flarerty, the beautiful Mexican-born Guadalupe Natalia, better known as Lupita, traveled to Hollywood where she appeared in the last of the silent movies. In 1931, she co-starred in Universal's Spanish-language version of *Dracula,* directed by George Melford. According to *Leonard Maltin's Classic Movie Guide* (New York, NY: Penguin Group, 2010), "much of the staging and camerawork is actually better [than the Tod Browning–directed English-language version]! Other major difference: the woman are dressed more provocatively." Lupita returned to her native Mexico where she starred in *Santa* (1931), the first Mexican sound film. During her career, she performed in more than thirty movies on four continents and was honored by the motion picture academies of Mexico and Hollywood. She married producer (and later agent) Paul Kohner and gave up her career to raise their children, Susan and Pancho. Susan Kohner received an Academy Award nomination as Best Supporting Actress for her role as Sarah Jane in *Imitation of Life* (1959) opposite Lana Turner. Pancho Kohner produced five films with then-reigning international action star Charles Bronson; he also directed the acclaimed film version of *Mr. Sycamore* (1975) starring Jason Robards. Lupita's grandsons Paul and Chris Weitz directed and produced the *American Pie* series of coming-of-age comedies. Chris directed the second installment of the *Twilight Saga*, and directed Mexican actor Demian Bichir in his Oscar-nominated Best Actor performance in *A Better Life* (2011). *Lupita Tovar: The Sweetheart of Mexico*, as told to her son Pancho Kohner, was published in 2010, the year of that remarkable lady's centenary. She died, aged 106, in 2016.

LUPE VÉLEZ (1908–1944)
ACTRESS

Lupe Vélez, born in San Luis Potosi, was a Mexican actress who attained success in silent and sound films. Douglas Fairbanks brought her to the attention of Hollywood by casting her opposite him in *The Gaucho* (1927). Vélez went on to work for some of the most important directors of the time, including Cecil B. DeMille (*Stand and Deliver*, 1928), D.W. Griffith (*Lady of the Pavements*, 1929), and Tod Browning (*Where East is East*, 1929, starring Lon Chaney). A talented, vivacious actress, Vélez starred in a classic series of Mexican Spitfire comedies for RKO. One of her last films was the Mexican production of *Nana* (1944) directed by Roberto Gavaldon. That same year she committed suicide, by intentionally overdosing on Seconal, in her Beverly Hills home; she was thirty-six.

ISELA VEGA (1939–   )
ACTRESS/SINGER/SONGWRITER/PRODUCER

Isela Vega is a beautiful and talented Mexican actress who became a popular sex symbol in Mexican cinema in the sixties and seventies. Vega often portrayed strong-willed women who would not allow themselves to be totally dominated by men. After a successful modeling career, she made her film debut with Pedro Armendáriz in *Verano Violento/Violent Summer* (1960). Vega's first Hollywood film was *The Deadly Trackers* (1973), which was shot in Durango and starred Richard Harris and Rod Taylor. She co-starred with Warren Oates in Sam Peckinpah's *Bring Me the Head of Alfredo Garcia* (1974); she also wrote "Bennie's Theme," which was used in the picture. The July 1974 issue of *Playboy* featured a nude photo spread of Vega, the first Mexican actress to appear in the American publication. In 1976, she starred in the Dino De Laurentiis–produced *Drum*, a sequel to 1975's notorious *Mandingo*, a film mixing themes of slavery and sex. In the follow-up, Vega plays a white prostitute who is raising (with her black lesbian lover) a teenaged son. She was seen most recently in the Mexican films *Herod's Law/La Ley de Herodes* (1999) and *Saving Private Perez* (2011).

JACK WAGNER (1891–1963)
SCREENWRITER/PRODUCER

Wagner was born in Monterey, California, but raised in Torreon, Mexico, where his father was an American railroad engineer who was later killed during the Mexican Revolution.

Jack moved to Los Angeles in 1909 where he found work in the film industry and developed a reputation

Cinematographer Alex Phillips Jr. checks a shot on the set of *Luminarias* **(2000).** *Photo courtesy of Carol Petersen, Evelina Fernandez, and Jose Luis Valenzuela.*

as a "gagman" who constructed visual comedy segments for silent screen comedians. Completely bilingual in Spanish and English, he directed and produced Spanish language versions of Fox studio movies during the transitional years from silent to sound films.

He was the co-writer of the Mexican themed Academy Award winning Technicolor Best Short Subject *La Cucaracha* (1934). Wagner was nominated with John Steinbeck (a longtime family friend) for an Academy Award in the category of Best Writing (Original Story) for the Mexican-American World War II drama *A Medal For Benny* (1945). He is the credited screenwriter along with Steinbeck and Emilio Fernandez of *The Pearl* (1948).

In Mexico he produced a number of films, most notably *La Otra/ The Other One* (1946) starring Dolores Del Rio in the dual role of conniving sisters that was later remade in English as *Dead Ringer* (1964) with Bette Davis.

ALFRED C. YBARRA (1905–2001)
ART DIRECTOR/PRODUCTION DESIGNER/ARTIST

Born and raised in Los Angeles, Alfred C. Ybarra was a direct descendant of the original Californio families. He traveled to New York to study architecture. Upon his return to L.A., he found work in the art department at Warner Bros. John Wayne noticed his work on John Ford's *The Fugitive* and hired him for his production of *The Bullfighter and the Lady* (1951), which was to be filmed in Mexico. Ybarra's numerous credits include such made-in-Mexico films as *Hondo* (1954), *Run for the Sun* (1956), *Kings of the Sun* (1963), *Major Dundee* (1965), and *Hour of the Gun* (1967). His other credits include *The High and the Mighty* (1954), *The Alamo* (1960), and *The Comancheros* (1961).

Bibliography

Adams, Les, and Buck Rainey. *Shoot-Em-Ups* (New York, NY: Arlington House, 1978).

Agnew, Jeremy. *The Creation of the Cowboy Hero* (Jefferson, NC: McFarland, 2015).

Andrade, Alberto Tejada. *Historias Del Cine filmado en Durango* (Durango: Gobierno Del Estado de Durango, Herfa Impresores S. A De C. V., Gomez Palacio, 2004).

Arce, Hector. *Gary Cooper: An Intimate Biography* (New York, NY: William Morrow, 1998).

Arau, Alfonso. *That's Life: Conversations with Armando Casas* (Guadalajara: Universidad de Guadalajara 2016).

Ayala, Blanco Jorje. *La Adventura del Cine Mexicano: En La Epoca de Oro y Despues* (Mexico City DF: Grijallbo Press, 1993).

Benshoff, Harry M., and Sean Griffin. *America on Film: Representing Race, Class, Gender, and Sexuality at the Movies* (New York, NY: Blackwell, 1986).

Bergan, Ronald. *The United Artists Story* (New York, NY: Crown Publishers, 1988).

Boetticher, Budd. *When in Disgrace* (Santa Barbara, CA: Nelville Press, 1989).

Brothers, Caroline. *War and Photography: A Cultural History* (New York, NY: Routledge, 1997).

Brownlow, Kevin. *The War, the West, and the Wilderness* (New York, NY: Knopf, 1978). Buford, Kate. *Burt Lancaster: An American Life* (New York, NY: Knopf, 2000).

Buhle, Buhle, and Ed Georgakas. *Encyclopedia of the American Left* (Urban and Chicago: University of Illinois Press, 1992).

Buscombe, Edward. *The BFI Companion to the Western* (New York, NY: Athenium, 1988). Calow, Simon. *Orson Welles, Volume 2: Hello Americans* (New York, NY: Viking, 2006).

Debroise, Olivier. *Mexican Suite: A History of Photography in Mexico* (Austin: University of Texas Press, 2001).

De Orellana, Margarita. Filming Pancho Villa: How Hollywood Shaped the Mexican Revolution. With a foreword by Kevin Brownlow. (Brooklyn, NY: Verso, 2009).

DeOrellana, Margarita. *How Hollywood Shaped the Mexican Revolution* (New York, NY: Verso, 2004).

DeUsabel, Gaizika. *The High Noon of American Film in Latin America* (Ann Arbor: University of Michigan Research Press, 1982).

Douglas, Kirk. *The Ragman's Son* (New York, NY: Simon & Schuster, 1988).

Eames, John Douglas. *The MGM Story* (New York, NY: Crown, 1976).

———. *The Paramount Story* (New York, NY: Simon & Schuster, 2002).

Essoe, Gabe. *Tarzan of the Movies* (Secaucus, NJ: Citadel Press, 1978).

Eyman, Scott. *Print the Legend: The Life and Times of John Ford* (New York, NY: Simon & Schuster, 2007).

———. *John Wayne: The Life and Legend* (New York, NY: Simon & Schuster, 2014).

Fine, Marshall. *Bloody Sam: The Life and Films of Sam Peckinpah* (New York, NY: Donald L. Fine, Inc., 1991).

Ford, Peter. *Glenn Ford: A Life* (Madison: University of Wisconsin Press, 2011).

French, Philip. *Westerns: Aspects of a Movie Genre* (New York, NY: Viking Press, 1973).

Fury, David Arthur. *Johnny Weissmuller: Twice the Hero* (Minneapolis, MN: Artists Press, 2000).

Gallagher, Tag. *John Ford: The Man and His Films* (Los Angeles: University of California Press, 1986).

George-Warren, Holly. *Public Cowboy No.1: The Life and Times of Gene Autry* (New York, NY: Oxford University Press, 2004).

Green, Douglas B. *Singing in the Saddle: The History of the Singing Cowboy* (Nashville, TN: Vanderbilt University Press, 2005).

Hall, Linda B. *Dolores del Rio: Beauty in Light and Shade* (Redwood City, CA: Stanford University Press, 2013).

Hammen, Scott. *John Huston* (Boston, MS: Twayne, 1985).

Hannan, Brian. *The Making of The Magnificent Seven: Behind the Scenes of the Pivotal Western* (Jefferson, NC: McFarland, 2015).

Hanson, Peter. *Dalton Trumbo, Hollywood Rebel* (Jefferson, NC: McFarland, 2003).

Hardy, Phil. *The Western* (New York, NY: Overlook Press, 2004).

Harris, Warren G. *Clark Gable* (New York, NY: Harmony Books, 2002).

Heston, Charlton. *The Actor's Life* (New York, NY: E. P. Dutton, 1976).

Hirshorn, Clive. *The Columbia Story* (New York, NY: Crown, 1979).

Huston, John. *An Open Book* (New York, NY: Knopf, 1980).

Isaac, Alberto. *Conversaciones con Gabriel Figueroa* (Guadalajara: Universidad de Guadalajara y Colima, 1993).

Isaac, Alberto. *Conversaciones con Gabriel Figueroa Testimonios del Cine Mexicano.* (Guadalajara: Universidad Guadalajara, 1993)

Janis, Maria Cooper. *Gary Cooper Off Camera: A Daughter Remembers* (New York, NY: Harry N. Abrams, 1999).

Kagan, Norman. *The Cinema of Oliver Stone* (New York, NY: Continuum, 1995).

Kaminsky, Stuart. *John Huston: Maker of Magic* (Boston, MA: Houghton-Miflin, 1978).

Katz, Freidrich E. *The Life and Times of Pancho Villa* (Redwood City, CA: Stanford University Press, 1998).

Kazan, Elia. *Elia Kazan: A Life* (Cambridge, MA: Da Capo Press, 1997).

Keenan, Richard C. *The Films of Robert Wise* (Lanham, MD: Scarecrow Press, 2007).

Leemann, Sergio. *Robert Wise on His Films* (Beverly Hills, CA: Silman-James Press, 1995).

Long, Robert Emmett. *John Huston: Interviews* (Jackson: University Press of Mississippi, 2001).

Maltin, Leonard. *The Disney Films* (New York, NY: Crown, 1977).

Manfull, Helen. *Additional Dialogue: Letters of Dalton Trumbo, 1942–1967* (New York, NY: M. Evans & Co., 1970).

McBride, Joseph. *Hawks On Hawks* (Berkeley: University of California Press, 1982).

Meyers, Jeffrey. *John Huston: Courage and Art* (New York, NY: Crown, 2001).

Miller, Arnold. The Films of Robert Aldrich (Knoxville: University of Tennessee Press, 1986).

Mirisch, Walter. *I Thought We Were Making Movies, Not History* (Madison: University of Wisconsin Press, 2008).

Mizrachi, Susan L. *Brando's Smiles*. (London, New York: W.W. Norton & Co. 2014).

Mora, Carl J. *Mexican Cinema: Reflections of a Society, 1896-2004* (Oakland: University of California Press, 2005).

Moss, Marilyn Ann. *Raoul Walsh: The True Adventures of Hollywood's Legendary Director* (Lexington: University of Kentucky Press, 2011).

Mraz, John. *Photographing the Mexican Revolution: Commitment, Testimonies, Icons* (Austin: University of Texas Press, 2012).

Munn, Michael. *John Wayne: The Man Behind the Myth* (New York, NY: New American Library, 2004).

Pilcher, Jeffrey M. *Cantinflas and the Chaos of Mexican Modernity* (Lanham, MD: Roman & Littlefield, 2000).

Pratley, Gerald. *The Cinema of John Huston* (New York, NY: A. S. Barnes & Co., 1976).

Prime, Rebecca. *Hollywood Exiles in Europe: The Blacklist and Cold War Film Culture* (New Brunswick, NJ: Rutgers University Press, 2014).

Quinn, Anthony. *One Man Tango* (New York, NY: Harper Collins, NY, 1996).

Railsback, Brian, and Michael J. Meyer. *A John Steinbeck Encyclopedia* (Westport, CT: Greenwood Press, 2006).

Rivera, Miluka. *Legado Puertorirqueno en Hollywood*: *Famosos y Olvidados* (Burbank, CA: Kumaras, 2010).

Roberts, Randy, and James S. Olson. *John Wayne: American* (New York, NY: Free Press, 1995).

Server, Lee. *Robert Mitchum: "Baby, I Don't Care"* (New York, NY: St. Martin's Press, 001).

Seydor, Paul. *Peckinaph: The Western Films* (Champaign: University of Illinois Press, 1980).

Seydor, Paul. *The Authentic Death and Contentious Afterlife of Pat Garrett and Billy the Kid* (Evanston, IL: Northwestern University Press, 2015).

Schickel, Richard. *Elia Kazan* (New York, NY: Harper Collins, 2006).

Skretvedt, Randy. *Laurel and Hardy: The Magic Behind the Movies* (Irvine, CA: Bonaventure Press, 2016).

Taymor, Julie. *Frida: Bringing Frida Kahlo's Life and Art to Film* (New York, NY: Newmarket Press, 2002).

Tunon, Julia. *Los Rostros de Un Mito: Personajes Femininos en las peliculas de Emilio "Indio" Fernánadez* (Mexico: CONACULTA Y Dirrecion General de Publicaciones IMCINE, 2000).

Wallach, Eli. *The Good, the Bad and Me: In My Anecdotage* (New York, NY: Harcourt,, 2005).

Weddle, David. *If They Move . . . Kill 'Em!: The Life and Times of Sam Peckinpah* (New York, NY: Grove Press, 1994).

Welles, Orson, and Peter Bogdanovich. *This is Orson Welles* (Cambridge, MA: Da Capo Press, 1998).

Weissmuller, Johnny Jr. *Tarzan, My Father* (Toronto, ECW Press, 2000).

Young, Jeff. *Kazan: The Master Director Discusses His Films* (New York, NY: New Market Press, 1979).

Index